Thunder on the River

UNIVERSITY PRESS OF FLORIDA

Florida A&M University, Tallahassee
Florida Atlantic University, Boca Raton
Florida Gulf Coast University, Ft. Myers
Florida International University, Miami
Florida State University, Tallahassee
New College of Florida, Sarasota
University of Central Florida, Orlando
University of Florida, Gainesville
University of North Florida, Jacksonville
University of South Florida, Tampa
University of West Florida, Pensacola

THUNDER
ON THE RIVER

THE CIVIL WAR IN
NORTHEAST FLORIDA

Daniel L. Schafer

UNIVERSITY PRESS OF FLORIDA

Gainesville · Tallahassee · Tampa
Boca Raton · Pensacola · Orlando · Miami
Jacksonville · Ft. Myers · Sarasota

Library of Congress Cataloging-in-Publication Data

Schafer, Daniel L.

Thunder on the river : the Civil War in northeast

Florida / Daniel L.Schafer.

p. cm.

Includes bibliographical references and index.

ISBN 978-0-8130-3419-5 (cloth: alk. paper)

ISBN 978-0-8130-6054-5 (pbk.)

1. Jacksonville (Fla.)—History, Military—19th century.

2. Jacksonville (Fla.)—Social conditions—19th century. 3. Saint Johns

River Region (Fla.)—History, Military—19th century. 4. Saint Johns

River Region (Fla.)—Social conditions—19th century.

5. Florida—History—Civil War, 1861-1865. I. Title.

F319.J1S35 2009

975.9'1205—dc22

2009023128

The University Press of Florida is the scholarly publishing agency
for the State University System of Florida, comprising Florida
A&M University, Florida Atlantic University, Florida Gulf Coast
University, Florida International University, Florida State University,
New College of Florida, University of Central Florida, University of
Florida, University of North Florida, University of South Florida, and
University of West Florida.

University Press of Florida

15 Northwest 15th Street

Gainesville, FL 32611-2079

http://www.upf.com

Dedicated to the Memory of Richard A. Martin

Richard A. Martin was born in Brooklyn, New York, in 1927. In 1949, after serving in the United States Navy, Richard made Jacksonville his home and newspaper work his vocation. He was a reporter and editor for the *Jacksonville Journal* for many years before going to work for the City of Jacksonville. Later, he put his talent with words to good purpose in the field of advertising. Throughout his years in Jacksonville, Richard made writing the city's history his passion. His legacy is the long list of articles and books on local history that he wrote before his death on March 27, 2003, at age seventy-five.

Contents

Preface

More than twenty-five years ago, I was asked to edit a draft of Richard A. Martin's two-volume history of early Jacksonville. The Florida Publishing Company had commissioned the draft several years before with the intention of publishing it during the American bicentennial celebrations. The nearly twelve-hundred-page draft was instead placed in storage until 1981, when I was asked to prepare a manuscript limited to the Civil War chapters. I added insights from a number of primary source documents and, with assistance from Richard Martin and James Robertson Ward, completed the manuscript in summer 1984. *Jacksonville's Ordeal by Fire: A Civil War History*, with Richard A. Martin as primary author, was published in August 1984 by William Shivers Morris III, the chief executive officer of the Florida Publishing Company. To the surprise of everyone involved, all five thousand copies sold in less than a week.

With the book out of print, editors of academic presses asked me to revise the book with a more scholarly focus. Mr. Morris indicated by telephone that he did not intend to republish the book and gave me permission to proceed with a new manuscript as I thought appropriate. Since Mr. Martin had no continuing interest in the book, I began work on a new manuscript, but put it aside when other obligations intervened. In 2005, I returned to the project with the help of history majors at the University of North Florida who enrolled in sections of my Local History Seminar. Grants from the UNF Board of Trustees made it possible for students to assist with the research at the National Archives and the Library of Congress in Washington, D.C.

The result is *Thunder on the River: The Civil War in Northeast Florida*. The narrative is intended to be engaging yet scholarly, reflecting the academic emphasis requested by publishers two decades ago. *Thunder on the River* is a local history placed in a national context and informed by the remarkable array of Civil War scholarship that has appeared in recent decades. It draws on dozens of research trips to the National Archives and the Library of Congress and on hundreds of primary and secondary sources that were not consulted for the 1984 monograph.

With the help of Kevin Hooper and Jim Vearil, I attempted to balance use of Confederate and Union sources and to expand coverage of events beyond Jacksonville's boundaries to neighboring counties and along the St. Johns to farms and towns far to the south. Overall, Confederate defense strategy is emphasized, especially as it concerned the vital significance of denying the enemy access to the interior of Florida via the St. Johns River. Although woefully deficient in military manpower and war materials, Confederate soldiers and supportive civilians resisted with such resourcefulness that Federal land-based advances were turned back at the bloody Battle of Olustee in February 1864, and thereafter limited to the Jacksonville defense works until late July 1864. The Union navy continued to dominate the St. Johns, but skillful application of underwater explosives—called torpedo mines at the time—almost succeeded in closing the St. Johns to Federal gunboats and ending the Union occupation of Jacksonville. Thunder on the river reverberating from the explosions that destroyed the *Maple Leaf* and other Union vessels inspired the book's title. During my last conversation with Richard Martin, he said that "Thunder on the River" should have been the title of the original publication.

Serious attention is also given to contributions of the black residents of northeast Florida who seized the opportunities for self-emancipation provided by the presence of Federal occupation zones and the naval gunboats on the St. Johns. After finding sanctuary behind Union lines, more than a thousand former slaves from northeast Florida joined Union infantry regiments and fought for the liberation of other black men and women. One of those regiments captured Jacksonville in March 1863 and occupied it for nearly three weeks, prompting additional self-emancipations. Some of those same men returned to Jacksonville one year later, fought at the Battle of Olustee, and formed part of the subsequent Federal army of occupation in Jacksonville.

A fresh and intensive examination was given to the local evidence regarding slavery as the motivation for secession and war. It was concluded that the white residents of Jacksonville were so convinced that Northerners intended to limit the right granted by the U.S. Constitution to carry human property into the western territories, and eventually to abolish the institution of slavery altogether, that they embraced secession and war as their last desperate chance to preserve slavery. This may not be an entirely popular conclusion, but the evidence for Jacksonville, especially the words of its own citizens, sustains it.

When the war finally came to Jacksonville, it did so with an intermittent fury that destroyed much of the city and scattered its residents. Federal forces occupied and then abandoned Jacksonville three times prior to 1863, and one year later they commenced a permanent occupation. The city was burned once by Confederates, once by Federals; it was shelled often, destroying dwellings and businesses. Jacksonville's beautiful trees were felled as protection for one or the other occupying force. The history of Jacksonville and the St. Johns River during the Civil War is a compelling story that encompasses the most important events that occurred in Florida between 1861 and 1865.

SAMMIS' BUILDINGS

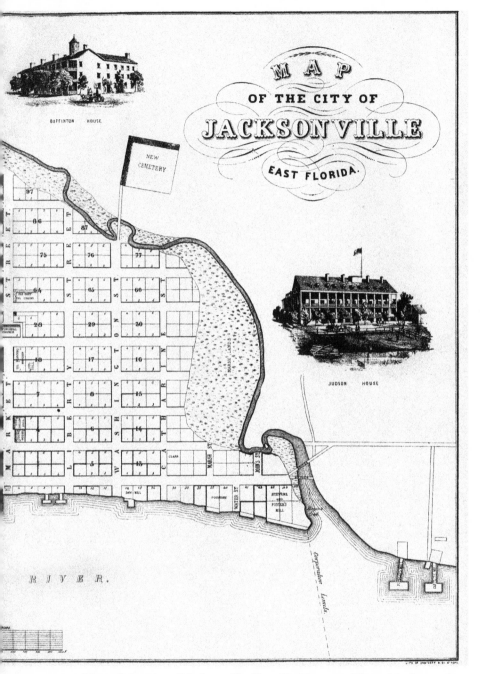

MAP 1. Map of the city of Jacksonville, East Florida, 1859. The original map is at the Jacksonville Public Library, a gift of G. D. Ackerly. The map was published in T. Frederick Davis, *History of Jacksonville, Florida, and Vicinity, 1513 to 1924* (St. Augustine, Florida: The Florida Historical Society, 1925).

"Raise the Banner of Secession"

Sectional Debates
in Jacksonville, 1845–1861

Why did seven states of the Lower South secede from the Union in 1861 to join the Confederate States of America and send men by the thousands to the battlefields of the Civil War? Few historical questions are more hotly debated, especially when defense of the institution of slavery is considered as the prime motivation for secession and war. This chapter again seeks answers to that question by examining the reports, editorials, and opinions of the residents of Jacksonville, Florida, that were published in the town's antebellum newspapers. Based on that evidence, it is clear that the prime motivation among Jacksonville residents was fear that abolitionists in the Northern states intended to take away the rights of slaveholders to carry human property into the western territories, and to eventually abolish the institution of slavery throughout the United States.

Two rival weekly newspapers were published for most of the 1840s and 1850s: one pledged to support the Whig Party (or its successors), the other the Democratic Party. Newspaper evidence for antebellum Jacksonville documents that white residents, correspondents, and editors participated in hearty two-party competition, spoke out at public meetings, and vigorously debated all political issues of the day. On all issues of contemporary importance, differing opinions abounded, with one vital exception: on matters related to slavery, whites closed ranks and passionately insisted on the legitimacy of the institution of slavery, branding all who favored abolition as heinous and evil.[1]

In 1835, the town's first newspaper, the *Jacksonville Courier*, reacted in alarm to rumors of looming slave uprisings inspired by the slave rebellion in Southhampton, Virginia, led by the slave preacher Nat Turner four years before.[2] The *Courier* reported rumors of abolitionist-inspired plots and impending uprisings among slaves and free blacks in northeast Florida, and on August 27, 1835, it informed Northerners of the "true" nature of slavery: "The good and faithful negro on a plantation at the South is no more a manual slave than the hired white man, who labors from sunrise to its setting, on a farm at the North."[3] For the next quarter century, every Jacksonville newspaper justified slavery as a benign and patriarchal institution, of benefit to black slaves as well as to their white owners; anyone who thought differently was denounced.

Even before the Nat Turner rebellion, the nation had experienced a major crisis over the extension of slavery into the western territories. The year was 1819, East Florida was still a Spanish colony, and the future site of Jacksonville was known as the Cowford, denoting the northern terminus of a ferry crossing on the road running north to Georgia. The controversy that threatened dissolution of the Union erupted over the proposed admission of Missouri as a slave state. Northern states were opposed, citing the immorality of slavery and its incompatibility with free labor, and also the worry that voting power in the U.S. Senate would tilt in favor of the South. The charges of immorality infuriated Southerners and aggravated fears that admitting Missouri as a free state would lead to abolition of slavery in the Southern states.

The crisis was averted with a compromise that admitted Missouri as a slave state and Maine as a non-slave state. Congress drew a line at the southern boundary of Missouri, marking for the future the permissible limits of slavery in the remaining unorganized land of the Louisiana Territory. South of that line slavery would be permitted, but to the north it would be "forever prohibited."[4]

The troubling sectional crisis reappeared in 1845 in congressional debates over annexation of Texas, again in 1846 during the war with Mexico, and yet again in 1848 over the role of slavery in the territory acquired after that war. The crisis was unresolved during the national election of 1848. Supporters of the Whig Party had opposed annexation of Texas; Democrats had given unquestioned support. The controversy was intensified by the determination of Southern Democrats to move human property into the new territory. Anti-slavery advocates in the North insisted that the western territories must be preserved for free white farmers.

Pennsylvanian David Wilmot, a House Democrat, tacked an amendment onto an appropriations bill stating "neither slavery nor involuntary servitude shall ever exist" in territory acquired as a result of the war. Wilmot had been advised of probable voter alienation in the North if the Mexican War was perceived as a Democratic Party ploy to open new fields for slavery. The proviso passed in the House and failed in the Senate, but it became a controversial rallying point for sectional disputes during the 1848 election debates. In the South, both political parties denounced attempts to ban slavery from the western territories. In the North, many Democratic voters defected to the new Free-Soil Party, prompted by fears that white yeoman farmers would not be able to compete economically against slaveholders whose workers were exploited and not paid wages. At the time it was not uncommon for Free-Soilers to express anti-black biases; in the antebellum years, racial discrimination was common in the North and Midwest.[5]

The 1848 Democratic candidate for president, Lewis Cass of Michigan, supported national expansion schemes and proposed "popular sovereignty" as a way to settle the controversy over expansion of slavery. Cass's plan, whereby each new territorial legislature would decide whether or not to permit slavery, had strong appeal for Southern Democrats. The Whig Party candidate was a Mexican War hero, General Zachary Taylor, a slaveholder from Louisiana who seemed safe to Southern voters. Taylor avoided discussion of divisive issues during the campaign and, aided by the popularity of Free-Soil candidate Martin Van Buren among Democrats in the North, won the election.[6]

Jacksonville voters engaged in the debates over the Wilmot Proviso with gusto. Florida had been admitted to the Union in 1845, and Duval County had grown to a population of 3,114, including 1,625 whites, 1,325 enslaved blacks, and 164 free persons of color.[7] Columbus Drew, editor of the *Florida Republican*, backed Zachary Taylor and followed the traditional Whig policy of moderation and compromise regarding slavery and state sovereignty. Drew acknowledged slavery as "the greatest landed interest in the South" but stressed that militant commitment to slavery to the exclusion of everything else was both provincial and detrimental to the total population. He rhetorically accused the Democrats of being aristocratic slaveholders who cared not for "the humbler planter who owns no slaves—the man who fulfills the primal decree of earning his bread by the sweat of his brow . . . [or for] the white mechanic of the South, who has no interest in land, none in slaves." In a statement that succinctly captured the moderate, compromise-oriented, and Unionist sentiment of Jacksonville's Whigs, Drew wrote that, if threatened, his party brethren would "not fail to give his vote and lift his voice in opposition to the schemes of the Northern incendiaries; but few will be found rash enough to propose disunion for a remedy."[8] Historian Herbert J. Doherty Jr. accurately characterized Drew and the Florida Whigs as "Union men" who were also ready to "stand up for the rights of the South."[9]

Felix Livingston, editor of the *Florida News*, backed the Democratic Party candidate, popular sovereignty, and national expansion, and excoriated "Whiggish doctrines" that would "wrap the Union in flames and blood." He believed that a working man was as much interested in protecting slavery as was a wealthy owner of "a thousand slaves. And the poor man, who has none, only considers it a misfortune, and his only hope is by industry and economy, to purchase a working hand." The editor was convinced that "the life and property of every resident in a slaveholding State . . . is entirely dependent upon this institution," and warned that electing Zachary Taylor would provoke "insidious attacks upon us. Insurrection will speedily accompany the prospect of emancipation. The brand and the butcher knife will be in the hand of the slave, but yet the Whigs cry moderation! Until they wake up of a morning and find their throats cut, and their houses burnt, so long will they believe in the virtue of moderation."[10]

Echoes of the radical and incendiary sentiment expressed by Livingston would be heard repeatedly in Jacksonville for the next thirteen years, but in 1848 his was not yet the dominant voice. A majority of voters chose the candidate pledged to compromise and loyalty to the Union, Zachary Taylor, a pattern repeated throughout Florida and the nation. The election results proved that Union sentiment still had deep roots in the area.[11]

With important issues concerning the territories still unresolved, voters entered the 1850s with apprehension concerning the fate of slavery. Once again, political battles left over from the Mexican War were divisive. Residents of California were maneuvering to come into the Union as a free state without going through a territorial stage, prompting fears that the South would henceforth have only a minority role in the U.S. Senate. The leading voice of secession, Senator John C. Calhoun of South Carolina, issued a call for delegates from the Southern states to meet at a convention at Nashville, Tennessee.

Some of Jacksonville's Democrats responded to Calhoun's invitation. At a public meeting in March 1850, thirty-eight locals signed a petition urging their neighbors to stand in defense of "Southern Rights" and chose a twelve-member delegation to represent them at the Nashville convention. A future Confederate general, Joseph Finegan, was the unofficial head of a delegation that included South Carolina–born Henry D. Holland, a physician, and Vermont native John P. Sanderson, a lawyer and planter. Beyond vehement speeches, little of importance was accomplished at Nashville. Calhoun died before the conclave began, and only nine states sent delegates.[12]

More important debates were heard in Washington, D.C., where Senator Steven Douglas, a Democrat from Illinois, managed passage of a bill known as the Compromise of 1850, which provided for admission of California as a free state and the creation of two new territories, New Mexico and Utah, where the question of slavery would be decided by popular sovereignty. In addition, the slave trade was abolished in the District of Columbia, and a stringent new Fugitive Slave Act was agreed to.[13]

Democrats in Jacksonville were outraged by the compromises. Oscar Hart, son of Jacksonville founder Isaiah D. Hart and well known for his mercurial temperament, had served as sheriff and clerk of court and generally supported Whig policies. Thoughts of moderation and compromise were far from his mind when he decided the Compromise of 1850 would surrender California to abolitionists and deprive slaveholders of their "inalienable rights" by abolishing the slave trade in Washington, D.C. In a letter to the *Florida News* he repudiated surrender to the Northern abolitionists, who intended to "place about our necks the galling chains of perpetual servitude and slavery."[14] He warned Jacksonville residents to beware lest their own "chains be forged and riveted. . . . The day for conciliation and compromise has passed. . . . We will retreat no further." The choices were now "Southern liberty or Southern annihilation."[15]

Other Jacksonville incendiaries accused the town's Northern-born residents of being abolitionists, until the editor of the *Florida News* encouraged people to cool their tempers and remember that Northern birth did not automatically make a person an abolitionist. If someone elected to political office supported laws "so mean and cowardly" as abolition, however, they should be voted out. He added that some local Whigs could not be trusted, especially Ozias Budington, James W. Bryant, and rival editor Columbus Drew, who was "perfectly rotten."[16]

Drew was not intimidated. During the fall 1850 elections for local and Florida-wide offices, he urged voters to choose Whig candidates and stand up for Union and accused Democrats John Broward and Thomas Ledwith of favoring secession. After Whig candidates emerged victorious, Drew wrote:

"The people have declared for Compromise—have chosen peace—have spoken in thunder tones for Union."[17] The Florida Whig Party triumphed in this campaign, but as Doherty observed, the victory was not in the "thunder tones" that Drew pronounced. Democrats gained voting majorities of the Florida General Assembly, lowered the secessionist volume of their political rhetoric, and became more conciliatory on national disputes.[18]

The inflamed political debates of the 1850s occurred during a period of general prosperity in northeast Florida. Newspapers published accounts of successful Jacksonville businessmen and area planters, and of merchants profiting from sales of wagons, horses, tools, and supplies to planters from other states transporting slaves to vacant lands in the interior of Florida.[19] Sawmills established on the St. Johns River prospered in the early 1850s: the Byrne and Moody Company mill was cutting 13,000 to 14,000 board feet of lumber a day; the Alsop, Mooney and Company mill and the Panama Mill were also experiencing "heavy business." The *Florida Republican* reported sixty cargoes of yellow pine timber and sawed lumber shipped to out-of-state buyers in June 1850. In ten months merchants shipped 2,500 bales of Sea Island cotton worth $150,000, along with 250 hogsheads of sugar and numerous bales of hides and Spanish moss. On June 27, 1850, more than 600 barrels of virgin turpentine dip worth $2.75 each were stacked on town wharves. The price of turpentine gave a corresponding boost to the value of pineland in the area.[20]

More than 130 ships carried five million board feet of sawed lumber, squared timber, and other forest products away from St. Johns River sawmills in 1850. Additional mills were built, some with the newest circular saw machinery. Mills were erected at Doctors Lake and the mouth of Black Creek, with a total of twenty-one sawmills on the St. Johns between Palatka and Mayport. George Mooney erected the Mooney Machine and Engine Manufactory to provide products for the mills. Dozens of new dwellings were constructed, and brick business buildings went up along Bay Street. In October 1851 the *Florida Republican* reported "vast numbers of strangers who flock to East Florida from the North during the winter" to lodge in the newly constructed hotels and boardinghouses.[21]

Prosperous times continued throughout most of the 1850s. On December 18, 1856, the *Florida News* wrote that sawmills on the lower St. Johns produced 2,500,000 board feet of sawed lumber each month, along with "many cargoes of ranging timber and cedar timber and live oak." Exports of lumber had increased to 350 cargoes a year, and the value of cotton, tobacco, and sugar cargoes passing through the Jacksonville port topped $500,000 in 1856, making "Florida's crop greater in quantity of cotton, and aggregate values, than any State in proportion to its population."[22]

Reports of labor shortages and advertisements from employers seeking workers were common in the 1850s. On December 13, 1851, James S. Baker placed an ad in the *Florida News* for eight to ten men, "either white or colored." By the mid-1850s, railroad construction projects in northeast Florida heightened the labor shortage. In October 1855 the Florida Railroad sought two hundred workers and promised the "highest wages will be paid."[23] Three months later the search was still under way, and prospective workers were tempted with offers of up to a dollar per day without board.[24]

F. F. L'Engle wrote to his son Edward in September 1856 asking for help finding workers for the railroad track he was constructing. The elder L'Engle, a Duval County planter and lumberman, had only been able to hire eighteen white men, including fourteen Irishmen, and twenty-two black slaves. Four months later L'Engle's wife, Charlotte Porcher L'Engle, informed Edward that his father had "failed in every quarter in getting Negroes to carry on the work," despite offering twenty dollars a month for every slave he could hire. Mrs. L'Engle wrote that a rival contractor, Hal Sadler, "has a large gang and is grading with Irishmen . . . [who] are feeding on Ham and Eggs and other dainties."[25] When the Florida, Atlantic and Gulf Central Railroad began laying rails in 1858, competition for laborers intensified. T. E. Buckman, the railroad's superintendent, promised "good wages paid quarterly" for thirty men.[26]

Other employers sought the return of enslaved workers who had escaped. Most issues of the local newspapers carried advertisements calling for the return of runaway slaves like Hampton, his wife, Nanny, and their five children, said to have a "large connection in Jacksonville . . . where they may be harbored for any length of time," or from where they might have been sneaked out on a vessel.[27] A solicitation for the return of John Butler, a runaway from Orange Mills, was compelling. Butler was described as a "bright mulatto with straight hair of yellowish brown colour" who was "fond of changing his name and passing for a white man, can read and is quite intelligent, and is a good home carpenter."[28]

The booming economy and labor shortages explain the increase in prices paid for human property during the decade. In January 1857 an auction in Tallahassee drew the attention of the editor of the *Florida Republican* when prices ranging from $1,100 to $1,300 were paid for enslaved men between the ages of sixteen and twenty, and $1,200 to $1,500 for enslaved women between fifteen and eighteen.[29] There was even talk in the newspapers of reopening the trade in slaves from Africa as a way to make affordable laborers more available.[30]

Slaveholders were able to profit from the labor shortage by either selling their chattel at high prices or hiring them out to other employers. Following the death of John Haddock in 1856, the thirteen slaves left in his estate (three men, ages sixty-five, fifty, and twenty-eight; two women in their early twenties; and eight children under sixteen) were valued at $5,525. Over the next three years these slaves earned $1,368 in hire-out wages paid to the estate. When another inventory of the Haddock estate was conducted in 1859, the combined value of human property had risen to $9,575. The two elder males were dead, but five more children had been born.[31]

Owners were outraged when slaves were stolen by white criminals. In January 1856, Jacksonville residents were apprised of the hanging death of Stephen P. Yeomans, a violent man with a record of stealing slaves and free blacks. Vigilantes had captured and hung Yeomans without benefit of a trial by jury. The editor of the *Florida News* condemned this act as an uncivilized abuse of the law despite Yeomans' criminal record.[32] Two years later posters were displayed in the town offering a $100 reward for the capture of another thief, John Barden, age thirty-five, convicted of robbery and arson and awaiting punishment for jailbreak and abduction of slaves during the escape.[33]

It is hard to determine from some reports if missing slaves were stolen or if they liberated themselves. In July 1850, Edwin R. Alberti, owner of Woodstock Mills on the St. Marys River, offered a $300 reward for the recovery of Stephen Harmon, a free black man who had been found guilty of "a violation of the Laws of the State" and had been "sold" by order of the Nassau County Circuit Court to labor for Alberti "for a brief term of years." Accusing unknown individuals of abducting Harmon and selling him "as a slave for life," Alberti offered the reward for his return and for the arrest and conviction of the "vile wretches concerned in the outrage. . . . Stephen is by profession a sailor—for over a year has been engaged about a sawmill—[He is] quite short (about five feet high)—dark brown complexion—about 25 to 30 years of age—rather slow in replying when spoken to—and can, in the negro style, (imperfectly) read and write."[34]

In the same advertisement, Alberti offered a $300 reward for the recovery of Rebecca, a slave woman believed stolen "by the same party engaged in the abduction of Stephen." Rebecca's owner was J. W. Banely, who lived at White Oak Plantation. Alberti said Rebecca was "of a yellow complexion, about five feet high—28 to 30 years of age—has several front teeth decayed or broken—quick in reply when addressed—has been the mother of five children, three of which are still living. She has a number of relations living in Savannah, to which place she was desirous to return, and the pretence of aiding her to do so, enabled the party to perfect arrangements for carrying her off."[35] Alberti was convinced that "a gang of desperadoes" had carried out the two thefts and urged other white persons in the region to capture the criminals responsible for the acts. "If permitted to escape with impunity," he warned, the criminals "will extend their ravages in this respect, and add other depredations thereto."[36]

Alberti apparently did not consider the possibility that Stephen and Rebecca acted in a joint conspiracy to liberate themselves. Stephen's court-imposed enslavement, coupled with Rebecca's desire to return to Savannah, represented sufficient motivation to abscond. Stephen, despite his imperfect literacy, was a sailor with experience traversing the St. Marys River from Woodstock Mills to Fernandina, Florida, and St. Marys, Georgia. No further information on the fate of Harmon and Rebecca has been found. Judging from the pair of $300 rewards offered for their recovery, Alberti and Banely apparently placed great value on them as human property.

In the November 14, 1850, issue of the *Florida Republican*, W. H. G. Saunders, guardian of a free woman of color named Matilda, who lived with her children near the juncture of Black Creek and the St. Johns River, offered a reward of $100 for the return of Matilda's two children. Saunders said that on the evening of November 7 five white men came to Matilda's house and abducted Judy, age fifteen, who was "very black, stout and well grown," and Charles, age ten, of a "rather yellow complexion." The newspaper's editor commented on the incident, citing a letter he received from Colonel Lewis Fleming with pertinent news of the abduction. Fleming said five disguised men were guilty of the act, and that on the same evening they stole Judy and Charles they also stole one of his slaves, who "feigned lame" and was released by the men as they made their escape. The newspaper linked this abduction with the report of the still-missing slave family of F. W. Sams (Hampton and Nanny and their five children) reported in the October 3, 1850, issue of the newspaper. "There is another instance in which two negro men are missing, and from their character and habits it is not supposed they have absconded," the editor asserted. He warned readers to be on the lookout for a "set of villains about."[37]

Slave runaways and abductions, the booming economy and resultant labor shortages, and escalating anger over the sectional crisis were all featured at a series of explosive meetings in May 1852. The meetings were prompted by a runaway attempt by three slaves employed at the Bellechasse and Finegan sawmill in Jacksonville. After loading lumber at the mill, the schooner *Lady of the Lake* sailed downriver bound for a port in the North. At Mayport the captain discovered three runaways hiding in the ship's hold and sent them back to Jacksonville. The Duval County sheriff, suspecting something seditious, arrested the entire crew of the schooner. The case was promptly brought before Judge Oliver Wood of the circuit court, who investigated and dismissed all charges against the captain and crew. The vessel was released and permitted to proceed. The editor of the *Florida News* was so outraged by the judicial decision, however, that he pronounced his own verdict:"there cannot be the slightest doubt that at least two of the sailors enticed off and secreted the negroes."[38]

A huge crowd gathered for the first meeting on May 22, presided over by Dr. Henry D. Holland. Participants called for measures to defeat"the nefarious projects of persons who are from time to time attempting to entice our slave population to abscond."[39] Speakers emphasized the difficulty of stopping slave runaways in Jacksonville because so many ships left the port for northern destinations. Some town residents believed local abolitionists were secretly following the impulses of their"mawkish sentimentality" by helping slaves abscond.

Several speakers denounced the practice of"self-hire," arguing that slaves should only be hired out to work when their legal owners or guardians conducted the transactions and collected the wages. When slaves were allowed to come and go without proper restraint, speakers warned, the result was a "larger freedom" that promoted"bad associations" and encouraged slaves to "contract idle and vicious habits." The negative results intensified "when the appointed time for the payment of their wages arrived, should they have been unsuccessful, or wasted or squandered them, they will be induced to, or voluntarily resort to, the commission of crime to supply or replace what their idleness or vicious habits have led them to misappropriate." Tougher laws and tighter restraints were needed, or else slaves working under the supervision of their masters would be corrupted by the bad examples of"self-hire" slaves who were"allowed to go at large, under little or no restraint, having ample leisure for their own amusements, and engaging only in such employment as may be congenial to their tastes. . . . [Others] are thus rendered *disobedient and discontented* with their condition," and become a danger to the community. After vigorous debate, the attendees resolved to change the "long dormant and slumbering sentiment with regard to a proper protection of our property, and resist'unto the death' all aggressions upon the same."[40]

Several formal resolutions were adopted. A proposal for an ordinance that would forbid "Negroes to hire their own time" was drafted and approved for presentation to the town council. The group resolved to find ways to stop abduction of slaves, to foil attempts by slaves to escape to the Northern states, and to promote "the greatest vigilance of our citizens and the most efficient legislation." A judge and four attorneys were assigned the task of studying state laws for the purpose of revising and toughening local legislation. Finally, a five-member "Committee of Vigilance" was appointed.[41]

The Jacksonville Town Council responded swiftly to the resolutions, enacting municipal ordinances intended to tightly regulate the life and labor of all black persons living in the town. The first ordinance was aimed at free blacks. White Americans in the Southern states generally limited avenues to freedom for slaves, believing that free blacks incited unrest and rebelliousness among slaves. Free blacks were discriminated against in nearly all aspects of life. This was in contrast to race policies in effect in Florida under the Spanish, when a more flexible system encouraged manumission and even permitted slaves to purchase their own freedom. Spanish owners of slaves who remained in Florida under American rule encouraged manumission as well, expecting the freedmen to become allies of their former owners and thus maximize control of the larger population of slaves. The new American territorial government passed rigid laws imported from neighboring Georgia and South Carolina making emancipation extremely difficult and recognizing only two castes: free whites and enslaved blacks. Free blacks were an anomaly, and over time their numbers declined markedly as discriminatory laws limited their possibilities of emancipation and freedom.[42]

It was undoubtedly demoralizing to free blacks that the first regulatory ordinance was aimed at them. The ordinance made it mandatory for all "free Negroes or Mulattoes" between the ages of ten and sixty living in Jacksonville to pay an annual fee ($10.50 for males and $5.50 for females) and to be registered by the town marshal. Failure to abide by this law was punishable by five days in jail or by corporal punishment: a public whipping of thirty-nine "stripes" of a lash.[43] The second ordinance made it unlawful for a slave to hire him- or herself to an employer in the town. In the future, only the slave's owner would be permitted to make hiring arrangements. Noncompliance by a slave would result in thirty-nine "stripes" from a whip. The third ordinance forced whites to observe the slave-hiring regulations. Anyone who hired a slave without permission from the slave's owner was subject to a fine of $20 or a jail sentence of five days.

Slaveholders were also subject to municipal regulation by the new ordinances. The fourth ordinance read: "It shall not be lawful for any slave or

slaves to live in any building within the limits of said Town, unless said building be under the enclosure" of their owner, guardian, or other white person
"responsible for their good conduct." Violations were subject to a $20 fine
or five days in jail. The final ordinance also regulated living arrangements. It
forbade any slave or free black to "keep a boarding, eating, or dancing house"
within the town limits. Violators could be fined $20, be incarcerated for five
days, or receive thirty-nine "stripes" of a lash.

Passage of these ordinances reduced the fear and hysteria that dominated
events in Jacksonville in May and June of 1852. With tension still elevated in
the aftermath of passage of the Compromise of 1850, residents of the town
turned their attention to the presidential elections scheduled for later in the
year. By the time the Whig nominating convention was convened, the death
of Zachary Taylor had elevated Millard Fillmore to the nation's highest office. Fillmore, a conservative Whig from New York, had alienated Northern
Whigs by vigorously enforcing the Fugitive Slave Act and by supporting
popular sovereignty. To retain vital support in the North, delegates bypassed
Fillmore and nominated General Winfield Scott instead.

For Florida voters, the choice of Scott had negative consequences. In
1836, during the Second Seminole War, Scott had briefly commanded Federal forces in Florida and made remarks highly critical of Florida planters and militia volunteers. He was bitterly attacked at the time by Joseph
White, Florida's territorial delegate to Congress. Scott's public support of
the Compromise of 1850 further limited the effectiveness of his campaign in
Florida.[44]

Florida's Democrats overwhelmingly backed Franklin Pierce of New
Hampshire, a man who had been publicly sympathetic to Southern causes
and advocated the annexation of Cuba. In addition to solid Democratic support in the North, winning all but two of the slave states resulted in a victory for Pierce and the Democrats. In a prelude to election results for the
remainder of the decade, Democrats in Florida won the gubernatorial and
congressional contests and both houses of the general assembly. In a glee-
ful postmortem, the News pronounced the Whig Party dead "by political
suicide."[45]

"Political suicide" might have been an overstatement, but the Whigs
had waged their last campaign for the presidency. Irreparably divided by
the Compromise of 1850 and driven by the political passions of their regions, Northern and Southern Whigs moved in different directions. Many
Northern Whigs, especially those who had supported the Free-Soil Party in
1848, joined the Republican Party when it was founded in 1854. In 1856 they

backed Republican John C. Frémont. Another branch of the Whig Party in the North embraced the American Party (popularly known as the Know-Nothing Party). Caught up in a virulent nativist movement sparked by the influx of Irish and German immigrants in the late 1840s and 1850s, American Party candidates supported anti-immigrant, anti-Catholic policies that called for legislation to extend the naturalization period, restrict immigrant office holding, and ban tax support for parochial schools.[46]

Southern Whigs were adrift in stormy political seas without the anchor of a national party. They found the policies of both Free-Soilers and Republicans calling for banning slavery from the territories so repulsive that many of them cautiously voted for the Democratic candidates. Others longed for a revival of their old party and contemplated whether the American Party could be made to fit Southern circumstances. With the exception of New Orleans, Baltimore, Louisville, and St. Louis, immigration had not been a significant political issue in the South, but events became so inflammatory that voters in the region had to make immediate political choices.

In 1854, Congress passed the Kansas-Nebraska Bill and further exacerbated the controversy generated by the Compromise of 1850. Led again by Stephen A. Douglas, supporters of a transcontinental railroad initiated a debate that resulted in the Kansas-Nebraska Act. Railroad backers appealed to Southern interests by proposing to repeal the Missouri Compromise and open the huge territory west of Iowa and Missouri (later the territories of Kansas and Nebraska) to popular sovereignty, and thereby open the territories to slavery. Southern politicians voted overwhelmingly for passage without realizing the consequences would be political chaos leading to secession and war. The Democrats flourished as a result, but passage of the Kansas-Nebraska Act spelled disaster for Florida's Whigs. Devoted party members tried valiantly to run local and state campaigns but suffered devastating losses.[47]

Democratic Party numbers increased throughout the 1850s as migrants from South Carolina and Georgia settled in northeast Florida. This was true in Clay County, part of Duval County until 1858, where residents born in Georgia and South Carolina constituted 60 percent of the total heads of household. Florida natives accounted for 19 percent. Fully 90 percent of the heads of households in 1860 were natives of one of the slave states; only one in ten was from a non-slave state or Europe.

The contrast with previously settled Duval County, especially the town of Jacksonville, is striking. Seventy-one percent of the heads of households in Duval County were natives of one of the slave states: four in ten from

Florida, three in ten from Georgia or South Carolina. Inside the Jacksonville boundaries, however, 44 percent of the heads of households originated in one of the non-slaveholding states or in a foreign country.[48]

Perhaps the relatively high percentage of Northern-born residents of Jacksonville explains why, despite the increasing popularity of Democratic Party candidates in the 1850s, the principles embraced by the Whig Party—moderation, compromise, and Union—continued to appeal to the town's voters. During the 1854 Duval County elections, William K. Cole, editor of the Democratic *Florida News*, had confidently predicted victory for his party. Campaign efforts were directed at the rural residents of the county, where the largest slaveholders resided. Cole called for "Equal rights in the Union to every portion of it, and no geographical lines for the exclusion of any portion of our people and their property [including enslaved human property] from the common domain."[49]

After the Democrats triumphed at both national and state levels, Cole boasted: "Write Florida down a Democratic state for ever and aye."[50] Democrats had indeed won a decisive statewide victory, but results in his own town and county should have tempered Cole's enthusiasm. The Democratic candidate for state representative from Duval County, Milton Haynes of Mayport Mills, won the election, but defeated Whig rival Columbus Drew by the slender margin of 391 votes to 385. The results of the election revealed serious differences between residents of the town of Jacksonville and voters who lived on rural farms and plantations. Drew had a strong majority inside town boundaries (223 to 170), but the rural precincts went solidly for Haynes. In the Clay Hill District (today part of Clay County) the vote was 17 for Drew and 73 for Haynes. Drew charged that "fraud and illegal voting" at Clay Hill swung the vote in Haynes's favor, but the allegations went unproven.[51]

In a region of limited choices, Jacksonville and Florida Whigs tentatively embraced the American Party and attempted to implant their old Whig political values in an organization that was grounded on the anti-immigrant and anti-Catholic biases of the Northern wing of the party. Historian Arthur W. Thompson demonstrated that in Florida "the state party would have nothing to do with anti-Catholicism" diatribes beyond "demands for more rigid naturalization laws."[52] Vague references can be found in local newspapers to "foreign" influences in Washington and in the North, along with letters to newspapers from individuals that included negative stereotypes about the Irish, but Florida employers were experiencing labor shortages and recruiting foreign workers. In Florida, American Party candidates minimized the importance of anti-Catholic and anti-immigrant planks on the national platform and instead emphasized moderation, compromise on issues related to slavery in the territories, and patriotic affiliation with the Union, precisely the issues that resonated with former Southern Whig voters.

The first test of the viability of American Party strength in Jacksonville came in the municipal elections of May 1855. To everyone's surprise, American Party candidates claimed every seat on the town council. Against long odds, a party sharing the principles of the old Whigs stepped into a local political vacuum with a strongly pro-Union stance.[53] Anticipating similar success in the forthcoming fall elections for Duval County offices, the *Florida Republican*, formerly a Whig advocate, published editorials that were patriotic and reverential of the past, still expressive of Whig values but formulaic and deliberately vague to avoid the poisonous web of sectional crisis.[54]

The *Florida Republican* ridiculed Jacksonville Democratic candidates as "foreigners" and praised the American Party candidates as true "Americans" and patriots. Being labeled a foreigner may have come as a surprise to one legislative candidate, Charles Broward, whose family ties in the region stretched back to the eighteenth century when Florida was a Spanish colony. Nevertheless, political trickery prevailed in a carefully orchestrated campaign of obfuscation that avoided the troubling sectional controversies and said little of substance about slavery. Behind a smoke screen of vigorous attacks on non-patriotic foreigners and vague appeals to a heroic past, the *Florida Republican* extolled the idea that "Americans shall rule America" and parlayed this strategy into a convincing victory. On October 1, 1855, American Party candidates won all four seats on the county commission, judge of the probate court, clerk of the circuit court, sheriff, tax assessor, tax collector, coroner, and land surveyor. It was a stunning victory for the new party.[55] Casually blaming the loss on voter apathy and the "usual Whig majority in this county," the *Florida News* predicted the revival and ultimate triumph of the Democrats. But American Party candidates were triumphant again in the April 7, 1856, municipal elections, winning all open seats on the town council.[56]

These local successes were impressive, but the American Party faced the same obstacle that had previously doomed the Whig Party: controversy over the future of slavery in the western territories. Northern candidates opposed expansion of slavery, while Southern candidates denounced limitations on the ability to carry slave property into the territories, considering this a denial of their rights as free American citizens that would ultimately doom their cherished institution. No single party could reconcile these diametrically opposed views. By the time of the next presidential campaign, Northern American Party voters would have thrown their support to the Republican Party.[57]

Violence in Kansas in March 1855 was the next crisis to galvanize the nation's attention. Carrying weapons and threatening to crack the heads of abolitionists they encountered, pro-slavery "border ruffians" from Missouri, led by Senator David Atchison, crossed into Kansas to seize polling places and stuff voting boxes with fraudulent ballots and thus ensure that Kansas would enter the Union as a slave state. Meeting at Lecompton, they installed a pro-slavery territorial legislature and constitution proclaimed legitimate by President Franklin Pierce.

"Free-Soilers" from the North responded by setting up their own legislature based at Lawrence and writing an anti-slavery constitution (which was disregarded by the president). Armed bands from Missouri invaded Lawrence, and abolition extremists from New England, led by John Brown, retaliated with a murderous raid on a pro-slavery settlement at Pottawatomie Creek in May 1856. News reports of "bleeding Kansas" prompted adventurers from both sides of the ideological divide to rush into the fray.

Edward Hopkins, a former Florida Whig and wealthy Duval County planter, traveled to Kansas in 1856 and returned with an urgent plea that his friends and neighbors answer the call that "bleeding Kansas makes upon us." He had witnessed "our ruthless foe, who puts to the sword our kindred, and robs and plunders and burns their homes," and returned to deliver "a Southern message," one that advocated "love [for] our institutions, for we see in them the hand of Providence, which is to conduct us through the quicksand of agrarianism to a stable republicanism, and to elevate the African to a participation of the common heritage of the Gospel." Hopkins urged one hundred good men to "leave the comforts of home" and go to the frontier to protect "our just and legal rights" by establishing pro-slavery communities. Hopkins was still a Whig at heart, but he was a quintessential Southern Whig who wanted to settle Union-loving men in Kansas to plant the flag of slavery in the western territories and defend fundamental states' rights within the Union.[58]

The American Party ventured into national and state electoral arenas once more in the fall of 1856 with President Millard Fillmore of New York as its candidate for president. The death of President Zachary Taylor in 1853 had brought Vice-President Fillmore into the presidency. Jacksonville's *Florida Republican* printed the party's anti-Catholic and anti-immigrant planks and, more importantly, displayed the plank that endorsed "the perpetuation of the Federal Union as the palladium of our civil and religious liberties and the only sure bulwark of American Independence."[59] By 1856 the American Party had become a temporary political haven for Southern Whigs like Edward Hopkins, who still endorsed the sanctity of Union but fervently believed that the Constitution entitled American citizens to carry their human property into the western territories.

Northern Whigs had briefly supported the American Party, but in 1856 they backed the Republican Party candidate, John C. Frémont. Unequivocally opposed to expansion of slavery into the western territories, the Republicans had become the largest political party in the Northern states. Such a stance was unthinkable for American Party brethren in Jacksonville.

Only the Democratic Party could count on supporters in both regions of the fracturing nation in 1856, but even this seeming unity in support of James Buchanan of Pennsylvania was under threat from growing North-South fissures. Popular sovereignty was still the bedrock policy of the Stephen Douglas wing of the Democratic Party, but opposition to that policy had prompted some Northern Democrats to join the Republican Party. In the South, radicals denounced the policy as "squatter sovereignty" and a deceptive ploy. Since the Missouri Compromise barred slavery from the western territories, only non-slaveholders could take up residence before a legislature applied for statehood, thus dooming the possibility of slavery ever gaining a foothold. This radical position gathered such momentum that it soon severed bonds of party unity and left behind northern and southern branches of a once dominant party.

During the 1856 election campaign, Democrats in Florida called for immediate secession in the event of a Republican Party victory. American Party supporters, while standing firmly for the rights of slaveholders, urged voters to reject such extreme demands and choose instead policies of moderation, reason, compromise, and Union. Florida's voters embraced the Democrats' message. Buchanan won in all of Florida's counties except Duval, Santa Rosa, and Columbia. He also carried all the other slave states except Maryland; victories in Pennsylvania, New Jersey, Indiana, Illinois, and California assured him of the presidency. Democrat Madison S. Perry was elected governor of Florida, and George S. Hawkins was chosen to represent Florida in the U.S. House.[60] Party organizers in Jacksonville held a torchlight parade, complete with music and bonfires and a 101-gun salute, followed by a macabre ceremony in which an effigy of the Republican candidate for president, John C. Frémont, was "hanged, drawn and quartered."[61]

Reeling from the defeat, American Party regulars put forward a slate of candidates in the April 1857 municipal elections for the Jacksonville Town Council. Only two of their candidates were elected, by the scanty margins of three and one votes over their opponents. Only three months earlier, American Party candidate Oscar Hart had been chosen in a special election to fill the vacant Probate Court judgeship, but by then Hart had become such an outspoken supporter of radical causes that he must have seemed a safe choice for Democratic crossover voters.[62] The elections of 1857 marked the end of the American Party in Jacksonville. Followers of the Whig Party again searched for a party compatible with their moderate and Unionist principles.

Events of such importance occurred between 1857 and 1860 that it became impossible for any national party to mediate the extreme demands. Pleas for moderation and compromise were barely discernible above the clamor generated by the sectional controversies. The first crisis was the U.S. Supreme Court's March 1857 decision in *Dred Scott v. Sanford*, denying the Scotts' claim to freedom based on their having lived in the free Territory of Minnesota. Writing for the majority, Chief Justice Roger B. Taney ruled that as black persons the Scotts were "beings of an inferior order [who] had no rights which white men were bound to respect." As inferior beings, they were not lawful citizens and had no right to sue in federal court. By this opinion, no free blacks had legal rights in America.[63]

Taney further ruled that the Missouri Compromise was illegal because it represented an unconstitutional denial of the rights of slaveholders to carry human property into the territories. The congressional legislation represented seizure of property without due process of law, as protected under the Fifth Amendment. A key plank of the Republican Party was invalidated as a direct consequence, along with the bedrock plank of the Democrats, popular sovereignty, since the ruling meant that neither Congress nor a state legislature could bar slavery from a territory.

Later in 1857, President Buchanan pressured Congress to admit Kansas as a slave state, after the majority of Kansans had clearly stated through the ballot that they opposed slavery. Abraham Lincoln worried that the Supreme Court and the president were willing tools of the "Slave Power Conspiracy" and that slavery would soon be extended into the northern states and the territories alike. Even fellow Democrat Stephen Douglas broke with the president, hoping to strengthen his party's chances in the North, but instead destroyed its chances in the South. Radical Democrats in the South were demanding that Congress pass a federal slave code for the territories to protect human property from the aggressive designs of abolitionists.

Secessionist rhetoric was also increasing in stridency and popularity among Jacksonville's Democrats. Dr. Holmes Steele, editor of the Democratic *Jacksonville Standard*, spoke for the radical cause. Steele was chosen mayor in April 1859, only a month after he arrived in town from South Carolina. His paper expressed the outrage of Jacksonville's Democrats following abolitionist John Brown's attempt to seize the United States arsenal at Harpers Ferry in October 1859 and to lead armed bands of former slaves in attacks on plantations throughout the South. Governor Madison S. Perry addressed the Florida legislature in December 1859, blaming the "villainy" of Brown's insurrection on the Republican Party and calling for "eternal separation from the Union."[64]

In early 1860, Florida's Democrats moved to block Douglas as the party's nominee for president. Events in Kansas had convinced them that popular sovereignty jeopardized the cause of extending slavery into the western territories. Delegates chosen to attend the Democratic Party nominating convention at Charleston in April were instructed to insist on strict enforcement of the Fugitive Slave Act and to "withdraw from the Convention unless a clear and emphatic recognition be given to the South, through both the nominee and the platform, that her institutions, when threatened by the usurpation of power, are to be protected by the strong arm of the Government wherever the American Flag waves."[65]

Delegates at the Charleston convention were unable to agree on either a candidate or a party platform. When Northern delegates held out for a Douglas candidacy, Southerners left the assembly hall and held separate meetings. Eventually, each region put forth its own candidate: Douglas for the North and John C. Breckinridge for the South.[66] As the 1860 presidential elections drew closer, newspapers from across Florida published increasingly shrill predictions that arrogant Northern politicians were intent on denying Southern rights, and the Democratic Party became overwhelmingly popular among Florida voters.

Unionists in Jacksonville and throughout Florida continued to seek a compromise that would prevent the dissolution of the United States. Guided by the principles of the defunct Whig Party, a new political party was created, the Constitutional Union Party. Historian Arthur Thompson called the organizational meetings the "last attempt to grasp political power and resist the growing . . . sentiment for secession."[67] The major planks of the new party tried to balance the interests of national unity and regional commitment to the institution of slavery: "maintenance of the Union, reduction in the price of public lands, internal improvements, and opposition to squatter sovereignty."[68]

In April 1860 the new party managed a shocking upset in a Jacksonville election. Democrats, expecting to claim all of the town council seats, captured only two. Jacksonville voters chose six men from the Constitutional Union Party to fill council seats, all migrants to Florida and all pledged to moderation, compromise, and Union. Five had supported the Whig and American parties in the past. Halsted Hoeg, a native of New York, was chosen mayor. He would be reelected in April 1861, three months after Florida seceded from the Union. For a brief moment in April 1860, the possibility of remaining within the American Union remained alive in the minds of a majority of Jacksonville's voters.[69]

Building on this encouraging impetus, Unionists called for a public meeting at the Duval County Courthouse on May 21 to discuss the Constitutional Union Party. Handbills announced "a meeting of all persons who are for the 'Union, the Constitution and a faithful administration of the Laws,' as well as those who are opposed to Florida taking the initiatory steps toward a disruption of the Union." Incensed by the handbills, local Democrats held their own public forum on May 15 and issued an ultimatum: "Regardless of who may be elected President, if it appears from such election that a majority of the people or the states of this Union deny to the South the amplest protection and security to slave property in the territories owned by the General Government, or . . . [refuse] to surrender fugitive slaves when legally demanded . . . then we are of the opinion that the rights of the citizens of Florida are no longer safe in the Union and we think that she should raise the banner of secession and invite her Southern sisters to join her."[70]

At the Union meeting on May 21, Democrats in the audience were eager to advocate for secession but were denied permission to speak. Edward Hopkins, the Constitutional Union Party's candidate for governor, gave a "patriotic speech containing Union sentiments and Southern Rights doctrines," according to one prescient observer.[71] Hopkins evidently gave such a stirring speech that several Democrats decided to join with members of the new party in an unplanned coalition. Conservative Democrats and former Whigs and American Party members agreed on a pro-slavery and states' rights position that also embraced support for the Union and the Constitution. A formal resolution endorsed that evening declared: "The Territories of the

United States are common property, in which the States have equal rights, and to which the citizens of every State may rightfully emigrate with their slaves, or other property recognized as such in any State of the Union, or by the Constitution of the United States."[72] It was also resolved that territorial legislatures lacked the power to "abolish slavery or to prohibit the introduction of the same within the territories." It was the fundamental obligation of the federal government to defend the rights of slaveholders residing in the territories.[73] The editor of Jacksonville's Democratic newspaper endorsed the resolutions "as good and sound Democratic ones" but questioned why the Constitutional Unionists were leading a "movement against the Democrats who are fighting the battles of the South upon these principles."[74] He encouraged Jacksonville residents to instead organize militia companies in case it became necessary to defend the state and its institutions.

Five months later, Dr. Steele challenged other communities in Florida to follow the example of his own "gallant corps," the Jacksonville Light Infantry, and organize militias for state service: "The times, gentlemen, are ominous; and while viewing the signs, let us 'in peace prepare for war,' for though no evil may come, yet it is the imperative duty of the state to arm." On November 1, Steele paraded the Light Infantry through Jacksonville in new "black cloth pantaloons" and dress hats in a demonstration designed to rally Jacksonville voters to the cause of the Southern Democrats and of secession.[75]

On the eve of the presidential election, four daughters of Colonel John Broward, an outspoken Duval County secessionist, warned men going to the polls to resist the lure of the "submissionists and Unionists in our midst." The Broward sisters advised Jacksonville's male voters that the most important issue they would decide was whether they were willing to "submit to all the degradation threatened by the North toward our slave property and be made to do what England has made white people experience in the West India Islands—the negroes afforded a place on the same footing with their former owners, to be made legislators, to sit as Judges." Faced with "aggression against the South" and the threat of the "final emancipation of our slave property, which would carry in its pathway all the evils of Haiti to the whites," submissionists were still "devoted to the Union." The Broward women announced they would be sending crinolines to adorn the bodies of submissionists with apparel appropriate to their timid natures.[76]

On November 6, voters participated in the most consequential presidential election ever conducted in the United States of America. Four political parties put presidential candidates forward, but all were regional parties. No party was able to bridge the explosive sectional divide. To add to the confusion, names of the candidates of only three parties were on ballots in Florida. Voters could choose between Stephen A. Douglas, a Northern Democrat; John Breckinridge, a Southern Democrat; and John Bell, a Constitutional Unionist. The name of the Republican Party's nominee, Abraham Lincoln, was not printed on the ballot in Florida.

When the votes for president were counted in Florida, John Breckinridge tallied 8,543, John Bell 5,437, and Stephen Douglas 367 votes. The contest for governor of Florida was closer than anticipated. Democrat John Milton tallied 6,994 votes, followed by Edward Hopkins of the Constitutional Union Party with 5,248. The number of votes cast for Hopkins indicates that preservation of the Union remained a compelling cause.

In the rest of the nation, Douglas gathered 1,375,157 votes to finish second. Breckinridge's count was 847,953, and Bell's 589,581. The vote tally for Lincoln was 1,865,000, about 40 percent of the total, sufficient to win 180 electoral votes and the presidency.[77] For the first time in the nation's history, a president had been elected by only a single section of the country.

"The cup of insolence and vanity of the North is full to overflowing," wrote the editor of the *Jacksonville Standard* in reaction to Lincoln's election.[78] The North would soon have a balance of power in the Congress, he predicted: "Slavery and the South must then go down in internecine war, with insurrection attended with all the horrors of conflagration, poison and rape."[79] Newspapers across the state reported the burning of effigies of Lincoln, secession flags flying in defiance, and politicians urging Floridians to dissolve the Union and form a confederacy of Southern states to defend against Republican and abolitionist aggression.[80]

During a November 26 address to the Florida General Assembly, Governor Perry said: "The only hope the Southern states have for domestic peace or for future respect of property is . . . secession."[81] The governor urged immediate withdrawal from the Union: further delay would make Floridians vulnerable to slave uprisings like those the white citizens of Saint Domingue suffered in the bloody slave rebellions in that former French colony. The assembly responded by calling for a "People's Convention" at Tallahassee on January 3, 1861, to decide whether to secede or remain within the Union. An election to choose delegates was scheduled for December 22. The *Jacksonville Standard* supported the assembly's actions, urging Floridians to "resist Black Republican rule, and seek safety in the only ark left—the withdrawal from the Government of enemies. . . . There is under the Sun no other way for the Southern States to protect their Rights . . . excepting in seas of blood."[82]

As political tensions increased, bands of vigilantes and regulators began organizing, supposedly to protect against slave insurrections and abolition-ist sympathizers. Some regulators openly intimidated pro-Union merchants and property holders. In Tallahassee, the daughter of former governor Rich-ard Keith Call feared "a war in which all the evil passions of our nature will be excited." The wife of a Jacksonville merchant complained that the word "Yankee is meaner than nigger, the lowest name a person can have," and added that some vigilante types in the city "call every person born north of Mason and Dixon's line by the meanest names they can command."[83]

Washington M. Ives, a Columbia County youth, kept a diary in these troubled times that recorded numerous violent incidents. On May 7, 1860, Ives wrote, a man was stabbed to death and a man known as "Britton George was whipped by the Regulators." Ten days later a huge fight broke out in Lake City, prompting Ives to predict that six men would be arrested. On the twenty-third a cabinetmaker named Peter Pent and a man named Keene were severely beaten by the regulators. In the following months Ives recorded men fighting with fists, knives, guns, and "loaded whips." In September the regulators met amid speeches and great excitement, and a vigilance commit-tee was organized. Less than a week after its inception the committee began examining Lake City residents and banishing those who failed to meet its standards of Southern patriotism. In October, the local newspaper editor shot himself, and a man named Roderick tried to cut the throat of Ives's father.[84]

On the day of the election, November 6, one man was paralyzed as a result of a fight. Two weeks later Ives recorded: "Tonight there was great excitement. The militia was called out to suppress a supposed revolt of the slaves. Some say it was a fact that sixty negroes were missing off one plan-tation and another negro confessed knowing about Lincoln's election as a thing to free him."[85] Ives recorded that tensions continued high in Lake City when he moved to Jacksonville in April 1861.

Elsewhere in Florida, citizens experienced similar acts of violence. At Mayport Mills, several fishermen were thrown out of town for their pro-Union attitudes. A New England tutor was escorted to the train depot in Tallahassee and told to leave Florida after she expressed anti-secession senti-ments. In Jacksonville, Union supporters learned that "men who were born and reared in the South could speak against secession long after it was un-safe for Northern men to do so."[86]

On December 6, 1860, the *Jacksonville Standard* reported the establish-ment of the "Minute Men . . . [an organization] which now numbers some seventy of the yeomanry of the county." The officers were Captain Paul B.

Canova, sheriff of Duval County, and Lieutenants H. M. Sadler, Dr. Emile T. Sabal, and Charles Seton Fleming. Organized as an association of "true sons of the South," the Duval Minute Men was a "semi-political, semi-military" organization whose members "were not only pledged to take up arms in the defense of the State, but to vote for Secession, and to do all in their power to promote its passage."[87]

A *Standard* editorial assailed the U.S. Constitution as a vehicle for injustice through which Northern states had "razed our cities to the ground, poisoned the waters of our wells, corrupted the hearts of our servants, placed murderous weapons in their hands to turn against the breasts of their masters . . . [and] stimulated insurrection." It was time for Florida to join in the establishment of "a separate slave-holding Confederacy to build up our own commercial mart and manufactories." Unless the move to secede was carried out at once, "it never can be done hereafter except in seas of blood."[88]

The men of the Jacksonville Light Infantry already had determined the path they would follow. They had met in November and decided "without a dissentient voice" that the results of the presidential election were "antagonistic to the domestic peace, the safety and property and the happiness and prosperity of the people of the Southern States," thereby justifying "a dissolution of the present Federal Government, through the secession of Southern States . . . [and] that in the event of the secession of the State of Florida, we pledge to her defense our arms, our fortunes, our lives and our sacred honor."[89]

For the convention scheduled January 3, 1861, the people of Duval and Clay counties elected James Madison Daniel and John P. Sanderson. Daniel was a fifty-four-year-old native of South Carolina, slaveholder, attorney-turned-educator, lumberman, planter, and clerk of the circuit court.[90] Sanderson, a forty-six-year-old attorney, was from Vermont, the owner of a mercantile store on Bay Street, director and president of the Jacksonville and Alligator Plank Road Company, partner in the St. Johns Steam Saw Mill, president of the Florida, Atlantic and Gulf Central Railroad, and owner of Ortega plantation and eighty-three slaves. His large brick home at the northeast corner of Forsyth and Ocean streets was Jacksonville's showplace residence.[91]

Daniel and Sanderson had campaigned on promises of compromise and moderation. When the convention was called to order on January 3, however, their commitments to moderation vanished. Swept up in the secession mystique, they voted against all measures designed to delay secession or submit the issue to a referendum of the people. Daniel served on several important committees, and Sanderson coauthored the secession ordinance.

The city's Unionists met and dispatched three representatives to Tallahassee to remind Daniel and Sanderson of their pledges to moderation. One of the negotiators reported: "We found it was as useless to talk to our delegates as it would have been to plead with the lamp-posts in the streets."[92] Sanderson said later that he had acted to protect the institution of slavery in the South, anticipating that to prevent secession, the Union government would agree to "permanent guarantees for the interests and institutions of the South."[93]

On February 4, delegates from Florida, South Carolina, Mississippi, Georgia, Alabama, and Louisiana began organizing a provisional government of the Confederate States of America. Compromise efforts were quickly initiated by Senator John J. Crittenden of Kentucky to revive the Missouri Compromise line and extend it westward, with a guarantee that Congress could never abolish slavery in the states. When that plan faltered, a thirteenth amendment to the U.S. Constitution was passed with a two-thirds margin. The amendment would have prohibited the federal government from abolishing slavery. Republicans, including Abraham Lincoln, agreed to the amendment even though it would have permitted slavery to exist forever in the Southern states, protected by the U.S. Constitution.[94]

Southern politicians insisted on stronger concessions: strict enforcement of the Fugitive Slave Act, repeal of personal liberty laws, and legalization of slavery in the western territories.[95] Northern congressmen agreed to all provisions, with one exception: they refused to permit slavery in the western territories. Southern Democrats were committed to the view that the extension of slavery into the territories was an inviolable part of their sacred "Southern rights." Consequently, the proposed thirteenth amendment was not ratified. Further attempts to reach compromise failed. Firing on Fort Sumter commenced in April 1861. Four years and more than 600,000 deaths later, the Civil War ended.[96]

Near the end of that war, on January 31, 1865, another thirteenth amendment was approved by the House and Senate and sent to the individual states for ratification. This version of the amendment abolished slavery in its entirety. In pondering the irony of the two versions, historian Michael F. Holt concluded that the inability of Americans in 1860 to reach compromise on the extension of slavery into the territories "speaks volumes about the causes of the American Civil War. Most historians . . . now agree that the issue that most aggravated sectional conflict during the fifteen years prior to 1861 was slavery's extension beyond the existing slave states, not demands for its abolition within them."[97]

Holt's insight has relevance for understanding why so many residents of Jacksonville insisted on secession. Judging from the evidence of political meetings, debates, and elections printed in the local newspapers between 1845 and 1861, the unhindered ability of Southern slaveholders to legally carry their human property into the western territories was central to their perception of "Southern rights." Closing the territories to slavery represented a fundamental violation of their constitutional rights as American citizens and a self-evident justification for dissolving ties to the Union. It raised the further fear that a Northern congressional majority would eventually force the Southern states to abolish slavery. The tempestuous Oscar Hart had warned Jacksonville residents in 1850 that compromise efforts would prove futile because Northern abolitionists intended to "place about our necks the galling chains of perpetual servitude and slavery."[98] Hart's prophecy that Jacksonville residents had only two choices, "Southern liberty or Southern annihilation," was impetuous and rhetorical in 1850. A decade later, however, the city's residents had moved beyond rhetoric and were calling for action.

2

Jacksonville
Prepares for War

For the people of Jacksonville, Florida's secession ushered in what would become four years of tragedy and terror. Otis Little Keene, born in Bremen, Maine, moved to Jacksonville in 1855 to manage the Judson House Hotel. Built in 1854 at the corner of Julia and Bay streets by another native of Maine, A. Judson Day, the Judson House was Jacksonville's premier hotel at the time. Keene and his wife, Abbie, hosted the Fourth of July Ball, the Regatta Ball, and the celebration marking the completion of the Florida, Atlantic and Gulf Central Railroad in 1860.[1]

On April 30, 1859, Keene volunteered for the Jacksonville Light Infantry, joining Aristides Doggett and Dr. Holmes Steele as charter members. Doggett, a migrant from Massachusetts, and Steele, from South Carolina, were coeditors of the *Jacksonville Standard*, a newspaper pledged to fervent support of secession and the Democratic Party. Richard R. Rushing, a clergyman from North Carolina, also joined the Light Infantry, along with William Grothe, a watchmaker from Prussia; George Flagg, a jeweler from Massachusetts; Loudwick Warrock, a saloonkeeper from South Carolina; Lewis Fleming, an attorney and the grandson of an Irish immigrant who arrived in East Florida when it was a Spanish colony; and A. A. Ochus, a German-born musician and owner of a music store. Also joining were the sons of the Haddock, Houston, Papy, Smith, and Wilson families, all from families whose roots in the region extended back for generations. Formed at a time when sectional tensions were increasing, the Light Infantry's roster was representative of the diverse population of northeast Florida.

Keene remembered that the militia's armory was a frame building located east of his hotel and that the men's "favorite place for drilling was in a grove of trees between Hogan and Laura on Forsyth Street. We had handsome uniforms, coats of blue cloth, with three rows of brass buttons in the front, and high caps with black pompons." The company had its first street parade on July 4, 1859, marching to east Jacksonville for target practice, and back "through deep sand to the armory . . . on a hot July day, and with our heavy coats and guns you can imagine that we looked and felt as though we had been in a bath, but we all enjoyed it."[2]

The ranks of the Light infantry began to swell during the election year of 1860. Among the new volunteers were gunsmith John Oliveros, a Florida native; James J. Daniel, born in South Carolina but raised in Jacksonville; and railroad superintendent Thomas E. Buckman, from Pennsylvania. The likelihood of secession had seemed remote when the Light Infantry was formed in 1859, but now war seemed imminent. Keene boarded a steamer bound for Mayport Mills when the Light Infantry was called into state service and ordered to prepare fortifications at the mouth of the St. Johns River, but his thoughts were not on stopping an invasion. Otis Keene was praying that the United States and the Confederate States would not go to war.[3]

Other Jacksonville men were openly loyal to Union. Dr. J. D. Mitchell, a thirty-seven-year-old native of Maine and graduate of the Harvard Medical School, had moved to Jacksonville in 1852. An elder in the Presbyterian Church, Dr. Mitchell became such a strong supporter of Union that he was sometimes ostracized by his professional colleagues. He refused to compromise, however, and would later become a surgeon in the Union army.[4]

Southern-born men were also praying the nation would not be plunged into a civil war. Columbus Drew, a successful printer and publisher from Virginia and a leading Whig politician and advocate of Unionism, was still hopeful that a compromise could be reached. Although severely criticized for his moderate policies before the war, Drew served in the Treasury Department of the Confederate States at Richmond. Ironically, Otis Keene would reside nearby, but a nation apart, in Washington, D.C., where he found work as a clerk in the United States Treasury Department.[5]

There were also Northern-born men in Jacksonville who supported secession and faithfully served the Confederacy. John P. Sanderson served in the Confederate Congress and later won a citation "for valor and daring" during the Battle of Olustee.[6] George Flagg and Cyrus Bisbee (both from

Massachusetts), Henry Clark from Scotland, Thomas Buckman from Pennsylvania, and Dr. Abel S. Baldwin from New York also served in the Confederate cause. "There are among us Northerners and Foreigners," the editor of the *Southern Confederacy* wrote, "who from length of residence, identity of interest, and attachment to our institutions, are willing to shed their heart's blood in the defense of the South. . . . We are proud to receive them into our ranks."[7] Southern-born men who prepared to defend Southern honor with their lives included James J. Daniel, Holmes Steele, Aristides Doggett, Lucius Hardee, the sons of John Broward of Cedar Creek, and the men of the L'Engle, Fleming, and Canova families.[8]

Few would be untouched by the war that was to come, regardless of their place of origin, gender, or age. Francis Hudnall of Locarno Plantation, on the south side of the St. Johns, took the family slaves to Middleburg for safety while his German-born wife, Eliza, remained behind with their children. George Bardin, born in Duval County in 1849, was too young to enlist for Confederate service, but he was old enough, and foolish enough, to snipe at Federal soldiers. He barely escaped with his life when a reward was posted for his capture or death. Maxey Jaudon was studying law in Jacksonville in 1861, but even though he was only sixteen, he helped organize the Davis Cadets and was elected to a lieutenancy. Robert A. Mickler, a St. Augustine resident whose family moved to Duval County in 1858, was fighting Union troops by the time he was fifteen. Harrison Starratt worked horses and drove oxen at a Dunns Creek lumber camp from the time he was twelve. At age seventeen he made an ideal recruit when Captain John Haddock organized a company of cavalry in 1861.[9]

On the eve of the Civil War, the persons most worried about their future were the Northern merchants and businessmen who controlled much of Jacksonville's commercial wealth and property. Calvin Robinson, born in 1828 at South Reading, Vermont, and a graduate of Vermont University, entered the wholesale commission field in Boston at the age of twenty-five. Failing health prompted him to move to Jacksonville in 1857. By 1860 he owned most of the waterfront block south of Bay Street between Hogan and Laura, a two-story wholesale and retail store that opened to a wharf at the rear, and a two-hundred-foot warehouse. To the east adjoining his lumberyard and planing mill stood another two-level building where he sold sawmill equipment. Further east was a tin shop and retail outlet for stoves, hollowware, and tinware. Robinson also operated a waterfront steam sawmill at Bay and Catherine streets. By stocking his stores with merchandise shipped direct from New York, Robinson boasted, he could sell at lower prices than

Jacksonville merchants who purchased goods wholesale at Charleston and Savannah.[10]

Robinson refused to believe the South would actually leave the Union, and he continued to import supplies. After returning from a buying excursion in New York in November 1860, however, he discovered that rumors were circulating that he was an abolitionist, which he said "signified everything that was vile and abhorrent to Southern people." Business associates defended him, but after Florida seceded Robinson noticed that "gradually, one after another, . . . [people] joined the current sentiment . . . until one hardly knew whom to trust. Men with whom you talked freely today, and who were firm in their opposition to the prevailing madness, would tomorrow boldly declare themselves in favor of secession, until the number of friends of the Old Flag became so small, and [their] stability so uncertain, that it was dangerous to talk Union Talk with anybody."[11]

Many of Robinson's bombastic detractors were harmless, and others were opportunists or debtors seeking an escape from their obligations, but some were malevolent and dangerous. Eventually, "it came to a point that silence was a crime," that "he who was not for secession was against it, and he who did not openly avow himself in favor of secession was counted an enemy of the South. For this reason many who were heartily in sympathy with the Union would utter sentiments of hostility to the Old Flag, especially in the presence of those . . . eager to catch something from their . . . lips that could be used against them . . . and they did this for their own personal safety."[12]

One group in the town was in an even more precarious position. On February 1, 1861, the *Southern Confederacy* reported: "A number of free persons of color left our city on Monday last, for the purpose of assisting in erecting a Battery at St. Johns Bar. These colored men were among the first persons in our community to offer their services as laborers to the Engineer who has charge of the works." Thumbing his nose at the Northern newspapers, the editor wrote: "We understand that their patriotic example will be followed by all the other free colored men in this place. What will Messrs. Seward, Greeley, and Co. say to this? Gentlemen, are we not reposing on a mine?" The mockery captured the optimistic sense of mastery common in the white community at the time.

Free African Americans in Jacksonville, on the other hand, lived restricted lives in a community where secession was seen as a heroic effort to defend the right of slaveholding, and where vigilantes daily stalked the streets harassing even influential white residents. The Florida slave code was harsh, and the system of race relations that accompanied it was equally severe. Slaves and free blacks were lumped together as degraded members of a despised race, and rigid institutional and social barriers existed between whites and blacks. African American slaves were seen as inferior beings incapable of existing outside the bonds of slavery, and free blacks were thought of as aberrations, as threatening to the general theory of slavery that prevailed, and as incendiary inspirations for slave insurrections. The rigid social-control laws passed to regulate slaves generally applied to free blacks as well: they were forbidden to assemble or to carry firearms, were disenfranchised, were barred from jury service and from testifying against whites in court proceedings, and were prohibited from interracial marriage. Discriminatory head taxes were levied on all free black males over fifteen years of age; they were subject to being drafted for mandatory manual labor projects, and after 1842 they were required to place themselves under a white guardian and pay an annual tax. During the 1850s, as the sectional tensions increased, the position of free blacks throughout the South grew more and more precarious.[13]

Perhaps Jacksonville's free black males saw contributions of labor on the battery at the entrance to the St. Johns River as a way to gain goodwill from the ruling whites, or more precisely, as a way to accommodate and survive in these trying times. Jacksonville's thirty-one free black males between fourteen and ninety could have made only a small contribution to the work at the battery—which was named Fort Steele—no matter how willing their participation. In May, Captain Holmes Steele asked Duval County slaveholders to contribute their enslaved men for the work under way at the mouth of the St. Johns River. Throughout the war slaves were routinely impressed from their owners and forced to labor on fatigue duties for the Confederate armies.[14]

The battery under construction was part of a fortification being prepared under the direction of a retired army engineer, Captain John C. L'Engle. The work was anything but pleasant according to Massachusetts-born Willie Bryant, the twenty-two-year-old son of merchant and newspaper publisher James W. Bryant, who complained about the "poor grub" and "dirty smutty work going on" at "Rebel Hall" at Mayport Mills. Suffering from a fever so severe that even quinine would not relieve his symptoms, Bryant was pleased when one of the officers went to Jacksonville with a subscription list to "try to get Negroes to do the heavy work."[15] Bryant was able to find some pleasurable activity along the river. While rowing to Mayport Mills he had five-hour stops at Yellow Bluff to visit with Miss Aggie Tombs, whose father farmed and operated a shipyard at Dames Point. As enjoyable as these visits were, they could not counter the incessant mosquitoes and disagreeable work at Mayport, which led him to conclude that "soldiering is boring."[16]

Otis Keene thought less about the boredom than about his predicament as a Unionist in a Rebel militia unit. He described Fort Steele as located near Mayport Mills lighthouse, atop "a ridge of sand dunes in some places twenty-four feet high, covered with palmetto and other growth." The fort was fashioned from earthworks made of sandbags reinforced with palmetto logs and heavy timbers supplied by the Parson and Hoeg sawmill on the St. Johns at Mayport. Initially mounted with four 32-pounder guns brought on log carts from old Fort Marion in St. Augustine, three more were eventually added. Although the fort was not garrisoned in force until April 1861, work details rotated between Mayport Mills and Jacksonville throughout that year.[17]

While the work continued at Fort Steele, residents of Duval County learned of the contest between Confederate and Union authorities for the Federal military installations in the state. On January 6, 1861, five days before Florida withdrew from the Union, the Quincy Guards overwhelmed a four-man garrison at the U.S. Arsenal at Chattahoochee. On the following day, the lone Union soldiers occupying Fort Marion at St. Augustine turned the ancient fort over to Confederates. On January 12, seven companies of Florida and Alabama militia marched against the U.S. Navy yard at Pensacola and were welcomed by its executive officer, Commodore Ebenezer Farrand, a militant secessionist. Meanwhile, a company of U.S. artillerists under Lieutenant Adam Slemmer retreated from Fort Barrancas on the mainland and dug in at Fort Pickens on Santa Rosa Island, which commanded all of Pensacola Harbor and could be reinforced from sea by naval vessels. Forts Barrancas and McRae, vulnerable to assault from the mainland side, were abandoned. Two forts were gained for the Confederate States of America, along with weapons and ordnance supplies and the extensive facilities of the U.S. Navy yard at Pensacola.

On Santa Rosa Island, however, the artillerists under Lieutenant Slemmer's command jeopardized these gains. Fully aware that Fort Pickens was in disrepair and had not been occupied for more than a decade, Confederate volunteers on the mainland prepared an assault. The Civil War might have started in Florida but for the intervention of U.S. senators David L. Yulee and Stephen R. Mallory, who urged that bloodshed be avoided since an attack on Fort Pickens might be "fatal" to the Confederacy's cause. Consequently, the situation at Pensacola Harbor settled into a stalemate similar to the one that was developing at Charleston Harbor, where Major Robert J. Anderson was holding Southern forces at bay from behind the walls of Fort Sumter.[18]

As war fever rose, John Darby of Baldwin published a notice offering a $400 reward "to the first company or regiment who gets or takes possession of Fort Pickens."[19] Nathan B. Sadler, the editor of Jacksonville's *Southern Confederacy*, challenged Carolinians on February 1 to "Talk no More! Take Fort Sumter at once! Take it, if it should cost the lives of 100,000 men!" The editor offered the "hundreds of Volunteers in this State only too ready to fly at a moment's notice to the relief of a sister State. Our 'cow-boys' may not be well-drilled; but they are brave, and they know well how to handle the rifle, and the knife."

Colonel Lucius A. Hardee, born in Georgia and the owner of Rural Home Plantation three miles west of Jacksonville, was a leading Duval County radical. Hardee's honorary military title was the result of leading a company of local volunteers during the Third Seminole War in the 1850s. In April 1861 he penned the broadside "God and Our Rights," in which he declared: "the crisis which has been so long impending . . . overshadows as a dark cloud this once sacred and hallowed Union." Southerners had been "traduced, slandered and insulted in the very halls of Congress" as well as on their own soil; "there is no retreat left to us—it is simply do or die." Hardee had called for men "true to the South" to join a cavalry corps that would offer its services to the first Southern state to secede from the Union.[20]

Late in 1860 Hardee recruited and was elected captain of the Duval County Cowboys. One observer of the Cowboys' drills said they camped and mustered in "Colonel Hart's Grove" to the west of downtown and that half the members were boys under eighteen. In June 1861 Hardee's men installed cannons at Talbot Island, and a year later they mounted heavy guns at St. Johns Bluff.[21]

At the Duval County Courthouse on March 8, 1861, the Duval County Minutemen were reorganized as the Perry Artillery, in honor of Florida's governor, Madison Perry. Officers elected that night were Paul B. Canova, captain; Albert J. Russell and Francis F. L'Engle, lieutenants; and William D. Dowell, clerk. The men filed out of the courthouse, formed ranks in the streets, and "at once proceeded to drill."[22]

Duval County had enrolled 250 men in three companies of volunteer militia. Convinced that Southern men would become the lifeblood of a powerful nation, editor Sadler of the *Southern Confederacy* wrote: "If any one thing were wanted to convince the world, and the North particularly, that the

South is in earnest, and is not wanting for resources, the rapidity with which thousands of men have been put in the field, forts repaired, batteries erected and defenses of all kinds organized, would, we think, convince them."[23]

At 4:30 a.m. on April 12, 1861, Confederate gunners opened fire on Fort Sumter. Men and women crowded the rooftops overlooking Charleston Harbor and applauded as shells burst against the fortification. Thirty-three hours later, the Union commander capitulated. After years of stormy threats and vigorous posturing, the war had finally come. War fever then spread rapidly through the North as well as the South. Abraham Lincoln called for seventy-five thousand militiamen from the Union states, and Northern governors were soon pleading for increased quotas.

In Jacksonville, the charter members of the Jacksonville Light Infantry were anxious to fight, but Otis Keene did not share their enthusiasm. Keene had reluctantly joined his comrades at Fort Steele, but he had been relieved when he was ordered to reopen the Judson House to accommodate the growing number of Confederate soldiers in the town. He was pleased to return to the "business as usual" spirit that again prevailed in the town.

On the morning of April 12, the fateful day of the Confederate attack on Fort Sumter, the telegraph line that carried the sensational news to Jacksonville went dead after the operator had decoded only part of the story. Word spread frantically through the town and people rushed to the station for more details, but the line was down at Savannah and would remain inoperative for two days. Anxious residents of the town would not have long to wait for eyewitness accounts of the bombardment, as the steamboat *Cecile* arrived the following day from Charleston with passengers lining the rails shouting out the news. When the telegraph lines began humming again the tales were confirmed: "HIGHLY IMPORTANT! THE WAR COMMENCED! Bombardment of Fort Sumter, Surrender of that Fort!"[24]

Confederate flags waved defiantly from Jacksonville rooftops and local men flocked to the colors. Colonel Hardee opened a new recruitment drive to fill the ranks of the Duval County Cowboys. Captain Steele of the Jacksonville Light Infantry appealed to the patriotism of local citizens for "the contribution of slave laborers, for a week or ten days, for most important work on the fort at the mouth of the river."[25]

Northern-born men were greatly worried by the inflamed passions they observed among the local citizens. An editorial in the *Mirror* advised that "as a prudential measure of safety, it might not be amiss to adopt some plan by which every man's true sentiments may be put upon record in the shape of an oath or affirmation. . . . If there are any persons among us whose citizenship and allegiance are with our enemies, it will enable us to know them and to treat them accordingly."[26] The loyalty proposal was vigorously debated at public meetings before being firmly repudiated. The town's leaders would have no part in a proscription against men who had been friendly neighbors and business associates for years. Calvin Robinson noted in his diary that "the idea was soon quietly dropped," but he also noticed that the feelings of bitterness and animosity persisted. He acknowledged that "sincere motives and pure patriotism" were involved but warned that "the drunken, idle and brutal, many of them the scions of pretentious families become impecunious from indolence and dissipation," had rejected the magnanimity of the majority. It would be some time before this group operated openly; for the time being they organized vigilance committees and began spying and harassing when opportunity permitted.[27]

Fear then began to stalk the streets of Jacksonville. Robinson noted that agents were sent to watch and interview Unionists "for the purpose of discovering some act or drawing out from us at an unguarded moment some word or expression that could be construed as hostile to the Southern cause." He resented that eavesdropping made Unionists fear talking to one another "without first examining to see that there was no possibility of our words being picked up through some keyhole, door crack, or around a corner."[28]

At the tiny village of Magnolia, which counted fewer than two hundred residents in 1860, supporters of Union were also stalked by zealous partisans of secession. After verbally defending a Northern-born Clay County resident, farmer and livestock herder James Taylor was warned that a mob would hang him. Jack Knowles was told he would be shot unless he joined the Confederate army. Known Union supporters Dr. Nathan Benedict, a New York native, and Thomas Hendricks, born in Duval County, were informed that they "would be harmed or troubled" if they did not move away from Clay County.[29]

Unionists were not the only ones frightened by the times. Faced with a war they were ill-prepared to fight and confronted with the possibility of slave uprisings, even Confederate patriots were apprehensive and fearful, sometimes to the point of hysteria. On April 26, three runaway slaves convicted of the murder of planter Richard Plummer of Mandarin were hung in Jacksonville. The murder and hanging of three men found guilty of the crime was shocking, although not surprising, but the severe sentences imposed on four slaves found guilty of complicity suggests hysteria was in the air. One man was given 160 lashes, two others received 100, and the fourth suffered 50 strokes. Considering that prior to the war Florida had imposed a 39-stroke limitation to prevent crippling or killing an offender, the sentences served as a warning to the slave population, as well as reassurance to an uneasy white population that they were still in control.[30]

One young man recorded the events of April 26 in his diary. Washington M. Ives was attending the St. Johns Grammar School, an institution for boys run by Episcopalian preacher John Hewitt. Classes had begun that morning amid a hubbub of excited conversation about the murder committed three days before at the Plummer Plantation on the St. Johns River near Mandarin. Seven slaves went on trial that morning at the courthouse, accused of murdering Richard Plummer when he apprehended them after they escaped from the Fairbanks Mills in Jacksonville. At 11 a.m. the boys interrupted their recess games to watch the Jacksonville Light Infantry lead a procession of three hundred men and the three slaves who had just been found guilty of the murder. Ives identified the convicted men as "Ephraim, Wesley, and Ed, the actual murderers, having shot Mr. Plummer and beat him with wooden paddles." The three men were hung at a grove beyond the school. "I did not go to see them hung," Ives wrote, "although I could see them on the gallows from my seat."[31]

After school, Ives walked to the courthouse to observe the trial of the other four slaves, who were accused of throwing Plummer's dead body into the river. That evening Ives walked back past the school and beyond to the gallows. It was rainy and just turning dark when he saw the bodies, "the two outside ones were hanging yet but the middle one had just been cut down by Dr. Saddler to be dissected, they were hung with plough lines and some boys say that one had his neck cut by it, neither had his neck broken, and one died very hard it is said." The three bodies were left hanging throughout the night. They were buried the following day.

The following day, a school holiday, Ives walked to the Judson House and watched several boatloads of men fish in the river. Porpoises were jumping at Captain Willey's wharf. That evening Ives enjoyed a theatrical performance at Washington Hall and listened to musicians play violins and a harp. The gruesome executions of the murderers and the sentences of corporal punishment for the men accused of complicity had not long occupied his mind. Ives had seen plenty of violence in the previous year at his hometown, Lake City; in April 1861 his mind was mainly concerned with dances and teas with the young ladies of Jacksonville. Adults were not able to brush the troubling events from their minds that easily.

The local economic conditions also troubled the residents of Jacksonville. Early indicators in February had passed almost unnoticed. The Judson

House had scrimped through the month with only one in every four of its rooms occupied, and Claudia Villard had sold a nine-year-old slave boy to pay the bills of her boardinghouse.[32] During March and April, Esther Haddock, a widow with two minor sons, was forced to sell land at her "Hunger and Hardship" farm to meet expenses, and the lumber firm of Wilson, Miller and Company was dissolved. As the prospects of war grew imminent, soldiers in uniform listed their property for sale. Oscar Hart, colonel of the 16th Regiment of Florida Militia, offered to sell "two gentle work horses, accustomed to plow or other harness." N. B. Sadler advertised his five-hundred-acre riverfront plantation, eight miles below Jacksonville, at "a low price." Thomas E. Buckman offered his cottage on Forsyth Street. John S. Sammis put Strawberry Mills Plantation on the block as he began liquidating assets, hoping to move his family to the North. A flurry of advertisements announced the appointment of business agents acting on behalf of men who were fleeing to safer climes in the North or departing for military service.[33]

Major changes were visible in May. The large fleet of Northern vessels that served Jacksonville's lumber industry had disappeared, leaving piles of lumber stacked on wharves. The mills began to work shorter shifts until, one by one, they closed. Other port-related businesses were affected: merchants were unable to replenish merchandise from Northern suppliers, and as unemployment soared small stores began to close.[34]

By May 1861, food shortages had become a subject of concern. Items such as salt, tea, coffee, wines, and liquors were also in short supply. In order to reassure residents of Duval County, who were already feeling the bite of inflation and runaway prices caused by hoarding and profiteering, the *St. John's Mirror* reported great quantities of foodstuffs being received daily in Savannah. The editor advised consumers who encountered merchants selling bacon for more than thirteen cents a pound to "Let the unprincipled extortioner fatten on his own bacon."[35]

Scarcity was the least concern of merchant Calvin Robinson. In April 1861 he had $70,000 worth of merchandise on his shelves. When Florida and Confederate States war currency began to circulate, along with "railroad money" he believed to be worthless, Robinson cut his workforce to two loyal clerks, concealed the most valuable stock, and left only a small selection on display. Robinson tried to avoid Confederate war taxes, but before he could ship his stock to Savannah for trade on the British Exchange, Confederate agents levied his picks, shovels, and camp and entrenching equipment and notified him that "they were ordered to 'press' these goods whenever they could be found." When the regular steamship lines suspended operations, Robinson contacted owners of independent steamers, but Port Collector Thomas Ledwith ordered him to make no further attempts to ship anything out of Jacksonville.[36]

Robinson continued to operate a lumber mill long after the other mills in Jacksonville had ceased operations. He purchased logs with Confederate and railroad notes, piled the finished lumber in the mill yard, and covered it, "believing that when the war was over Southern pine lumber would bring high prices, and at all events it would be a safer investment" than the prevailing currency. He converted other war currencies into "Southern bank money" and stuffed it into wine bottles until about $12,000 accumulated. Fearful that his treasure would become "a sort of an elephant on my hands" if Confederate authorities jailed him, he buried the bottles in what he hoped would be "the safest bank in the South"—his garden.

Robinson secured permission to travel to Louisville, only to return to greater troubles. Vigilantes threatened his life, accusing him of plotting with the enemy. From that moment on, Robinson "lived constantly in fear" that he would "be shot down in the night or in the day, and have left my dear home in the morning not knowing as I should ever return—have kissed my dear wife and little boys, feeling that it might be the last time I see them."[37]

Otis Keene had also encountered vigilante intimidation, and faced the added worry of the severe economic recession that endangered the financial stability of the Judson House. The brief resurgence of business during March and April was mitigated in the first two weeks of June when only eighty-one guests registered. On June 15, 1861, Keene wrote in the hotel register: "The House closed this day for the first time since it was opened—and when it will be open again no one can tell."[38]

Events of a more tragic nature would soon envelop Keene and the Judson House. In August 1861 the Jacksonville Light Infantry mustered into Confederate service as Company A, 3rd Florida Infantry. Keene did not muster with them. In July the state of Florida requested that he reopen the Judson House to accommodate the hundreds of volunteers assembling in Jacksonville for induction into the Confederate army. Keene resigned from the Light Infantry while concealing the relief he felt from avoiding formal enlistment in the army of the Confederate States of America.[39]

The Judson House reopened on July 6. Three hundred guests registered that month, mostly soldiers from the ten companies of volunteers assembling for induction at Camp Virginia. The St. Johns Grays, the seventh company of volunteers raised in Jacksonville, was one of the units inducted.

Organized by J. J. Daniel and Andrew M. Jones, the ranks of the Grays included attorneys, engineers, merchants, and well-known public figures such as Uriah Bowden, former sheriff of the county, and John C. and Edward M. L'Engle, whose sister Emily (Captain Daniel's wife) had suggested the company's name.[40]

Washington Ives watched the daily drills of the local companies, recording the names of the commanders: Dr. Holmes Steele, Lucius Hardee, John Broward Jr., John G. Haddock, Milton Haynes, John B. DaCosta, and James J. Daniel. The militia leaders were all between twenty-seven and thirty-nine years of age and were moderately wealthy owners of slaves, all Southern-born.[41]

On May 3 the St. Johns Light Infantry, better known as the "Boy's Company," was formed. Led by Captain Albert Willard, the unit was composed of twenty boys from the Jacksonville vicinity. Their first drill was in a large room above Dr. Webster's drugstore, and within two weeks Ives could record that the "Boy's Co." was making remarkable progress "for the time they have been organized. Maxey Jaudon is first and Albert Shattuck second lieutenants."[42]

May 25 was an exciting day for Ives: all the militia companies mustered for public parades and demonstrations. John Haddock's cavalry company of fifty-four men paraded with "Capt. L. Hardee's Cow Boys" and the "Boy's Co." Later in the afternoon the St. Johns Grays marched from their camp one mile south of town dressed in the uniforms sewn at the Judson House by Jacksonville ladies. Ives judged it "the best military maneuvers ever displayed in this place."[43]

By the following week the militia companies were moving in and out of the town attempting to buttress river defenses against possible attacks by the Yankees. The Jacksonville Light Infantry was "almost continuously at the Bar," Ives noted, and Broward's company, the Leon Rifles, was sent to Fernandina. On June 22 the Duval Cowboys suffered its first casualty when one of the men was "mutilated when a cannon exploded" at Talbot Island.[44] Entranced by the militia drills, Ives returned home to Lake City to join a militia company. He was seventeen years old at the time.

During the first months of the war, policy for defense of Florida had been plagued by confusion, competitive factionalism, disorganization, and conflict between the state and national governments. These were trying times to establish new governments in a region that prided itself on independence and states' rights. Florida voters had chosen John Milton to be their governor in November 1860, but he was not scheduled to be inaugurated until the following October. State government was also compromised by conflicts between an elected assembly and a holdover body from the People's Convention (called to consider secession), which insisted on conducting official business as if it were the state's legally designated legislative body. Florida was without an effective Confederate military commander until November 1861, when Brigadier General James Heyward Trapier finally arrived, and even then it was unclear whether Florida or the Confederate States of America would assume responsibility for recruiting, equipping, and training an army.[45]

In the early months of the war, enthusiastic support for secession had prompted hundreds of Florida volunteers to join local militia companies. Responsibility for local defense had been exercised at the local level until April 1861, when the state of Florida was first given authority to defend coastal areas with state militia units. Before that time the Jacksonville units had acted on their own authority, arranging for arms and clothing and deciding on policy with neither advice nor interference from officials in Tallahassee or Richmond. With Confederate officers in town to induct local units into national service, there was a feeling of permanence and stability present in Jacksonville for the first time in months.

The establishment of Camp Virginia in July 1861 brought the possibility of war to the attention of the citizens of Jacksonville. Located west of the city at what had been a quiet pasture near the present intersection of Myrtle Avenue and Adams Street, the campground was soon bustling with the noise and martial activity of a thousand men eager to get on with the war. Dressed in colors and uniforms distinctive to their units, they crowded into restaurants and shops and registered at the Judson House as "C.S.A." and "the Reg't for Virginia." Companies from other counties at Camp Virginia included the Alachua Guards, Columbia Rifles, Hammock Guards, Gulf State Guards, Hamilton Blues, St. Augustine Rifles, Davis Guards, and Madison Rangers.[46]

On July 12 and 13, Major William T. Stockton mustered officers and enlisted men from the volunteer companies into the Confederate States Army as the 2nd Regiment of Florida Infantry. Hundreds of relatives and friends attending the historic ceremonies at the brick Baptist church heard Colonel George T. Ward of Leon County announce that the 2nd Florida Infantry was ordered to Virginia, the first Florida regiment to serve with a Confederate army in the field.[47] On July 15, bands played as the men of the 2nd Florida boarded cars of the Florida, Atlantic and Gulf Central Railroad to head west for Baldwin, and a large crowd assembled to wish them godspeed. By

September the regiment was in the front lines at Yorktown on the Virginia Peninsula.[48]

Enthusiastic patriotism inspired a continuing parade of Jacksonville volunteers for the Confederate armies. On August 10 the Jacksonville Light Infantry and the Duval County Cowboys were mustered in at Amelia Island as Companies A and F of the 3rd Florida Infantry Regiment. The 4th Florida was organized simultaneously, commanded by Colonel Edward Hopkins and Lieutenant Colonel M. Whit Smith. The Milton Artillery was commanded by Captain George A. Acosta, a former Jacksonville city councilman. Captain Noble A. Hull's mounted volunteers and John W. Brady's Bartow Cavalry mustered into the 1st Florida Cavalry on October 14. Both companies were composed of local men: Brady's outfit included the three sons of Elias Jaudon and sons from the Bigelow, DaCosta, Hudnall, and Turknett families. Other units would form later, including a home guard company known as the Silver Grays, composed of older men who remained home during the fighting. Of the eight hundred white men in Duval County reported in the 1860 census to be of fighting age (sixteen to sixty years), approximately three-quarters would see service of one kind or another during the war. At least one-fourth would be under arms before the conflict was four months old.[49]

One woman was not impressed by the hubbub of martial activity in Jacksonville during the summer and fall of 1861. Octavia Stephens and her infant daughter, Rosa, had ridden a steamship to Jacksonville to visit her parents, James W. and Rebecca Bryant. Octavia left her husband, Winston, at home to supervise the family's seven slaves during cotton harvest while she traveled from Welaka, stopping en route to visit with the Fleming family at Hibernia and the Reed family at Mulberry Grove. Only twenty-one years old at the time, Octavia had lived in Jacksonville much of her life, moving from Boston when her father opened a law office in Florida in 1850. She had married Winston in 1859 at Welaka, Florida, and moved to his plantation at the mouth of the Oklawaha River.

Octavia was stunned by the changed circumstances she found in Jacksonville. Her father was away from home on an extended business trip to Cuba, and her brothers Willie and Davis had mustered into Confederate service. Reports of a Union fleet off Fernandina had so alarmed Jacksonville residents that some were packing their goods and contemplating abandoning the town. Worried about her mother and two younger brothers, Octavia made plans to move them to her home in Welaka until her father's return from Cuba. She was also deeply disturbed by the militia activity she witnessed. On September 7, after watching a company drill in front of the courthouse, she wrote to her husband: "I declare it made me feel dreadfully to think what they were drilling for. You do not know how glad I feel when I think you are not in any company, and I hope and pray you may never be in any."[50]

By the time Octavia's letter reached Welaka, her prayers had fallen short; Winston had joined the St. Johns Rangers and been elected first lieutenant. He told his wife, "I do think it is the duty of every man to help drive back the invader when he is so near," but reassured her that the Rangers were all local men who had volunteered only for home service.[51] In October, Lieutenant Stephens was stationed at Camp Porter, drilling in a former pasture five miles from Palatka and complaining about shortages of blankets, clothing, and shoes. Even this early in the war, the pinch of the Union coastal blockade was felt as far upriver as Palatka, where Winston was unable to buy clothing or brooms and could not find a merchant with change for a one-dollar bill.[52]

For the next three years, Stephens's cavalry company ranged from the Indian River on the south to the St. Marys River on the north. Mustered as Company B of the 2nd Regiment of Florida Cavalry in November 1862, the unit would be associated in some way with nearly every important military action in northeast Florida in the months ahead. His letters to Octavia provide invaluable eyewitness accounts of Confederate activities in and around Jacksonville. Octavia was never reconciled to the war or to the prolonged absences of her husband; her letters to Winston are of great significance as a chronicle of the hardships of life on a St. Johns River plantation and the growing disillusionment of a young wife and mother with the realities of war.

With so many militia companies forming and Confederate patriotism at such a fever pitch, Unionists in the city began to worry about their safety. Calvin Robinson observed that "a reign of terror gained full swing and the time came when for a Northern man to utter openly his love for the Union would be almost suicide." One townsman shouted on the street, "Robinson, you d——d traitor, you ought to have your throat cut." For one group of Unionists, the pressure of being placed under surveillance became so great during the winter of 1861–62 that they went into the woods every Saturday "with the ostensible purpose of hunting squirrels, but really in order that we could gather under some wide spreading oak and sitting or lying on the thick carpet of autumn leaves, talk Union Talk freely and with none to molest or make us afraid."[53]

Some Unionists joined a newly organized home guard company late in 1861, after concluding that "carrying a gun for an hour per day was very harmless exercise" as long as they were not required to give allegiance to the Confederacy. It also occurred to Robinson "that possibly, at some future time, we might have to make a stand for the Old Flag we loved, and should this be the case we knew that any skill that we might acquire in the use of arms would be of no damage to us." But wartime passions could not be assuaged that easily. The schism in the city's population became more pronounced, feelings grew increasingly bitter, and a band of "ruffians" began to harass openly, threaten lives, and attempt to extort money from Unionists in exchange for safety. One young merchant sent a prominent attorney to pay $1,500 to the "ruffians." Robinson refused to negotiate, saying he "did not scare worth a cent," but after learning the vigilantes had labeled him an enemy of the South and planned to kill him, he realized "the extreme hazard and . . . hopelessness of the condition I was in."

To protect his family, Robinson rigged an alarm system around his house. Into the floor was cut a trapdoor through which Robinson could descend to a ground-level view and fire a pistol or a new Sharps rifle with enough vigor to "disperse any crowd of men. . . . I could load and fire the breech loader ten times a minute, with great accuracy . . . and make them think there was a squad of men under the house." The alarm rang only once during the night: Mrs. Robinson hurried out the back with the children (they slept fully clothed) while he leaped through the trapdoor and confronted a lone trespasser with a cocked rifle. A few days later the town marshal reported that "Robinson has some d——d fool infernal machine about his house . . . and it would not do to go fooling around there in the night." After that evening, visits from the vigilance committee ceased.[54] Robinson realized that the existence of the fanatical and occasionally criminal vigilance committee "was not known to many of the citizens of the town," but he also observed that the citizens who sympathized with the plight of the Northerners tended to become "more and more silent and careful as the political sky . . . darkened."[55]

Other Unionists also chose to risk the "reign of terror" rather than flee the city and leave behind their valuable assets. Otis Keene considered hiring a business agent to operate the Judson House until the war ended, but he instead trusted in the goodness of his fellow citizens and remained in Jacksonville. Calvin Robinson, a Jacksonville merchant and avid Unionist, looking back on those dark days, recalled that after the 2nd Florida Infantry left Jacksonville for Virginia, "the mails ceased coming, and the town began to subside into inactivity, only interrupted by the exciting war news. Yet no one thought of leaving, thinking that Florida, especially Jacksonville, would not be attacked or taken possession of."[56] Years later, those who survived the terror that followed would realize that remaining in the town had been a tragic mistake.

After the Union navy launched a blockade of Southern ports along the Atlantic and Gulf coasts of Florida in April 1861, Jacksonville residents began to experience the escalating impact of the war. Most of the steamboats between Jacksonville and Savannah or Charleston were pressed into military service, running arms, medical supplies, and provisions into Georgia and Florida ports where the Union blockade was relatively weak. The *Cecile* made twenty-five successful runs, and the *Carolina* (renamed the *Kate*) made forty before wrecking in 1862.[57] Two Savannah steamers, *St. Johns* and *St. Marys*, also evaded the warships of the Union's South Atlantic Blockading Squadron, occasionally running in and out of Jacksonville. The *Darlington*, commanded by Captain Jacob Brock, tied up at Cyrus Bisbee's wharf with the first shipment of smuggled provisions into the city after the blockade was established. Both Brock and Bisbee were New Englanders, but they were thoroughly committed to the Confederate cause.[58]

Louis Coxetter, one of the most popular steamboat captains on the St. Johns before the war, commanded a Confederate privateer, the *Jeff Davis*, that captured or destroyed eleven Yankee merchantmen in July and August 1861. When Coxetter's vessel was lost in a storm off St. Augustine, he and his men were rescued and brought to Jacksonville, where "church bells were rung, homes were thrown open to the privateers, and great feasts were prepared" to celebrate their victories. Crowds gathered outside the Judson House to catch a glimpse of the heroes.[59]

On October 25, a newcomer to Florida waters crossed the St. Johns River bar and reported to Customs Inspector Thomas Flotard that she was the *Camilla*, out of Cowes, England, carrying dispatches for the Confederate government at Richmond. Seafarers were not fooled by the vessel's name; they recognized by her graceful lines that she was the yacht *America*. Built a decade earlier to carry the challenge of American seamanship to England and international waters, the *America* was one of the most famous ships afloat. In 1851 she had defeated England's best and had gained glory for American yachting in international competition, giving her name to an illustrious symbol in yachting competition—the "America's Cup."[60]

The *America* had not returned to home waters since her triumph of 1851. In July 1860 she was purchased and renamed the *Camilla* by a mysterious

English adventurer, Henry Edward Decie, who sailed for America when news of the Civil War reached England. At Savannah in May 1861, Decie sold the yacht and his services to the Confederate States government for $26,000. On November 2, 1861, Otis Keene entered a cryptic notation in the hotel register: "Yacht America arrived from England with dispatches and the bearers left at once for Richmond, Va. The yacht anchored in the River just in front of Hotel."[61]

Blockade-running activity decreased after November 7, 1861, when a Union fleet commanded by Flag Officer Samuel F. Du Pont captured Port Royal, South Carolina, and increased the number of warships off Florida's shores. Once the South Atlantic Blockading Squadron had its ships in place, two schooners operating out of Jacksonville's port were captured, and only the swiftest sailing ships and steamers succeeded in slipping through.[62] By February 1862, with Union gunboats stationed permanently at Mayport Mills, most blockade running off Florida's Atlantic Coast focused at the Mosquito Inlet.

In Jacksonville, a race against time was taking place involving the city's shipbuilders and Confederate naval and marine officers. Commander Ebenezer Farrand directed efforts to construct a six-hundred-ton gunboat before the Union blockade grew strong enough to block off the St. Johns River. The vessel was to be a fifty-foot-long wooden gunboat with a twenty-five-foot beam, powered by two engines, and rigged as a schooner. The vessel was expected to cost $59,000 when completed at the George Mooney Shipyard.[63] The shipyard and adjoining Jacksonville Foundry and Machine Works formed a small industrial complex on the waterfront near the eastern boundary of the town at Bay and Water streets. Calvin Robinson wrote in his diary that "the construction of this vessel required considerable iron," exhausting "the little of this material which the town afforded." A second drive was launched, and Jacksonville was stripped of everything from nails to iron fences and cooking utensils. With the pinch from the Union blockade being felt more acutely, agents returned to appropriate any hidden items.[64]

While the gunboat was being built, Fort Steele was completed at the entrance to the St. Johns River. It consisted of two batteries mounting four guns each, including four heavy 32-pounder seacoast guns capable of firing 26-pound explosive shells more than a mile. Six miles upriver, at St. Johns Bluff, the Duval Cowboys were hurriedly preparing another fortification of "two earthworks, one intended for four and the other for three guns . . . and seven houses for the accommodation of troops."[65] The ordnance at the bluff, more powerful than that at Fort Steele, included two 8-inch Columbiads, a rifled 30-pounder, two 32-pounders, and three pieces of field artillery. The two forts were thinly garrisoned by inexperienced troops and vulnerable to assault from the rear. Their combined armament was not sufficient to stop a strong, determined enemy fleet.

No fortifications were erected at Jacksonville, where only a token force of Confederate troops patrolled the area. Instead of fortifying Jacksonville, which commanded a river that provided easy access into the heart of the peninsula, Florida's coastal defenses were concentrated at Fernandina, a town situated on a coastal island that could easily be bypassed or isolated. By the time the error in this strategy became apparent, it was too late to defend either town. Florida had withdrawn from the Union, in the words of historian Rowland Rerick, "with a mighty enthusiasm and Patriotic outburst of feeling [but] without a dollar in the treasury, and little money in the hands of the people save irredeemable paper."[66]

On the verge of bankruptcy in January 1862, the state passed an emergency ordinance obligating the governor to either transfer all of Florida's militia men into Confederate service or to disband the entire state militia. Jacksonville resident James M. Daniel had sponsored the measure to eliminate the "confusion and weakness" inherent in dividing military powers and decisions between the state and national governments. Daniel was also aware that Florida did not have enough money to arm and equip the state militia, let alone maintain it on active-duty status. Consequently, Florida's state militia units were officially abolished. Merging them into Confederate regiments became difficult when the Confederate army refused to accept militia units unless they were fully armed and equipped.[67]

While Florida struggled with problems of finance and supply, Confederate armies in Kentucky and Tennessee suffered serious defeats that would have significant impact on Jacksonville residents. A combined Union navy and army expedition on the Tennessee and Cumberland rivers, led by Commodore Andrew Foote and General Ulysses S. Grant, led to the capture of Forts Henry and Donelson in February 1862. The Confederacy effectively lost all of Kentucky and parts of Tennessee. Foote's gunboats then steamed unopposed on the Tennessee River through northeast Mississippi and to Muscle Shoals, Alabama.

On March 1, General Robert E. Lee, then in command of the coastal defenses of South Carolina, Georgia, and Florida, ordered all available troops in those states to the threatened front. Lee's order to abandon the defenses at Fernandina and to evacuate military personnel from Amelia and Cumberland islands reached General Trapier the following day. "The only troops to be retained in Florida," Lee wrote, "are such as may be necessary to defend Apalachicola River, by which the enemy's gunboats may penetrate far into the state of Georgia."[68]

Florida responded with emergency authorization for militia units. Local volunteer companies continued to protect their home territories, but there were not enough troops available to oppose an invading army. Winston Stephens and the St. Johns Rangers roamed widely in late 1861 and early 1862, when in a four-month period they moved from camps at Palatka to Fernandina, Dunlawton, Enterprise, Volusia, and Ocala. But with Confederate regulars hurriedly evacuating the state, the enthusiasm of militia companies would be no match for the Union army that was already forming in the Sea Islands off the coast of South Carolina.[69]

On February 28, 1862, Admiral Du Pont set sail from Port Royal with a fleet of thirty-three ships. Aboard was General Horatio G. Wright's 3rd Brigade, U.S. Expeditionary Corps, consisting of the 9th Maine, 4th New Hampshire, 6th Connecticut, and 97th Pennsylvania infantry regiments. Also along were a battalion of marines, volunteer engineers, and two sections of Hamilton's Battery, from the 3rd U.S. Artillery.[70]

General Wright was well informed on enemy operations as he approached the Florida coast. For weeks, Union supporters from the threatened areas had been slipping into Union lines with reports of Confederate defenses. One of the most valuable informants was an escaped slave named Isaac Tatnall, who had been pilot of the Jacksonville-to-Savannah steamer the *St. Marys*. The Federals had already been given a detailed account of Confederate defenses south of Fernandina by Dr. Henry Balsam, founder of New Berlin on the St. Johns. A Prussian by birth and onetime Jacksonville Port physician, Balsam, who had residences at New Berlin and Fernandina, conveyed an accurate account of Fort Steele's armament, the incomplete state of the fortification at St. Johns Bluff, and the lack of fortifications at Jacksonville, noting that defense of that crucial city consisted of only two companies of militia.[71]

On March 3, Du Pont's fleet arrived at Cumberland Sound in time to exchange shots with the last Confederate soldiers abandoning Fort Clinch. When an escaped slave brought news that "the Rebels had abandoned in haste the whole of the defenses of Fernandina, and were even at that moment retreating from Amelia Island," Du Pont ordered his forces to attack with "utmost speed to save public and private property from threatened destruction." The effort was redoubled when it was discovered that a train of cars on the Florida Railroad was about to depart Fernandina.[72]

For days, residents of the town had crowded aboard the railcars, hoping to escape across the trestle bridge to the mainland and along the track to Baldwin and beyond as far as Cedar Key on the Gulf Coast. As the gunboats hurried on the Amelia River, one last train was frantically preparing to depart, jammed with civilians and escorted by a detachment of Florida cavalry. Du Pont ordered the gunboat *Ottawa* to head it off. Belching black smoke from her stack, the *Ottawa* chased the fleeing train along a two-mile stretch where the track ran parallel to the shoreline. As the train neared the railroad bridge, passengers and cavalrymen began firing at the gunboat. The *Ottawa* returned fire, but the train clattered out of range, scattering household goods and baggage from the roofs of its cars and throwing sparks from its stack and grinding wheels. A *New York Times* correspondent described the action: "The Ottawa, thinking that the train was freighted with soldiers, discharged a shell, which struck the rear car—a platform car, loaded with furniture— and burst, scattered the furniture on all sides, and instantly killed two young men named Savage and Thompson, who were seated on a sofa. . . . The rebels loosened the rear car, and the train immediately proceeded on its way and succeeded in getting over the bridge."[73]

While the last train out of Fernandina was making its escape, the Confederate steamboat *Darlington* was captured. That night the Confederates managed to burn the mainland end of the bridge, and the next morning, March 4, the Federals occupied Fernandina. "Upon reaching the town we found it nearly deserted," the *New York Times* reported, "not more than a hundred white people remaining in the place. A small portion express themselves Union men, while others are either silent or openly avow themselves disloyal."[74] Fernandina would remain in Union hands until the end of the war.

News of Fernandina's fate spread quickly throughout Florida. Governor Milton reacted in fury. It was his opinion that the "immense expenditures of money and labor" for fortifications on Amelia Island had been foolishly wasteful. Those same resources "would have been sufficient to have made the defenses complete on the St. Johns River." The governor blamed David L. Yulee, a former U.S. senator and the president of the Florida Railroad, which headquartered in Fernandina, for using his influence to selfishly protect his personal interests by concentrating defenses in that town. This action demonstrated a "culpable ignorance of military science [in] utter disregard of the general interest of East Florida . . . to the great and irreparable injury of the citizens of St. Augustine and Jacksonville." All the Federals could gain at Fernandina was the "use of a few buildings," the governor contended, whereas "access to Jacksonville and the St. Johns opened a pathway into the heart of East Florida."[75]

On March 7, General Wright made a decision that would have fateful consequences for the people of Jacksonville. He gave orders for eight companies of Federal infantry to board naval vessels and to proceed on a reconnaissance in force up the St. Johns River to destroy defensive fortifications and claim the guns, and to "capture"—if only temporarily—Jacksonville. In a message to General Thomas W. Sherman, commander of the Department of the South at Hilton Head, Wright said that he and Admiral Du Pont had agreed to conduct a joint reconnaissance and to withdraw the gunboats and the troops when the mission was accomplished.[76]

On the very day General Wright made this decision, the men of the Jacksonville Light Infantry buried the guns of Fort Steele and hastily withdrew toward Jacksonville. Although Wright had no way of knowing it in advance, when the gunboats assembled offshore on the morning of March 8, "the pathway into the heart of East Florida" would be wide open. The reconnaissance would proceed without opposition.

A Pathway into the
Heart of East Florida

"When the news came to Jacksonville that the gunboats were off Fernandina great excitement prevailed in our city," Calvin Robinson recalled. The excitement continued for days as refugees streamed into the city. Refugees had been quietly settling in the town since February 1862, but the numbers had increased sharply when dozens of families escaping aboard the last train out of Fernandina arrived in Jacksonville. They had boarded cars of the Florida Railroad that normally traveled between Fernandina and Cedar Key, but on this run passengers disembarked at Baldwin to transfer to cars of the Florida, Atlantic and Gulf Central Railroad and continue on to Jacksonville. They had barely alighted from the cars before soldiers straggled into the city with tales of narrow escapes from Union gunboats that reportedly could "run anywhere there was a heavy dew." The stories were so alarming that "many families at once commenced leaving Jacksonville, hurrying their effects toward Lake City and other points along the railroad."[1]

On March 5, 1862, Washington Ives wrote in his diary of "the Great Excitement" in Lake City "when about 2 hundred persons came up from Jacksonville and Fernandina." Before breakfast the next morning Ives watched as another trainload of frightened migrants arrived and filled the town to capacity. Many of those in flight traveled with the slaves they owned. Five days later Ives wrote that Governor Milton had come to Lake City to give cheering speeches to the town's beleaguered citizens and to the disheartened souls fleeing from the Yankee invaders.[2]

Most Duval County residents, including the Confederates, decided to remain at home on the chance the Yankees would not move up the St. Johns River. Union supporters made it clear they had no intention of leaving, even if the Union gunboats steamed all the way to the Jacksonville wharves. According to Robinson, Unionists stayed in town, waiting quietly, "their very souls . . . ready to burst with joy at the thought" of nearby Union forces.[3]

Rooms at Jacksonville's Judson House filled quickly as refugees and Confederate staff officers and couriers arrived. Manager Otis Keene noted in the hotel's register that Brigadier General James Heyward Trapier was among the new guests. Trapier, a West Point graduate, had served for a decade as an artillerist and engineer before leaving the U.S. Army in 1848. Later, as a South Carolina militia officer, he supervised construction of the batteries in Charleston Harbor that fired on Fort Sumter in April 1861. Appointed to command of Confederate troops in the Department of Middle and East Florida in late 1861, Trapier had encountered needless conflict with Governor Milton over military policy and suffered from a severe shortage of men and arms. As late as January 30, 1862, his command had consisted of only 2,127 infantry, 1,126 cavalry, and fewer than a hundred artillerists spread along the entire eastern coast of Florida.

Trapier had been in the process of moving his command to the west when the unexpected Yankee attack on Fernandina commenced. He was in Jacksonville to see that all military supplies that could aid the enemy cause were disposed of before Confederate troops departed, and, following General Lee's orders, to consider the feasibility of concentrating military forces "at the point liable to be attacked." It appeared to Trapier that Jacksonville was to be that point, but it was not clear that the town could be held.[4] To clarify that issue, he met at the Judson House with Commander Ebenezer Farrand of the Confederate navy, Colonel Edward Hopkins and Lieutenant Colonel M. Whit Smith of the 4th Florida Infantry Regiment, and Brigadier General Samuel R. Pyles and Colonel Oscar Hart of the 16th Regiment of Florida Militia.

Jacksonville's mayor, Halsted Hoeg, was also involved in the strategy sessions. Hoeg was a native of Burlington, New York, who had moved to Duval County in 1840 and prospered as a merchant and sawmill owner. After the war commenced, his pro-secession critics complained that the city was "cursed with a Mayor who will do nothing but oppose what others suggest" and that under his leadership "at least one half of the population of the city would tamely submit to Lincoln."[5] Hoeg did not bother responding to his critics. He had to deal with the fact that nearby Fernandina had been invaded and that Jacksonville would probably be attacked next. There was little he could do but cooperate with the military and call on residents to maintain law and order. On March 6 he coordinated an emergency meeting of civil and military authorities to determine a policy to "best promote the safety, comfort and happiness of the people." Attending the meeting at city offices at the Sammis Building on Bay Street were the military officers, members of the town council, and the town's leading citizens. On May 7 Hoeg published a proclamation to his "fellow citizens" informing them that it had been the "unanimous decision" of those attending the meeting that, because "all the Confederate troops, arms, and munitions of war upon the St. John's River and in east and south Florida generally are ordered away, and that the east and south are to be abandoned, it is useless to attempt a defense of the city of Jacksonville." He urged residents to remain at home, to maintain good order, and to follow the advice of Jacksonville's "most experienced and intelligent citizens . . . that if the enemy meet with no resistance, private property will be respected, and unarmed citizens will be allowed to pursue their usual occupations."[6]

That same evening, General Wright, commanding the 3rd Brigade, Expeditionary Corps, and Admiral Du Pont, in charge of the naval flotilla, issued orders for "an expedition to the Saint John's River . . . to start tomorrow morning."[7] Under the command of Colonel T. J. Whipple, eight companies of the 4th New Hampshire Regiment received orders to accompany the naval vessels. Wright warned his officers to watch for "a battery at the mouth of the river, another at Saint John's Bluff, and a third . . . at Dames Point. To destroy these batteries, take possession of the guns, and to capture Jacksonville are the objects of the expedition."[8] He informed Adjutant General Lorenzo Thomas that he planned to occupy "some of the most important harbor outlets" in order to stop blockade runners from bringing guns and supplies to Confederate troops. "St. Simon's, Fernandina, the mouth of the Saint John's, and possibly Saint Augustine, would I think, be sufficient," he wrote Thomas. "Other places of some little importance could be blockaded by the Navy."[9]

The agreement reached between Wright and Du Pont specified that Union forces were "to land and occupy Jacksonville or other points for a few hours for purposes of reconnaissance or other necessary service," after which "the troops shall be withdrawn and return with the gunboats when this shall have been accomplished."[10] Du Pont had ordered the man in charge of naval operations, Lieutenant Thomas Holdup Stevens, "to examine the condition of things in Jacksonville, taking any public property that may be of military importance to the rebels, but respecting to the utmost private property."[11] Du Pont emphasized that the expedition was "a reconnaissance in force" and that he did not intend to permanently "occupy any point on St. John's River."[12]

On March 8 the Union flotilla arrived off the entrance to the St. Johns River. Entry was delayed when even the "light vessels" were unable to cross the treacherous sandbars and shallow water at the entrance. For the next three days Stevens fretted while soundings were conducted to find a channel deep enough to permit the vessels to cross. He had no way of knowing that Confederate scouts had sighted his vessels as soon as they arrived at the bar and had immediately transmitted the news to Jacksonville over a temporary telegraph line.[13] Town residents knew that once the gunboats crossed into the river, they would need only a few hours to steam upriver and trap them behind Union lines. Residents with valuable property, especially human property, began hurriedly moving to safe locations in the interior of the state.

No one left with greater style than John P. Sanderson. Having previously closed his local law office while serving as a legislator in Tallahassee, Sanderson returned to put his house in order. Standing three stories tall at the northeast corner of Ocean and Forsyth, Sanderson's mansion was one of the most impressive structures in Jacksonville. Bowing to the inevitable, Sanderson strolled through his rose gardens, made sure a supply of fine wines was available, and instructed his house servants to seek out the Federal commander when the troops landed and offer him the comforts of the mansion.[14]

South of Jacksonville at Millwood, James M. Daniel was joined by Francis F. L'Engle in boarding up windows and doors and packing personal belongings on wagons and carriages for a journey to Madison, Florida. L'Engle then moved to his own home to repeat the experience. Items that would not be damaged by the experience were buried, and the house was boarded up and abandoned. It was a scene being repeated throughout Jacksonville and along the lower St. Johns River. For most residents preparing to depart, their self-imposed exile would last for the duration of the war.[15]

Attorney Rodney Dorman, mayor of Jacksonville in 1851, buried several hundred dollars in a jar under his Bay Street home. When he returned four years later the money was still there, well concealed by the pile of charred debris that had once been the Dorman home. Arthur M. Reed, the founder and president of Jacksonville's Bank of St. Johns, hurried to his plantation at

Mulberry Grove (today at Jacksonville Naval Air Station on the St. Johns) to bury the family silver and other valuables. With his treasures safely concealed, Reed remained at Mulberry Grove.[16]

Colonel John Broward had already decided to make a spirited fight if the Federals ever advanced up the river. Although most of his sons had enlisted in the Confederate service and were no longer at home to assist him, the old colonel recruited his neighbors in a plan to delay the approaching gunboats and give people more time to move their slaves and other property to safe locations in the interior of the state. Logs were mounted on a waterfront promontory to resemble cannons, forcing the gunboats to halt their advance and shell the supposed fortification. One of the Broward sons, Napoleon Sr., rode from Fernandina to the St. Johns with the first warnings of the Federal presence and then carried out orders from his brother, Montgomery, to take men to Yellow Bluff and "fire into the first Yankee vessel that should come within range."[17]

Lucius Hardee and the Duval Cowboys were engaged in another kind of work with authentic artillery at St. Johns Bluff. Having been ordered to evacuate, the men were doing their best to conceal or bury the cannons they could not cart away. They finished on March 9 and marched to Jacksonville to join men of the Jacksonville Light Infantry, who had finished similar work at Fort Steele. Otis Keene had already noted the arrival of the latter company with a brief entry in the Judson House register: "Jacksonville Light Infantry came from Fort Steele and took cars for Lake City."[18]

Calvin Robinson claimed that the "ruffian portion" of the town, "members of the Vigilant Committee" who had "little or no property of their own . . . insisted on burning the town, and that everybody should flee to the country. Now the wildest excitement prevailed. Every sort of vehicle was pressed into service hurrying household goods and merchandise towards the depot." Robinson noticed that nearly all of the town's residents who supported the Confederacy were desperately seeking a means to depart. "Most of the Northern citizens and some of the large property holders among the Southern people objected to leaving the city. . . . There was no terror in those gunboats or the Old Flag to them."[19]

On the same fateful night, a grim drama was being enacted at the East Bay Street shipyard, where Commander Farrand and his men had been rushing their gunboat to completion. With machinery newly installed and decking almost completed, the gunboat was only three weeks from launching. Sitting away from the water, high on her stocks on the banks of the river, the unnamed vessel could not be scuttled and sunk. As darkness settled over Jacksonville, torches were applied to the gunboat's hull.[20]

It would be three days before the gunboats reached Jacksonville. On March 9, the same evening the flames from Farrand's ill-fated gunboat rose above Jacksonville, Lieutenant Stevens placed his ships in formation off Mayport to await sufficient daylight before risking a crossing of the treacherous sandbars at the entrance to the river. Stevens had decided to proceed cautiously upriver after receiving reports that "the St. Johns River was strongly defended and that the gunboats would have all the fighting they wanted."[21]

At daybreak Stevens sent a landing party under direction of Lieutenant Daniel Ammen to inspect locations near the mouth of the river. Ammen returned with the four black men who had informed him that all Confederate troops had been evacuated from Florida and that no defense would be made on the river. The citizens of Jacksonville who remained were reportedly anxious to send a flag of truce to greet Stevens's fleet.[22]

At age forty-two, Stevens was a veteran of a quarter-century of naval service. With a flotilla consisting of four gunboats (*Ottawa*, *Seneca*, *Pembina*, and *Huron*), two small armed steamers (*Isaac Smith* and *Ellen*), the armed transport *Boston*, and assorted armed launches and cutters for amphibious operations, he was in charge of a formidable force. The gunboats were less than six months old and armed with a variety of ordnance, from large-caliber Dahlgren smoothbores, to 20-pounder Parrott rifles, to 24-pounder howitzers. The *Ellen* was a diminutive side-wheeler, but it carried heavy ordnance, and its launches and cutters were armed with small but effective swivel guns.[23]

On the afternoon of March 10, Stevens sent a shore party to occupy the abandoned Fort Steele. An accompanying correspondent for the *New York Tribune* reported the capture of four 32-pounders with cartridges and shot, along with evidence in the camps located to the rear of the fort indicating the battery had only recently been evacuated. One of the departing Confederates left a note "in chalk on the door of one of the huts record[ing] that the Rebels had left 'from force of circumstances,' but [they] hoped to meet the Yankee . . . at another point."[24] Undeterred by the challenge, the men of the shore party crossed to the north of the St. Johns seeking shelter for the night in "four ruinous old houses, rejoicing in the name Pilot Town." The *Tribune* reporter said the men were so tormented by mosquitoes that they "gave up the notion of sleeping after one or two attempts, and bestowed their undivided attention on [the pesky critters]."[25]

After conducting experimental soundings and sending smaller craft bouncing across the barriers, Stevens lost patience on the afternoon of March 11 and took the controls of the *Ottawa* himself. The *Tribune* reporter said he approached "under full steam" and rammed the gunboat at the bar, striking twice in the crossing, but making it safely across without damaging the vessel. Stevens's record of the crossing is a less exciting rendition of the event. He informed Du Pont that the *Ottawa*, *Seneca*, and *Pembina* crossed the bar at "about 4 o'clock, having no water to spare under our keels. The *Isaac Smith* arrived half an hour afterwards, and crossed without a pilot."[26] By nightfall, all the Federal vessels had followed Stevens's example and were across the bar.

By the time Stevens made arrangements to land a company of the 4th New Hampshire Regiment to occupy the abandoned Fort Steele and guard the entrance to the river, it was too late to steam upriver safely, and the gunboats anchored in the river for the night. At "near 10 o'clock," Stevens "discovered large fires bearing W.S.W., from the anchorage, which proved to be on my arrival here [the next day at Jacksonville], the burning of mills, houses, and property belonging to Northern men with suspected Union proclivities, burned by order of the rebel commander."[27]

At dawn on March 12, signals were sent to the other captains to "move at daylight, taking precedence according to rank. Should it be necessary to engage the enemy the vessels will form in line ahead at a distance of a cable's length."[28] Jacksonville was to be the immediate priority, but after traveling only six miles up the St. Johns, Stevens sent orders to Lieutenant Ammen to anchor the *Ellen* beneath the abandoned Confederate battery on St. Johns Bluff and send a shore party to search for possible weapons left behind. Stevens's orders from Du Pont were to secure Jacksonville, reduce any enemy fortifications, and "to go as far as Palatka, 80 miles beyond to reconnoiter and capture river steamers . . . accompanied by the armed launches and cutters of the *Wabash* . . . and by a light-draft transport, with the Seventh New Hampshire Regiment."[29]

As the gunboats continued upriver a white flag was seen hoisted above a house on the shore, prompting Stevens to send a party to the wharf with assurances that no harm would come to peaceful and unarmed citizens. As the squadron proceeded, more houses were seen flying white flags, giving the illusion of peace and calm, but the Federals grew increasingly apprehensive when they saw smoke from the fires of the previous evening still lingering in the skyline ahead. The *Tribune* correspondent recorded his fear that "the town might already be destroyed."[30] Stevens cast caution aside and ordered the squadron to proceed at full steam toward the clouds of black smoke. He would soon learn the full extent of the terror that Jacksonville's remaining residents had experienced on the infamous night of March 11, 1862.

As long as the gunboats had remained outside the bar at the entrance to the river, Mayor Hoeg was able to avoid wholesale panic in Jacksonville. But as soon as word arrived that the gunboats had entered the St. Johns River, conditions turned chaotic. Refugees began streaming out of town carrying their belongings. The town's small railroad depot became the scene of near-riotous confusion as hundreds of panicked people contended for places near the track in hopes of boarding one of the special trains operating during the emergency.[31]

With the departure of many of the city's older and more influential Southern residents, Jacksonville's Unionists were left to the mercy of a mob that was beginning to range through the streets with increasing belligerence. Calvin Robinson was warned by friends of a plan to murder him and destroy his property. Also singled out for execution was attorney Philip Fraser, a forty-two-year-old Pennsylvanian who had lived in Jacksonville since 1841 and served as mayor in 1855. That evening Robinson arranged for a safe house on the south shore of the St. Johns for Fraser and his family. Robinson and his wife decided to risk one more night in their home—hoping that Union gunboats would arrive in time to save them from the rampaging mob.[32]

Otis and Abbie Keene were aware of the panic and terror, but for several days they had been too busy at their hotel to worry about their own fate. On March 8, twenty-three new guests had registered. On the ninth the hotel register listed many familiar names, among them Holmes Steele, W. A. Bryant, and John Butler, all of the Jacksonville Light Infantry. Many of the other guests were either refugees from Fernandina or men whom Otis Keene recognized as the most violent of Duval County's secessionists. That night, Keene made note of two historic occurrences: the burning of the Confederate gunboat at the Mooney Shipyard and Foundry, and the retreat of the Light Infantry. On the tenth he bade farewell to two old friends, Calvin Oak and John P. Sanderson.[33]

On March 11 the Keenes greeted an unusual assortment of guests, including four men from Fernandina who registered as Judge Woodward, J. V. Rumly, Charles B. Futch, and Captain Fred Clark. In addition, four men registered as Confederate officers with the "Special Battalion, C.S.A." The

Special Battalion had marched into town early that morning with orders from General Trapier to destroy strategic facilities and supplies to deny their use to the enemy.[34]

Shortly before noon on the eleventh, Major Charles Hopkins and five hundred men from the Special Battalion formed a square at the railroad depot at Clay and Adams streets. Hopkins told the troops their mission was to destroy the sawmills and stockpiles of lumber, the foundries and machine shops at both ends of Bay Street, and the railroad depot. The men were expressly forbidden to molest civilians or damage properties other than those specifically designated. This briefing took place in full view of the Keenes and some of their guests, watching from across the street on the hotel's upper piazza.

The railway depot now attracted even larger crowds of strangers and residents. When it was verified that the soldiers had been ordered to destroy property, some of it owned by Southerners, agitators shouted to the mob: "Why should Southerners lose all they owned and Unionists remain in possession of the town with their property intact?"[35] This and other questions, along with provocative taunts shouted by the agitators, ignited the passions of many in the mob and produced a state of frenzy.

Unionists recognized individual faces in the crowd and were chilled by what they saw. Many in the mob were bitter and angry refugees from Fernandina, but there were even more firebrands from Jacksonville, including the extremists from the vigilance committees who had harassed Unionists for months and were now clamoring for the destruction of the entire city. Soon, rumors circulated that Jacksonville would be burned to the ground that night. Runners roamed the streets warning that all who valued their lives must leave within twenty-four hours. Whether friend or foe, the provocateurs warned, anyone remaining in town would be in danger of death. Meanwhile, the word was passed that the regulators meant to kill Judge Fraser, Mayor Hoeg, Calvin Robinson, and others.

Calvin Robinson had no idea what was going on in the town that afternoon until his neighbor rushed to the back of the store to warn him to leave immediately. Hurrying to his home, Robinson gathered his family and survival rations and ran to a boat at the wharf behind his store. He had rowed only a few yards away from the wharf when he and his wife witnessed "a column of troops march down Bay Street and another column down the back of the town and in a few minutes the city was under close military guard." Next came the ruffians of the vigilance committee, who saw Robinson and cursed at him as he and his family crossed the river to join his friend Philip

Fraser in a cabin on the south bank of the river. Later that evening, they "were startled by the sudden illumination of the surrounding woods, and on looking out discovered that the Confederates had begun their work of burning the steam mills. . . . There were eight or ten of these mills, with millions of feet of sawn lumber, within sight of where we stood. Soon, all of these were in flames and their light reflected back from the sky, then overcast with heavy clouds, was a fearful sight to look upon. The whole heavens seemed like billows of flames."[36]

Elizabeth Robinson had the impression that not more than a dozen families were left in Jacksonville that night. "The past week has been a perfect reign of terror—such sights and sounds I pray my Heavenly Father I may never see or hear again," she wrote. "This trouble has nearly broken our hearts. To think that people who have so long professed such friendship . . . [could] become such bitter enemies without any cause."[37]

While the Robinsons fled across the river, the Keenes watched the Special Battalion file by the Judson House, followed by a mob of armed civilians that included four men registered at the hotel: Woodward, Futch, Clark, and Rumly. The four men were greeted by Mrs. Keene, who inquired about the safety of the hotel. "They set her fears all at rest by assuring her that there was no truth in the reports that the hotel was to be burned, ordered supper, and partook of one especially prepared under the superintendence of the hostess herself." After finishing the meal, however, "they began their work of destruction by applying the torch. . . . Mr. and Mrs. Keene, seeing their all was about to be destroyed, rushed to their private room, and began bringing out some of their choice articles, among them a fine old mirror, a valuable heirloom . . . which Mrs. Keene prized very highly. . . . Seeing one of the young men standing near, whom she had fed that night . . . she handed him the mirror and begged him to carry it to a place of safety. He took the glass from her hands and turning from her deliberately smashed it to fragments on his knees, and then ordered her not to move anything from the house." The Keenes were able to carry some items to a nearby hiding place, where they waited in fear throughout the night.[38] The destruction of the Judson House seemed to accelerate the frenzy of the mob. Soon, the town's sawmills and lumber storage sheds, the foundries and machine shops went up in flames. Their fury not yet sated, the mob moved on to apply the torch to several stores and homes.

Eliza Hudnall watched the conflagration from across the river. Her husband, Francis, had just left for Middleburg with the family's slaves. As she scanned the distant waterfront with binoculars, she saw pinpoints of light suddenly appear in the dark, spawning flames that flickered and raced over black buildings outlined in the light that was consuming them. She realized that the pinpoints were torches. What she did not know, however, was that her sister, Maria, was trapped in the burning district. Maria, an ardent secessionist, was the wife of Dr. Miles J. Murphy, a physician and South Carolinian, and a lieutenant assigned to the Special Battalion then in the town. When his duties prevented him from assisting his wife, he turned for help to the family's closest friend, Dr. J. D. Mitchell, a migrant from Maine and an ardent Unionist.

Mitchell escorted Maria, her son, and Miss Belle Buddington to the depot, only to learn that the train would be delayed for hours. Around them, armed soldiers and civilians were silhouetted against sheets of flame. Mitchell found a vacant house near the depot, from where they "sat through the night . . . while almost over our heads the Judson House . . . was in flames," Maria recalled. "From time to time we went out . . . and near morning my husband and others arrived to take us to a place of safety."[39]

Across the river the Robinsons and Frasers also watched the torches "pass up and down the river," dreading the inevitable moment when the Robinson warehouse would burst into flames. That moment came soon enough, followed by mob looting at Robinson's store before it, too, was consigned to flames. Two clerks inside the store fled through the rear door that led to the wharf, from where they leaped into a boat and rowed for their lives under a hail of rifle shots. "They sought to kill me that night," Robinson remembered. "Now we knew that the rumors brought to us were true, and they would murder us if they could find us. We began to realize the hopelessness of our situation." Thinking that the Yankee gunboats had turned back toward the mouth of the river, the merchant wrote, "It was a dark hour."[40]

It was also a terrifying night for Otis and Abbie Keene. As they stood amid their salvaged possessions and watched the Judson House burn, they saw that all around them the city was ablaze. They watched as the mob surged through the streets after burning the mills and railroad wharf to loot and burn at least a half dozen Unionists' homes and shops along Bay Street. Far into the night the shouts of the mob and the sounds of shooting echoed over the river. Fortunately, a brief early morning downpour checked the wind-driven flames that were spreading from one structure to another, and prevented the total destruction of Jacksonville.[41]

While the event was still fresh in his mind, Keene wrote that those responsible were "Rebel soldiers, commanded by Major Chas. F. Hopkins," and in the hotel register he managed to save he circled the names Wood-ward, Clark, Futch, and Rumly, and wrote: "Parties who burned the Judson House after taking supper there." At the bottom of the page he added: "Judson House was burned at 8 o'clock by parties from away and others, and the Military here in command would lend no aid to protect the property. . . . A terrible night. . . . A night of terror."[42]

As the last of General Trapier's soldiers and the civilians boarded the last train to leave the depot, flames still flickered from the wreckage of the platform and the overhead canopy. It was after daybreak before the town's remaining residents emerged from shops and houses where they had been hiding. Aaron W. Acosta and his wife and four children could be seen in a large rowboat being poled downriver by an Acosta slave. At Ortega they found a temporary haven in an abandoned home, where they rested before proceeding on foot to Baldwin.[43]

Along the plank road and the railroad right-of-way between Jacksonville and Baldwin, abandoned baggage and furniture lay scattered in the wake of those who fled. Scores of families still wandered about or huddled in make-shift shelters. Most of these disheartened souls were cold, wet, and hungry. Unionists who fled to the south side of the river stared back in disbelief at a skyline they no longer recognized. Much of their community had vanished in fire and smoke and madness.[44]

As the Union flotilla approached Jacksonville on the afternoon of March 12, Lieutenant Stevens saw from the deck of the *Ottawa* that "the fires of the mills and houses were still burning, and the smoke hung heavily." Following in the wake of the flagship, the other gunboats formed a line of battle, their broadsides presented to the city, guns on targets and crews at the ready, but no signs of hostility were detected. Gradually, people began to appear near the river, and several small boats with passengers waving white flags approached the flagship. Satisfied that the Confederates were not going to contest their approach, Stevens ordered his cutters and launches to land companies of the 4th New Hampshire.[45]

Stevens was greatly encouraged by the warm reception his men received from the inhabitants of Jacksonville. The town's "corporate authorities" greeted the gunboats with a flag of truce and a surrender of the town. After conversing with these "intelligent citizens," Stevens concluded that "the inhabitants are seeking and waiting for the protection of our flag; that they do not fear us, but their own people, and from the occupation of this important point I am satisfied, if our opportunities are improved, great results will follow."[46] General Wright was also pleased that the remaining residents had "hailed with joy the arrival of our forces and their relief from the oppressive rule of the rebel authorities."[47]

With the Union navy now in control of Fernandina, Jacksonville, and St. Augustine, and regiments of the Union army in occupation of all three towns and Union gunboats roaming up the St. Marys and St. Johns rivers at will, Rebel enthusiasts in East Florida looked desperately to the Confederate government in Richmond for emergency assistance. General Trapier was replaced in command by a man who had lived in Duval County for much of his life, Brigadier General Joseph Finegan. The new commander was instructed to "pay particular attention to defense of the interior of the state and the lines of interior communication with both the Apalachicola and St. Johns rivers."[48]

Winning back East Florida's coastal cities must have seemed like an impossible challenge to Finegan, since he had fewer troops than Trapier had commanded. He subsequently complained about insufficient men and weapons, and learned he would have to recruit on his own. "For all intents and purposes," historian William H. Nulty has observed, "Florida found herself abandoned by the Confederacy she had been so eager to join, isolated and vulnerable to the enemy."[49]

4

The First Occupation
of Jacksonville

On March 12, 1862, Lieutenant Stevens stopped the Union vessels short of the Jacksonville wharves to scrutinize the town's streets for signs of Confederate soldiers. As soon as he was convinced the Confederates had evacuated, a shore party was dispatched to secure the town's streets and perimeter. The squadron remained at battle stations while the troops searched the town for public property and military supplies that might later aid the enemy. Stevens intended to depart in the morning "to penetrate, as far as prudent, the upper waters of the St. John's."[1]

The upriver journey to Jacksonville had been without incident, and the reception at Jacksonville was greatly encouraging. Municipal government was restored on the day the Union ships arrived, and although "many of the citizens have fled, many remain, and there is reason to believe most of them will return."[2] Nevertheless, Stevens intended to carry out Admiral Du Pont's orders to carefully investigate conditions at Jacksonville, travel as far up the St. Johns as appeared prudent, and return all Union forces to a planned gunboat base at the mouth of the river.

Du Pont's orders were as yet unknown to the Union loyalists who remained in the town. Otis Keene, watching the shore party search the town, felt he had been delivered from "imprisonment from rebel despotism . . . and thrilled to the sight of the glorious Old Flag once more." Philip Fraser was so excited he began jumping and shouting on the riverbank. When cautioned to stop lest the gunboats shell him, Fraser shouted: "Let them fire. It would be glorious to be killed with shells from under that Flag." Fraser and

Calvin Robinson jumped into a rowboat and made for the nearest gunboat. Only later did it occur to Robinson that after suffering through the previous sleepless "night of terror" his resultant "wild and haggard looks" might cause the officer to think he "had gone 'daft' or would soon."[3]

Sheriff Frederick Leuders boarded the *Ottawa* believing he was the only elected official left in the city, but instead he found a twelve-man delegation headed by Connecticut-born Judge Samuel L. Burritt already in conference with Stevens. The two men were old friends from their younger years in New England. The town's municipal officials surrendered the town and requested personal and property protection for the residents. Their main worry was that regulators might come in from the countryside and attempt to kill Unionists or burn their property. Stevens accepted the surrender and assured the delegation that town residents were safe as long as Federal forces were present, but he also informed them that his mission did not call for a permanent occupation of the town.[4] Burritt and his colleagues repeatedly told Stevens that if Union forces were withdrawn "the town [would] lay at the mercy of the traitors who meant to burn it, and every man who uttered a word of loyalty to the Union would be certainly murdered." A correspondent for the *New York Tribune* who heard the conversations wrote: "the people in Jacksonville fear nothing so much as their own people."[5]

The delegation so impressed Stevens that he invited the men to meet with his senior staff. Robinson told the officers of the "many citizens in Jacksonville who were loyal to the Old Flag, or would be should the threatening power of the Confederacy be lifted from them." When all the delegates had been heard, Stevens and his officers held a private consultation. They emerged to announce that, although their orders were to the contrary, they had decided "to take possession of the town." Stevens later explained to Du Pont: "the inhabitants are seeking and waiting for the protection of our flag," and asked the admiral to confer with General Wright about sending reinforcements to hold the city.[6]

The unauthorized occupation began immediately. Landing forces carried six companies of the 4th New Hampshire and a regimental band ashore. With the band playing "Yankee Doodle," Colonel Whipple's men marched from Pine Street (now Main) to Bay Street, past the smoking ruins of Calvin Robinson's wharf and stores, the remains of Paran Moody's sawmill, the railroad wharf, and the Judson House before drawing up in formation at the public square. Stevens joined them while the Stars and Stripes were raised and Jacksonville was formally surrendered.

Colonel Whipple posted his troops and established a provost guard, and then got "publicly and shamelessly drunk." The *New York Tribune* correspondent reported that while drinking that evening Whipple caroused with a local "negro woman on his arm, and made drunken speeches to his men until daylight."[7] The following morning Stevens arrested Whipple and sent him to Fernandina.

Stevens pulled anchor at dawn on March 13 to carry out his orders to reconnoiter upriver. He stopped briefly at Palatka, where an informant provided the surprising news that the yacht *America*, recently employed as a blockade runner, had been trapped in the St. Johns when the Union fleet arrived. With his path back to the open sea blocked, the captain of the *America* had it towed upriver by the steamer *St. Marys* to Dunns Creek, where both vessels were scuttled. After Stevens resumed his journey, "a boat was discovered with two persons in it, to which we gave chase, when as we neared the shore the boat was abandoned. Upon searching the boat a letter was discovered from a Mr. Hemming, the person employed to sink the yacht and the steamer, giving all the information desired."[8] Colonel J. C. Hemming had been at the tiller of the *America*, assisted by his eighteen-year-old son, Charles. English born, the forty-five-year-old Hemming had been in Jacksonville since the 1840s and had held a variety of public offices and jobs, including town councilman, public auctioneer, and purser of the steamboat *Welaka*. Charles was a private in the Jacksonville Light Infantry.[9]

Stevens then returned to Jacksonville and reported to Du Pont that he had encountered "no hostile demonstrations; on the contrary the assurance I gave that we did not come to molest peaceable citizens has had a good effect. I am induced to believe from the result of my visit up the river and from my intercourse with the citizens here, if a sufficient force is left at this point to protect the Union sentiment, which is showing itself more and more, the State of Florida will soon be disenthralled."[10] Stevens met with General Wright in Jacksonville to inform him of widespread Union sentiment in the town. After the meeting he reported: "I am happy to say our views fully accord."[11]

The following day, Stevens and a team of Union sailors found the *America* at the bottom of Dunns Creek "in three fathoms of water, only her port rail being above water."[12] They also found the steamer *St. Marys* sunk at Haw Creek, 140 miles above Palatka. Stevens then returned to Jacksonville to assemble ships and crew to raise the scuttled vessels and tow them back to Jacksonville. Stevens wrote: "it is asserted and generally believed she [the *America*] was bought by the rebels for the purpose of carrying Slidell and Mason to England."[13]

While the men of the reclamation party labored to raise the *America,* they were unaware that a Confederate cavalry detachment under command of Captain Winston Stephens had been watching from secure hideouts in trees only two hundred yards away, with rifles sighted on the Union men. The sailors were easy targets, but Stephens could not bring himself to authorize his men to fire. After ordering his men down from the trees, he turned to J. C. Greeley and said, "I can't shoot them. I just can't do it—it would be murder," and ordered a withdrawal. The Union salvagers raised the yacht and returned it to Jacksonville. Still seaworthy, the yacht was refitted and assigned to Du Pont's South Atlantic Blockading Squadron.

Stevens was careful to not antagonize citizens who lived along the St. Johns. On one occasion he loaded "a quantity of resin, sirup, moss, hardware, . . . leaving word with ex-Governor Mosely, at Palatka, if the property belonged to persons not in arms or not inimical to the authority of the Government of the United States, it would be returned, or if used, paid for at a fair market value."[14] If the owners of the property happened to be Confederates, however, Stevens wanted it confiscated without compensation.

By pursuing a conciliatory strategy toward citizens along the St. Johns, Stevens was following the policy of the Lincoln administration in early 1862, which was to act with magnanimity and protect the property of locals with the hope of winning back their allegiance. Stevens was also determined to protect pro-Union residents along the St. Johns. On March 27 he posted a warning "to the owners of property at Orange Mills," a sawmill on the east shore of the river near East Palatka. Stevens had heard that a Union supporter named "De Costa, while in charge of the Orange Mills . . . has been maltreated and incarcerated for holding intercourse with persons belonging to the naval forces of the United States by some lawless person or persons."[15] Stevens informed residents of the Orange Mills area that failure to return De Costa would result in the destruction of their property.[16]

By the time the *America* was returned to Jacksonville, a few businesses had reopened their doors. The Union gunboat *Ellen,* damaged while raiding plantations along the river, was soon refitted locally. Stevens informed Du Pont that repairs could be done in Jacksonville "at reasonable prices and by experienced workmen. The rebels in destroying by fire the frame of a gunboat being built for their service . . . left untouched the berth deck planking of the vessel, which is now being used for repairing the *Ellen's* hurricane deck."[17]

The increase in ship traffic prompted the return of additional local merchants. A *New York Times* correspondent noted that it had been a year since so many ships had assembled in Jacksonville, and the presence of hundreds of sailors and soldiers with money to spend brought merchants hurrying back from self-imposed exile. Eliza Hudnall initiated an entrepreneurial career by bartering her home-baked goods for various scarce supplies possessed by Union sailors. She loaded her young son and an assortment of delicacies in a rowboat and ventured amid the Union vessels anchored in the river. Her daughter, Phena, remembered that "the officers were delighted, and they took all of her offerings and gave her in return flour, salt, coffee, tea, and sugar," even a pair of shoes for the boy. The Hudnalls became a familiar sight to the sailors at Jacksonville.[18]

The promise of a business revival prompted some merchants with Confederate sympathies to disguise their true feelings and feign allegiance to the Union. William A. Young, proprietor of the Cowford Ferry, was one such opportunist. Young wanted his ferry service to continue under Federal authorization while he secretly smuggled secessionists and Confederate spies back and forth between Jacksonville's business district and the south bank of the river. He was eventually arrested and jailed as "a suspected and dangerous individual."[19]

The Federals permitted a flow of refugees between the city and the Confederate lines a few miles beyond. Incoming refugees brought information about Confederate forces, while the departure of dissidents minimized security problems within the town. Yet, when Colonel Oscar Hart requested permission to enter Jacksonville in order to determine how many residents wanted to leave, he was refused. General Wright was not about to allow the residents to be intimidated by uniformed Confederates, not even under a flag of truce. Those wishing to leave the town were given passes. Wright announced: "We do not profess to wage war upon women and children, nor upon quiet, unoffending citizens; but, on the contrary, have done all in our power for the protection of their persons and property."[20]

Captain Stephens did not believe such protestations. When the gunboats first arrived off Mayport, he sent a warning message to his wife: "I am nearly crazy to think of what might happen to you—take to the woods, anything but disgrace by the polluting touch of those scoundrels." A week later he was still worried: "I will not trust them and I don't want you to trust them. Don't be uneasy about my safety as we will fight them Indian fashion and can have a better chance to save ourselves."[21]

Despite the presence of Federal troops in Jacksonville, the danger to Unionists was not over. Calvin Robinson was told that "the Rebels would give more to catch me and Judge Fraser than the highest Federal officers."

A friend visiting the city on a pass warned Robinson that the regulators planned to "dash into the town and capture him." Facing such dangers, the Robinson family set up housekeeping on a guarded wharf; later they moved nightly from one vacant house to another. Secessionists who had remained in town to protect their property also lived in fear of regulator vengeance in the event of a Federal withdrawal, prompting some to petition for safe passage out of the town. Fear of the regulators became so intense that civilians began clamoring for weapons to protect themselves.[22]

Newspaper reports of these developments praised the Unionists for their perseverance and for being "loyal men whom no arts could seduce, no influence lead astray." As for the secessionists, the *New York Times* contrasted the peaceful surrenders of Fernandina, Jacksonville, and St. Augustine with the conduct "of those ferocious rebels and humbugs who met in Tallahassee fifteen months ago and swore that they would all die in the last ditch rather than recognize the National authority." The reporter also expressed the hope that soon "a loyal and legitimate Government shall be given to the deluded people of the peninsula."[23]

This was exactly what Jacksonville's Unionists had been waiting to hear. At every opportunity they reminded the occupation authorities that Jacksonville was the center of loyal sentiment in East Florida and that it would be a grave mistake to abandon it to Confederate control. They urged the occupation forces to hold the city permanently and allow the citizens to reestablish a loyal state government. General Thomas W. Sherman, commander of the Department of the South, was not convinced. He had already advised Washington that Jacksonville was occupied "contrary to the tenor of my instructions to General Wright."[24]

On March 19 Sherman arrived in Jacksonville on a personal inspection tour and was greeted aboard his transport by a delegation that included Mayor Hoeg, Judge Burritt, John S. Sammis, Paran Moody, John W. Price, Philip Fraser, Calvin Robinson, and Otis Keene. A *New York Times* correspondent summarized the conversation: "They proclaimed their anxiety for the restoration of the United States Government and assured Gen. Sherman that a similar sentiment was widespread through this region of the State." Three or four hundred people were residing in the town at the time, with deserters from Rebel arms arriving each day, professing their eagerness to pledge loyalty to the United States. The Jacksonville delegation assured Sherman that many of the deserters were "willing to take up arms to defend themselves against the tyranny to which they have lately been subjected, and on one occasion, when the Regulators were expected, even the women seized arms."[25]

Sherman requested an exact count of the number of loyal citizens in town. That afternoon notices were posted throughout the city calling on all loyal citizens to register their names at the office of the provost marshal on the following day. The register was opened at 8:30 a.m., and within two hours, eighty-two names had been inscribed. Thirty minutes later, one hundred loyal citizens met at the courthouse. When their work was completed, it seemed apparent to the *Times* correspondent that the speakers had openly avowed their Union sentiments for the first time in more than a year, knowing "they were taking their lives in their hands" in doing so.[26]

A committee of citizens elected at the meeting issued its own declaration of rights and resolved that no state had the right of secession. Speaking for the citizens, Judge Fraser said that Florida was still "an integral part of the United States," having survived tyranny, despotism, and a "mad and barbarous policy which has punished us for remaining in our own homes by sending a brutal and unrestrained soldiery to pillage and burn our property, threaten and destroy our lives." But with the arrival of Federal troops the "reign of terror" had passed and "Law and Order" again prevailed. The committee then resolved to call a "convention of all loyal citizens" to organize a Unionist Florida government, and appealed to General Sherman to permanently occupy Jacksonville with "a sufficient force to maintain order and protect the people in their persons and property."[27]

Sherman praised the citizens at the meeting for clinging to Union and promised to protect property and personal rights. He urged every Florida resident to throw off the Confederate government, swear allegiance to the Union, and elect a loyal government of the state of Florida. Peaceable and loyal Floridians would be protected, Sherman said: "The sole desire and intention of the Government is to maintain the integrity of the Constitution and the laws and reclaim States which have revolted from their national allegiance to their former prosperous and happy condition."[28]

Jacksonville Unionists sent copies of their own proclamation through the Federal lines to other communities where they thought loyal sentiments were strong. Copies were also dispatched by Union gunboats to Fernandina and St. Augustine, and delegates were invited to attend a convention to establish a loyal state government. The convention was to be held in Jacksonville on March 24.[29]

As the date for the convention drew near, the *Times* observed that "the citizens . . . invited the National Officers to their houses and tables . . . and never tired of the endeavor to convince the Nationals that their loyalty was real. They insisted that the Union sentiment was shared by thousands of others; and that many of the rebel troops are ready to desert."[30] Lieutenant Stevens agreed, claiming that he had found the people living along the river above Jacksonville to be "peaceable and apparently well disposed toward their old flag. . . . All along the route the people would come out, claiming protection, waving white flags from their houses, and declaring themselves heartily sick of the rebel rule." Stevens had previously read a report written by Commander C. R. P. Rodgers on behalf of Admiral Du Pont to Judge William Marvin of the U.S. District Court at Key West, informing him "of evidence of a strong Union feeling, smothered, repressed, somewhat timid but susceptible of being cherished into a very genial loyalty." Rodgers felt that three of four people remaining along the river were happy to be under the U.S. flag and were tired of the rebellion. Du Pont had assured them that loyal citizens and their property would be protected but had found it difficult to "allay all apprehension"; he judged that it would require "much tact, and much knowledge of the community to bring about a thorough, cordial and *active* return to their allegiance."[31]

On March 24 the Union convention was held at the courthouse in Jacksonville, with local citizens and delegates from throughout northeast Florida in attendance. The delegates chose Calvin Robinson as chairman and Otis Keene as secretary. A resolution was approved that called for another convention to reorganize civil authority in all of Florida. The second convention was scheduled for April 10 at Jacksonville.[32]

The spirits of the Jacksonville Unionists were boosted the following day when the naval transport *Cosmopolitan* arrived in port carrying the 97th Pennsylvania Volunteers, under command of Colonel Henry R. Guss, to reinforce the Jacksonville garrison. General Wright was also aboard, having decided to relocate headquarters of the 3rd Brigade, Expeditionary Corps, from Fernandina to Jacksonville and to assume command in person. Three days after he arrived at Jacksonville, Wright brought Captain D. R. Ransom from Fernandina with two batteries of light artillery and ordered earthworks constructed on the outskirts of town. Guns confiscated at St. Johns Bluff were mounted in these defenses. Houses located near the outer limits of the town were demolished or burned, and shrubbery and trees were cut down to clear lines of fire.[33]

Reassured that the Federal command intended to hold Jacksonville, citizens who had previously been reluctant to profess their Unionism now lined up to take the oath of loyalty. Before long Calvin Robinson was receiving daily "congratulations and assurances [of loyalty] from parties coming through the lines." Overjoyed, Robinson reported that "nearly the whole country was in sympathy with us, and would support us, and would exhibit their support just as far as their safety from the rebel troops . . . would permit."[34]

Sherman had done all he could to reassure the Unionists and hold Jacksonville against any Confederate challenge. On March 21 he had authorized Wright to divert troops from Fernandina and St. Augustine to Jacksonville in order to repel any enemy force that might threaten his base. In a report to the War Department, Sherman wrote: "After thoroughly understanding the political situation of affairs there, and the reign of terror to which the Union men are still subjected, I not only confirmed Gen. Wright's acts, but have increased the force at Jacksonville [by] one regiment." With sixteen companies of troops in Jacksonville, Sherman was confident that "Florida will soon be regenerated."[35]

Alarmed by the increasing Federal presence, Confederate troops began concentrating in the area. By March 31 nearly three thousand Confederates were encamped ten miles north of Jacksonville. When Wright received intelligence reports that the Confederate command was considering sending two regiments from Georgia to Jacksonville, he requested two additional Federal regiments: "I shall, of course, hold this point to the last against any force that may be brought by the enemy, and am entirely confident, with the aid of the gunboats now here, of making a successful defense."[36]

The Confederates occupied positions along McGirts Creek thirteen miles west of Jacksonville to protect the rail line leading to Baldwin. Colonel W. S. Dilworth, in command of the Confederate troops, conducted "a thorough reconnaissance of the city," which convinced him that his forces could not retake the town in the face of the firepower of the Union gunboats. He instead mounted a campaign of "annoyances" against picket lines and foraging parties. One attack occurred at the edge of town at the old Brick Church, near the present intersection of Myrtle Avenue and Monroe Street. On March 27, jittery Federal pickets fired on a party of black men and women from Lake City who were seeking freedom behind Union lines. One of the escapees was killed and another was wounded.[37]

On March 29, concerned about intelligence reports of an imminent Confederate attack on Jacksonville, Wright joined five companies of the 4th New Hampshire on a reconnaissance mission. He later reported: "We examined the country as far as [McGirts Creek] and pushed . . . some three-quarters of a mile beyond without seeing anything of the enemy, but we learned that a party (horse and foot, numbering 100 perhaps in all) had been in that vicinity earlier in the day."[38] The following day, Wright sent two companies of the 97th Pennsylvania to penetrate even further into enemy territory. Again, they failed to make contact with the enemy. By March 31, Wright had gathered sufficient information to convince him the Confederates had moved up to twenty-seven hundred men into defensive positions north and west of Jacksonville.[39]

Confederate sharpshooters were sniping at Union gunboats and supply ships at various points along the St. Johns, chiefly in the Yellow Bluff area, where some of the Broward family were allegedly involved. Lieutenant Ammen reported that during an upriver mission to Jacksonville a party of "between twenty and thirty small-arms men" fired on the *Seneca* from Yellow Bluff, at a distance of approximately one hundred yards, and "about fifty balls struck the ship," wounding three sailors. Gunners on the *Seneca* shelled the bluff with a howitzer and rifled guns before proceeding. During the return voyage to Mayport Mills, Ammen ordered his men to "fire one round of great guns into the ambuscade, and came to out of the range of small arms." The *Seneca* was then transporting twenty-two Union refugees (white) and eight contrabands (black) from the vicinity of Palatka. From Mayport the white and black refugees were transported safely to Hilton Head. As a result of Rebel sniper activity, sailing vessels traveling upriver were convoyed by navy gunboats and the pilothouses on Union vessels were protected with wood planking.[40]

The Federal military force at Jacksonville proved more than adequate for defense of the town. Stevens was buoyant in April: "we are perfectly secure here; but it would hardly do to leave the place without naval protection. . . . Everything about us looks promising and we all hope before long that Florida will once more be under the protection of the flag we all delight to honor."[41]

Planters in the vicinity were so encouraged they requested permission to bring agricultural products to the port for shipment to markets in the North. John S. Sammis brought in fifty-five bales of cotton. Wright recommended appointment of a federal district judge and marshal to reside at Jacksonville, and postmasters to serve the troops posted at camps from Fernandina to St. Augustine. Wright also authorized the citizens of Jacksonville to renew their practice of holding annual municipal elections, starting on April 7.[42]

One of the most enthusiastic supporters of the Jacksonville occupation was Admiral Du Pont. He had earlier criticized General Sherman for being "very lukewarm about holding the city. . . . The fact of the people having remained must override all military ideas; these must yield to the moral and political ones, and if you leave these people without protection you will never hear the end of it, and protect them I will, if you don't." Du Pont even wanted an army sent to the interior of the peninsula in an effort to bring Florida back into the Union; in the admiral's opinion, "the moral effect of holding a whole state was more important than taking Savannah."[43]

Du Pont's assessment of Jacksonville's importance for the overall Union war effort was not shared by Major General David Hunter, appointed March 15, 1862, to replace General Sherman as commander of the Department of the South. After reviewing troop dispositions in his command, Hunter decided that Union lines were overextended. With large numbers of troops needed for an upcoming campaign in South Carolina, he concluded that further occupation of Jacksonville would serve no useful military purpose, and on April 2 he ordered that the 1,470 men posted at Jacksonville and Mayport be evacuated within two or three days.[44]

Hunter sent assurances to the citizens of Jacksonville that Union gunboats would continue to patrol the St. Johns and protect them from Rebel harassment and that "order and quiet" would be preserved. Rebels were warned that "any outrages upon persons or property contrary to the laws and usages of war shall be visited fourfold upon the inhabitants of disloyal or doubtful character nearest the scene of any such wrongs when the actual and known perpetrators cannot be discovered."[45]

The residents of Jacksonville were informed of the impending evacuation on April 7, the very day they had scheduled the resumption of municipal elections and only three days before the second Union convention was to occur. For loyal Unionists who had lived through the "night of terror" when Confederate forces and violent regulators had rampaged through the streets of the town with torches, Hunter's promise of protection provided no comfort. Unionists in Jacksonville and at farms and plantations along the St. Johns feared they would be killed if they remained in their homes. Wright and Du Pont shared their fear and permitted them to evacuate along with Union forces.[46] "This intelligence fell on our ears like a death knell," Calvin Robinson remembered. "Suddenly like a thunder bolt from the clear sky, this order comes, crashing to earth the last hope, and banishing us from our homes . . . and sending us out, refugees and wanderers, to what we know not where."[47]

With only ten hours' notice to evacuate, the desperate families gathered their remaining possessions. Those wishing to go north to Fernandina were assigned space on the transport *Cosmopolitan*, while those heading to St. Augustine were sent aboard the *Belvedere*. Abbie and Otis Keene took a few pieces of silver, some bedding, carpeting, a piano, and various items of furniture aboard the *Cosmopolitan*, most of it property of the Judson House. Watching the departures, Robinson observed: "It was sad to see them hurrying down to the wharf, each carrying some article too precious to forsake."[48] The Robinson and Fraser families boarded the *Seneca* at the invitation of Lieutenant Ammen, and at 9 a.m. on April 8 the ship steamed for Hilton Head.

Troop embarkation began at noon on the ninth and was completed five hours later. Civilian passengers crowded the railings to look back at their abandoned homes after the gangplanks were raised and the ships pulled away from the wharves. Their attention was drawn to smoke rising from piles of burning military equipment that had been left behind to make room for the refugees and their belongings. A brisk wind whipped plumes of black smoke across the sky and created turbulent conditions on the river that prevented the transports from heading downriver until sunset—too late to safely maneuver the tricky channel of the lower St. Johns River. Stevens ordered the captains to anchor their vessels in the river until morning.

When the vessels got under way on the tenth, the *Ellen*, *Ottawa*, and *Pembina* convoyed the transports *Cosmopolitan* and *Belvidere*, the yachts *America* and *Son of Malta*, and five supply schooners. As the fleet departed, Union officers watched Confederates move into positions along Bay Street and at posts on the wharves. When the fleet reached Mayport Mills, the Federals burned the gun carriages and platforms and otherwise destroyed the abandoned Confederate batteries at Fort Steele. Union gunboats remained on station, however, blockading the entrance to the St. Johns and patrolling upriver well beyond Jacksonville.[49]

General Wright's report of the evacuation explained that it had been necessary for the security of the Unionists to transport them to Fernandina. He tried to arrange housing for them in Fernandina, and ordered emergency provisions to feed them, but it was clear that they still faced major problems. "The necessity for the withdrawal of the troops from Jacksonville is to be regretted," he wrote. "These persons could not remain with their families with any safety, the enemy having threatened the lives of all who should show us the least favor or even remain in town after our occupation. . . . Many of these people have abandoned all, and are without any means than the worthless paper currency in circulation before our arrival. Their condition not only appeals strongly to our sympathies, but they have a claim to present assistance from the Government."[50]

Most of the refugees who had traveled on the *Cosmopolitan* remained on board for the week they were in Fernandina awaiting transfer north. Housing was so scarce in the town that many of them slept in makeshift shelters on the shore of the St. Marys or crowded into whatever space could be found in the town, with as many as thirteen persons sleeping in one small room. Fifty Jacksonville refugees, including the Robinsons, Frasers, and Keenes, boarded the *Star of the South* on April 17, bound for New York City. They were accompanied by Colonel J. F. Hall, the provost marshal at Fernandina at the time. Hall, a native of New York City, arranged a rousing welcome for the Jacksonville refugees. In a special appearance before the New York City Council, Mayor George Opdyke described the Jacksonville Unionists as "destitute fugitives from a relentless despotism" and appealed for funds to help meet their needs. Newspapers published accounts of Jacksonville's occupation and evacuation, rallying the city in support of the refugees. Hotel keepers provided lodging, the city council allocated $1,000 for a special relief fund, and the New York Board of Trade made additional cash gifts to each family.[51]

The publicity generated by the plight of the refugees focused national attention on the terminated Federal expedition up the St. Johns. Influential Northerners demanded to know why a town occupied by so many loyal citizens had been evacuated voluntarily if the enemy was too weak to drive them out. Critics wanted to know what could justify the abandonment of a town after its residents had taken the first steps toward reorganizing a loyal state government.

On April 24 the House of Representatives passed a resolution directing Secretary of War Edwin M. Stanton to "communicate all the facts and circumstances . . . in regard to the late evacuation of Jacksonville." Stanton's April 28 reply was noncommittal. President Lincoln had instructed him to disclose only that "Jacksonville was evacuated by the orders of the commanding general for reasons which it is not deemed compatible with the public interest at this time to disclose."[52]

There the matter rested until several Florida men visiting in Washington managed to extract unofficial information from highly placed sources. Calvin Robinson wrote in his journal that even President Lincoln considered the evacuation of Jacksonville to have been "a great blunder . . . done without orders from the War Department, and that it was a great mistake and he was sorry it had occurred; that, in his opinion, the point should have been held and made a base of operations for the center of our State; that it should be retaken again as soon as troops could be spared from other operations for the duty."[53]

The *New York Times* judged the troop withdrawal "unfortunate" because it exposed Jacksonville's Unionists to "the vengeance of implacable enemies" and forced them to abandon their homes, but the evacuation had been "inevitable" because the Department of the South lacked sufficient troops to hold Jacksonville against a determined enemy attack. Wright and Stevens strongly disagreed. They knew that as long as the Union gunboats controlled the St. Johns—and they did so for the duration of the war—only a massive and costly assault could dislodge even a token Federal garrison in Jacksonville. Almost a month after the Federal withdrawal, the *St. Augustine Examiner* declared that within Confederate circles the reason for "the evacuation of the City of Jacksonville by the Yankees . . . still is a mystery."[54]

Late in May, Admiral Du Pont was still furious about the evacuation. While the troops were in the town he had urged Washington to expand operations in Florida, believing that five thousand infantry and a single cavalry regiment could carve the state away from the Confederacy in less than two months of campaigning. Along with Captain Percival Drayton, Du Pont believed that the eastern portion of Florida, with Jacksonville, St. Augustine, and Fernandina occupied by Federal troops, would have rejoined the Union whether or not the rest of the state joined them. He branded Hunter's decision to abandon the town as "silly beyond measure" and was outraged that "two weeks after the forces were withdrawn General Hunter let sixty officers go on leave."[55]

The evacuation of Jacksonville would remain one of the mysteries of the war in Florida. The war had been in progress for only one year, but most of the town's residents were refugees scattered to disparate locations. The town's Confederate supporters sought safety at vacant farms and plantations or in towns in the interior of Florida. The town's Union loyalists had traveled further; many returned to their childhood homes in the North or frantically sought employment in Washington and other northern cities. Most Confederate and Unionist refugees would suffer a three-year exile before they saw their homes again.

Freedom Was as Close
as the River

On April 10, the day after the Union evacuation of Jacksonville, gray-clad soldiers from the Duval Cowboys, the Jacksonville Light Infantry, and the 3rd Florida Infantry stood at sentry points on the wharves and along Bay Street. These were local men, returned to find their families gone, their homes locked and barred, and the town's shops boarded. Only a few dozen women and children remained, down from the twenty-one hundred who resided in the town when the war began twelve months before.

After the Federals withdrew from Jacksonville, Lieutenant Stevens posted gunboats at Mayport Mills. Union ships would continue on station at the entrance to the St. Johns River to stop blockade runners and to conduct patrols as far upriver as they could safely navigate. Jacksonville would remain an open city, its people free to come and go, but the Confederate military would not be permitted to fortify or garrison the town without facing retaliation from the gunboats.

Only hours after the Federal transports evacuated the city, Stevens ordered the commander of the *Ellen*, Master William Budd, to approach Jacksonville under flag of truce to communicate these plans to the Confederates. Stevens wanted it understood that the Union navy intended to protect Unionists even if it meant inflicting four-fold retaliation on anyone who harmed citizens for cooperating with Union forces. The visit was marked by courtesy on both sides. Lieutenant Colonel John Maxwell of the 3rd Florida, C.S.A., informed Budd that his troops would occupy the town to prevent further violence and preserve property. Budd left the town confident the truce would be honored. Stevens wrote later that he had not "discover[ed] any intention on the part of the enemy to interfere with our occupation of the waters of the St. Johns."[1]

Stevens's successor, Lieutenant Ammen, was less confident the Confederates would observe the truce. He was alarmed by the large numbers of soldiers he saw in Jacksonville, a "company of sixty or a hundred" one day and "groups of men, evidently soldiers or officers" on another. Only the presence of women on the shore prevented him from opening fire.[2]

Confederate deserters, Union refugees, and escaped slaves all told Ammen that three infantry companies had moved into Jacksonville and that violent regulator bands were again at work along the river. A leader of the regulators was captured and placed in double irons on April 25, an event that led to another series of conferences. Ammen and Colonel Edward Hopkins eventually came to an understanding that mitigated tensions on both sides, at least temporarily. Hopkins explained that he had been sick and unable to act decisively when parties of armed men appeared on the banks of the river, and he emphatically "disavowed the acts . . . of regulators." He further agreed to Ammen's demand that "no batteries would be erected within the distance of a mile above or below the town."[3] Confederate soldiers would occupy the town only to protect the residents and their property.

When the two officers met again on April 28, Ammen advised Hopkins that "the removal of women and children from the immediate presence of hostile forces is always desirable," but conceded: "If it is not your object to erect batteries within 1 statute mile of the city, or to throw large masses of men into it, or if we are not fired upon in the vicinity, no danger need be apprehended by the peaceable inhabitants, and a removal will not be necessary."[4] If violations of the truce occurred, however, he advised "the earliest removal of all who do not expect to share the fate of those who are in arms."[5]

Confederate companies remained in Jacksonville throughout April and May. Washington M. Ives was one of the soldiers. Ives, an eighteen-year-old from Lake City who had attended school in Jacksonville, joined Company C of the 4th Florida in April and was surprised to discover that three of every four men in his company were his age or younger. For the next four weeks Ives was assigned picket duty at what remained of Mooney's foundry and other waterfront locations. He counted five gunboats on patrol during this time, often with guns targeted on the town as they passed by or anchored in the river. Ives recognized one of the vessels as the former Confederate blockade runner *Darlington*, which had been captured by the Federals and given a new mission. Ives could hear the bells on the gunboats and the voices of sailors as they called watch. On occasion he even "conversed with several Yankee sailors," but the tenor was generally hostile as armed adversaries eyed each other suspiciously. Ives continued to serve on picket duty until late in May, when he received orders to travel to Corinth, Mississippi, a railroad terminus crucial to the Confederacy's chances of holding the Mississippi Valley.[6]

Officers aboard the *Seneca* and the *Pembina* noticed in May and June that their river patrols were being interrupted with increased frequency by refugees seeking protection from harassment by regulators. Ammen investigated conditions in the vicinity of Black Creek after three escaped slaves reported that their owner, a man they called "Capt. Huston," was in command of a body of men who had stretched a "boom" across Black Creek four miles from the mouth. At a nearby hiding place, they installed coverts to snipe at Union gunboats. When Ammen's ship returned downriver it carried away the three contrabands who had provided the intelligence, along with five more black escapees.[7]

Correspondents for three New York newspapers reported that regulator bands were "murdering and destroying property" and orchestrating "a reign of terror" along the St. Johns. Unionists in St. Augustine were reportedly afraid to wander outside the town "because bands of guerrillas are everywhere organizing . . . and do not hesitate to kill those who differ with them." The partisans, known as "guerrillas" and "regulators," were a combination of civilians, state militia members, and Confederate soldiers, men like Captain J. W. Pearson of the Ocklawaha Rangers. In April 1862, Pearson described his activities: "I am now a Guerrilla in every sense of the word. We neither tell where we stay or where are going or when we shall return. We assemble the company at the sound of a cow's horn. We have made some arrests, both black and white, and hung one negro belonging to Mr. Mays last week. . . . We have three men spotted that ought to be hung. Three-fourths of the people on the St. Johns are aiding and abetting the enemy."[8]

To escape the guerrillas, some Unionist refugees fled overland to Fernandina and St. Augustine, while others quietly flagged down the gunboats on the St. Johns. Mrs. Vandegrift of Jacksonville told a gunboat captain that "she had been abused and that her life had been in danger" because of her husband's Union sentiments. Confederate cavalry officer Davis Bryant wrote that "Old man Tomb [a resident of Dames Point] has been driven to the Gunboat by the Browards. He has *no doubt* acted badly. I am very sorry for the family."[9]

A very different sort of refugee arrived at the Union gunboat base at Mayport in early May. James W. Bryant, a businessman and planter with property in Duval County and upriver at Welaka, had launched a new career as a newspaper publisher in Cuba from 1860 to 1862. When he returned to Jacksonville to join his wife and children, he found the town occupied by Confederate soldiers. Bryant's attempts to reunite his family were complicated by the fact that his two oldest sons were in Confederate regiments outside Florida, and his wife and two youngest sons were in Welaka at the plantation home of his only daughter, Octavia, the wife of Confederate cavalry officer Winston Stephens.

Bryant persuaded a sympathetic gunboat captain to carry him along on an upriver patrol on the chance they could make it as far as Welaka, where he expected to arrange a meeting with some of his family. The boat ran aground at Buffalo Bluff, just south of Palatka, and the captain refused to travel further. Bryant's wife, Rebecca, learned later that the St. Johns Rangers had laid a trap to shell the vessel Bryant was aboard. Bryant's son-in-law, Captain Stephens, was then in command of the company hidden upriver and around the bend from the point where the gunboat foundered. Stephens was unaware that his father-in-law would have been one of his targets.[10]

Bryant was able to send a letter through the lines to his daughter, informing her that it was too risky to try again to reach Welaka. From Jacksonville he traveled north to engage in efforts to restore the Union in East Florida and to reopen the ports of St. Augustine, Fernandina, and Jacksonville to commerce. "The blockade will be withdrawn so soon as a civil government is established," he predicted, with more hope than assurance.[11]

Winston Stephens and members of his Confederate cavalry company continued to monitor gunboat activities along the St. Johns River, setting traps and sniping when possible. At one point he joined seventeen armed men at battle stations along a wharf, hoping to intimidate two approaching gunboats. For weeks, Stephens had eagerly stalked the Yankee vessels, stating repeatedly in his letters his desire "to shoot a Yankee."[12]

It may have been Stephens and his cavalry company that fired on the *Isaac Smith* during an upriver patrol on May 18. Lieutenant J. W. A. Nicholson commanded a ship that had traveled to "within 5 or 6 miles of Lake George" before being "fired upon by a party of concealed riflemen."[13] Nicholson returned to the gunboat base, stopping in passage at Orange Mills, where he learned that twenty-five Confederates were stationed in the vicinity and that one hundred more were camped near the juncture of the St. Johns and Ocklawaha rivers. Five miles above Jacksonville, Nicholson observed a flag of truce and stopped to pick up three white refugees seeking passage to the

North. He also took aboard a contraband who had escaped from Dr. Mays, a zealous Rebel partisan. Nicholson wanted "the whole establishment about Orange Mills destroyed, as it is a hotbed of traitors, who are now all in arms against their country. As there is considerable valuable property (now abandoned), it might be seized for the benefit of the Government and the houses burned."[14]

With regulators, vigilantes, and Confederate troops moving freely throughout northeast Florida, conditions deteriorated to the point that Union supporters were in constant danger. Conditions were not much better for Confederate partisans still living in Jacksonville. From intelligence gathered during river patrols, Ammen learned of a serious shortage of food in Jacksonville, noting on May 21 that the city appeared to be "almost entirely deserted." Ten days later he reported: "the poor people, of whom I see a number, are very much troubled . . . and do not know which way to turn."[15] In June, the last units of the 4th Florida left the city and civilians were without any protection for a ten-day period.

By June 8, Ammen had become convinced that most people living along the river "would gladly acknowledge the authority of the Government of the United States were they not in fear of violence" from bands of Confederate regulators. He decided to send a message to the regulators by assigning Lieutenant John G. Sproston and seventy armed sailors the task of capturing George Huston, leader of one of the most notorious regulator bands in northeast Florida. Huston had earlier led an ambush of two gunboats at Mosquito Inlet that claimed the lives of two Federal officers and five seamen. He later boasted of having hung a black river pilot who had joined the Federals as a guide.[16]

The arrest ended with tragic results: "Lieutenant Sproston landed at early daylight and proceeded rapidly with his party to the house of Huston. The latter, it appears, was apprised of his coming and met him at the door armed with a double-barreled gun, two pistols, and a bowie knife."[17] When Sproston demanded Huston's surrender, the Rebel leader instead discharged his weapons, killing Sproston instantly. Huston was wounded during the ensuing gunfire and was captured by the Union sailors. He died on June 19, 1862.[18]

Black refugees, both free persons and escaped slaves, were also harassed by the regulators. Nicholson reported that in the early evening of June 12 he was aboard the *Isaac Smith* about fifteen miles above Jacksonville when suddenly "the contrabands commenced coming in, and when I started on my return . . . I had 43 on board."[19] Twelve children were among the forty-three escaped slaves. Nicholson also took aboard four free blacks, designating them refugees rather than contrabands.

As the vessel continued downriver, Nicholson observed a flag of truce being waved at Jacksonville. He "sent a boat for two ladies, both widows, one of whom had four children. They had been nearly two months trying to get away, but as they were from the North [they] could not get a pass. Fortunately all troops left town on Saturday eve for Tennessee, and the town is, therefore, unoccupied by the rebels." Nicholson described the two widows, "Mrs. Pickering and Ms. Fleming," as "ladies" who he hoped would "meet with courtesy the whole way North, for they have endured enough of suffering from the rebels to last them."[20]

On June 17 Nicholson commented on the vital importance of slavery to the economy of the region and suggested a means to weaken the resolve of the enemy. "The whole of the banks of the river as far as one can see is planted with corn," he informed Admiral Du Pont. "They say corn enough is in Florida for all of the Southern rebel States. If we carry their darkies off they can not gather it."[21] On a subsequent patrol, Nicholson reported, "numbers of contrabands continue to come in. I house and feed them on shore, allowing their owners, on application, if they satisfy me that they are not disloyal, to go on shore and get them if they can, as no assistance is given them. Thus far but two persons have been allowed this privilege." Nicholson also provided lodging and provisions for free black refugees. On June 27 he wrote: "Attempts having been made to run the free blacks into the interior, several have come to me for protection. I have sent to Fernandina this day four white and eleven black refugees, also fifteen contrabands. I should like to have some instructions on the contraband question."[22]

Only six days later, Du Pont responded to Nicholson's request: "In reference to the contraband question, my instructions are to surrender none, no matter whether the parties asking for them profess to be loyal or not. There has been so much abuse of this privilege that it can no longer be granted. A glaring instance of it occurred in the case of the murderer Huston, whose slaves were returned to him on the false pretense of a neighbor that they belonged to a Union man. Even supposing the claimant may be loyal, yet if he takes his slaves among the rebels he is liable to be seized at any moment and put to work in erecting fortifications against our forces." Du Pont instructed Nicholson to record the names of claimants in the ship's logbook and to inform them that "the Government will determine the case after the war is over."[23]

Finally, Du Pont's order clarified what had been a confusing and inconsistent Federal policy concerning escaped slaves seeking Union protection on the St. Johns River. Until the summer of 1862, naval officers had generally followed the Lincoln administration's policy of conciliation toward slaveholders. Lincoln's policy was motivated by his efforts to retain support for Union in the border states and to regain the allegiance of locals in the zones of occupation in the Confederate states. Citizens were to be treated justly, with compensation provided when confiscation of foodstuffs or other materials became a military necessity. A citizen's right to own private property, including human property, was to be protected.[24]

The First Confiscation Act, passed by Congress on August 6, 1861, had authorized commanders to refuse requests for the return of slaves only if they had been employed in some way by the Confederate military. As applied in the field, the act provided wide latitude for officers to make individual decisions: pro-abolition officers could refuse to return slaves to owners regardless of their loyalties, while more conservative colleagues could go so far as to exclude all black refugees from Union lines. This act, while important, had little direct relevance for slaves who escaped from plantations in northeast Florida.

The policy in practice on the St. Johns during the first half of 1862 had evolved in response to local conditions and to enslaved blacks' initiative to change their circumstances. As Union forces moved south in January and February 1862, it became apparent that relations between masters and their enslaved men and women were undergoing profound changes. The naval blockade of the Atlantic and Gulf coasts, coupled with Union occupation of portions of Southern states, created opportunities. Slaves seized the initiative; they gathered as refugees wherever a Union military presence could be found, then performed invaluable labor services and provided information to Union troops. As Union vessels proceeded toward Fernandina in February 1862, for example, Du Pont learned from an escaped slave that the enemy was abandoning the defensive works at the south of Cumberland Island and the entry to the St. Marys River. With this intelligence, the ships moved immediately upriver to Fernandina.[25]

On March 4, Du Pont had sent Lieutenant Stevens on a reconnaissance mission up the St. Marys aboard the *Ottawa*. Stevens traveled all the way to the Alberti plantation and sawmill at Woodstock Mills, a distance of fifty miles by water, stopping at plantations along the way to convey Du Pont's message "to protect all peaceable citizens in their persons and property, and inviting those who had fled to return to their homes."[26] Before Stevens commenced his return to Fernandina, an escaped slave informed him that the

Rebels intended "to cut us off with their light batteries and infantry." Stevens consequently took precautionary measures that saved the ship and crew from an ambush at a place known locally as the Brick Yard. Stevens reported: "the reign of terror rules everywhere."[27]

Naval officers had reported that contrabands boarded their vessels as soon as they arrived in area waters. S. W. Godon, in command of the *Mohican*, reported to Du Pont on March 30 that he had "sent a number by the *Potomska* to Fernandina, and also several by the *Connecticut*. On the 26th I started for Brunswick . . . and on my way up the river twenty-seven more contrabands came to me." Godon had accumulated forty black refugees by then, and it had become his responsibility to find provision for them. He proceeded to St. Simons Island and landed all the contrabands and supplies, provided them with tools and housing, and "set them to work. Already they have planted potatoes. Tomorrow they begin to prepare the land for corn. They have set up their mill, and I have told them they are to plant cotton and thus to become of use to themselves. . . . A thousand blacks could be usefully employed here and made self-supporting. Such a colony, properly managed, would do much good."[28]

On March 10, General Wright had reported similar occurrences at Fernandina: "The contraband question also presents itself and will soon require to be decided by the military authority, as regards their support. Some of these people were left behind, and others are presenting themselves daily, coming in from different directions."[29]

The Union navy's presence on the St. Johns further challenged the ability of northeast Florida slaveholders to control their human property. During the Federal occupation of Jacksonville in March 1862, owners repeatedly complained of slaves absconding to Union gunboats. Waving white flags from shore, paddling canoes and poling rafts, slaves and free blacks hailed Union vessels. For the enslaved men and women of northeast Florida who could escape to the Union gunboats, the possibility of freedom was suddenly as close as the St. Johns River.[30]

Jacksonville slaveholders had been given advance warning early in March that Federal forces were coming their way when the Union gunboats were delayed for two days at the entrance to the St. Johns River. Many were consequently able to move their slaves to more secure locations in the interior of the state. Samuel Fairbanks took his slaves upriver to a Clay County plantation, but two of the men—John and Frank, a sawmill engineer and a laborer—stole a boat and rowed back to Jacksonville after the Union occupied the town. Fairbanks found them, but they refused to return to Clay County.

With the cooperation of the military, the town's civilian authorities, many of whom were both slaveholders and Unionists, had the men jailed for their "saucy" behavior.

Subsequently, the jail was broken open and, assisted by sympathetic sailors, John and Frank boarded a Union gunboat traveling to Fernandina. In this second escape they managed to bring John's wife, Charlotte. Frank made it to Fernandina, but Fairbanks caught up with John and Charlotte at Mayport, where he persuaded a Union officer to return them to his custody. While Fairbanks looked for a boat to carry them back to Clay County, gunboats departed for Fernandina carrying white Unionist refugees and slave escapees. John and Charlotte, along with seven other contrabands formerly owned by Fairbanks, had been secreted aboard one of the gunboats.[31]

John and Frank later joined Company A of the 1st South Carolina Loyal Volunteers, the first unit of black men organized by the Union army. The unit later became Company A, 33rd Regiment of United States Colored Troops, and participated in several campaigns in northeast Florida. When Fairbanks heard in July 1863 that John, "our engineer," had been wounded in action, he wished the same fate for Frank. By the end of the war both Frank and John were dead.[32]

Friends of Fairbanks suffered even heavier losses in March 1862. In one escape, twenty-three men and women from three neighboring plantations fled together, pursued by an armed posse that shot and killed one of the men during the chase. The man killed was known to the whites on the posse as "Old Banjo," an elderly and previously loyal servant and the father of Burrell, also a slave and the manager of Winston Stephens's Welaka plantation. With his wife, mother-in-law, and three young children the only white persons at his rural plantation, living with nine slaves, Stephens was worried about the safety of his family. He instructed his wife to inform Burrell and the other slaves of the draconian measures being employed to discourage runaway attempts. He also warned her to watch carefully for three fugitives thought to be lurking in the Welaka area searching for the slave wife of one of the escapees. Stephens warned his wife to secure all weapons at the estate and to send a message to his brother, Clark, whose rural estate was a few miles distant, to shoot the runaways if they appeared in the vicinity of Welaka.[33]

Union military records provide the names of some of the enslaved men and women who escaped to the Federals during the first occupation of Jacksonville. Joseph Cryer and his son Andrew escaped to Union lines from the Palm Valley plantation of Jacob Mickler. Andrew Murray, a native of St. Augustine, was the property of Joseph Finegan when he fled to freedom in Fernandina after hearing rumors of Federal forces there. For James and Henry Adams, property of Francis Richard and living at Little Pottsburg Creek and the St. Johns, the route to freedom was a three-mile boat ride to the Union-occupied town. Thomas Long and Charles McQueen also made their way to Jacksonville and were aboard the Union transports when the city was evacuated on April 9, 1862. All of these men later volunteered for service in the Union army.[34]

The free blacks of northeast Florida also sought protection behind Union lines, with several later volunteering for Union military service. Benjamin Williams was living in Jacksonville in 1860, listed in the census of that year as having been born in the free state of Maine. Alonzo H. Phillips, born in Jacksonville, became a commissary sergeant in Company A, 3rd South Carolina. Henry Hanahan, born free in 1833 at Pablo Beach, became a sergeant major in the same company. The eighty-four-year-old Cyrus Forrester, head of the only free black family in Clay County, was a small farmer and herder who established a homestead in the vicinity of Magnolia. His eldest son, Lewis, married a free black woman named Affa in 1854 and settled at a homestead near his father. Lewis told investigators that early in the war his daughter and his sister-in-law and her three children were seized by "rebel ruffians" and sold into slavery in Georgia. They were eventually returned to Clay County, but the Forrester family felt so endangered in 1862 that they boarded a Union gunboat bound for Fernandina. Lewis volunteered for service in Company A of the 3rd South Carolina on June 3, 1863. George Forrester joined the Union navy in 1862, as did the freedmen Henry Johnson and James P. Lang. Other Duval County free blacks who joined Union regiments include Albert Sammis, George Floyd, Frank and Alexander Hagen, John Lacurgas, Charles Lang, Levi and William H. McQueen, Samuel Petty, John B. Richard, Walter Taylor, James Simmons, and Henry and James Williams.[35]

Abraham Lancaster was a free black from St. Augustine who enlisted in Company F, 1st South Carolina, in 1863. Other free blacks from St. Augustine who volunteered to serve in black Union regiments included Pablo Rogers, James Lang, James Hills, James Ash, George Garvin, William Morris, Alexander Clark, and the Pappy brothers: Antony, Frank, and William. Samuel Osborn and his son Samuel Jr., free black residents of St. Johns County since at least 1850, volunteered for service in Company D, 1st South Carolina. In an unusual occurrence, another Osborn son, Emmanuel, volunteered for the St. Johns Grays, a Confederate militia company formed in St. Augustine. It appears that free black families, like white families, could be divided by Civil War loyalties.[36]

The deck logs of Union gunboats and the letter books of their commanders document the inconsistent nature of contraband policy on the St. Johns. On April 2, 1862, while Jacksonville was still occupied, Lieutenant Ammen permitted to board the *Seneca* three escaped slaves who were property of the father of a Confederate army officer. The three escapees were returned to their owner after it was determined that he was too elderly to fight against Union forces. Later that same day, Ammen refused entreaties for eight more contrabands whose owners were identified as "rebels in arms." They were later carried to freedom at Hilton Head.[37]

Ammen's immediate superior officer, Lieutenant Stevens, told a Confederate officer that "no encouragement or inducement has been offered on my part, or on the part of any officer or man under my command, to entice slaves away. My orders are stringent upon this subject and I know of no violation of them."[38] Stevens tended to be cooperative with loyal slaveholders seeking return of their human property, while sternly forbidding the return of slaves to Confederates.

During the evacuation of Jacksonville, General Wright had ordered the removal of all escaped slaves from Union vessels; they were to be left at the town wharf for owners to reclaim. No regard was given to whether their owners were loyal Unionists or Confederates. Wright's men objected, however, and smuggled the escapees back aboard the ships and hid them during the journey to Fernandina. When Wright discovered the stowaways, he ordered them returned to Jacksonville under flag of truce. Fifty-two black men and women were unloaded at the Jacksonville wharf and placed under supervision of Confederate soldiers while they waited for their owners to appear. Two in the group, Jim and Sally, belonged to Samuel Fairbanks.[39]

By the time the Jacksonville evacuation fleet reached Fernandina in April 1862, the exodus of black laborers had reached alarming proportions. Two Duval County men—Fairbanks, the sawmill owner, and Stephen Bryan, a wealthy Clay County planter—traveled to Fernandina to test Union policy concerning confiscation of slave property. They carried a letter from Lieutenant Stevens describing them as "gentlemen of character and influence" and requesting Union officers in Fernandina to "give them whatever facilities your official position may afford toward securing the object of their mission."[40] Disdaining the letter and the men, an "abolitionist Lt. Colonel" refused to even grant an interview. Fairbanks and Bryan remonstrated that

General Wright on a daily basis "afforded every facility for masters to claim and take away their negroes," even "towing boats up the river with them."[41] Their protests were to no avail: the Union officer curtly sent Fairbanks and Bryan back to Jacksonville, alone.

This late in the war, contraband policy should have been consistent. By March 13, 1862, the growing power of radicals in Congress had resulted in a tougher and unambiguous Second Confiscation Act, which forbade the return of any slaves, no matter whether the owners were loyal to the Union or the Confederacy. If the guidelines were ambiguous and subject to individual interpretation before March 13, they were as clear as a possible court-martial after that date. And this resolve deepened in the months ahead. What is perplexing about events in Florida in April 1862 is the failure of an officer like General Wright to follow the recently established rules. If the orders had not been disseminated into the field as far as Jacksonville by April 10, they had certainly reached Admiral Du Pont by July 3, and henceforth no escaped slaves who reached Union gunboats would be returned to their owners.[42]

Jacksonville slaveholders nevertheless persisted in efforts to reclaim their human property. In late April, Judge Burritt traveled to Hilton Head to confer with General Hunter, hoping to obtain an order for the return of all slaves who had escaped from their Jacksonville owners. Hunter refused to cooperate. The audacious Burritt continued on to Washington, where he arranged to meet with President Lincoln. According to Samuel Fairbanks, Burritt found the president still a reluctant emancipator who would "not commit himself. But Burritt says that he thinks Lincoln is not an abolitionist and that the negroes will be returned at the end of the war."[43]

Burritt must have been surprised to discover later that year that he had misjudged the president. At the time of his appointment, Lincoln was still worried that border states might secede and join the Confederacy. In August 1861 he had rescinded John C. Frémont's declaration of martial law in Missouri, which would have emancipated the slaves of Confederate owners in that state. Lincoln's action was accompanied by commentary about the importance of retaining Kentucky as a Union state. In October 1861 he had forced Secretary of War Simon Cameron to retract a statement advocating the emancipation of Rebel-owned slaves and arming them to fight for the Union. As late as May 1862, Lincoln rebuked General Hunter and revoked his order abolishing slavery in Florida, South Carolina, and Georgia. Publicly, Lincoln was playing a cautious hand to avoid alienating residents of the border states.

The president was also being pressured by radicals in Congress, who wanted him to free the slaves as a military necessity. For months Lincoln had privately contemplated an emancipation proclamation, but in public he attempted to persuade congressmen from the border states to accept gradual and compensated emancipation. On March 13, 1862, when his moderate policy was rejected, Lincoln privately embraced the more radical position and waited for a dramatic Union victory before announcing the Preliminary Emancipation. In September 1862, following the Federal victory at Antietam, Lincoln proclaimed that all slaves in regions still in rebellion on January 1, 1863, would be forever free. On New Year's Day he made the Emancipation Proclamation official. The president also announced that day that the United States would begin enlisting black men in its armed forces.

The vagaries of Union contraband policy were thereby clarified for Burritt: in the months ahead, Federal armies would free his slaves. Like many abolitionists in the North, Burritt had misinterpreted the political intentions of the reluctant emancipator. The president embraced the more revolutionary position, and henceforth would be an enthusiastic abolitionist.

Slaves in northeast Florida had not waited for Lincoln to announce his position on emancipation. Despite inconsistencies in Union policy, slaves had continued to run away from their owners. As Union vessels pulled away from the wharves at Jacksonville, thirty contrabands were standing on the decks of the yacht *America* when it was towed downriver. All thirty were carried to freedom at Hilton Head.[44] Union gunboats continued to take aboard both black and white refugees following the evacuation of Jacksonville. Acting Master Robert Lelar of the *Patroon* permitted twenty contrabands to board his vessel in late May.[45] Late in May, a gunboat anchored off Stephen Bryan's Laurel Grove plantation at St. Johns River and Doctors Lake, galvanizing "twenty-four of his negroes to escape and take refuge." Bryan drove the remainder of his chattels, along with sixty-two black men and women from neighboring estates, to unoccupied land in the interior. Although Winston Stephens was able to capture two runaways from Ocala who were trying to get to the gunboats near Jacksonville, he estimated that fifteen hundred black refugees had gathered in Fernandina by late July 1862.[46]

So many contrabands, free black refugees, and white refugees were being picked up by the gunboats that Lieutenant Ammen had to establish residential quarters at the mouth of the St. Johns until the refugees could be moved to Fernandina or Hilton Head. On May 3, Ammen reported that twenty people were at Mayport Mills, "families of refugees and of the soldiers who deserted. They are wholly destitute and I am obliged to feed them or see them starve." He complained that his resources were inadequate to protect them, since he was in charge of "a large extent of river and the force is of two gun boats."[47]

Captains of the Union gunboats established a colony for contrabands at Batten Island on the north side of the St. Johns River, across from the naval station at Mayport. Before the war a half-dozen families had lived at a settlement on the island known as Pilot Town, in recognition of the river pilots who resided there. The pilots earned their living guiding oceangoing vessels across the shallow sandbars that endangered traffic at the entrance to the river. In June the *Patroon* delivered fifteen refugees and contrabands and provided them with food. Between May and November 1862 the *Uncas, Paul Jones, Patroon, Water Witch,* and other gunboats brought contrabands and refugees to Pilot Town, which was guarded by military pickets and provided with food rations. The incomplete records found in the gunboat logbooks and the registers of their commanders document that more than 220 former slaves were accommodated at Pilot Town between May and November. Free black and white refugee families were lodged there as well. Maxwell Woodhull, in command of the Union naval forces on the St. Johns, reported that feeding the residents of the growing colony presented a serious challenge. It is clear from his letters that he was a fervent supporter of the current union policy regarding contrabands, and pleased that the still enslaved men and women of the area were discovering that freedom had become as close as the Union vessels that patrolled the St. Johns River.[48]

Samuel Fairbanks had viewed the growing colony at Pilot Town and considered it a major threat to the continuation of slavery along the river. He predicted that between fifteen and twenty thousand bushels of corn in the coastal area would not be harvested in the current season for lack of laborers. Winston Stephens agreed, saying planters would "not be able to save their crops." Late in August, Fairbanks complained that "Negroes are gradually getting away—singley and by two's and three's—the coast is pretty near drained."[49]

In Tallahassee, Ellen Call Long received a letter from a friend in Jacksonville who wrote that it was "impossible to keep negroes on the river now." Soon after the Yankees arrived, "Father discovered our servants about to bid farewell to the place; so next morning he packed them all off to the interior. Can you imagine how we get along without a single servant? Father determined it was better to have a home without servants than servants without a home. So we stay here living on cornbread and hope, our only consolation that we are no worse off than our neighbors."[50]

The Jacksonville-area slaveholders would have empathized with the anguish of a former St. Augustine merchant who lost fifteen slaves to Union contraband policy. Writing to his son, Christian Boye explained: "Those slaves of mine were worth to me a year ago, seventeen thousand dollars and there was some 10 young ones among them who increased in value every day. My yearly income from them was not less than $2000.00 to $2500.00. I could afford to send you and your sister to expensive schools." Without the income he earned from the labor of his slaves, Boye lamented: "This income is stopped, and God knows when it will begin again. I am obliged to use strictest economy, turn a penny a dozen times before I spend it. The loss of our slaves forces me to take Mary from school . . . as I cannot make enough to pay her school bills."[51]

Another man who could sympathize with Boye was Brigadier General Joseph Finegan, a longtime slaveholder in northeast Florida who lost bondsmen to Union gunboats. Finegan understood the importance of slavery to Florida's economy and was willing to tailor Confederate strategy to protect that vital connection. In May 1862 he began moving men and artillery to the lower St. Johns in an effort to stop the Union gunboat incursions. If he succeeded, future escapees would be forced inland through military security and vigilante patrols, and the numbers lost would be dramatically decreased.

Federal commanders may have had suspicions of Finegan's plans, but they were not fully aware during the summer of 1862 that the increase in guerrilla activity along the river, the sniping attacks on their gunboats, and the upsurge in numbers of white and black refugees were the direct result of a major change in Confederate policy. Finegan had been appointed to command of Confederate troops in East Florida on April 8, with orders from General Lee to give "primary importance" to protection of the state's interior, especially the Apalachicola and St. Johns rivers. By the time Finegan settled into his new headquarters at Lake City, he realized the drastic shortage of men and material under his command made it nearly impossible to defend the interior of Florida without a means to stop the gunboats from running at will on the St. Johns.[52]

Finegan sent Colonel John C. Hately to Jacksonville on June 25 in command of two hundred men of the 5th Florida Infantry. On his first day in Jacksonville, Hately met under a flag of truce with Lieutenant Nicholson to renew the agreement reached earlier in the year that barred fortifications within one mile in all directions from the town market. After conferring with Finegan, Hately raised another white flag two days later. He informed Nicholson that Finegan "disapproves of the arrangement, and it therefore becomes my duty to notify you that the agreement must henceforth be considered as of no effect. The general instructs me to inform you that the threat of shelling our undefended town, containing only women and children, is not consistent with the usages of war between civilized nations."[53]

Nicholson asked Hately to "inform the general that no threat has been made of shelling the town containing women and children. On the contrary, my request was made that no batteries should be erected there for the express purpose of saving them from the horrors of war.... So long as the gunboats are not fired upon from that vicinity the town is safe from the shells of the gunboats."[54] After this second meeting, Nicholson increased the number of patrols on the river.

Finegan had already decided to install artillery on St. Johns Bluff and Yellow Bluff in order to close the river to the gunboats, knowing the plan could succeed only if he was able to "evade the vigilance of the enemy." Convinced that Union sympathizers were the enemy's main source of intelligence, he ordered all small boats belonging to Unionists confiscated or destroyed and decreed that anyone even suspected of harboring a Union sympathizer was to be moved at least ten miles inland, away from the river and the Federal gunboats.[55]

On July 1 Nicholson learned of Finegan's order from an informant. As a consequence, he sent the *Isaac Smith* to pick up "the family of Mr. Myers (who is in Fernandina), consisting of his wife and nine children; also Mr. Tombs and family, of eight persons, they having been ordered off or to the interior."[56] One week later Nicholson ordered the *Uncas* to carry eighteen white refugees and eleven contrabands to Union-occupied Fernandina.

Before the month was out, regulator hostilities had become so troublesome that Nicholson decided to retaliate. After Dr. Balsam, a Union loyalist residing at Dames Point, was ordered off his property by a guerrilla band headed by members of the Broward family, Nicholson told Balsam to remain at his house and shoot anyone who "approached his dwelling at night." In the meantime he ordered the gunboat *Uncas* to proceed "noiselessly" to the Broward plantation at Cedar Point and shell the surrounding woods. Captain Lemuel G. Crane "performed the duty handsomely," Nicholson reported, "and the next day threw a shell at the Breward [Broward] house, upon which a party of eight mounted men fled to the woods." Nicholson then took control himself. He left an anchorage at Jacksonville on July 31 aboard the *Isaac Smith* and steamed directly to the Broward home to "fire thirty shells, completely tearing it to pieces; then sent an armed party on shore . . . to destroy the buildings, stable, etc., by fire." He later reported with satisfaction: "Thus has been destroyed the residence of one who has both before and since the rebellion, been a leader in every unlawful act, and a source of annoyance to every respectable inhabitant."[57]

Within a week of the destruction of the Broward property, another gunboat commander felt compelled to take defensive action to protect "five or six Union families" at Batten Island, also known as Pilot Town, where the St. Johns River pilots and their families had resided before the war. The inhabitants had fled Batten Island earlier in the war, but they returned when Edward McKeige, commander of the *Patroon*, encouraged them to resume their old vocations. McKeige also pledged to provide protection for the "former bar pilots [who] are willing to return with their families. . . . They were driven away from here by threats, and are now living in great distress in temporary shanties in the woods." But McKeige said it would first be necessary to destroy a sixty-foot-long, "strong and substantial bridge . . . to cut off all communication with the mainland, keep the guerrillas away—whom these people so much dread—and prevent them from disturbing the Union citizens who wish to remove here for protection."[58] On August 9, McKeige sent thirty men to destroy the bridge. Three hours later it no longer existed. McKeige judged the island safe for families of refugees and bar pilots alike. "The inhabitants are now safe and feel more easy and comfortable."[59]

With great ingenuity General Finegan began pulling together a military force from around the state. It would include ten pieces of artillery that he had found scattered from Volusia on the upper St. Johns to Tallahassee and St. Marks. Finegan intended to "relieve the valley of the St. Johns from the marauding incursions of the enemy and . . . establish a base for operations against St. Augustine," but he was plagued from the start by a shortage of men and arms. On May 7, 1862, he complained to General Pierre G. T. Beauregard's headquarters at Charleston that one of his regiments was entirely without arms and that no weapons were on hand for several companies of conscripts being mustered into service. In the next two months demands on other war fronts required him to send so many men out of the state that his command was reduced to only 1,374 men, and these were scattered over too large an area. Finegan issued a proclamation to "the People of Florida" asking them to surrender any shotguns, muskets, or rifles in their possession: "The battles on which your rights and liberties depend are to be fought by armed men, and your Government now earnestly exhorts you to place the arms which you have hitherto kept for your own convenience in the hands of our brave soldiers who are destined to meet your enemies on the field of battle."[60]

By September, Finegan was ready to act, even though his troops were relatively few in number and insufficiently supplied. He understood that control of the St. Johns River was essential if the interior of Florida was to remain safe. In September 1862, a campaign to close the river to Union forces was initiated.

No. 671.—REBEL STEAMER DARLINGTON, CAPTURED IN FERNANDINA HARBOR.

FIGURE I. Side-wheel steamship *Darlington*, built at Charleston, South Carolina, in 1849. Owner Jacob Brock used the ship for civilian transport until the Confederates acquired it in 1861–62. The *Darlington* was captured on March 3, 1862, in Fernandina Harbor by the Union navy and was employed as a Federal transport for the remainder of the war. (Courtesy of Florida State Archives.)

FIGURE 2. William H. Haddock joined two Jacksonville militia companies in 1859 and 1860, the Jacksonville Light Infantry and the Duval Cowboys. He saw garrison duty at Fort Steele and St. Johns Bluff on the St. Johns River, and was mustered into the 3rd Florida Infantry in August 1861. Haddock attained the rank of second lieutenant and was mustered out of Confederate service on April 26, 1865. (Courtesy of Dr. Wayne W. Wood, from the Jacksonville Historical Society.)

FIGURE 3. Mayport Mills, Florida. The tiny sawmill town at the south shore of the entrance to the St. Johns River became a gunboat base for Union vessels patrolling the river. The sketch depicts the sawmill owned by Amander Parsons and Halsted H. Hoeg. Sketch by Alfred R. Waud, 1864. (Courtesy of Library of Congress.)

FIGURE 4. Pilot's house, St. Johns River. Located on the north shore of the river across from Mayport Mills, Pilot Town was home to ship captains who guided vessels across the shifting sand bars. During the war years the Union navy established a temporary camp for white and black refugees picked up by gunboats patrolling the river. Sketch by Alfred R. Waud, 1864. (Courtesy of Library of Congress.)

FIGURE 5. USS *Pawnee*, a sloop-of-war assigned to the South Atlantic Blockading Squadron. The *Pawnee* participated in the first Union occupation of Jacksonville in 1862. Sketch by Alfred R. Waud, 1864. (Courtesy of Library of Congress.)

FIGURE 6. USS *Belvidere*, one of the vessels assigned to the South Atlantic Blockading Squadron that patrolled the St. Johns River. Sketch by Alfred R. Waud, 1864. (Courtesy of Library of Congress.)

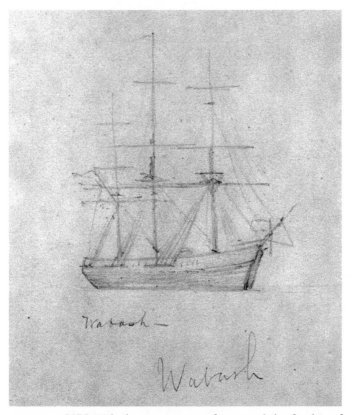

FIGURE 7. USS *Wabash*, a steam screw frigate and the flagship of Admiral Samuel F. Du Pont, commander of the South Atlantic Blockading Squadron. The *Wabash* saw action on the St. Johns during the first Union occupation of Jacksonville. Sketch by Alfred R. Waud, 1864. (Courtesy of Library of Congress.)

FIGURE 8. Admiral Samuel F. Du Pont, commander of the South Atlantic Blockading Squadron, was in charge of naval operations during the first three Federal occupations of Jacksonville. (Courtesy of Library of Congress.)

FIGURE 9. General Horatio G. Wright, commander of Union land forces during the first occupation of Jacksonville in 1862. (Courtesy of Library of Congress.)

FIGURE 10. Brigadier General Joseph Finegan. Born in Ireland, Joseph Finegan came to Florida in the 1830s. He became a planter, sawmill owner, lawyer, and railroad executive before commanding Confederate forces in Florida from April 1862 through February 1864. (Courtesy of Library of Congress.)

FIGURE 11. Major General David Hunter, commander of Union forces in the Department of the South. Hunter organized the formation of a regiment of black soldiers known as the "Hunter regiment," and he ordered the controversial evacuations of Jacksonville in 1862 and 1863. (Courtesy of Library of Congress.)

FIGURE 12. "Contrabands" in Virginia employed as teamsters by the Union army. Thousands of slaves escaped from their owners in Florida and Virginia to seek refuge aboard Union gunboats and behind Federal lines. Labeled "contrabands of war" by Union officials, many of the men joined regiments of United States Colored Infantry and fought for the liberation of their still-enslaved brothers and sisters. Photograph by James F. Gibson. (Courtesy of Library of Congress.)

Debacle at
St. Johns Bluff, and
the Second Occupation
of Jacksonville

Captain Lemuel G. Crane, commanding the Union gunboat *Uncas*, detected "a company of rebels" on a St. Johns River bluff south of Jacksonville on September 1, 1862. Crane ordered his gunners to open fire, "killing and wounding several . . . and scattering the rest." Over the next week Crane saw other guerrilla bands "passing through these woods and doing all sorts of mischief" to Unionists living along the river. In a raid at Mayport, where a number of refugees were sheltered, guerrillas set fire to a house before being driven off. Crane concluded that infantry, cavalry, and guerrilla bands were concentrating in the area, carrying orders from General Finegan to fire on the gunboats whenever they could. He informed Admiral Du Pont: "I am perfectly satisfied that the rebels in this vicinity are getting stronger and bolder every day."[1]

Crane's observation was accurate. Finegan had been preparing for months, moving men and material from distant points in Florida, waiting for an opportune moment to open a campaign to terminate Union gunboat patrols on the St. Johns. On September 4 Finegan ordered twenty-five men of the 2nd Florida Cavalry to raid the Union base at Mayport and pin down the gunboats while other Confederate units installed artillery atop St. Johns Bluff. Situated six miles from the river's entrance and at the highest elevation along its course, the bluff towered over a site where the channel narrowed and forced ships to pass within easy range of an enemy's guns.[2]

While the raids were under way at Mayport, Confederate forces at the bluff rushed to prepare gun emplacements for the artillery that was en route from Tallahassee. Finegan, Lieutenant F. L. Villepigue, and a detachment of artillerists left Tallahassee by train on September 6 carrying two 8-inch siege howitzers and two 12-pounder rifles. At Lake City they added two 32-pounder rifles. The train reached Jacksonville at 2 a.m. on the seventh. Both men and materials were placed under command of Captain Joseph L. Dunham of the Milton Light Artillery Battalion and ferried across the St. Johns to a wagon road leading east to the bluff.

Wagon master Richard Joseph Adams had been aboard the train supervising the fifty-two mules and ten wagons that transported the artillery to the fortification at the bluff. In the early months of 1862, Adams had been an employee of Hubbard L. Hart's steamship line, routinely sending ships between Jacksonville and Enterprise on Lake Monroe as if a war were not in progress, but on March 14 his life had changed abruptly. He wrote in his diary: "Federal Gunboat arrived at Palatka at 8½ A.M.—I took to the woods."[3]

When Adams emerged from the woods, he roamed from the interior of Florida to Indian River, carrying merchandise smuggled through the Union naval blockade for deposit in a warehouse he maintained at Orange Springs. During June and July he was employed primarily in obtaining horses and mules for Confederate armies, purchasing them in Georgia and sending them by rail and steamer to the Chattahoochee River and to Savannah. On September 7 he was back in Florida, harnessing mules to wagons and hauling cannons and ammunition over a dirt road to St. Johns Bluff.

Five companies of cavalry and one company of infantry waited at the bluff to install the weapons. A large force of slaves drafted from area plantations had already dug caverns for the magazines and constructed gun emplacements. By the evening of September 9, six guns had been mounted. For the remainder of September, Adams obtained corn and fodder for the draft animals and cavalry horses in the area. His mules were also used to haul timber and ammunition to the batteries and to carry baggage to the infantry camps protecting the land approaches.

When the fortifications were nearing completion, Finegan learned that two 8-inch columbiads, capable of firing 65-pound projectiles, and two more 8-inch siege howitzers had arrived at Jacksonville. On September 10 the cannons were rafted and towed to St. Johns Bluff by the steamer *Governor Mil-*

ton. By then, the element of surprise had slipped from Finegan's grasp. On the evening of the ninth, an escaped slave named Israel had boarded the *Patroon* with news of clandestine Confederate activities under way at the bluff. The following day the story was related to Captain Crane, who decided to investigate. Under cover of darkness, Crane took the *Uncas* to within five hundred yards of the bluff and fired nine shells at the position. When the shots were not returned, Crane anchored the *Uncas* directly below the bluff, not realizing the Confederates withheld return fire, aware that the muzzle flashes of their guns would have revealed their positions and invited a return attack.

At daybreak the Confederates launched a devastating bombardment on the ship anchored below, striking her five times before Crane was able to maneuver into position to return fire. One shell pierced the hull at the waterline and penetrated through the magazine, but did not explode. Another passed through the pilothouse, barely missing Crane, and others raked the decks, blowing away gear and anchor chains. Miraculously, none of the crew was hit: defective Confederate shells had saved them from a worse disaster.[4]

Stung into action, the gunboat launched two 32-pounders and a 20-pound rifled piece, while another gunboat, the *Patroon*, armed with four 8-inch guns and a 30-pounder, steamed to her assistance. Together, the gunboats fired more than two hundred rounds in the ensuing five-hour battle. Crane said that once the *Uncas* got up steam and began maneuvering she was not hit again. At least ninety of the Federal shells "exploded within and around" the batteries on the bluff, driving the Confederate gunners from their positions "for nearly an hour."[5]

Finegan claimed an unqualified Confederate victory and praised a Jacksonville man, Lieutenant Thomas E. Buckman, for his part in the action. One gunboat had been crippled and the other driven away, the Confederate commander boasted, while "little or no damage" was inflicted on his batteries. One artillerist was lost in the exchange, and others were wounded, among them an officer who fell down the steep embankment and impaled himself on a bayonet held by one of his own men. Aware that control of the bluff was necessary to "relieve the valley of the St. Johns from the marauding incursions of the enemy," Finegan wired Richmond an urgent request for reinforcements. Given only one more regiment of infantry, he was sure he could save the bluff and even "take St. Augustine and hold it."[6]

When news of the attack reached Port Royal on September 15, Admiral Du Pont reacted angrily: "I had intimated in various ways to the citizens and authorities of Jacksonville that if the gunboats were molested from the banks of the river, or Union people maltreated and their property destroyed, that I would adopt retaliatory measures by destroying Jacksonville." He sent Commander Charles Steedman and the gunboats *Paul Jones, Cimarron,* and *E. B. Hale* to "warn responsible persons of the consequences" of the attack and the punishment that was sure to follow for violating his warning of retaliation if the Confederates fortified positions along the river. Steedman was to "destroy all the works on the banks which might be used or occupied by the rebels at any future time against us" and to take extra measures to protect his men and boats from snipers.[7]

Steedman's squadron anchored off Mayport the evening of September 16. At daybreak, led by the *Paul Jones,* five Union vessels entered the river and steamed to positions two thousand yards short of St. Johns Bluff. The *Paul Jones* and the *Cimarron* opened fire with their 100-pounder Parrotts while Steedman studied the fortifications and admired the calm and efficiency of the Confederates, remarking that despite the noise and smoke from exploding shells that tore huge holes in the fortification, the defenders "received our fire for some time with indifference, taking care, however, to seek cover in their pits at the flash of our guns."[8] Bombardments drove them temporarily from their posts, but as soon as the shelling ceased the gunners returned to the batteries.

Steedman moved the gunboats in line about sixteen hundred yards from the bluff, near the mouth of Sisters Creek where the effective range of the Confederate guns ended, and initiated the offensive. Over the next five hours the gunboats were hit several times but suffered neither serious damage nor casualties. Steedman surmised that the fixed positions were the hardest hit and that "the enemy must have suffered considerably from the incessant shower of shells and projectiles."[9] There was no doubt in his mind that if ground troops had been available to him a landing could have been made and the bluff taken that day, but Steedman ordered the boats to return to Mayport without steaming further upriver to Jacksonville. He feared that the Confederates would quickly repair their defenses and wreak havoc when the gunboats returned to Mayport. A "combined land and naval attack" would be necessary to reopen the St. Johns.

Captain Dunham's men had returned a "quick and well-directed fire" and prevented the gunboats from passing upriver. The Rebels might have inflicted heavier damage on the wooden gunboats had their two longer-range guns been operative, but these had arrived too late to be installed before the attack began. After the Federal bombardment ceased, Dunham immediately sent crews to repair damages and improve the defenses. Wagon master Adams wrote in his diary that evening: "Battery attacked by five Gunboats—Gunboats repulsed after five hours hard shelling. . . . Two men killed at battery and 4 or 5 wounded."[10]

Finegan received Dunham's report of the duel in Tallahassee and immediately boarded a train for Jacksonville. In a terse dispatch to Richmond, he reported: "the enemy, having failed to pass our batteries, may attempt a land attack. I am preparing for it, and will be there tonight. Can you send me one regiment of infantry from the coast of Georgia or Carolina? I need them very much."[11] Finegan decided to fortify a second strategic location at Yellow Bluff on the north bank of the St. Johns, upriver and across from St. Johns Bluff. Yellow Bluff was situated at a promontory thirty feet above the water where swamps and a creek protected the land approaches, and from where artillery could pose a threat to ships in the river's channel. On September 23, Finegan sent Company H of the 2nd Florida Cavalry Regiment, under Captain J. J. Dickison, to Yellow Bluff. Three days later, Dunham led the Milton Light Artillery and two additional companies of cavalry into positions at Fort Yellow Bluff, ready to fire on Union ships in case they slipped by the defenses at St. Johns Bluff.

While the artillery duel was under way at St. Johns Bluff, Confederate cavalry companies of the St. Johns Rangers had been in camps located at the rear of the bluff protecting ground approaches to the fortifications. Captain Stephens was confident that the artillerists had driven the Federals from the area. "We have the game played out with the gunboats on this river. Shell and shot fell like hail," Stephens said, but the Confederate guns had not been damaged.[12] In addition to 227 mounted cavalry, Stephens counted 300 infantry in a battalion under Captain John C. Richard, 117 infantry in an independent company, and 150 men to work the guns. The total manpower of 794 was sufficient to withstand an attack, Stephens said, as he scoffed at Finegan's request for a regiment from Georgia and called him an "old granny" and political "credit-seeker" who could better expend his energies finding Enfield rifles and sabers for the Florida troops already in place.

Lieutenant Colonel Charles F. Hopkins, who replaced Dunham as commander at St. Johns Bluff on September 26, did not agree with Stephens's assessment. What Hopkins saw at the entrance to the river when he looked through the lenses of his field glasses shook him to the core: "When I arrived there were five gunboats in the river; on September 29 another came over the bar, and on the 30th another, making in all seven gunboats. . . . I became apprehensive that forces would be landed and the batteries attacked by land troops."[13] Hopkins immediately put his men to work installing four cannons and sent an urgent message to Finegan requesting more ammunition and a regiment of infantry to augment the small force under his command.

While Hopkins secured Confederate defenses at the bluff, a land force of nearly sixteen hundred Union men boarded transports and headed for the St. Johns River. The plan agreed upon by Du Pont and Brigadier General John M. Brannan called for the infantry to attack the batteries from the rear while the gunboats pounded the bluff from the river. Steedman was told to "disturb the rebels by an occasional shot and keep them from improving the works until the troops arrive."[14] Du Pont wanted to initiate the campaign as soon as possible in order to avoid storms on the Atlantic during hurricane season that might hamper efforts to resupply ammunition for Steedman's big guns and delay departure of the land forces.

General Brannan, as a veteran of the Second Seminole War and commander of Union installations at Key West, was familiar with Florida terrain. The infantry force he assembled at Beaufort, South Carolina, consisted of 825 men of the 47th Pennsylvania led by Colonel Tilghman H. Good and 647 men of the 7th Connecticut under command of Colonel Joseph R. Hawley. In addition, he attached a section of the 1st Connecticut Light Artillery, which contained 41 men and two small fieldpieces, and 60 men of the 1st Massachusetts Cavalry. Troop strength totaled 1,573 men.[15]

The troops left Hilton Head on September 30 aboard the transports *Boston*, *Ben DeFord*, *Cosmopolitan*, and *Neptune*. They arrived at the entrance to the St. Johns at 8 a.m. the following day and waited for the tide to raise the water over the bar before hazarding a crossing. Inside the bar Steedman's squadron of five ships lay at anchor, although crossing the sandbar and unloading troops proved to be a lengthy and difficult exercise. Men, armaments, rations, baggage, and other equipment and supplies had to be transferred from the transports to smaller vessels and brought ashore. The horses were forced over the rails of the ships. Most survived and swam to a sandbank near the transports. Some drowned, others had their legs broken and were shot, and hundreds of men waited for hours before food could be prepared and campfires lit.[16]

One of the soldiers described Mayport as "a small timber village . . . of two or three large sawmills supplied with gang saws, which gave evidence of cutting a large amount of lumber." The small village had "a Catholic Church and two light houses" located close to the river, "one of them a very beautiful and costly structure, nearly new, apparently never having been used, and . . . several small cottages, containing three or four rooms, were built on the sand and had most probably been occupied by the lumbermen; they appeared as though they had been standing empty six or seven months." The soldier was surprised to see white sand drifts surrounding the cottages, "some of the drifts were 25 feet high and so compactly made that it was possible for the comrades to walk up the sand drifts and on the roofs of the houses and look down the chimneys. . . . One of the comrades . . . lighted a pine torch and commenced setting the houses on fire."[17] The soldier with the pine torch was surprised when officers ordered him to cease the destruction and had him arrested.

While the transports were being unloaded, the gunboats were able to approach St. Johns Bluff to test the firepower and accuracy of the Confederate batteries.[18] Captain Valentine Chamberlain of the 7th Connecticut recorded his impressions from aboard one of the transports: "About four miles up the river the bank on the left rises into a high bluff . . . [forming] an arc of a circle around which the St. Johns finds its way, so that all boats are brought close under the bluffs."[19] The danger was obvious, and one soldier standing at the rail near Chamberlain remarked: "Guess they mean to fight."

It was 9 p.m. before the entire expeditionary force was ashore. Earlier that day, while the horses were being driven over the rail into the river to swim ashore, scouting parties had explored the terrain east of Pablo Creek. They discovered that an advance from this position would require the troops to march south to the head of the creek before turning inland toward the bluff. The route would have exceeded forty miles.

Brannan decided instead to load the 47th Pennsylvania aboard smaller vessels at daybreak on October 2 and send them beyond the mouth of Pablo River to tiny Buckhorn Creek. At Greenfield plantation (today a residential neighborhood known as Queen's Harbor), approximately three-fourths of a mile inland, they found a solid landing site. To speed up the shuttle operation, Brannan put the troops still at Mayport back aboard the transports and moved them closer to Buckhorn Creek.[20]

From an observation post at the top of St. Johns Bluff, Colonel Hopkins watched through field glasses as Union troops shuttled back and forth throughout the day. He dispatched orders to Captain Dunham at Yellow Bluff to "dismount the three cavalry companies under your command and send them over tonight by the steamer." In response, approximately 110 dismounted cavalry were sent immediately. Later in the day Hopkins rushed another dispatch: "The enemy landed this afternoon . . . about 3,000 men; also artillery. You will repair without delay to these headquarters with your whole command. We need your artillery immediately." When Hopkins learned that Dunham's horses and caissons were located at too great a distance to permit him to move the eight fieldpieces in time to help at St. Johns Bluff, he requested that all the artillerists be sent across the river to be armed and used as infantry.[21]

Reports of Hopkins's predicament reached Finegan in Lake City as he searched for arms and reinforcements. Having despaired of getting help from Beauregard, Finegan fired off a dispatch to the Confederate Congress at Richmond, saying he was "hard pressed on the St. Johns River. The Commanding officer at St. Johns Bluff reports 3,000 Federals . . . at Mayport Mills. . . . Enemy engaged our batteries again yesterday for the third time and were repulsed . . . have not sufficient men to resist a land attack if made in force. Do go at once to the Secretary and get one or two regiments of infantry from the coast of Georgia. If I had them for a few days it might save the St. Johns River and perhaps East Florida."[22]

Meanwhile, Hopkins ordered the infantry to form a line of battle at the rear of the batteries. Two companies of cavalry were further out skirmishing with the Federals as they advanced. From a base camp near what Stephens called "Tyger Hole," his men had been scouting on horseback between the bluff and Pablo Creek for the previous three weeks. Without protection of either tents or raincoats, they had slept at night in the woods in wet clothing and wet blankets while heavy rains pounded them relentlessly. In an October 1 letter to his wife, Stephens complained that for the two previous days his men had only dry bread for sustenance. "Despotism" and "military dictation" had replaced "civil law," he griped: "We have been treated badly in some respects since we were moved on this side of the river." He asked his wife to send him the oilcloth from their kitchen table so he could fashion a raincoat and gain some protection from the storms.[23]

Stephens was wet and bitter, but he had not lost his enthusiasm for battle. He lamented that he had not yet been able "to kill a Yank." He was convinced the Federals would have to bring "an overwhelming land force" to dislodge his men from the bluff, "as we have good guns and a plenty of them and then we have a battery on Yellow Bluff to keep them back if one or more should pass this bluff. We are not as strong as we wish to be but we can kill four to one in these woods."[24]

Captain W. E. Chambers's company of St. Johns Rangers was deployed further north, scouting through terrain that alternated between rolling hills covered with pine forests and wetlands dotted with dense swamps. Sensing that a Federal advance through this terrain would drain the marchers' strength, Major T. W. Brevard sent a message to Hopkins on October 2, "asking leave to proceed with command in the direction of the enemy and contest his passage through the swamps." Hopkins consented, but with-drew permission after receiving an alarming report from Chambers that the enemy "had passed through his camp and were within a few miles of the infantry in rear of the batteries." Based on exaggerated reports from Chambers, Hopkins was convinced that he was facing almost five thousand men. He stripped the batteries of all but four detachments of artillerists, gave them muskets, and ordered them into the rifle trenches at the rear of the gun emplacements.[25]

While Hopkins desperately deployed his units, the men of the 47th Pennsylvania moved out from their beachhead at Greenfield. Colonel Good sent skirmishers to the south and west to bypass the head of Greenfield Creek and then turn back northwest toward the bluff. The march through swamp and brush exhausted the Pennsylvanians, but by noon they had driven Chambers's cavalry from a place known locally as Parker's Plantation. Chambers ordered his men to retreat before the superior Federal force but to harass them and slow their advance.

One of the Pennsylvania men thought of the march as the most exhausting and frightening event of his life. He recalled landing at six o'clock that morning "in one of those great Florida swamps and marshes, among rattlesnakes, copperheads, centipedes, alligators, and many other poisonous reptiles and insects. We were informed that the natives never dare venture into that swamp except in mid-winter, and even then they selected the coldest days when no sun was shining."[26] While coffee was being prepared at one of the regiment's stops "near a large palmetto jungle . . . out crawled a huge rattlesnake from the palmetto grove. . . . Everyone who saw the reptile had a shot at him with pistols, making him surrender very quickly. He measured nine feet in length and had ten rattles."[27]

Good remembered one portion of the day's excursion as "one of the toughest marches I ever experienced, for ten miles, through chaparral so thick and matted that a weasel could hardly have creeped through. Again wading through swamps up to our hips in mud and water . . . and by the middle of the afternoon we had marched thirteen miles to gain one and a half." Joined by the 7th Connecticut that afternoon, the Federals marched west to Mount Pleasant Creek. After repairing a damaged bridge, they crossed over and followed a road to Mount Pleasant Landing at the head of the creek, passing through one of the Confederate cavalry camps en route. Good was surprised by what happened next: "After marching one mile down the bank of [Mount Pleasant] creek my skirmishing companies came upon a camp which evidently had been very hastily evacuated, from the fact that the occupants had left a table standing with a sumptuous meal already prepared for eating. On the center of the table was placed a fine, large meat pie still warm, from which one of the party had already served his plate." Good's men resumed the march, traveling another mile to a second camp, which also had been evacuated hastily. Here the men of the 47th found nearly fifty rifles and shotguns, and knapsacks for an entire company. "We drove the enemy's skirmishers in small parties along the entire march," Good said, but the approximately one hundred men who opposed him never closed for sustained combat.[28]

One of the Pennsylvania men in Good's regiment summed up the day as "unusual . . . always through bush, marsh, swamp and water and a few times we were under water and in much rain. We worked through with sixty bullets per man on the side, and five days rations on the back, but we made it." Led by "a negro, who escaped from the fort but four weeks previous" (Israel, the same man who had informed the gunboat commanders of efforts to install artillery at the bluff), the regiment pushed on through terrain so swampy that horses could not follow, until they reached a landing at Mount Pleasant Creek where they camped for the night with plans to resume the march at daybreak, after being reinforced by a detachment of the 1st Connecticut Battery with two pieces of field artillery. General Brannan felt a delay would also allow time for the 7th Connecticut to move into place and for three hundred infantry reinforcements to arrive from Fernandina.[29] Writing in German, one of the soldiers remembered the events of the day: "the march was a difficult one, in consequence of meeting so many swamps almost knee deep. . . . It rained all day and much of our way was through swamps. I was glad to stop and get hot coffee and dry stockings."[30]

The day had been equally difficult for Captain Stephens. His company had reported the enemy landings at Greenfield plantation and had skirmished while retreating and protecting their flanks. Stephens expected to mount a spirited resistance at his campsite, but Confederate cavalry units were instead ordered to return to St. Johns Bluff for a hurried conference with Hopkins. Stephens received permission to reposition two field howitzers on a high hill to fire down on the advancing enemy. While this work was under way, the cavalry units were ordered to remount and ride to the left flank to block the road the Federals were following from Mount Pleasant Landing toward the bluff.

At 9 p.m. Stephens was called in from the front and told that the ranking officers had unanimously decided to abandon St. Johns Bluff. Caught between a probable gunboat bombardment from the water and a superior land force that would surely reach the infantry trenches the following day, and with the field howitzers hopelessly mired in heavy mud and inoperative, Hopkins had decided to evacuate the bluff. He later said he "was convinced that unless I made a retreat my small command would be captured, as the guns from the batteries afforded no protection to the rear." Two of every three Confederate soldiers left in East Florida were concentrated in the bluff fortifications, all subject to capture if the Union advance succeeded. Hopkins decided to slip away in the night, quietly, so as to avoid alerting the enemy and provoking an attack. All the officers at the bluff agreed with the decision, and "the post was reluctantly abandoned."[31]

Stephens's company was ordered to protect the rear as the Confederates retreated toward Jacksonville. His sick, lame, and exhausted men and horses did not reach the ferry landing opposite Jacksonville until nine o'clock the following morning, and by then it was too late to cross safely. With the guns of St. Johns Bluff silent and useless, the river was again open to the Union gunboats, and men making the slow crossing on the ferry would have been vulnerable to shelling or capture by the fast-moving enemy vessels. Rather than risk detection as a group, Stephens released his men to escape on their own. He went upriver all the way to Fort Gates and crossed there. Along the route he crossed several streams, nearly drowned at Haws Creek, and lost his horse. Safe at last, but sorry that the enemy had not been driven back as he believed they should have been, Stephens took consolation in the fact that he had survived the "fierce situation" at the bluff and had led his men in a "masterly retreat"; although he was not sure, he thought it possible that he had finally killed a Yankee.[32]

While Stephens made his dramatic escape, his wife expressed the anxieties of thousands of Florida women who waited helplessly in their homes. Octavia had received a letter from her husband dated October 1, informing her that he was wet and miserable but alive. Next she heard a rumor that the bluff had fallen and the Confederates had escaped by swimming across the river. Terrified that Winston had been either captured or killed, she penned a letter to him before realizing that she had no idea where to send it, or whether it would ever be opened. She closed the letter: "Heaven only knows where you are now. Oh my dear husband I don't know what to do or say. All I can do is pray for your safety."[33]

Wagon master Adams made a less dramatic escape from St. Johns Bluff. His diary contains a single sentence in the October 2 entry: "Retreat from St. Johns Bluff commenced."[34] For the next nine days, accompanied by five men and teams of mules, he evaded the gunboats by carefully picking secluded roads east of the river, crossing Sampson Creek, McCullough Creek, and Moccasin Branch before reaching the ferry opposite Palatka on the tenth. Along the way he purchased more than two thousand pounds of fodder and approximately one hundred barrels of corn to keep his draft animals alive.

It was not until the morning after the Confederates abandoned the bluff that the Federals realized the fortifications had been deserted. They had halted the advance the night before to wait for reinforcements, not realizing that additional troops would not be needed. Captain Chamberlain reported: "the gunboats went up to feel the rebels but they would not answer our fire. The boats ran by the battery, frowning with guns, but silence—the rebels had fled." Chamberlain and his men landed and marched over the shortest route to the batteries, but it was evening before they reached the bluff. He "wandered around among the guns in the clear moonlight. It was certainly a strong place and well protected in the rear by thick undergrowth and commanding hills. But they had left, and we were glad. We could probably have taken the place, but if compelled to storm it we must have lost heavily."[35]

General Brannan's assessment of the Confederate position was more revealing. He found the batteries "skillfully constructed, well armed, and well supplied with ammunition," and noted that they "appear[ed] to have been deserted in great haste, the guns being all mounted, loaded, and in good condition, the ammunition served, and everything in excellent fighting order. I am in fact utterly at a loss to account for this sudden evacuation on the part of the rebels, as, in addition to a most skillfully constructed line of defense, the position possesses natural advantages which render it almost impregnable." The batteries on the bluff could only be approached by one route, which led through "a winding ravine immediately under the guns." Noting that "most of the guns were mounted on a complete traverse circle" and could have been reversed and fired inland at the approaching troops, Brannan concluded: "I have no doubt but that a small party of determined men could have maintained this position for a considerable time against even a larger force than was at my disposal."[36]

Finegan was embittered by the precipitous Confederate retreat. He had hurried from Lake City to join Hopkins on the night of October 3, only to learn that the bluff had already been abandoned. His report to Richmond claimed there had been a "sufficient force to hold the place" and blamed Hopkins for a "gross military blunder." Finegan also charged that the evacuation occurred "eighteen or twenty hours before the approach of the enemy by land. The guns were not spiked, nor the ammunition, of which there was a large quantity, destroyed."[37]

Stung by the accusations, Hopkins demanded a court-martial. In his defense he pointed out that his small infantry force was only "partially armed with the almost useless arms turned over by Captain Dickison." One company was "unprovided with ammunition," Hopkins said, and the ammunition of another was "damaged by the rain, which fell constantly during the day." He also claimed that his men could not have dismounted or spiked the guns without creating a great deal of noise, which would have alerted the Federals and endangered their route of retreat. Nor could they have removed the ammunition, as only a single wagon was available for transport.[38]

Finally, Hopkins said he had dispatched troops to destroy the magazine, and that charges had been placed, along with a linking trail of gunpowder that was poured for several yards beyond. The plan was for the men of the rear guard to wait until the retreat had proceeded for a prudent distance before igniting the powder. The flame was expected to follow the trail back to spark an explosion of gunpowder in the magazine of sufficient strength to destroy everything of military value. But the powder trail was so poorly prepared that the rain extinguished the flame short of the magazine. In the dark and soggy fortification, amid the haste and panic of the retreat, this important work was bungled.

Finegan and Hopkins also clashed over the number of troops available at the bluff. Hopkins said only five hundred Confederates had been available to oppose a force at least three times that number. Finegan, who was not at the bluff during the battle, insisted that Hopkins commanded seven hundred men, enough to hold off the Federals. Unless desertions were rampant and unreported, or sickness depleted the ranks, the evidence supports Finegan on this disputed point.

But even if Hopkins had had seven hundred inadequately armed men under his command, that number would have been insufficient to hold off the Federals. It was Finegan who had requested an additional regiment from Georgia or South Carolina on September 19, thirteen days before Brannan's troops landed at Greenfield plantation. While the Federals were advancing toward the bluff, Finegan had again wired Richmond to say he lacked "sufficient men to resist a land attack." What caused him to change his mind? With approximately sixteen hundred men, Federal land forces were clearly far superior, and the firepower from the gunboats exceeded the capacity of the artillerists on the bluff. Assessments by Brannan and Chamberlain were accurate: the bluff defenses were formidable, and had they not been abandoned, Federal casualties might have been heavy if Hopkins had decided to stay and fight. But undoubtedly the men from Pennsylvania and Connecticut would have prevailed, and when they came within firing range of the entrenchments, routes of escape for the Florida men would have been cut off. Stephens's charge that Finegan was a political "credit seeker" may have merit in this situation. His denunciation of Hopkins might have been better directed had he pointed blame at Richmond and a Confederate command that failed to send either adequate arms and ammunition or reinforcements. Once again, Florida had been left, in the words of historian William Nulty, "isolated and vulnerable to the enemy."[39]

Hopkins was exonerated at the court-martial. Lieutenant Colonel William D. Mitchell, writing for the court of inquiry, concluded that Hopkins could not have effectively defended the batteries with the men and material at his disposal. Evacuation "was positively necessary for the safety of the men under his command," and Hopkins was "wholly justifiable in the course he pursued in abandoning the batteries on the Saint John's."[40] President Jefferson Davis believed Finegan's version of events. Based on a report of the episode, Davis wrote, "Florida regiments in Virginia and elsewhere have uniformly acted with gallantry and have received the applause of their commanding generals. The bad conduct of the garrison at the battery can only be explained, therefore, in the manner reported. . . . The loss of the position was a serious calamity."[41]

Angry postmortems mattered little to the Federals. They had taken a formidable position without a fight, and the river was again open to their gunboats. As soon as Steedman learned that the bluff was not defended, he ordered the *Hale* and *Paul Jones* to steam to Jacksonville to prevent Hopkins and his men from crossing the river to safety. It was 7 p.m. on October 3 before they arrived, too late to hinder the retreat, Steedman said, as "the greater part of the rebel army had crossed during the midnight and morning."[42]

The fall of St. Johns Bluff was followed by a second Federal occupation of Jacksonville, which lasted for less than a week and was of little military significance. The goals of the army-navy expedition had been to capture the guns and destroy the fortifications at St. Johns Bluff in order to reestablish Union supremacy on the river. These goals had been achieved before Union troops landed at Jacksonville on October 5 to find the town "nearly deserted, there being but a small portion of its inhabitants left—chiefly old men, women, and children."[43]

There was only a brief engagement between the landing forces and Rebel cavalry before the town was secured. Chamberlain was escorting Israel, the escaped slave who had reported Finegan's bluff fortifications, to a reunion with his family when the Confederate cavalry swept around the ruins of the railroad depot. He stopped to watch his comrades "yell and pour a volley into the advance of the enemy consisting of some fifteen horsemen . . . [from a total of fifty]. They brought up in a hurry, took a hasty glance and retreated. We saw no more of them in any force. . . . The negroes afterwards told us that the rebels lost two men and three horses [and] claimed they had killed three of our men. None of us even got a scratch." Picket lines were immediately established, but Chamberlain and his men experienced "no further trouble while we were in this place," although on occasion "the gunboats threw a few shells in the direction of the rebels, and the boat howitzers were also brought ashore."[44]

During his free hours Chamberlain wrote letters describing the "desolation and distress" the war had brought to the town. "Before reaching the city you see ruins of large steam saw mills. . . . Grass and weeds grow rank & tall in the principal streets. Houses with blinds closed attest the absence of inmates. Stores with shelves but no goods. Churches deserted and gloomy. Depot, but no cars. Such is the general look of the city."[45] In the parts of town where people still were in residence, Chamberlain found "darkies, a few women, a few men." He was told the white men were "away up the country, but you know they are in the rebel army." But what most fascinated the young soldier was the town's female population, especially those who "dipped" snuff. While patrolling one morning, he stopped to converse with a group of Jacksonville's ladies. "There they were, one quite decent looking young woman, married, husband gone, she said he was not in the rebel army. She sat in a rocking chair, with a tin box in one hand, looking like one of my old worm boxes, and a stick in the other. The stick she plunged into the box, in which was snuff, then into her mouth. After a little, she would spit from her mouth the collected saliva black with tobacco. How do you like the picture of the Jacksonville ladies?"[46]

Chamberlain was surprised to discover that a newspaper was being published in the town. Called the *Southern Rights*, it had begun on July 26, and the forms for the eleventh edition were still in the press when the Federals broke down the door. This final edition gave news of a forthcoming election with Joseph N. Haddock, I. V. Garnie, and W. A. MacLeans as candidates for state offices. It also printed a list of lawful exemptions from conscription, an item describing counterfeit Confederate currency, and an advertisement offering a reward of twenty-five dollars for the capture of a slave runaway named Ned, the property of E. O. Aulon Sr.[47]

Brannan ordered Chamberlain to "fire the printing office of the Secesh paper and to gut it." But first, Chamberlain indulged in a little fun. Stripping a few blocks of type from one column, he set a few replacement items of his own and ran copies of the revised *Southern Rights* before demolishing the plant and confiscating the press. Two of these items brought guffaws from the occupation forces and probably stirred anger among Southerners still in the city. "The friends of Col. Hopkins are informed that the Colonel declines to run as candidate for the office of Senator, not withstanding the good time he made running from St. Johns Bluff. The Editor of this paper is absent from town for a few days on urgent business in the interior. It is therefore announced that the publication of this Paper will hereafter be weekly suspended. . . . The taking of our battery after a loss of courage, but no blood, and the presence of the Yankee Fleet, and the fearful proximity of General Brannan and his forces, render the *Southern Rights* precarious."[48]

Some other fun got out of hand. On the second day of the occupation "almost every store on [Bay] Street was broken into." Chamberlain thought the looters cut comic figures tearing open packages and scattering merchandise. Summary punishments quickly ended the looting, and the troops settled down to a routine of equipment repair and preparation for the sea voyage back to Hilton Head.

There were other arrests during the brief occupation. Sailors aboard the *Patroon* became sufficiently "demoralized and insubordinate as to render her totally inefficient," and four men were arrested and confined aboard the *Paul Jones*. A few civilians were placed under arrest, among them Mr. Young, the ferryman at Jacksonville, whom Commander Maxwell Woodhull of the *Cimarron* described as "a rabid secessionist and . . . one of the most active and persistent rebels in these parts."[49] Amander Parsons and one of his slaves were arrested for refusing to reveal information about Confederate activities. Parsons was taken into custody and held in confinement for being "so thoroughly a rebel that no threats could induce him to give information." In October, his property was seized and quantities of lumber and other valuable articles found at his Mayport sawmill were confiscated and shipped north by the navy.

Events of greater importance transpired on the river. On October 6, Union gunboats located the *Governor Milton* on a small stream more than one hundred miles south of Jacksonville. She was returned and pressed into Federal service as an auxiliary gunboat. The navy scoured the St. Johns for small boats and rafts, destroying several hundred in order to prevent their use by Finegan's troops. During these operations the gunboats roamed at will along the St. Johns, shelling potentially dangerous structures and drawing return fire from snipers and guerrillas. Rebel-owned property was destroyed or confiscated, and endangered Union supporters were evacuated. At Palatka, Woodhull was concerned for the safety of several black refugees who served as river pilots and guides for the Union vessels. Threats had been issued that they would be hung and their families abused if ever the gunboats abandoned them. Woodhull evacuated them, along with their "wives, sons and daughters, and even grandchildren, to the number of about thirty persons."[50]

Woodhull also pondered Florida's future importance to the Confederacy. Impressed by the rich grazing lands and the corn and sugar crops he saw along the banks of the St. Johns, he observed: "The cattle of Georgia, Alabama, North and South Carolina have all been consumed. Texas and the rich grazing country to the westward of the Mississippi being cut off, the whole dependence of the Confederate Government to feed their Army now rests on this State." It would take more than a year for the Federal high command to reach the same conclusion and to decide to do something about it.[51]

By October 9 the Union command felt confident that the river had been reopened to their gunboats and that safe passage was again possible from Mayport to Palatka and beyond. Consequently, the second Federal occupation of Jacksonville ended after only five days. News of the fall of St. Johns Bluff and the subsequent chaotic retreat of Confederate forces spread rapidly, especially in places where black slaves in clandestine gatherings shared news of vital importance. Conditions were again favorable for runaway attempts, and black refugees soon appeared on the riverbanks, in boats and canoes, and in Jacksonville. Summarizing the importance of the campaign, Lieutenant S. W. Preston reported to Admiral Du Pont that more than "2,000 negroes from the territory adjacent to the river have sought the protection of our arms."[52]

Samuel Fairbanks wrote of the second Yankee occupation: "They shall probably steal what few negroes there are left and destroy at will."[53] He was furious to learn that the Federals had destroyed a thousand boats along the St. Johns. After reconsideration, the Confederate slave owner welcomed the act, saying that it might keep the blacks from rowing to the gunboats.

One group of enterprising contrabands found it possible to gain freedom without small boats. Lieutenant S. S. Snell and a small naval force worked in the Palatka area for two days, raising two barges sunk by the Rebels. As soon as the barges were floating, forty-nine runaway slaves appeared on the shore, boarded the barges, and were towed downriver to Mayport.[54] Mass runaway attempts were atypical, however, as most escapees traveled alone or in family groups. Such men as James Bagley, James Bagley Jr., Henry Harrison, Jackson Long, Lewis McQueen, and Benjamin Turner made their escapes to Jacksonville. Thomas Holzendorf and his wife, Harriet, escaped to Fernandina with their two children. All of these men would later join Union regiments.[55]

Some slaves discovered that vigilance on individual plantations was still operational. At A. M. Reed's Mulberry Grove plantation south of Jacksonville, a mass runaway attempt was thwarted when a neighbor discovered the conspirators as they prepared to depart. Winston Stephens described the event to his wife: "All of Mr. Reeds negroes had packed up to go off at night and they were seen by [Peyre] Pearson and he ordered one of the men to stop and he then got Mr. Reed up and he went in the kitchen and there everything was ready and Perry attempted to run off and he was shot in the legs and I think they are sent off to be sold. Long legged Jake got to the Gunboat and the Yankees went back with him after his family but they had moved out in the country and Jake made a terrible fuss."[56]

A. M. Reed recorded the same event in his diary on October 5: "About 12 p.m. found my negroes preparing to leave. In the melee, Jake and Dave escaped carrying off my boat, the Laura Shaw." Reed acted swiftly. His diary entry for October 6 states: "Started all the negroes . . . for the interior." He was astonished the following day when Jake returned in the company of Union troops. He wrote: "U.S. Gunboat, Patroon, stopped at my wharf. Sent up Lieutenant Potts of the flagship, [and] Captain Steedman, with a file of men bringing the runaway, Jake, to get his family and things."[57] When he learned that his wife, Etta, had been sent into the interior, Jake could only remonstrate and return to Jacksonville. A. M. Reed had not seen the last of Jake.

Looking back from the deck when the Federals evacuated on October 9 was the man Stephens called "long legged Jake." Also aboard were 276 other enslaved men and women who had escaped from their owners. Numerous other contrabands had already been carried to Mayport and Fernandina. After the evacuation, Stephens complained that the Yankees stole and vandalized, acting "more like black hearted scamps in Jacksonville than they ever have on the river."[58] The Yankees, Finegan lamented, "have taken all the negroes, free and slave, they could find in the place." He ordered cavalrymen under Captain Dickison to round up all blacks—free or slave—and remove them "from the St. Johns River into the interior at a safe distance from the enemy." Stephens reported that several blacks were shot in Jacksonville in mid-October and that others were captured. Samuel Fairbanks concluded that slave property was no longer safe on the St. Johns. He took his two remaining slaves to be sold in Georgia, and other planters followed his example.[59]

Fairbanks, Finegan, and Stephens now realized the lesson that Florida's enslaved African Americans had learned soon after April 1861: self-emancipation was no longer an impossible dream. Although the dangers were still daunting, freedom was now as close as the St. Johns and as sure as the power of the Federal gunboats that stood ready to receive and protect black Floridians who were able to escape to the river. Finegan would work diligently in the months ahead to keep escaping slaves from reaching the gunboats, but his range of options had narrowed substantially. After the attempt to bar the gunboats from the St. Johns River failed at the bluffs south of Jacksonville, the Union navy was on the river to stay.

Unionists in Exile

Jacksonville's exiled Unionists followed the news of the successful army-navy campaign to reopen the St. Johns River in October 1862 with great interest. Scattered among many Northern cities, the refugees who had left their homes to board Union transports when the navy evacuated the town in April 1862 communicated with one another and pressured military and political officials to mount another campaign to bring Florida back into the Union. Men like Judge Philip Fraser, Calvin Robinson, John Sammis, Paran Moody, William Alsop, and Otis Keene had attempted to reestablish a loyal government in East Florida and been forced to flee with their families to escape what the *New York Times* called "the vengeance of implacable enemies."[1]

From exile, the men addressed political rallies, published reports of their experiences in newspapers, spoke to mayors and governors in their native states, and carried their message to Congress, cabinet officers, Vice-President Hannibal Hamlin—even President Abraham Lincoln. In the summer of 1862 the president told Jacksonville refugees that abandonment of their town was "a great blunder"; it should have been held and used as a base of operations against other points in the state, and "as soon as troops could be spared from other operations," the town will be occupied again.[2]

Further encouragement came on June 7, 1862, when Congress passed the Direct Tax Law, intended as a punitive measure in the parts of the South occupied by the Union army. The law was to be administered by Secretary of the Treasury Salmon P. Chase and called for appointed members of a Direct Tax Commission in the occupied regions of each Southern state. The three commissioners were empowered to tax abandoned Rebel property and sell it at public auction if the owners failed to pay taxes. Some opportunists saw the commission as a chance to profit from the misfortune of Rebel property owners, but the Jacksonville exiles believed it would lead to reoccupation of their town by Federal troops.[3]

Otis Keene, manager of the Judson House Hotel before it was burned, was a prominent member of the coterie of exiled Jacksonville Unionists working actively for the return of Federal forces to Florida. After Union troops departed the town in April 1862, Keene returned to his hometown of Bremen, Maine. By January 1863 he was living in Washington, D.C., working for the Treasury Department. Keene's diary entries for 1863, 1864, and 1865 document numerous meetings at the Willard Hotel in Washington attended by Judge Philip Fraser, Calvin Robinson, John Sammis, Paran Moody, Dr. J. D. Mitchell, Miles Price, A. M. Reed, John Clark, William Alsop, and other exiled Jacksonville Unionists. They persuaded Vice-President Hamlin to join them for dinner on at least one occasion. They were also joined by a pair of controversial Northerners, Lyman D. Stickney of Vermont and Eli Thayer of Massachusetts, who were agitating for an experimental takeover of confiscated land in Florida. Stickney and Thayer were convinced that the application of Yankee enterprise in Florida would produce agricultural riches sufficient to attract a dense population of thrifty farmers to the state.[4]

Thayer was well known to Florida secessionists as the man who organized the Massachusetts Emigrant Aid Society to promote mass migration of free farmers and laborers from the North into slave states and territories that he felt "had not yet responded to the influence of Yankee civilization."[5] He established colonies in Kansas, Texas, and Virginia, and after the Civil War began he called for "complete social and political reconstruction of the Southern States" through economic means. The first step would be "confiscation of rebel property," followed by colonization of the confiscated land by free farmers and artisans from Northern states who would enlist for nine months of service in the Union army to establish occupied strongholds in the Southern states. Half the volunteers would remain under arms to protect the other half, who would form "an army of production in the rear."[6] In 1861 Thayer urged Lincoln to apply his plan in the border states, but he changed his target to northeast Florida after Federal forces occupied coastal towns in the winter of 1862. Thayer boasted he could return the state to the Union with only twenty thousand volunteers.

Stickney joined forces with Thayer following passage of the Direct Tax Law in June 1862. In 1843 Stickney had left his home state of Vermont to join the utopian community at New Harmony, Indiana, founded by Robert Owen. Later, he settled alongside the Caloosahatchie River near Fort Myers,

Florida, to cultivate tropical plants before moving to Tennessee to engage in railroad speculation and edit a newspaper. In 1860 Stickney returned to Fort Myers, intent on establishing a colony of Northern men. Secession and the outbreak of war, however, prompted him to hurry to Washington, where he established a close relationship with Chase that resulted in his appointment to the Florida Direct Tax Commission. Both men viewed the Florida tax commission as a means to advance Chase's political ambitions.[7]

Also appointed to the Florida Direct Tax Commission was John S. Sammis, a native of Dutchess County, New York, who had lived most of his adult years in Duval County, Florida. Married to Mary Kingsley Sammis, the daughter of Zephaniah Kingsley Jr. and his African wife, Anna Madgigine Jai Kingsley, Sammis became a wealthy planter, slaveholder, sawmill owner, and merchant. He and his large family had sought protection aboard the naval transports that departed Jacksonville in April 1862. Sammis had been one of the leaders of the movement to establish a loyal government at Jacksonville during the first Union occupation. He was the only man from East Florida appointed to the first Florida tax commission.[8]

Chase's third appointment to the Florida commission was Harrison Reed, a New England native who migrated to Wisconsin and became a newspaper publisher and Whig Party leader before becoming a Republican in 1860. Reed had never been to Florida and had no knowledge of its people or politics, but he was destined to become the state's first postwar governor. An employee of the Treasury Department in 1862, Reed was recommended for the tax commission appointment by Wisconsin governor Louis P. Harvey, numerous state legislators, and more than thirty U.S. congressmen.[9]

Jacksonville's exiled Unionists endorsed the appointments of Reed, Sammis, and Stickney to the tax commission and supported the Thayer colonization plan. At an October 24, 1862, rally in Brooklyn for the radical faction of the Republican Party, a former judge and mayor of Jacksonville, Philip Fraser, was introduced to the crowd as a victim who had been ground underfoot by the "iron heel" of Rebel tyranny. Fraser confessed that he had once been a slaveholder but that he now recognized the injustice of enslaving human beings and said he wanted nothing more than "a Union where every man shall be free, both North and South."[10]

The New York Times reported the tax commission appointments in a style that must have been encouraging for the Jacksonville exiles. "This is the commencement of a most important experiment, and one which, if successful, will result in the speedy return of rebel landholders to their allegiance, or replace them with the new and loyal population to whom their estates will fall a cheap prize, by reason of their alienation for taxes." To encourage Union supporters to participate in the experiment, the U.S. government had promised to execute the Direct Tax Law and to provide protection for individuals who purchased land at the auctions conducted by the tax commissioners. The *New York Times* reported that the new law was "designed to carry out Hon. Eli Thayer's scheme of white colonization, and all powers needed to insure success."[11]

Before leaving for Florida, the tax commissioners drafted a petition to Lincoln calling for Thayer's appointment as military governor of Florida. The petition stated that "Judge Fraser and the other prominent and loyal citizens of Florida" supported the measure. It had also been endorsed by Hamlin and 134 senators and representatives, and was presented to Lincoln with a request that "Thayer be authorized to enlist 20,000 volunteers for the armed colonization of the state."[12]

Lincoln had previously heard from a nine-state delegation of German Americans that "thousands of German citizens were ready and anxious to share the fortunes of the enterprise."[13] The president assured the delegates that he and his cabinet had carefully considered the Florida colonization plan and decided to implement it as soon as military campaigns then under way were concluded and troops were available to reoccupy areas of northeast Florida abandoned earlier in the year.[14] The plan was endorsed by the House Committee on Military Affairs, whose members were confident Jacksonville's Unionists would soon "return to their desolated possessions and rebuild their once beautiful homes and throw the old flag again to the breeze."[15] The congressmen also saw Florida as a refuge for the thousands of slaves who were escaping to Union lines, "a place at once ready, cheaply reached, and where they [escaped slaves] may find . . . abundance of employment in labors with which they are familiar, and in a climate admirably adapted to their wants."[16]

A group of influential New York politicians and businessmen invited Eli Thayer and Judge Philip Fraser to discuss the colonization plan at a mass meeting on January 23, 1863. A public meeting was held at the Cooper Institute in New York on February 7. One of the speakers, the famed abolitionist Cassius M. Clay, extolled the plan for Florida as "a great proposition . . . calculated to solve the question of slavery as well as the rebellion." The editor of the *New York Evening Post*, William Cullen Bryant, called for Florida's immediate restoration to the Union "by means of the organized immigration of armed free labor colonies, who are now ready to become permanent residents in that state."[17]

Despite this widespread support, Lincoln found the plan troublesome, especially the provisos for arbitrary confiscation of private property and the forced resettlement and permanent subjugation of the Southern white population. The president had also read editorials in the *New York Times* and the *New York Tribune* warning that the conquest of Florida would not strike a lasting military blow against the Confederacy. Ultimately, both the Thayer plan and the proposal to open regions of Florida for occupancy by free black settlers died a quiet death, but the lure of potential Union votes to be gained if Florida were restored as a loyal state continued to reverberate in the halls of power in Washington.[18]

In March 1863, Stickney, Reed, and Sammis were in Fernandina organizing the Florida Direct Tax Commission, with a plan to expand its area of operations as soon as they persuaded Federal officers to initiate a campaign to secure the inland farmlands and towns along the St. Johns. What they did not know was that the Union presence on the St. Johns had degenerated precipitously in the months after October 10, 1862, when the second Union occupation of Jacksonville ended.[19] Admiral Du Pont was aware of the situation. On March 9 he ordered Commander Steedman to conduct a reconnaissance of the St. Johns and to "make the best disposition of the force you have and assume a bold front on the St. Johns, or we shall be forced to abandon that river."[20] Du Pont was aware that Jacksonville continued to be a focal point for guerrilla bands and a small Confederate force under the command of General Finegan. Union gunboat captains observed several hundred inhabitants in the city in late 1862 and early 1863 and had received intelligence that a Confederate force of approximately four hundred men, led by Colonel Hopkins, was eight miles to the west at Camp Finegan.[21]

Cavalry officer Winston Stephens was at the camp, writing often to his wife to inform her of conditions in the town she had called home during her teen years. Stephens visited with families in Jacksonville and dutifully sent news to his wife, even if that news would not be well received. After a visit during the summer of 1862, prior to the second Yankee occupation of Jacksonville, Stephens commented that the men in his company were pleased to be posted so near the town and its pretty girls. He hastened to assure Octavia that at age thirty-three he was "too old for such things." Duty did call him to an establishment called the "Crespo Boarding House" that piqued his aging imagination. "What kind of people live there?" he asked his wife. "I rather think from appearances that things are conducted rather loosely as they were very familiar with some of the male gender. Some of them are good looking and rather fascinating to some but I am all right and you may rest easy, but I think some wives are cheated of some affection they should have."[22]

Octavia was furious when she learned her husband had been to the Crespo House. After receiving his letter, she was quick to reply: "I think you must have been bad off to go to those Minorcans. For pity sake don't go there again. I think it pretty queer that you the paymaster went there. For your sake as well as mine don't get your name out for going to such places." When Stephens next wrote he again asked his wife about the "girls" he had seen at the Crespo House. Octavia replied, in a revealing insight into ethnic prejudices of the time, "I know the family are low Minorcans. . . . I hope there is no particular attraction there. Mrs. Wallace has been married four times and I think all of her husbands but one are alive."[23]

Duties for Confederates were apparently not onerous in the days after the Yankees evacuated Jacksonville the second time. On November 20, 1862, Stephens told his wife that Camp Finegan was "in an uproar with fun and the noise would indicate contentment. . . . You would be amused at some of the tricks they fix upon one another and some of them get the hardest falls and bumps you ever saw, but as it is in fun they have to laugh it all off and try to pay off in the same coin."[24] Stephens was not participating in the merriment at the moment; he had just returned from a day in the saddle after riding more than thirty miles to inspect troop dispositions along the St. Johns.

Stephens reported that his men were "generally well but on short allowance which makes soldiers in bad humor, but I am in good humor as I have just had dinner—baked beef, potatoes . . . and rice with a little sugar for desert. . . . We have to purchase feed for our mess servants which makes bill of fare pretty high."[25] He avoided the burden of preparing his own food by forming a mess group with twelve other men to share the cost of provisions and the twenty-six-dollar monthly rental fee for a skilled cook named Felix, a slave owned by Benjamin Hopkins.[26] When they were in camps near the St. Johns River, meals often featured bass, catfish, and oysters.

Lieutenant Adolph Ochus recruited thirty-six new men in early February 1863, and Stephens filled the ranks of his 110-man Company B, 2nd Florida Cavalry.[27] Despite the improving morale at the camp, Stephens was growing tired of what he called "a wicked war" that had already caused "much unhappiness and distress." Chafing at the "strict military rule" at the camp, Stephens dug in his heels when Finegan attempted to convert the status of his men from state militia to regular Confederate soldiers: "I will not make regulars out of my men and they will not accept [my] resignation, and I don't care much what happens."[28] Stephens's dislike of Finegan had intensified to the point that Stephens was attempting to have the general removed from command. He blamed Finegan for "letting the Catholic religion . . . [control] the organization of the Regiment."[29] Stephens said he and Finegan met face-to-face at the end of October and "had quite a tongue lashing and every one standing by said I got the best of him," but the tension between the two men was never fully dissipated.[30]

The men's prime nemesis continued to be the Union gunboats that conducted regular patrols on the St. Johns. By early 1863, however, the Confederates had scored a few victories. On January 12, pickets stationed on the marsh adjacent to the Nassau River near what is today the town of Yulee "discovered one gunboat and two large transports with two schooners in tow going up Nassau River." Davis Bryant, Stephens's brother-in-law, concluded they were heading for Henry F. Holmes's sawmill, where the manager had stockpiled a large quantity of seasoned lumber. Traveling through the marsh in a fog so dense it forced the Union vessels to anchor and wait for better visibility, Bryant's men reached the mill in time to destroy the entire stockpile before the Union vessels were able to resume their journey.[31]

Following this triumph, Bryant and his companions hurried to a bluff to wait in ambush for the ships to return. He wrote with satisfaction that the gunboat "came 'tearing' back and imagine our satisfaction on seeing the other boats turn about and follow in her wake, disappointed as they must have been, returning empty." When one of the boats passed the bluff, Bryant said, Union sailors who had been protecting themselves from enemy fire came on the deck, whereupon "the fellows in the gulley opened fire on them, and of all the falling down and scrambling below you never saw the like, but before our boys had time to reload they commenced firing small arms from the boat. . . . The thing might have been bettered had we known the ground well, but I think all considered it was a 'glorious victory.' "[32]

While this action was under way, Stephens was at his upriver home at Welaka on furlough for one month to assist his wife during the birth of their second child, a daughter named Belle.[33] There would be little happiness in the months ahead for Stephens and his wife. Their newborn daughter became extremely ill and suffered intensely before dying on January 24, 1863. Octavia wrote one week later that the Lord "saw proper to take our darling . . . oh how hard the grief is to bear, but it is a blessing to know that she was perfectly pure and unspotted from sin and will go to Heaven where she will feel no more pain."[34] As Octavia suffered from intense grief and loneliness, her letters reflected a need for comfort from her husband and disgust with the ongoing war. On February 14 she wrote: "when will all these scouts end? Seems to me the war is no nearer the end now than it was months ago, seems to me we had as well live together under Lincoln's Government than to live separate most of the time under this Government, and are you now much more free than negroes, and the discipline becoming more and more strict. I suppose before long none of the soldiers will be allowed to go home at all."[35]

In an effort to break the spell of depression, Octavia made plans to meet her husband at Jacksonville. She was to travel by horse and buggy to Waldo accompanied by Felix, the enslaved man who cooked for Stephens and his mess group. Felix had been given permission to visit his enslaved wife and children at Welaka. From Waldo, Octavia and Felix were to travel by train to Jacksonville. On March 15, Rebecca Bryant, Octavia's mother, wrote in her diary that her daughter, "Tivie," and granddaughter, "Rosa," started in the buggy for Waldo, with "Felix walking."[36]

It was a well-intentioned plan, but the journey ended at Waldo, from where Octavia reluctantly returned to Welaka. An unexpected Union invasion of Jacksonville had occurred five days earlier. White Floridians reacted in fear and terror to the news that black Union soldiers had captured and were in occupation of the town. Expressions of outrage were heard, not dissimilar to the feelings heard in previous decades concerning rumors of slave rebellions. Davis Bryant warned that "the poor ill starred old place . . . is again taken possession of and occupied by the yankees and garrisoned with nigger troops. . . . If those niggers are brought out into the State as they say they intend, you'll hear some of the 'damdest fights' you ever heard tell of, as every man of us is determined to do his best towards wiping them out completely."[37]

That black troops would be used in a Union expedition up the St. Johns should not have come as a complete surprise to the Confederates of East Florida. In mid-1862, prompted by military reverses, serious shortages of fighting men, and realization that the conflict would likely become a long war of attrition, the Lincoln administration did an about-face and authorized the enlistment of black men—free blacks from the North—in regiments composed of black troops and white officers. Ironically, the first black regiment formed was made up primarily of black men from the South, including many escaped slaves from Duval, Nassau, and St. Johns counties. By early November these same black men had conducted successful raids along the Georgia and Florida coasts. Brigadier General Rufus Saxton saw in these expeditions the germ of a larger war policy, one that could cripple plantation production, deliver a psychological blow to the Confederates, and force the Confederate command to divert manpower from battlefields further north.

With thousands of escaped slaves crowded into refugee camps wherever Federal forces were in occupation, abolitionists increased pressure on Congress and the president to provide black males with arms and form them into army regiments. Aware of persistent racism among whites in the North, Lincoln proceeded cautiously, worried that an emancipation proclamation and enlistment of black men in the Union army would prompt border states to secede from the Union and join the Confederate States of America. Although he was personally an abolitionist by this time, Lincoln kept his feelings private while he pursued a policy he thought was vital to preserving the Union.[38]

A former U.S. senator from Kansas, James Lane, organized a black regiment in the summer of 1862, only to be informed by Secretary of War Stanton that he had no authority to organize black troops. In Louisiana an officer under command of Benjamin Butler organized five companies of free black men into a military unit in July and August 1862. Butler, in communication with Stanton, refused to provide arms to the recruits, and limited their activities to manual labor at Union fortifications. But even prior to these incidents in Kansas and Louisiana, an effort to organize a black regiment from refugees in South Carolina occurred that was destined to have far-reaching repercussions.[39]

Major General Hunter, newly appointed to command the Department of the South, initiated a series of dramatic actions that he thought had been authorized by the First Confiscation Act in August 1861. It was his understanding that the act made it legal to seize Confederate-owned property that had been used to aid the rebellion, including slaves who labored at Rebel fortifications.[40] On April 13, 1862, Hunter granted freedom to all slaves at Fort Pulaski and Cockspur Island, Georgia.[41] On May 9 he went even further, declaring that "Slavery and martial law in a free country are altogether incompatible. . . . The persons in these three states, Georgia, Florida, and South Carolina, heretofore held as slaves are therefore declared forever free."[42]

On that same day, May 9, 1862, Hunter sent soldiers to the Treasury Department plantations on Port Royal Island with the assignment of delivering "every able bodied negro between the age of eighteen and forty-five capable of bearing arms" to his headquarters at Hilton Head within twenty-four hours. The plantation superintendents condemned these recruiting tactics as "impressment" and "violent conscription," but a correspondent for the *New York Post* reported the recruits were settled into comfortable camps at Beaufort and were clothed, sheltered, and well fed while they engaged in routine military training activities.[43] The men were apparently armed, although unofficially, and were put through military training with the intention of providing protection for freedmen and -women who were plantation laborers in the Union-occupied coastal zones.

On May 19, Lincoln responded with a rebuke of Hunter's emancipation declarations. Still fearful of instigating secession in the border states, and possibly miffed that Hunter had acted without first consulting him, Lincoln declared that no Union official, including the president, had the authority to emancipate slaves. It was alleged at the time that Lincoln learned of the emancipation order by reading a newspaper account of it. Still hoping for a compromise on the slavery issue, Lincoln chose instead to support Congress's resolution: "That the United States ought to co-operate with any state that may adopt a gradual abolishment of slavery, giving to such State pecuniary aid, to be used by such State in its discretion, to compensate for the inconveniences, public and private, produced by such change of system."[44]

By the middle of 1862, many in the North believed that emancipation and the enlistment of the newly freed black men—if the Union army opened its ranks to black men—could be decisive in the outcome of the war. "Our army needs the 'aid and comfort,' which can be obtained from contrabands, and in accepting it we deprive the enemy of an element of strength," one man wrote to the *New York Times*. The author succinctly captured a current belief that without slaves to work the land and build fortifications, the Confederate army would quickly succumb to Union forces.[45] On August 6 the *Times* published another argument gaining in popularity: "Why should we fight the battles alone, while they stand ready to offer their help?" To reduce loss of life for white soldiers, citizens of the Union were becoming increasingly willing to consider options that had previously been unthinkable.

Many in the North feared a negative reaction from the border states if slaves were emancipated and enrolled in Union regiments. Others refused to believe that former slaves were interested in bearing arms or capable of performing military duty. Still others advocated a variety of compromise policies, such as allowing blacks to enlist and work on fortifications but not be provided arms. Another argument heard at the time was that the Confederacy used slave laborers to build fortifications and perform labor services at military camps, so the Union might as well arm blacks to balance the odds.[46]

On June 16 the House of Representatives finished an investigation and concluded that Hunter was not authorized to muster "fugitive or captive slaves" into military units. Three days later, Lincoln released a proclamation clarifying Union policy on "the Contraband Problem" and announcing that he did not intend to put rifles in the hands of former slaves. On August 6 the *New York Times* reported that Lincoln "would employ all colored men as laborers, but would not promise to make soldiers of them."

Without authorization or funding, Hunter recognized the futility of continuing what many saw as a quixotic effort. On August 10 he notified Stanton of his decision to disband the regiment known as the "Hunter Conscripts." He permitted only Company A, the first one hundred men recruited, to remain in Union service. Lieutenant Charles Trowbridge continued to command the company, with orders from Hunter to provide protection for the refugee blacks at labor on the abandoned plantations.[47]

Only two weeks after Hunter's troops were disbanded, the Union government reconsidered its objections to organizing black troops. On August 25, with the full support of the Lincoln administration, Stanton ordered Saxton to begin a campaign "to arm, equip, and receive into the service of the United States such number of volunteers of African descent as you may deem expedient, not exceeding 5,000, and ... detail officers to instruct them in military drill, discipline, and duty, and to command them."[48] It must have come as a shock to Hunter that while the news of his failed experiment was still being discussed around Union campfires, Saxton was already appointing officers and recruiting men for the first officially sanctioned black regiment in the Union army.[49]

As military governor of the District of Beaufort, Department of the South, Saxton made organizing and supervising life and labor at the tax commission plantations his first priority. A religious man keenly interested in the economic, moral, and civic advancement of the freedmen under his care, Saxton gave orders to the plantation superintendents that reflected his abolitionist principles. Each plantation superintendent was required to agree that slavery was morally wrong and to sign an oath promising to "use all means in my power so to educate and elevate the people under my control as to fit them to enjoy the blessings of freedom."[50]

Saxton was also in charge of the military activities of the black regiment being formed, although he visited the camps only occasionally and never went into the field with the men. When he formed the new regiment, he mustered in as Company A the first company inducted into the Hunter Conscripts and recruited nine additional companies to fill out the regiment. Because Company A had remained in active volunteer service during the months between the time the Hunter Conscripts disbanded and the new regiment was mustered into service, it would eventually establish the longest continuous service record of any black military unit in the war. Saxton recognized that Trowbridge was dedicated to the cause of freedom and had the respect of his soldiers, and therefore he promoted him to captain of Company A.

Trowbridge was in continuous contact with black soldiers for a longer period than any other white officer in the Civil War. He was appointed to the rank of lieutenant colonel and to command of the regiment late in the war. After the regiment mustered out he accepted an appointment to work for the Freedmen's Bureau.[51] The author of Trowbridge's obituary was of the opinion that "he was robbed of credit for organizing the first colored regiment by an official hocus pocus, which failed to recognize his organization until after one organized by Colonel Shaw of Boston had been officially mustered in."[52]

The soldiers of the regiment were recruited from among the thousands of contrabands and free blacks concentrated at tax commission plantations and at refugee camps at Union-occupied Fernandina, St. Augustine, and Key West in Florida and at Beaufort in South Carolina. While the men were undergoing military training in August, Saxton arranged a test of their fighting merit. In early November he sent them on raids along the Georgia and north Florida coast. At the conclusion of the expedition, the commander of the raid, Lieutenant Colonel Oliver Beard, said: "I started from Saint Simon's with 62 colored fighting men and returned to Beaufort with 156 fighting men (all colored). As soon as we took a slave from his claimant we placed a musket in his hand and he began to fight for the freedom of others."[53] Saxton told Stanton that the raids had been a "perfect success. . . . The negroes fought with a coolness and bravery that would have done credit to veteran soldiers. There was no excitement, no flinching, no attempt at cruelty when successful. They seemed like men who were fighting to vindicate their manhood and they did it well."[54]

Summing up the efficacy of the campaign, Saxton said one of its goals had been "to prove the fighting qualities of the Negroes (which some have doubted), and the other was to bring away the people from the main-land, destroy all rebel salt works, and break up the rebel picket stations along the line of the coast." He concluded: "the expedition was a perfect success. Rarely in the progress of this war has so much mischief been done by so small a force in so short a space of time. Thirteen different landings were made. The pickets in every case were driven in, the salt-works destroyed, and all the work finished up before the enemy could collect a sufficient force to overpower our men."[55]

Saxton captured Stanton's attention by writing: "I trust that you will appreciate the importance of the First South Carolina Volunteers. It seems to me one of the important events of the war—one that will carry terror to the hearts of the rebels. It discloses an objective point where the hardest blow can be dealt against the rebellion."[56] He urged the secretary of war to expand these coastal raids and to intensify pressure on the Confederates of the region by arming and fortifying a number of light-draft vessels, each manned by one hundred black soldiers, to run up the coastal rivers and capture plantations. Expecting hundreds of slaves to flock to the nearest wharf when they heard the gunboat whistles, Saxton could "see no limit to which our successes might not be pushed, up to the entire occupation of States."[57]

The man Saxton chose to command the regiment was Thomas Wentworth Higginson, a well-known abolitionist, graduate of the Harvard Divinity School, novelist, Unitarian minister, and a captain in the Fifty-first Massachusetts Regiment.[58] Sensing that a dramatic chapter in the history of the nation was about to be written, Higginson seized the opportunity to command the 1st South Carolina: "I had been an abolitionist too long, and had known and loved John Brown too well, not to feel a thrill of joy at last on finding myself in the position where he only wished to be."[59] Historian Dudley Cornish described Higginson as a man who "could no more ignore the opportunity of striking hard blows against slavery" than he could have "stopped breathing by an act of will."[60]

Higginson's motivations are revealed in a transcript of an interview he gave in 1863 to members of the Office of American Freedmen's Inquiry Commission, a government-sponsored panel charged with determining whether freedmen could properly serve the country as soldiers. Higginson said it was important to make soldiers of black men because the Union army was "the best school in the world" and "it makes men of them at once."[61] He further explained that "the more intelligent" of the former slaves "not only feel that it is their duty to fight for their own freedom, but by proper appeal many of them can be made to understand that only by proving their manhood as soldiers, only through baptism of blood, can they bring about such a change in public opinion as will insure for their race, from the present generation in this country, common respect and decent treatment in their social relations with whites."[62]

A stickler for drill and discipline, Higginson put his troops through a rigorous training schedule that stressed order and military discipline, but he also instilled abolitionist ideals in the recruits through his daily talks on the meaning of freedom. On November 25, 1862, he told the men: "You are fighting for your own liberty and the liberty of your children. Nobody can make you free unless you have the courage to fight for your own freedom. And if you resolve to be free nobody can make you slaves."[63]

Higginson lavished praise on the men of his regiment who were from north Florida, saying on one occasion that "the finest men physically were from Florida, and these men, having been pilots and fishermen, had more knowledge of the world than those from South Carolina, who had lived chiefly on isolated plantations all their days."[64] On December 2, 1862, Higginson wrote in his diary: "Today General Saxton has returned from Fernandina with seventy-six recruits, and the eagerness of the captains to secure them was a sight to see." The following day he commented on a special company of "all Florida men . . . the finest looking company I ever saw, white or black; they range admirably in size, have remarkable erectness and ease of carriage, and really march splendidly. Not a visitor but notices them; yet they have been under drill only a fortnight."[65]

Higginson might have been referring to Company G, which included 57 Florida-born men among the first 106 enrollees. The regimental muster rolls indicate that the three loyal regiments from South Carolina—known eventually as the 33rd, 34th, and 21st regiments of United States Colored Troops—enlisted more than a thousand men who had lived in northeast Florida prior to the war. Considering that the 1860 U.S. Census for Florida listed 11,756 slaves of both sexes and all ages for Clay, Duval, Nassau, and St. Johns counties, and that many owners either sold their chattels or moved them to more secure locations in the interior of Florida prior to the arrival of Union troops, the one thousand volunteers represent a significant percentage of the adult male slaves living in the region in 1862.[66]

The volunteers came from surprisingly diverse circumstances. Based on a sample of 364 recruits from the region, the median age was twenty-four, yet forty-two gave their age at the time of muster as between forty and sixty years. The majority of the recruits, 65 percent, were engaged in some form of agricultural enterprise; 10 percent were employed in skilled crafts, as carpenters, machinists, tailors, shoemakers, and bricklayers. Two who had been free before the war were engineers. Fourteen men gave teamster, drayman, wagon driver, hostler, or coachman as their occupation, while nine said they had been lumbermen or sawyers, and twelve said they were boatmen or sailors when enslaved. Fifty-seven had been cooks, waiters, or servants in towns that drew business travelers and tourists. From St. Augustine alone came twenty-five waiters and three cooks.

As Higginson prepared his men for battle, the government and the public followed the news of the regiments' activities with intense curiosity. Northerners wondered if former slaves would be able to cope with the strict rules of military discipline, given their background of servitude. The debate over whether black men possessed sufficient intelligence or bravery for military duty was a persistent staple of Northern newspapers and periodicals. According to Higginson, the officers of black regiments were aware that both they and their men were under intense public scrutiny.[67]

Higginson's first Florida expedition began at Beaufort on January 23, 1863, with 462 officers and men aboard the *John Adams*, *Ben DeFord*, and *Planter* headed for the St. Marys River on a mission to carry the Emancipation Proclamation into the interior and to plunder lumber mills and ransack the countryside. Higginson kept Corporal Robert Sutton close by his side to act as guide and adviser. Sutton knew from experience every bend of the river: before escaping to Union-occupied Fernandina, he was owned by Edwin Alberti of Woodstock Mills on the St. Marys River, a major target of the January 1863 expedition.

Both Higginson and Dr. Seth Rogers, the regimental surgeon, held Sutton in the highest regard. To Higginson, Sutton appeared "kingly" and was "the wisest man in our ranks"; his intellect was "meditative and systematic ... and lucid and accurate."[68] Rogers compared the black corporal to the Haitian revolutionary leader Toussaint-Louverture: "I never look at Robert without feeling certain that his father must have been a great Nubian king. I have rarely reverenced a man more than I do him. His manners are exceedingly simple, unaffected and dignified, without the slightest touch of haughtiness. Voice low, soft, and flooding, as if his thought were choking him, he is tall, straight and brawny muscled." In addition to his impressive physical attributes, Sutton's demeanor was dignified and commanding. Rogers felt that Sutton "ought to be a leader, a general instead of a corporal. I fancy him like Toussaint L'Ouverture and it would not surprise me if some great occasion should make him a deliverer of his people from bondage."[69]

At Township, Florida, a detachment of Higginson's men surrounded by a company of mounted Floridians lost one man killed and seven wounded, but not before "emptying at the first discharge thirteen saddles and killing and wounding many more."[70] The invaders proceeded up the "narrow, swift, winding [river] bordered at many places with high bluffs, which blazed with rifle shots" as Confederate riders galloped "through the woods from point to point to await us . . . so daring against musketry that one rebel actually sprang from the shore upon the large boat . . . where he was shot down." The black troops showed equal daring, "loading and firing with inconceivable rapidity, and shouting to each other, 'Never give up.'" When ordered below deck "they actually fought each other for places at the few port holes from which they could fire on the enemy."[71]

The expedition ended at Woodstock Mills, where Higginson met Mrs. Alberti, the widow managing the estate and the former owner of Corporal Sutton. Higginson felt she had a "courtly" bearing until he introduced her to "Corporal Robert Sutton." He later recalled the look on Alberti's face when she recognized the man: "I never saw a finer bit of unutterable indignation than came over the face of my hostess. . . . 'Ah' said she, after some reflection, 'We call him Bob.'" Sutton, meanwhile, took the introduction in stride: "He simply turned from the lady, touched his hat to me, and asked if I would wish to see the slave-jail."[72]

Dr. Rogers, who was also present when Mrs. Alberti was introduced to her former slave, wrote that "Madam Alberti spent much time trying to convince me that she and her husband had been wonderfully devoted to the interests of their slaves, especially to the fruitless work of trying to educate them." The surgeon lost all respect for the widow when he followed Corporal Sutton to a "strong slave jail" the Albertis maintained that contained "implements of torture which we now have in our possession, (the lock I have)."[73] The New York Times correspondent who accompanied the expedition recorded that "Madame Alberti's slave baracoon" contained "iron collars, bracelets for wrists and ankles for both sexes," and chains, stocks, and other devices used to punish slaves or keep them in close confinement.[74]

Sutton later described the expedition and the meeting with Mrs. Alberti to Dr. Esther Hill Hawks, a Yankee volunteer who traveled with the regiment to teach the soldiers during time away from their military duties. Dr. Hawks recounted the incident in her diary: "It was a proud moment for Robert when he placed a guard of colored soldiers around the house of his former owner, 'Madam Alberti' and one of great rage to the good dame when she discovered the outrage, and heard her own nigger, 'our Bob,' give the order to shoot anyone who attempted to leave the house without his permission!"[75]

While returning to camp aboard the gunboat, Dr. Rogers praised the courage, dependability, and trustworthiness of the black soldiers. He felt the expedition had been a "capital success. . . . We are satisfied that the blacks must help us in this war. The next question to solve, is, how to penetrate far enough into the interior to solve this problem. Give us a good gunboat and plenty of ammunition to help us into the midst of them and I think we may trust God and our determination for the result."[76] Winston Stephens, who confronted the invaders, thought differently. He called the mission a "general thieving expedition." Stephens's brother-in-law, Willie Bryant, wrote: "What makes it more maddening is they are all nigger soldiers, officered by white men."[77]

The success of the expedition convinced Higginson that others like it should be made in East Florida to establish posts where his black soldiers could rally the slave population and seize strategic materials. "No officer in this regiment now doubts that the key to the successful prosecution of this war lies in the unlimited employment of black troops," he wrote in his official report. Higginson singled out Sutton as "the real conductor of the whole expedition."[78] After reading Higginson's report, Saxton informed Stanton that the expedition "foreshadows clearly the very important advantages which might result to our cause by the extensive arming of the blacks. . . . In my humble opinion it would be no misapplication of the best energies of the Government should they now be directed toward the arming and disciplining of every one that can be brought within our lines."[79]

Lyman Stickney, the district tax commissioner at Fernandina, was delighted by the success of the expedition and added his voice to the chorus calling for the use of black troops in Florida. He argued that an expedition up the St. Johns was necessary to recapture Jacksonville and hold it permanently as a base to extend the tax commission's jurisdiction. Stickney no doubt mentioned the most recent reports of Commander Woodhull extolling a revival of Union sentiment among residents of the area "and a decided wish for the termination of the war."[80]

Du Pont's was the only dissenting voice to be heard at the moment. Short of men and gunboats, Du Pont informed his wife that "no Union man dare land in Florida except under the guns of my gunboats, and yet people are sent from home to tax lands which we do not hold. So to remedy this, they propose to send the black regiment to hold Jacksonville." The admiral scoffed at Stickney's boast that twenty thousand slaves could be easily gathered by black troops, and "told him and General Saxton that his regiment could not exist a week in Jacksonville unless I surrounded the place."[81]

Negotiations proceeded in spite of Du Pont's reluctance, and Higginson soon learned that Saxton's plan went far beyond another raid up a Florida river. Saxton told him, "It is my opinion that the entire State of Florida can be rescued from the enemy, and an asylum established for persons from other States who are freed from bondage by the proclamation of freedom."[82] Higginson's confidence that slaves would flock to his picket lines once his black regiment established a solid base in Florida convinced Du Pont that the plan had merit, and soon all the negotiators agreed that "it was worthwhile to risk something . . . to hold Florida, and perhaps bring it back into the Union."[83]

Early in March 1863, after receiving approval of his plan from Hunter, Saxton ordered Higginson and his regiment to proceed to Fernandina aboard the steamers *John Adams*, *Boston*, and *Burnside*. From Fernandina, the men of the 1st South Carolina were to venture up the St. Johns River to capture and occupy Jacksonville. The goals of the expedition were "to carry the proclamation of freedom to the enslaved; to call all loyal men into the service of the United States; to occupy as much of the State of Florida as possible with the forces under your command; and to neglect no means consistent with the usages of civilized warfare to weaken, harass, and annoy those who are in rebellion against the Government of the United States."[84]

Somehow, distorted reports of the planned expedition were leaked to the New York press. The nine hundred men of Higginson's regiment were transformed by the newspaper reports into a "liberating host" of five thousand, and the expedition fantasized into "servile insurrection" that will "swell to a wave so mighty that it will sweep both Rebellion and Slavery out of existence wherever it may roll."[85] These were phrases designed to terrify and infuriate Southern white men; it was inflammatory propaganda, and Higginson was incensed. He planned a freedom crusade, not a battle of attrition, and he wanted the third occupation of Jacksonville to come as a complete surprise to Florida's Confederate defenders.

"These Are United States Troops and They Will Not Dishonor the Flag"

The Third Occupation
of Jacksonville

Thomas W. Higginson, in command of the 1st South Carolina Loyal Volunteers, received confidential orders on February 25, 1863, to prepare his men for a voyage of at least ten days aboard the steamers *Boston, Burnside,* and *John Adams.* Higginson was subsequently told that his men were to capture and occupy Jacksonville. They would have the support of Colonel James Montgomery's volunteers, 125 black men recently recruited at refugee camps at Key West. Montgomery was planning to fill the ranks of what would become the 2nd South Carolina Loyal Volunteers by recruiting "in the field" at farms and plantations along the St. Johns River and in the interior of the state. As historian Stephen V. Ash has written, Higginson, Montgomery, and "the 1st South Carolina Infantry would invade Florida to make war on slavery."[1]

The ships departed Beaufort, South Carolina, at 4 p.m. on March 5, stopping first at Fernandina. On the morning of the ninth, the *Boston* and the *Burnside* dropped anchor outside the bar at the entrance to the St. Johns to wait for the transport carrying Montgomery's men that had been delayed in departing Fernandina. Higginson was frustrated by the delay. A full day passed with ships and men immobilized in hot and sultry weather, the breeze so calm that the surface of the river was like glass. The troops took advantage of the delay, fishing and shooting at pelicans while their officers visited Pilot Town and Mayport. Higginson also went ashore to inspect the "rather pathetic little gardens" of vegetables planted by the gunboat crews on permanent station at the river's entrance. He walked along the sand dunes viewing the wave-like sand drifts that almost covered some of the houses. Other officers ordered foraging parties into the countryside and rejoiced when the men returned "with a fat beef, slung on a pole, that had fallen victim to good marksmanship."[2] Chickens and fresh vegetables were also found by the foragers, who must have presented a comic sight as they straggled back toward the beach with their feathery burdens strung upside down, tied by their legs to the soldiers' musket barrels and cackling noisy protest at their treatment.

As the hours of the delay wore on, however, Higginson began to worry. Aware that parts of Jacksonville had been burned in March 1862, he feared it might again be burned: "It seemed as if the news of our arrival must surely have traveled thirty miles by this time. All day we watched every smoke that rose from the wooded hills, and consulted the compass and the map to see if that sign announced the doom of our expected home."[3] No sign was discovered that the expeditionary force had been detected, however, and the night passed without incident. Surgeon Seth Rogers was less forgiving than Higginson. Even after hearing of fog so dense at Fernandina that the captain of the transport, the *John Adams*, deemed it unsafe to pass over the bar, Rogers complained: "If the rebels are not duller than I think them, we shall suffer for this most annoying delay."[4]

Shortly after midnight on March 10, the *John Adams* arrived in time to cross the bar on a favorable tide. At 2 a.m., under a bright moon, the troop transports started upriver, led by the gunboats *Norwich*, *Uncas*, and *Paul Jones*. Though he was aware of danger from underwater explosives and snipers, Higginson described the cruise as a "bewitching" excursion through a "world of romance" as the ships proceeded upriver. His Florida-born recruits were "wild with delight, and when we rounded the point below the city, and saw from afar its long streets, its brick warehouses, its white cottages, and its overshadowing trees—all peaceful and undisturbed by flames—it seemed, in the men's favorite phrase, 'too much good,' and all discipline was merged, for the moment, in a buzz of ecstasy."[5]

It was 8 a.m. on the tenth when the gunboats drew near the Jacksonville wharves. Higginson saw "children playing on the wharves, careless men here and there, lounged down to look at us, hands in pockets; a few women came to their doors, and gazed listlessly upon us, shading their eyes with their hands." Higginson was fearful of a party waiting in ambush, "yet no sign of danger was seen; not a rifle-shot was heard; not a shell rose hissing in the air . . . the pretty town was our own without a shot . . . the surprise had been complete."[6]

A correspondent for the *New York Times* reported: "the first knowledge of the invasion only came to the townspeople when they saw the black soldiers marching past their dwellings."[7] A small Confederate picket force was barely able to escape capture as they fled westward to alert Rebel cavalry that black troops had landed and were "going in every direction trying to capture all they could."[8]

It was late in the day before the debarkation was complete and the troops were dispersed into defensive positions. Captain William Lee Apthorp, with Montgomery's regiment, had worried that "we should not land without wetting the gangplank with blood, but land we did, and peaceably. We found everything quiet. A few mounted pickets skedaddled and a few secesh ladies who came down to welcome us, seeing the dusky hue of our men, followed the example of the pickets."[9]

Montgomery's men moved to the outskirts of town to set up a line of defense. Montgomery found shelter in a deserted dwelling at the edge of town. Apthorp and the men of his company "lay on our arms all night, springing up at various alarms caused by nervous pickets, and when daylight came it found our men not at all refreshed by sleep."[10]

In the morning, Apthorp began teaching his raw recruits how to march and how to use their weapons, stopping abruptly when they heard the sound of horses galloping toward them. Two hundred cavalrymen had gathered in the woods opposite Apthorp's camp and surprised the untrained black infantrymen. "We waited there for fire and received it," Apthorp recalled. "One man fell severely wounded. . . . Our men returned the fire with some effect. The rebels wheeled and put on another volley as coolly and firmly as if it was not the first time they had ever smelt powder."

When his men ran out of ammunition, Apthorp ordered them to fall back to protective cover near the town. The men had never received training in this maneuver, yet they did not panic. They "rallied by a wood and marched steadily to again meet the foe they knew was twice their strength." Instead of facing a cavalry charge, however, they faced "a strong force of infantry stretched across the field and opened a hot fire." The black men held off the infantry charge and then "fell back under the [protective] fire of the gunboats . . . and the repulse begun by us was turned by a few shell and shrapnel into a rout." Apthorp reported that the "behavior of the men was impeccable, and this when they were entirely without drill and they had only had [weapons] two days." He thought the enemy had learned a valuable lesson: "that a black man could stand up and pull a trigger and that a bullet from his rifle was as deadly a thing to receive as if a white man had fired it."[11]

Higginson had not been at the outskirts of town while the encounter with the Confederates was under way. He was instead at the wharf supervising unloading and occupation efforts. The first night he took shelter in a grove of linden trees where "mocking birds sang like nightingales," but he kept his men under arms. Daylight gave him the opportunity to study the city and its surroundings. He found "the wharves were capacious, and the blocks of brick warehouses along the lower street [Bay Street] were utterly unlike anything we had yet seen in that region, as were the neatness and thrift everywhere visible."[12] He estimated that approximately five hundred civilians remained in the town, "semi-loyal only," and "very poor so that I shall have to issue rations to them." The provost marshal, Captain James Rogers, was instructed to set up police patrols to protect the residents. Dr. Rogers, Captain Rogers's uncle, provided medical treatment for the sick among them.

The residential sections of the town earned Higginson's praise: "There are fine rows of brick houses, all empty, along the wharf, and the houses and gardens are very pretty." He established command headquarters in the same dwelling he chose for his personal quarters, the "handsome brick house" owned by attorney and planter John P. Sanderson, a Vermonter who was absent on Confederate service. "My house, the chief one in town, is new and really magnificent, with beautiful gas fixtures and superb marble fireplaces. The streets are shaded with fine trees."[13] Higginson thought it "funny to go into a strange city & go to housekeeping in another man's house," calling the absent owner a "rich lawyer" and noting that whenever "the Union or Confederate troops have been here, this has been the Head quarters, but entirely uninjured. Brick kitchen adjoining with every convenience & lingering pickles, a brick office opening out of my private room, & accessible by another door from the street. The office is lined with great empty book cases, & we have furniture enough for the house. The field officers &c are with me."[14]

Dr. Rogers judged Jacksonville to be the one place in the South he would consider making his residence after the war ended (he instead chose nearby Green Cove Springs). "The town gradually rises from the river, back a third or half a mile. Streets and houses have gas fixtures, a New England look to everything, streets beautifully shaded by live oaks, now and then a cornus Florida, the ground paved with its white petals, peach trees in full bloom."[15]

Worried about security inside the town, Higginson ordered all white men to report to him to have their names recorded and take an oath of loyalty. Those who refused were locked up. All white males were required to carry passes when they walked the streets and to present the passes to the black soldiers on guard at the corners. To secure the approaches to the city, Higginson reluctantly ordered barricades constructed at strategic intersections, using many of the beautiful trees that lined the city's streets: "[It] went to my heart to sacrifice . . . several of my beautiful lindens; but it was no time for aesthetics. As the giants lay on the ground, still scenting the air with their abundant bloom, I used to rein up my horse and watch the children playing hide-and-seek among their branches, or some quiet cow grazing at the foliage."[16]

To create clear lines of fire for his riflemen, Higginson gave orders to clear heavy stands of pine and oak along the railroad line at the western outskirts of the town. Fifty dwellings "of an inferior class" that had sheltered free blacks and slaves prior to the war were torched. Two earthwork forts reinforced with large tree trunks were constructed on the vulnerable western approach to the town. Named Fort Higginson and Fort Montgomery, the earthworks were strategically placed on either side of the railroad track, near the present intersection of Broad and Adams streets. A correspondent for the *New York Tribune* compared them to the best earthwork fortifications he had seen the army erect anywhere in the South during the war.[17]

Higginson felt the soldiers' work put "the town in a pretty strong position . . . the streets are barricaded . . . [but] we do not go outside at night."[18] To protect against an enemy arsonist, troops not on picket were lodged in the second story of the brick buildings that lined Bay Street. Higginson realized he commanded too few troops to assault Camp Finegan, eight miles to the west and several miles beyond the protective range of the artillery aboard the gunboats. He also feared the Confederates would rush reinforcements to the area and attempt to retake the town. To discourage this, Higginson did his best to give the impression that he commanded more soldiers than were actually in the town. He ceased holding dress parades, did not allow groups of soldiers to congregate in any one location, and made "judicious use . . . of empty tents."[19]

Higginson was concerned about the reception his black troops would receive from the white residents of the town, but he was confident his men would conduct themselves with dignity. During training drills he reminded his men that they were fighting for a noble cause: for their own freedom and the liberty of their children and their children's children. Some of the men were returning as conquerors of the town where they had been slaves only a few months before: twenty-six men from Duval County were members of only one company of the 1st South Carolina. Others were scattered throughout the 1st and 2nd South Carolina regiments, among them Amos, Andrew, and Edward Forrester; Anthony, Stephan, and Boston Brani; William Noble, a former blacksmith in Jacksonville; Frank Hagan, a onetime St. Johns River boatman; and Simon and Smart Primus, August Creighton, and Adam Robinson, all born in Mandarin.[20]

One of the men in his regiment, a northeast Florida man named Private Thomas Long, best expressed the lasting meaning of black men serving in the Union army. "If we hadn't become sojers, all might have gone back as it was before; our freedom might have slipped through de two houses of Congress and Presient Linkum's four years might have passed by and notin' been done for us. But now tings can neber go back, because we have showed our energy and our courage and our naturally manhood." Thinking of future generations of African Americans, Long said: "suppose you had kep your freedom witout enlisting in dis army; your children might have growed up free and been well cultivated . . . but it would have been always flung in dere faces—'Your fader never fought for he own freedom'—and what could day answer? Neber can say to dis African Race no more."[21]

The return of these former slaves in uniforms of Union blue, come to subjugate Jacksonville and spearhead a movement to bring Florida back into the Union, had an immediate impact on the whites living in the city. Higginson said that on arrival the town's residents had been polite, "some overjoyed, some secretly cursing, some of the women hate the black soldiers, others say they have known many of the men all their lives, & it does not seem like being among strangers." Some residents regarded the occupation by their former slaves as "the last crowning humiliation . . . and they were, or professed to be, in perpetual fear."[22]

Many of his men "had private wrongs to avenge," but Higginson was confident they "took too much pride in their character as soldiers" to allow their "honor and dignity" to be tarnished "by any misdeeds." Nevertheless, tension developed between troops and civilians, with the latter charging the blacks with misconduct and abuses of authority. The soldiers complained about the civilians, especially about the women, who they said "insulted them most grossly, swearing at them, and the like." Higginson marveled at the self-restraint of the former slaves, especially when two of his men led him to the spot where "they had seen their brothers hanged by Lynch law."[23] Higginson said in addition: "My men have behaved perfectly well, though many were owned here and do not love the people as you may suppose. There has been no wanton outrage."[24]

Dr. Rogers also commented on the charges of misconduct white women leveled against the black troops, recounting one instance in which a soldier was accused of being "very much" insulting when in fact he had only taken a seat on the woman's front stoop. It pleased Rogers to write: "Many of our soldiers are natives of this place and meet their old mistresses here. On the day of our landing I was over and over implored, by those who knew their deserts [escaped slaves], to protect them from the 'niggers.' It was an awful turning of the tables. I quite enjoyed saying 'These are United States troops and they will not dishonor the flag.'"[25]

After a combination of warnings from Confederate officers that women and children would be in danger if an attack occurred and complaints from civilians who demanded to leave the city, Higginson permitted 150 white residents to depart under troop escort. Army wagons carried those who needed transport to a church near the brickyard west of town, where Confederate soldiers waited. Higginson allowed men to leave, although his own officers warned they might join General Finegan's army. Higginson said he "wished to have his enemies in front where he could fight them" rather than in town at his rear where they could be neither fought nor trusted. Finegan kept a tally of the departing residents and reported on March 20 that "all but a few families had been safely evacuated under flag of truce."[26]

Some local whites had good reason to fear for their personal safety. Hattie Reed, daughter of A. M. Reed of Mulberry Grove plantation outside Jacksonville, was startled to see a soldier who only recently had been the property of her father. She wrote to Confederate cavalry officer Davis Bryant that the former slave, known to her family as "long legged Jake," had returned as a "bold soldier boy" after escaping to a Union gunboat the previous spring. This time he was carrying a rifle and bayonet, and also harboring a bitter grudge against Hattie Reed's father for selling Jake's wife, Etta, into slavery somewhere in Georgia. Hattie said he "wants to meet Pa face to face to teach him what it is to part man and wife."[27] Jake later made a public threat to burn the Reed home and put a loaded gun to the head of a white man who had shot at him the night he had escaped. When Jake's behavior was reported to the provost marshal, Higginson had him arrested and confined to the guardhouse.

One local white man harbored grudges as bitter as Jake's toward A. M. Reed. Angry over events in the war that made it possible for so many slaves to escape from their masters, he took grim satisfaction from reports of injuries and death suffered by the escapees. He wrote to a friend to report that "Our negro Ted was among the troops at Jacksonville, also Mrs. Duval's boy Henry. Henry was mortally wounded in one of their skirmishes and has since died. So out of five who left our plantation last year only two are well and strong. . . . Does this not seem a just retribution?"[28] Aware of such sentiments, Higginson was surprised to hear from an "intelligent and lady-like woman," the wife of a Rebel captain, that she would rather be under the control of the black troops than white soldiers from the North. The former were men "whom they had known all their lives, and who had generally born a good character." Seeing familiar, although black, faces walking the Jacksonville streets with rifles was to this lady preferable to being "in the power of entire strangers."[29]

Not all the black soldiers under Higginson's command nursed personal grievances against their former owners. Albert C. Sammis of Company C, 1st South Carolina, was born free across the river from Jacksonville at the Sammis plantation, the son of an enslaved woman and her white owner, John S. Sammis. Albert's mother was freed by Mary Kingsley Sammis, the mixed-race wife of his father, when she learned of her husband's infidelity. Albert was raised in the Sammis household with his half brothers and half sisters, the legitimate children of John S. and Mary K. Sammis. At age twelve he was apprenticed to R. W. Biggs of Jacksonville to learn the blacksmith trade. He remained in Jacksonville for several years, working at his trade and rowing across the St. Johns to spend weekends at the Sammis home.[30]

Following the first Union evacuation of Jacksonville in April 1862, Albert traveled with the Sammis family to New York. When his father returned to Florida to become a member of the Direct Tax Commission, Albert accompanied him as far as Beaufort, South Carolina. In December 1862, Albert was enrolled in the 1st South Carolina, briefly as Higginson's orderly. After suffering an injury, he was discharged in July 1864. Albert remained close to the Sammis family after the war; both he and his mother received homesteads from Sammis. Albert lived in Jacksonville for decades and served as a constable for eighteen years.[31]

It may have been Albert Sammis whom Higginson referred to as a "young recruit" in a December 16, 1862, journal entry written at Hilton Head. "To-day a young recruit was sent out here, who had belonged to a certain Col Semmes or Sammys of Florida. Two white companions walked him out, who seemed rather inferior retainers of the Colonel—and I could do no less than ask them to dine." Higginson described one of the companions as "English born; the other Floridian, a dark sallow Southerner, well bred enough.

Later that day, Sammis appeared at Higginson's quarters. During the ensuing conversation, Colonel Sammis mentioned the "dark sallow southerner" who had walked to the camp with the recruit: "'Yes, that white friend of whom you speak is a boy raised on one of my plantations, he has traveled with me to the North and passed for white, & always keeps away from the negroes.' Certainly I never should have suspected," Higginson wrote in his journal, that "he may have been his own son."[32]

While he was in Jacksonville, Higginson purchased a horse that had been raised and trained at the Sammis plantation. He described the horse as "a sorrel named Rinaldo, belonged to a rebel cavalry officer & is perfectly trained, very fleet & perfectly gentle. By an odd coincidence he was reared by Col. Sammis, former master if not father of my young orderly Albert, who regards Rinaldo as a sort of foster-brother—younger brother I suppose by the severity with which he rides him."[33]

At least seventeen black soldiers, most of them in the 1st South Carolina, had known Albert Sammis before the war. They all grew up as slaves at the Sammis plantation or at neighboring estates, and most were in the habit of visiting the Sammis estate on weekends to attend dances and swim in the river. They all appear to have gone north at about the same time and enrolled in black regiments in 1862. Only a few months later they were back in Jacksonville as Union soldiers, sometimes giving orders to their former owners. Albert was Higginson's orderly at the time the regiment occupied the town.[34]

One of the strongest backers of the use of black soldiers was Lyman Stickney, head of the District Tax Commission at Fernandina. Stickney accompanied the troops to Jacksonville, along with his business associates—three silent partners—to begin publication of a newspaper, *The Peninsula*, and to open a mercantile establishment on Bay Street. He conferred with Higginson about the need for reinforcements and returned to Fernandina to urge Colonel Hawley to seek authorization to send some of the troops under his command to Jacksonville.[35]

On March 20, Stickney returned aboard the gunboat *Paul Jones*, along with 800 men of the 6th Connecticut, sent from General Saxton's command at Beaufort. Three days later, 850 men of the 8th Maine arrived with Colonel John D. Rust, who assumed overall command of the 2,500 Union troops in the town. Higginson worried that his loss of command would "defeat all of my plans and [diminish the black soldiers'] success," but he was determined to prove that black and white soldiers could "work in harmony together."[36] The arrival of the white troops represented a historic moment, since it was the first time during the war that "white and black soldiers had served to-gether on regular duty."[37]

Dr. Rogers was impressed by how well the white and black soldiers co-operated. On March 22 he recorded: "Our regiment and the 6th Conn. met harmoniously at church this morning. The prejudice of the white soldiers is very strong, yet I trust there will be no serious collision." He was particularly impressed by the black soldiers' ability to ignore heckling from the whites, and observed, "Our boys have seen hardships enough to unfit them for re-ceiving taunts very graciously."[38]

One of the white soldiers, Sergeant Charles K. Cadwell of Company F, 6th Connecticut, saw nothing unusual or historic in the occasion and rarely mentioned serving with black troops in his diary. Instead, he mentioned how impressed he was with the appearance of the city. Jacksonville "must have been an inviting retreat in its palmiest days," Cadwell wrote; "every-thing here seemed to have been laid out for comfort and convenience." But the Union occupation brought major changes: "Houses that were once the home of wealth and luxury were now the abodes of the Union soldier. Gar-dens laid out with the choicest flowers were trampled under foot by horses of our cavalry; the stores were closed, the goods removed; and business at a standstill."[39]

While the Federals established fortifications and picket lines around Jacksonville, General Finegan strengthened the Confederate defense lines eight miles to the west at Camp Finegan. The appearance of black troops along the St. Johns sent waves of panic throughout Confederate Florida, but with only 803 men in the infantry, cavalry, and artillery companies at his disposal, Finegan realized he would not be able to drive the Federal force out of Jacksonville. He alerted headquarters at Richmond "that the enemy are certainly in large force in Jacksonville; that they are negroes, with white com-missioned officers" whose primary mission was to "entice the slaves" along the shores of the St. Johns River to join their ranks. Finegan feared "the en-tire negro population of East Florida will be lost and the country ruined . . . unless the means of holding the St. Johns River are immediately supplied. . . . The entire planting interest of East Florida lies within easy communication of the river; that intercourse will immediately commence between negroes on the plantations and those in the enemy's service; that this intercourse will be conducted through swamps and under cover of the night, and cannot be prevented. A few weeks will suffice to corrupt the entire slave population of East Florida."[40]

Finegan also appealed directly to the citizens of Florida. He composed a proclamation announcing the dire emergency and circulated it throughout the State.

> Our unscrupulous enemy has landed a large force of negroes, under command of white officers, at Jacksonville, under cover of gunboats. He is attempting to fortify the place so as to make it secure against attacks. The purpose of this movement is obvious and need not be mentioned in direct terms. It is sufficient to inspire the whole body of the people with a renewed and sterner purpose of resistance. I therefore call on such of the citizens as can possibly leave their homes to arm and organize themselves into companies without delay and to report to me. Ammunition, subsistence, and transportation will be furnished them while they remain in service. I further ask the zealous co-operation of the whole people in forcing into service all persons within the conscript age who yet remain out.[41]

On this subject, but on few others, Winston Stephens was in agreement with his commanding officer. On March 16, after fighting an exhausting series of skirmishes with Yankee troops, Stephens wrote to warn his wife of the black troops and of the grave danger the Yankee gunboats would pose if they traveled upriver as far as Welaka. "Get the slaves ready to run to the woods on a moment's notice," he warned Octavia. "The negroes in arms will promise them fair prospects, but they will suffer the same fate those did in town that we killed, and the Yankees say they will hang them if they don't fight."[42]

On March 23, the Confederate secretary of war, J. A. Seddon, sent a telegraph to General Howell Cobb, commander of the Middle District of Florida, with orders to "render any aid in your power to General Finegan."[43] It was General Beauregard who responded, however, with news that Finegan did not appreciate receiving. As commander of the Department of South Carolina, Georgia, and Florida, Beauregard was faced with the prospect of a major Federal offensive against Charleston or Savannah, and he desperately needed every man and gun at his disposal. Regrettably, he could not send reinforcements to Florida.[44]

Finegan refused to be intimidated and began aggressively probing Union defenses around Jacksonville. Twice on March 11, elements of the 2nd Florida Cavalry and about two hundred men of the 2nd Battalion of Partisan Rangers clashed with Union pickets, driving the Federals back into the town. On both occasions, Finegan's men were driven off by shells fired by the gunboats *Uncas* and *Norwich*, anchored in the river adjacent to the town. "Every day after this," Higginson reported, Finegan's men "appeared in small mounted squads in the neighborhood, and exchanged shots with our pickets, to which the gunboats would contribute their louder share."[45] Confederate snipers were also posted in a line of cottages on the outskirts of town, and it was only after a series of determined attacks that they were driven out and the structures burned to prevent their return.

Finegan's tactics kept the Federals on the alert but failed to prevent the black infantrymen from making sorties into the countryside to raid plantations for provisions and supplies and to carry the Emancipation Proclamation to the enslaved. With the help of the gunboats, Colonel Montgomery and the 125 men he had recruited at Key West conducted several major raids along the river. Montgomery, a radical abolitionist whose first combat had been in the bloody prewar struggles on the Kansas border, advocated taking a "hard war" to the enemy homeland and was a controversial figure throughout the war. Captain Apthorp defended Montgomery's conception of how warfare should be conducted in the South. Apthorp, who moved through the ranks to become lieutenant colonel of the regiment, felt that the critics who professed to be "shocked" at Montgomery's raiding tactics, which led to destruction of private property, lacked understanding of the real and hard nature of warfare. "They prefer to meet the Enemy where he is strongest *and best prepared*, and to continue their attacks upon him to his armed forces in the field. They apparently forget that every dollar's worth of material resources, every negro, and every foot of inhabited land that is captured from the enemy, or is surrendered or laid waste, is so much taken from the support of the rebel armies, and it is a deeper and more lasting injury than any force of similar strength *could possibly inflict* in the field."[46]

Apthorp felt that critics of Montgomery's tactics were delusional. Southerners were in his view "a warlike people" who must be "assailed at their homes" and that "nothing short of a totally crushing defeat and annihilation of their army can seriously injure them."

As long as their determination holds out they can steadily supply the usual demands of the field, both in material and in men, from home. But let the foundation of their strength be assailed, let their agriculture be stopped, their territory diminished, and their population crowded inward, and they will soon have no surplus resources for the support of an army. The alternative choices of capitulation or starvation will soon stare them in the face, and the victor can dictate terms. And let it be remembered that a peace thus conquered, though causing for a time great inconvenience and suffering, is still won at the expense of fewer lives, and a shorter, less protracted struggle than if the contest would have been won in the field alone. This is not a friendly boxing match with gloves, where neither party wishes to really hurt the other. It is a struggle for life, and the quickest and surest conquest is the best.[47]

Higginson was not an admirer of Montgomery's tactics. He called him "splendid, but impulsive & changeable never plans far ahead, & goes off at a tangent."[48] Higginson preferred a "gentleman's war" that spared civilians and their private property whenever possible, but Montgomery, Apthorp, and the men of the 2nd South Carolina had other ideas. Apthorp described an upriver raid on March 17 that stopped at Laurel Grove plantation on Doctors Lake, the "plantation of a Colonel Bryant in the Rebel service." Montgomery noticed the plentiful stocks of poultry and livestock at the plantation and, according to Apthorp, told his men: "Boys I don't want you to interfere with private property but if any pigs or turkeys attack you, you must defend yourselves." Defend themselves they did, inflicting "great slaughter" after they were attacked by "strutting turkeys and swine." Before departing with their plunder, they captured Colonel Bryant and placed him in restraints aboard the armed transport *General Burnside*. They also considered imprisoning Mrs. Bryant after she told the black soldiers "she despised and abhorred them. She hoped every one of them would go to hell that they would sink down into the bottomless pit." Apthorp said "it required a stern word of command to restrain the men" after Mrs. Bryant said the soldiers' wives were "nasty old black things."[49]

Higginson was at the Jacksonville wharf when Montgomery returned from his first gunboat raid. He was not sure whether to be appalled or amused. "The steamer seemed an animated hen-coop. Live poultry hung from the foremast shrouds, dead ones from the mainmast, geese hissed from the binnacle, a pig paced the quarter-deck, and a duck's wings were seen fluttering from a line."[50] But the raids continued unabated. Apthorp described one raid that resulted in the capture of sixteen Confederates, large supplies of fine furniture and stores of cotton, poultry, horses, mules, and pigs.

Finegan saw nothing amusing in the raids, and neither did settlers along the river whose homes and farms were plundered. Reporting to his superiors, Finegan said the Yankees were "making prisoners of all male citizens found on the St. Johns River who refuse to take the oath of allegiance, and holding them as hostages for their negro troops. They are robbing and plundering everything on the east bank." But Finegan's major worry was that Higginson may have been planning "to occupy Jacksonville with white troops and send the negroes . . . to Palatka and then attempt to move amongst the plantations."[51]

Finegan had a fine cavalry arm under command of Captain J. J. Dickison, a hard-riding partisan from Marion County whose courageous exploits were earning him a reputation as the "War Eagle" of Florida. Dickison was assigned to monitor the gunboats from outposts along the river and to attack their shore parties when possible. With the forces remaining at his disposal, Finegan focused his attention on Jacksonville and on a deadly 64-pounder that could fire 8-inch explosive shells with a range of up to two miles. Cobb had sent the giant gun from middle Florida mounted on a flatbed rail car.[52] Lieutenant Thomas E. Buckman of Jacksonville, a former superintendent of the Florida, Atlantic and Gulf Central Railroad, rolled the gun to within firing range of Jacksonville and opened fire on Union military positions.[53]

The first bombardment came on the night of March 24. Private Francis Soule of the 1st Special Battalion, Florida Volunteers, was in charge of the gun crew located a mile and a half west of town. The projectiles were so enormous they could be seen in flight. Higginson observed that the artillerists "had the range well, and every shot fell near the post headquarters." Dubbing the gun a "Dantean monster," Higginson was relieved that damage was minimal and even found it "exciting to see the great . . . shell, showing a light as it rose . . . moving slowly towards us like a comet, then exploding and scattering its formidable fragments. Yet, strange to say, no serious harm was done to life or limb."[54]

The medical officer of the 8th Maine, Dr. Alfred Walton, reacted differently. "The first shot went through an unoccupied house next to our medical headquarters and exploded, turning us all out in a hurry," he wrote. "Just as I got out of doors the second one broke over our heads. The third one struck the roof of a house where a Union man and his wife were sleeping; the shell passed through the side of the house and imbedded itself eight feet in the ground without exploding."[55] Positioned on the river, the Union gunboats *Norwich, Uncas,* and *Paul Jones* took up the challenge, and the artillery batteries at Forts Higginson and Montgomery joined the duel. The bombardment destroyed buildings, uprooted trees, caused general havoc, and forced Buckman to withdraw.[56]

The following morning six hundred men of the 8th Maine and 6th Connecticut regiments were sent on a mission to push the Rebel gunners out of range of Jacksonville by tearing up the rail lines west of town. One of the Maine men, Captain William M. McArthur, recorded the events in a journal. "We advanced on the right of the [rail line], and Conn[ecticut] on the left and a car pushed by darkies & mounting a gun on the track. I covered the front of the regiment with my company as skirmishers and drove in the enemy's skouts [sic] and pickets." As the work detail began dismantling the rail line, McArthur saw Confederate troops approach them with an engine pulling the flatcar and its 8-inch gun. The men from Maine and Connecticut turned their attention to the engine and gun crew: "We advanced about six miles. The engine car & gun of the rebs kept receding before me, evidently being afraid of my skirmishers capturing the gun. After we had gone in 6 miles, Col. Higginson (in command) ordered his gun to retire and us to retreat. Immediately, the gun of the rebs came down into us. It being entirely on account of a sudden falling back and the drawing in of the skirmishers." The first shot fired by the Confederates landed "in the midst" of McArthur's company.[57]

Dr. Walton accompanied the soldiers on the mission and left a vivid account of the shelling: "the first shot struck in the center of the track just short of where Captain McArthur and myself stood, exploded and a large piece of the butt of the shell ricocheted to the right, making a high curve, cut off the top of a tall pine tree, and fell into the ranks of Company I, Eighth Maine, who were marching in four ranks. . . . It struck the musket barrel of Thomas Hoole of Brunswick, Me., taking off his head. Passing to the next rank it took off the shoulder of Joseph Goodwin of Lyman, Maine—he lived two hours. Passing to the next rank it took off the leg below the knee of another man."[58]

The following day McArthur was made "Chief of Arty [artillery] and put in command of the guns mounted on our platform car. I chose a crew of gunners from my own company and took the gun out on the track a mile and a half, dug a trench to cover my gunners and supported by two companies kept the town from being shelled that night. Our gun was a better one than that of the rebels and they did not dare to venture within shelling distance of the town." For the remainder of the occupation of Jacksonville, McArthur took the car and gun out of town each night and traded shots with the Confederates. He said he and his gunners stayed "out all of each night and we had no more trouble from them."[59]

Meanwhile, the Federal gunboats reigned supreme on the river. On March 27, Montgomery and 120 black troops boarded the *Paul Jones* and started on an expedition upriver to Palatka, raiding plantations along the way. Thomas T. Russell, a local planter, reported that at least six landings were made and that the black troops carried off slaves, horses, carts, poultry, hogs, cotton, salt, about "everything they could lay their hands on . . . and abused and insulted the women just as they pleased." When the gunboat docked at Palatka, Dickison and about fifty horsemen greeted it with a hail of fire, wounding Lieutenant Colonel Liberty Billings. A *New York Tribune* correspondent reported that the gunboat returned the fire and "the Rebels scattered in all directions and soon disappeared." After that a shore party was landed and managed to seize "all the cotton in the place and about 30 negroes." The expedition convinced Montgomery that he could easily recruit ten thousand soldiers among the slave population along the river, and he planned to return with a larger force to occupy Palatka permanently as a base for future operations. With equal determination, Dickison said: "My little command is again ready for them, and will contest every inch of ground if they should attempt another landing."[60]

President Lincoln was pleased with the reports he received of the black troops in occupation of Jacksonville. He wrote to Hunter: "I am glad to see the accounts of your colored force at Jacksonville. . . . I see the enemy are driving at them fiercely, as is to be expected. It is important to the enemy that such a force shall not take shape and grow and thrive in the South, and in precisely the same proportion it is important to us that it shall."[61] The success of the black troops in Jacksonville convinced Saxton "that scarcely an incident in this war has caused a greater panic throughout the Southern coast than this raid of the colored troops in Florida."[62] All involved felt the campaign in East Florida had been successful and that with increased troop strength, operations could be expanded and thousands of black recruits could be gained for the Union army. Dr. Rogers wanted to "make a big hole through the rebel lines so that the blacks can run back to us."[63]

On the morning of March 28, the gunboat *Boston* and a convoy of Union ships tied up at the city docks. Dr. Rogers was certain the ships carried artillery, supplies, and the troop reinforcements needed to expand the raids into the Florida interior and to hold Jacksonville until the end of the war. Instead, the ships carried orders from Hunter to terminate the Florida campaign and evacuate Jacksonville once again. This news took Higginson and the other Federal officers by surprise. Higginson felt his black troops had been denied the opportunity to engage the enemy in force, and he had not yet recruited as many men for the new black regiments as he had anticipated. His frustrations paled in comparison to the disappointment of the civilians in the city who had again chosen to side with the occupying forces. For the third

time, Federal troops were abandoning Jacksonville, leaving Union supporters without protection. Higginson wrote: "All of us felt keenly the wrongful-
ness of breaking the pledges which we had been authorized to make to these
people, and of leaving them to the mercy of the Rebels once more."[64] Residents who wished to leave were allowed to evacuate with the Union forces.

Montgomery and the men of the 2nd South Carolina were recalled from
Palatka, from where Montgomery believed he could recruit hundreds of
troops among the slaves who had been moved away from the coastal zones
earlier in the war. Apthorp said the withdrawal order was the most disap-
pointing news his men could have received. "On our way down [river] a floating object was seen which proved on examination to be a scow loaded with
furniture and three and a half bales of cotton. It was immediately 'gobbled
up,' swelling our captured cotton to nearly $4000, besides fifteen Enfield
Rifles, and other valuable property, and all the furniture. This property was
afterwards turned over to the Provost Marshall at Fernandina."[65]

Dr. Rogers, an avid abolitionist and a strong advocate for Montgomery's
raiding tactics, condemned Hunter's decision to withdraw. "I fail to see anything by that fatal vacillation which has thus far cursed us in this war," he
wrote. "We have planted ourselves here for the definite purpose of making
this state free, and have already so fortified the city that a small force can hold
it while the boats are making such raids up the river as may seem best."[66]

Saxton was as angry about the withdrawal from Florida as the officers
and men on duty in Jacksonville were. He considered the occupation a success and withdrawal premature: "We had complete and undisputed possession of Jacksonville and Palatka, and Colonel Montgomery was moving into
the interior when the order of recall from General Hunter was received."[67]
Saxton was impressed by "the moral effect of the presence of these colored
soldiers under arms" and by the way white and black soldiers had joined
hands to fight effectively against the common enemy. "I am glad to report
that the hostility which at one time existed among the white troops in this
department against employment of colored troops has passed away, and they
are now perfectly willing to go into action with them."[68]

Saxton deeply regretted the troop withdrawal and urged Secretary of War
Stanton to reinstitute the campaign. "It may require a somewhat larger force
at first to regain what we have abandoned," he wrote. "Should the Charleston expedition be successful such force can be recruited there[.] [W]ith
the Saint John's River for a base of operation the entire State can be readily
occupied by our forces and restored to the Union." According to historian

Stephen V. Ash, the expedition had a significant impact on the Union army and the future conduct of the war. He argues that "it contributed mightily to a shift in sentiment among the white soldiers in the Department of the South in favor of black troops," and lessened their prejudice about serving with black regiments in the field. Ash feels that the greatest achievement of the expedition was to convince Lincoln and his cabinet to begin "full-scale recruiting of black troops for the Union army. . . . There can be no question that the expedition . . . played a crucial role in this pivotal event of the Civil War." Eventually, nearly 180,000 black men served in the Federal forces, contributing a "crucial addition of manpower, without which the Union army might have been unable to subdue the Rebel nation."[69]

The reputation of Federal forces was tarnished by events that transpired on March 28 while the troops prepared for departure. Three gunboats were in the river off the town ready to protect the troops should a Rebel attack occur during embarkation of the six Union transports. Two companies of the 6th Connecticut formed the rear guard until they were signaled to move toward the wharves and board the transports. Shortly after 8 a.m., as the pickets were negotiating the gangplanks, first one, then another, and finally a third column of smoke rose from the city, quickly followed by flames that leaped high into the sky. A *New York Tribune* correspondent described the ugly scene he saw from the deck of the *Boston*: "On every side, from every quarter of the city, dense clouds of black smoke and flame are bursting through the mansions and warehouses. A fine south wind is blowing immense blazing cinders right into the heart of the city. . . . The whole city, mansions, warehouses, trees, shrubbery, and orange groves; all that refined taste and art through many years have made beautiful and attractive, are being lapped up and devoured by this howling fiery blast. . . . Is not this war—vindictive, unrelenting war? Have we not gotten up to the European standard?"[70]

Sergeant Cadwell of the 6th Connecticut was also standing on the deck of a transport, his attention focused on the piles of furniture, bedding, and household goods abandoned by the departing refugees when they were told that there was no more room on the ships. "An old lady appeared on the veranda of her house wringing her hands and sobbing as if her heart would break." Behind her, buildings on Bay Street were "burning like torches."[71]

Dr. Walton scrambled aboard a transport just ahead of the pickets. "Before we were ready to embark," he recalled, "the boys began to set fire to the city and soon we had to hurry up for the smoke was getting rather uncomfortable. On my way down I ran into . . . a church and groping through the smoke and fire I took from the altar a large gilt-bound prayer book with the inscription on the cover, *St. Johns Episcopal Church, Jacksonville*. Farther down on Market Street I entered a building that appeared to be some kind of office and from the table or desk I took a manuscript map of the city of Jacksonville. Farther down I saw some negro soldiers setting fires and from their songs and shouting they appeared to be having a good time."[72]

Calvin Robinson was one of the civilians evacuating with the troops. Robinson was no stranger to vandalism and arson; his extensive Bay Street properties had been burned by the Rebels only hours before Union troops arrived in Jacksonville for the first occupation of the city. Intent on reviving his mercantile operations, he had returned with troops for the third occupation, only to find himself caught up again in a devastating conflagration. He later pinpointed how and where he believed the fires had been ignited: "One fire was set by soldiers of the 8th Maine, who were quartered in the dwelling of Thomas Ledwith. Another by the 6th Connecticut quartered in the mansion of Judge Pierson. The third fire was kindled by a mulatto soldier of Col. Montgomery's Regiment, named Isaac Smith, in the second story of Bisbee & Canova's brick store." Robinson gathered information from numerous witnesses before concluding that the soldiers started the fires by lighting straw and moss from their bedding at the time they departed for the transports. A strong southwest wind spread the fire rapidly: "The fire of Bisbee & Canova's store communicated with Dr. Baldwin's office and residence, and so on in a strong northeasterly direction . . . through the middle of the town. The fire in Judge Pierson's house burned the Episcopal Church."[73]

Most Northern newspapers exonerated the black soldiers of involvement in arson. The *New York Tribune* reported that blacks "had nothing whatever to do with it and were simply silent spectators."[74] Others used the incident to discredit Lincoln's management of the war efforts. The *New York Times* defended the president: "It is certainly unfortunate that we should have among us a class of patriots who will twist and exaggerate an insignificant affair like this into one of the most shocking Union atrocities—to the infinite infamy of our army and the disgrace of the whole nation."[75]

As late as 1878, Higginson denied that blacks were involved in any way. In an article published in the *Atlantic Monthly*, he wrote: "the town was in flames, the streets were full of tongues of fire creeping from house to house; the air was dense with lurid smoke" when the Union transports pulled away from the city's wharves. "Our steamers dropped rapidly down the river, laden to the gunwale with the goods of escaping inhabitants. The black soldiers, guiltless of all share in the flames, were yet excited by the occasion, recalled their favorite imagery of the Judgment Day, and sang and shouted without ceasing."[76]

Dr. Rogers denounced the event as "shameful" and lamented that the incendiary incidents would likely be blamed on the black troops to tarnish their image in the North. The *New York Evening Post* placed the blame solely on the 8th Maine and gave credit to Colonel Rust for "trying to stop the vandalism."[77] Higginson said "Col. Rust is so unpopular that all but two of his officers have just resigned, and some said openly that they burnt the houses because they thought he didn't wish it."[78]

Given the eyewitness testimony, it is clear that both white and black soldiers participated in what Rogers called a "shameful" event that destroyed many large trees, dwellings, and commercial structures. The arsonists might have destroyed the entire town had not a timely rainfall mitigated the damage, and had not the men of Winston Stephens's cavalry company hurried into the town on the heels of the departing Yankees while the conflagration was still in progress. In a letter to his brother-in-law, Stephens wrote: "I sent them in every direction and they did all they could to arrest the fire. [We] saved Colonel Sanderson's house, Flemings['], and some others that were on fire." Stephens believed that the entire town would have burned had it not been for the hard rain that fell throughout the afternoon and evening.

With the devastation still fresh in his mind, Stephens summed up the fire's toll: "The block on which Mrs. Fosters house stood is destroyed all but the house on the South West corner & the block north of that is destroyed & Pearsons houses are destroyed & the Catholic and Presbyterian Churches are destroyed, Col Harts building and brick office Bisbee & Canova Store & the one nearest I think Hickmans then Parkhurst stores & the two brick stores on the corner next to Ochus Hotel & the shoe shop adjoining." As he plumbed his memories of that terrible night further, Stephens added: "Those are all the stores destroyed I think but in the vicinity of the dwelling of Col Harts place several houses are burnt, and in the other parts of the Town. I forgot to say the Court house was destroyed."[79]

An anonymous town dweller gave an even more precise inventory of the dwellings and commercial properties destroyed by the fire, including "the Episcopal and Catholic churches, the jail, Parkhurst Store, Miller's Bar Room, Bisbee's Store and dwelling house, Dr. Baldwin's house and that whole block, Mrs. Foster's house, Washington Hotel, one of Hoeg's stores—nearest Millers—and every house from the Judson House above the Railroad to Mrs. Collins old house, (Lydia Foster's House, Sadlers, etc. are among them)." The writer then cataloged the destruction between the depot and the Brick Yard, where the conflagration had been merciless: "not a house left—all there shared the conflagration besides other small houses which I have not heard of."[80]

The *New York Tribune* eyewitness account was published eleven days after the event. "Jacksonville is in ruins. That beautiful city which has been for so many years the favorite resort for invalids from the North, has to-day been burned to the ground, and what is sad to record, by the soldiers of the National Army." With some overstatement, the correspondent lamented: "scarcely a mansion, a cottage, a negro hut, or a warehouse remains."[81]

Southern newspapers registered outrage. The *Gainesville Cotton States* declared: "The miserable white, black and ginger-bread-colored troops have now evacuated Jacksonville and burned a portion of the city."[82] Colonel Rust attempted to counter the growing controversy by blaming the fires on "secessionists" or Rebel soldiers who sneaked into town. He estimated that no more than twenty-five buildings had been destroyed, although every other eyewitness account indicated far greater damage.[83]

Finegan stated in his official report that he arrived in the city "just after the departure of the last gunboat" and found "the town in great part consumed."[84] Beauregard was outraged. He sent a letter of protest to Union general Quincy Adams Gillmore, calling the acts a "savage and monstrous excess" and warning Gillmore that "the belligerent who wages war in that manner must justly . . . be regarded as carrying on war like a furious barbarian."[85]

In the aftermath of the evacuation, Higginson and his fellow officers debated the reasons for the evacuation of Jacksonville, the abandonment of the campaign to recruit enslaved black men for the 1st and 2nd South Carolina Loyal Volunteer regiments, and the effort to restore Florida to the Union. The reason given by Hunter was his urgent need to augment Union troop strength and to increase the number of naval gunboats to support his campaign against Charleston. Judging from the reports of troubles Union forces were experiencing at Charleston at the time, Hunter's rationale appeared to some of the officers to be a legitimate reason for calling off the Florida expedition. Higginson and his officers blamed the War Department for attempting to stifle and thwart the efforts of Saxton and other abolitionists to expand the role of black soldiers in the war effort: "It was commonly attributed to pro-slavery advisors, acting on the rather impulsive nature of Major-General Hunter, with a view to cut short the career of the colored troops, and stop their recruiting."[86] Dr. Rogers was similarly convinced that Hunter had been "influenced by pro-slavery counsels," although the regimental surgeon never identified the malefactors.[87]

A few shocked residents remained in the town to search the smoldering ruins for precious items that might have survived this latest inferno. They had learned from bitter experience the feel of "vindictive, unrelenting war." Perhaps it was fortunate they had no way of knowing the war would last for two more years, and that a fourth Union occupation of their town was less than one year away.

FIGURE 13. 1st U.S. Colored Infantry, also known as the 1st South Carolina Loyal Volunteers. In May 1862, Major General David Hunter, the devoted abolitionist then commanding the Department of the South, organized a regiment of black soldiers from among the thousands of "contrabands of war" residing in the Union-occupied Sea Islands. When the Lincoln administration refused to authorize the regiment, it was disbanded, with the exception of one company posted at St. Simons Island. Brigadier General Rufus Saxton, also an abolitionist, organized this regiment in August 1862. Photograph by Mathew Brady. (Courtesy of Library of Congress.)

FIGURE 14. Colonel Thomas W. Higginson described a special company of "all Florida Men" in his regiment as "the finest looking company I ever saw, white or black; they range admirably in size, have remarkable erectness and ease of carriage, and really march splendidly." The men shown in this image, although not from his regiment, match Higginson's description. (Courtesy of the U.S. Army Military History Institute.)

FIGURE 15. 33rd Regiment of United States Colored Infantry at dress parade. Originally known as the 1st U.S. Colored Infantry, this regiment was composed of former slaves and free African Americans from South Carolina, Georgia, and Florida. (Courtesy of U.S. Army Military History Institute.)

FIGURE 16. Thomas Wentworth Higginson, Unitarian minister, radical abolitionist, and commander of the 1st South Carolina Loyal Volunteers, believed that by serving in the Union army the black men under his command would drive a dagger into the heart of slavery. Higginson was in command of the 1st South Carolina when it captured Jacksonville in 1863. (Courtesy of U.S. Army Military History Institute.)

FIGURE 17. Charles T. Trowbridge, originally a white sergeant in the "Hunter regiment" of black men organized in May 1862 and disbanded soon after. The company led by Trowbridge continued to serve, however, and in August 1862, when the 1st South Carolina Loyal Volunteers was recruited, Trowbridge's unit became Company A. Trowbridge remained with the regiment throughout the war and was promoted to lieutenant colonel and commander after it became the 33rd U.S. Colored Infantry. He served with a black regiment longer than any other white officer during the Civil War. (Courtesy of U.S. Army Military History Institute.)

FIGURE 18. Major General Rufus Saxton, avowed abolitionist and a key supporter of recruiting former slaves as soldiers in the Union army. (Courtesy of Library of Congress.)

FIGURE 19. Dr. Seth Rogers, surgeon, 1st South Carolina Loyal Volunteers. Rogers kept a daily journal that recorded the early history of this famous regiment. (Courtesy of U.S. Army Military History Institute.)

FIGURE 20. Captain William Lee Apthorp. Born in Georgia in 1837, reared in Iowa, a Dartmouth College graduate in 1859, Apthorp became captain of Company B, 2nd South Carolina Loyal Volunteers, under Colonel James Montgomery, and was eventually promoted to Lieutenant Colonel of the 34th Regiment, United States Colored Infantry. For his version of life in that regiment see "Montgomery's Raids in Florida, Georgia, and South Carolina" at www.unf.edu/floridahistory online. (Photograph courtesy of Historical Museum of Southern Florida.)

FIGURE 21. Private Albert Sammis, the son of a wealthy white planter named John S. Sammis and a slave woman. Mother and son were emancipated when Mary Kingsley Sammis, the mixed-race wife of John, learned of her husband's infidelity. Albert was reared in the Sammis household at a plantation near Jacksonville. He joined the 1st South Carolina Loyal Volunteers and served as orderly to Colonel Higginson during the third Federal occupation of Jacksonville. (Courtesy of Eileen Brady, Special Collections, Thomas G. Carpenter Library, University of North Florida.)

FIGURE 22. Residence of John S. Sanderson. A migrant to Florida from Vermont, Sanderson left his home in Jacksonville in 1862 to serve in the government of the Confederate States of America. His dwelling became the residence of every Union commander during four Federal occupations of the city. (Courtesy of Library of Congress.)

FIGURE 23. Octavia Bryant Stephens. Born in Massachusetts, Octavia Bryant was reared in Jacksonville. She married Winston J. T. Stephens of Welaka shortly before the war. Their correspondence during the war captures poignant incidents in the life of a woman left in charge of a lonely rural homestead and the combat activities of a Florida cavalry officer. (Courtesy of Stephens-Bryant Family Papers, Special Collections, University of Florida Library.)

FIGURE 24. Winston J. T. Stephens, Welaka, Florida, husband of Octavia Bryant, veteran of the 3rd Seminole War (1855–58), and captain of the 2nd Florida Cavalry Regiment. Stephens was killed by enemy sniper fire at Cedar Creek, west of Jacksonville, on March 1, 1864. (Courtesy of Stephens-Bryant Family Papers, Special Collections, University of Florida Library.)

"To Redeem Florida
from the Rebels"

*The Fourth Occupation
of Jacksonville*

April 1863. Little more than a year had passed since the first Federal gunboats steamed up the St. Johns River in March 1862. The once bustling waterfront was silent. As Union gunboats passed by on patrol, sailors viewed empty streets, abandoned homes, stores with windows and doors shuttered, and weeds growing high on lots littered with charred skeletons of former buildings. Women and children could be seen, many waiting for the return of husbands and fathers. Small groups of Confederate soldiers were posted along Bay Street; hundreds more were located eight miles west of town at Camp Finegan. J. J. Daniel stopped at the posts on Bay Street that April; recently promoted to the rank of major and assistant commander of Florida conscripts, he was about to begin the unpleasant duty of searching for deserters from the army and men evading the state's tough conscript laws. After viewing the damage Jacksonville had sustained since March 1862, Daniel wrote a plaintive note to his father: "The people are weary of war. God help us all."[1]

Had Major Daniel stopped at Camp Finegan, he would have learned that desertion had become a serious problem at the northeast Florida camps. More than two thousand men from Florida deserted during the war, many lured home by the suffering of their families. Some became "layouts," men who farmed until conscript officers came looking for them, whereupon they fled into the woods and swamps to live off the land until it was safe to return again. Joined by perennial draft-dodgers, they sometimes formed renegade communities. Others renounced loyalty to the Confederacy and accepted arms and equipment from Federal agents to operate behind Confederate lines. By 1863, increasing numbers of deserters, refugees, and escaped slaves were seeking safety and employment at Union-occupied St. Augustine and Fernandina.[2]

Late in May, General Finegan attempted to boost morale among the soldiers at Camp Finegan by bringing forty women to watch the troops drill. Winston Stephens described the event: "the men formed [a] line of battle and our brass band struck up a lively tune and the Genl then passed down our line and after he had returned the Command was given by Plattoon right wheel and the whole line moved pass the Genl in review, the Cavalry first, the Artillery next and the Infantry in the rear, the drums beating and band playing."[3] The ladies then boarded railcars to attend festivities in Jacksonville.

One week later, Finegan was back with "100 Ladies" and a surprise guest, the dashing General Beauregard. The men marched that day under a "broiling sun and Dust that almost suffocated for about two hours."[4] Stephens described Beauregard as "45 to 48 years of age, hair quite Grey, keen eyes a little crossed just enough to notice, . . . rather good looking, small but erect and soldierly in his appearance but looks very Fancyfied, taking him altogether he does not look like the lion that he is."[5]

Davis Bryant, Stephens's brother-in-law, turned the events of late May and June into a series of convivial social outings, including a "big dancing affair and . . . two picnics." One evening he ate "dinner in the market and walked all over town. Had a splendid time." One week later he was in the company of "a very pleasant unassuming man," General Beauregard, who indicated he was "much pleased with the troops and affairs here generally. . . . He was charmed with the St. Johns."[6]

Octavia Stephens wrote to her husband from their farm at Welaka: "So you have seen the great yet little Beaureguard [sic], I think it was a hot sight, did you speak with him? Or were you not that much honored, but had to be satisfied with waiting on him. I should like very much to have been there to have seen my husband, better in my estimation than all the Generals, though I would have liked to see the Gen too."[7] She worried that Beauregard might initiate military action against the Union gunboats and prompt another invasion of Florida. "I hope he or any other Gen may never have the pleasure of leading you to battle, I hope those laurels may stay unwon, that the war may stop before there is a chance or need for that."[8]

Only twenty-two years old at the time, Octavia was struggling to manage slaves and a farm and was deeply worried about Yankee raiders and the health and safety of her family. The death of her infant daughter in January had triggered a deep depression, with spells of "gloomy" moods, of feeling "blue" and jealous of the women with whom the soldiers associated. More pervasive were fears that Winston might be killed.[9] "When will there be an end of this?" she wrote in July. "I wonder if we will ever live together at home any time again. Events look more gloomy. . . . I think the Confederacy nearly a goner. I had just begun to have a good deal of hope that we would gain our independence, but things are now worse then ever."[10] In August she wrote, "I think if we fight much longer we will come down as low as slaves, and I think we had better give up, and have our husbands with us, slavery if such it will be, will be much harder when we are subdued after our husbands are killed. Oh how I wish the war never had started."[11]

By July and August 1863, despair was widely shared by Floridians who supported the Confederate war effort. The disastrous defeats suffered in Tennessee by Braxton Bragg's Army of Tennessee and in Pennsylvania by Lee's Army of Northern Virginia were serious blows to morale. To make matters worse, Union forces under General Grant forced the surrender of Vicksburg, Mississippi, and effectively closed off Confederate food supplies from the West. Octavia's brother Willie wrote from Tennessee: "Affairs look gloomy for the Confederacy just now."[12]

Winston Stephens's spirits were also lagging at the time, stemming from poor lodging conditions. At Camp Cooper near Fernandina, sickness was so prevalent among the men of his company that only fifty-eight were fit for duty. Some were forced to stand guard for nine consecutive nights.[13] Stephens also groused about the high cost of food and accused speculators of driving up prices to line their pockets at the expense of hungry families of Confederate soldiers. "Who will stay and battle when he knows his family is starving? Not I."[14] In early August he decided: "We will never settle this question by arms—but we must stop fighting and talk it over and come to terms in that way—and the sooner the better for both North and South. We can maintain our position and so can the North for an indefinite time and nothing gained on either side—but every thing lost."[15]

On September 9 Stephens received a letter from his father-in-law, James W. Bryant, urging him to send his family to a safe location away from the St. Johns, as "the Yanks and negroes were coming out in a short time to try to overrun Fla."[16] Bryant remained loyal to the Union throughout the war, even though his wife, sons, daughter, and grandchildren were either in the Confederate army or behind their lines. The timely warning prompted Stephens to relocate his family temporarily to Thomasville, Georgia, where dependable kinfolk lived.

The move to Georgia did not lessen Octavia's anxieties. She wrote from Thomasville on October 30, "I guess I miss you more here than at home, I say home, I have no home." One week later she wrote: "Oh how many times a day I wish we never had left Welaka." By mid-December she was having premonitions of losing her husband. "If I should live to see the end of this war I fear I will be a widow and will have to knock about the first place I can get. If I knew the end of this war would find us as when it began, a living happy couple, I believe I would say go anywhere."[17]

In December and January, Stephens continued to complain about the living conditions afforded his men. Furloughs had been halted and clothing issues stopped, leaving his men "nearly naked and barefoot"; consequently, men were deserting daily. A bitter storm in January, coupled with rising food prices, compelled him to unleash his frustrations in a letter to his wife: "I fear unless things change very materially that I will not be able to feed you another year. . . . I want you to economize every thing. . . . I think you had better feed Jane from the table and perhaps others of the children and perhaps you can save in that way. You see, you have no dog to eat the cold provisions [so] you must give it [to] the negro children. I am glad you have no dog on that account."[18]

Stephens was troubled by thoughts of the fate of his wife and daughter if he should be killed. His special worry was of her marrying "some Yankee that had been instrumental in destroying me! I want you to promise that no matter what befalls me that you will never marry a yankee, no matter what his calling or position. I don't ask you to promise me never to marry again. I want to know that I am not leaving such a good wife for a cursed Yankee." Regarding his children, Stephens wrote: "I want them educated to hate a Yankee and glory in their Southern blood, and I want them never to go North and especially do I want them educated South and Southern principles instilled in their bosoms. . . . I hope God in his mercy will give us deliverance from such a people as the Northern people."[19]

In October the *Norwich* took aboard fourteen Confederate deserters in less than three weeks; its commander reported that "one [Confederate] company stationed at Jacksonville lost 32 out of 82 men."[20] Morale appeared to be so low among civilians along the St. Johns that gunboat commanders surmised it might be possible to persuade them to support the Union. To test that possibility, Admiral John Dahlgren, successor to Admiral Du Pont, sent the *Ottawa* on a mission to ascertain the extent of pro-Union sentiment among the residents. Dahlgren learned that the residents of the area "wish to be neutral, but are willing to take up arms against the enemy, provided they are not taken from their homes and are protected by gunboats."[21]

The widespread demoralization felt by Floridians who lived along the St. Johns in late 1863 and early 1864 convinced Lyman Stickney, head of the Florida Direct Tax Commission, that Union sentiment was reviving sufficiently to justify another Union military expedition up the St. Johns River. Stickney persuaded Secretary of the Treasury Salmon Chase that a permanent Federal presence on the St. Johns would produce "a free state, and forever extinguish slavery within its borders."[22] Chase, who was then exploring his chances of replacing Lincoln as the Republican Party's candidate for president in the 1864 elections, recognized an opportunity to advance his own candidacy. Support for Lincoln had dipped so low in the early months of 1863 that votes for Chase from a Florida delegation might prove decisive at the nominating convention.[23]

In August, Stickney directed the editor of his Fernandina newspaper to print articles and editorials favorable to a Chase campaign for the presidency. He returned to Washington in September to urge Lincoln to send an army to free Florida from "Confederate rule." He later traveled to Hilton Head to meet with Major General Quincy Adams Gillmore, commander of the Department of the South, to communicate his plans for Florida, "to make it a free State and forever extinguish slavery within its borders." Stickney told Chase that Gillmore "gave his cordial assent . . . [and] said he was ready and able to redeem Florida from the rebels with Colored troops if permitted by the Government."[24]

Stickney, always a self-promoter and influence-seeker, may well have underestimated Gillmore's sagacity. Before rushing troops to the state, Gillmore prudently considered troop strength in the Department of the South as well as the military and political goals of a Federal occupation of Florida. Not until January 15, 1864, more than a month after his conversation with Stickney, did Gillmore write to Secretary of War Edwin Stanton concerning another Florida campaign. Even then, he waited until Lincoln encouraged him to undertake the campaign.[25]

While Gillmore was considering his options, Stickney traveled to St. Augustine to generate local support for a Florida campaign and to build enthusiasm for Lincoln's recently declared amnesty proclamation. In December the president had offered amnesty and restoration of property, other than human property, to all former Rebels who pledged an oath of loyalty to the Union. Included in the proclamation was a formula for political reconstruction of a state that had seceded and joined the rebellion: if 10 percent of the total number of that state's residents who voted in the 1860 presidential election would take an oath of loyalty to the Union in 1864, a new government could be formed and representatives elected to Congress.

At a meeting of Unionists in St. Augustine on December 19, 1863, Stickney introduced a set of resolutions calling for disavowal of the existing rebellion and for a plan to reorganize Florida as a loyal state. He also put forward resolutions calling for the emancipation of all slaves and for a convention of state delegates to assemble at St. Augustine on March 1, 1864, to amend the Florida Constitution "with a view to the early restoration of the State to the Union."[26] Stickney, along with William Alsop, Calvin Robinson, and Philip Fraser from Jacksonville and Homer G. Plantz of Key West, were elected to a committee charged with making the arrangements.

On December 21 the Florida Direct Tax Commission held its first sale of property confiscated in St. Augustine for nonpayment of taxes. Prime real estate was auctioned off at bargain prices, including a house and lot surreptitiously purchased for Stickney by one of his aides. Another lot was purchased for John Hay, Lincoln's private secretary. Hay was advised, in confidence, that if a military expedition succeeded, Florida's Unionists might elect him to Congress. Stickney was apparently willing to ride to power in Florida on the coattails of either Lincoln or Chase, depending on who won the Republican nomination in 1864.[27]

After reading Stickney's letter, Hay met with Lincoln. The president recognized the political benefits a permanent occupation of Florida could bring, especially if it resulted in the first political reconstruction of a seceded state. Hay wrote in his diary that the president agreed to "appoint me a Commissioner to go to Florida and engineer the business there."[28]

On January 13, Lincoln informed Gillmore of his desire to reconstruct a loyal government in Florida: "I have given Mr. Hay a commission as major and sent him to you . . . to aid in the reconstruction. He will explain . . . my general views on the subject." Military objectives were given first priority, with the understanding that political goals were also important.[29]

The next day, Gillmore wrote a one-sentence note to the general in chief of the Union army, H. W. Halleck, informing him that, if authorized, he would initiate a campaign to "occupy the west bank of the Saint John's River . . . and establish small depots there preparatory to an advance west at an early day."[30] The following day he sent a similar letter to Stanton.

The tone of Halleck's response suggests a distinct lack of enthusiasm for the campaign. He told Gillmore that the Florida expedition "had been left entirely to your judgment and discretion, with the means at your command." From a military perspective, Halleck wrote, "I attach very little importance to such expeditions. If successful they merely absorb our troops in garrisons to occupy the places, but have little or no influence upon the progress of the war."[31]

Nine days later, Gillmore addressed Halleck's concerns with a letter outlining both the military and political goals of the forthcoming expedition to Florida.

First. To procure an outlet for cotton, lumber, timber, turpentine, and the other products of that State.

Second. To cut off one of the enemy's sources of commissary supplies. He now draws largely upon the herds of Florida for his beef, and is making preparations to take up a portion of the Fernandina and Saint Mark's Railroad for the purpose of connecting the road from Jacksonville to Tallahassee with Thomasville, on the Savannah, Albany and Gulf Railroad, and perhaps with Albany, on the Southwestern Railroad.

Third. To obtain recruits for my colored regiments.

Fourth. To inaugurate measures for the speedy restoration of Florida to her allegiance, in accordance with instructions which I have received from the President by the hands of Maj. John Hay, assistant adjutant-general.[32]

While planning was under way, Hay met with Gillmore at Hilton Head and informed the general that he would be expected to achieve political as well as military objectives in Florida. The political goals were "to initiate, guide, and control, such measures as may be necessary under the Presidential [Amnesty] Proclamation of December 8, 1863, to restore the State . . . to its allegiance."[33] Stickney, who was at the meeting, informed Chase: "Every day I am more convinced of the ease with which Florida can be restored to the Union. . . . Gillmore . . . is your friend."[34]

Hay next traveled to Fernandina and discovered "a most gratifying unanimity of sentiment" among the male residents. Even the former conservatives seemed ready to come back into the Union, while people in general seemed "ignorant and apathetic. . . . They will be very glad to see a government strong enough to protect them." Hay was given the "best assurances that we will get the tenth required; although so large a portion of the rebel population is in the army & so many of the loyal people refugees in the North, that the state is well-nigh depopulated."[35]

The man Gillmore chose to command the Florida expedition was Brigadier General Truman Seymour, age forty, a native of Vermont, a West Point graduate, and a veteran of the Mexican War and the Third Seminole War in Florida. Between 1861 and 1864, Seymour was at Fort Sumter, Mechanicsville, Malvern Hill, Second Bull Run, and Antietam, and he commanded the bloody frontal assault on entrenched Confederate troops at Battery Wagner, Morris Island, during the first attempt to capture Charleston in July 1863. Of the 5,264 troops Seymour led in that failed assault, 1,515 became casualties. Seymour, too, was seriously wounded. He returned to duty in December 1863; one month later he was selected to lead the Florida campaign.

The plan worked out between Gillmore and Dahlgren called for a fleet to depart Hilton Head early on February 6 and rendezvous at the entrance to the St. Johns River at dawn the following day.[36] Two days prior to departure, infantry and cavalry regiments began boarding ships, each man provided with sixty rounds of ammunition and rations for six days. Lieutenant Cyrus W. Brown, 3rd U.S. Colored Troops, wrote in his diary: "It is a matter of conjecture where we shall go. Probably to Florida." Private Milton M. Woodford of the 7th Connecticut wrote: "February fifth we had orders to get ready to go *somewhere* right away. No one, not even the Colonel, had any idea where."[37]

Twenty armed transports and eight supply schooners made up the convoy that departed Hilton Head on February 6, accompanied by eight gunboats and armed tugs.[38] Eleazer Crowell of the steamer *Harriet A. Weed* had previously been ordered to "buoy out the entrance and to stay and assist ships." The transport *Island City* arrived early on the sixth, carrying the first word of a pending invasion to commanders of the *Norwich* and *Ottawa*, already on station at the navy's coaling base at Mayport. Pickets were landed to prevent civilians from warning the Confederates, and four Union sympathizers were hired to cut telegraph wires and burn a railroad bridge outside Jacksonville.[39]

At dawn on the seventh, a Sunday, the first transports arrived. By 10 a.m. the entire fleet had gained entry to the river except for the transport *Burnside*, whose hull had been ruptured when the captain tried to ram the vessel across a sandbar. At 10:10 the *Norwich* and *Ottawa* began moving upriver in advance of the flotilla.[40]

Dahlgren was aboard the *Mahaska*, and Gillmore and Seymour were aboard the transport *Maple Leaf*. Sharing the view from the deck with the generals was Major John Appleton of the 54th Massachusetts Colored Troops and three New York newspaper correspondents: George Bowerem of the *Tribune*, Oscar Sawyer of the *Herald*, and Whit Whittemore of the *Times*. Appleton pushed aside thoughts of a Confederate army waiting at Jacksonville and instead focused on the sandy white beaches, the two lighthouses on the shore at Mayport, and the black-and-white pelicans soaring overhead.[41]

Late in the afternoon the *Ottawa*, *Norwich*, and *Mahaska* presented broadsides to the town, gun crews at the ready, while the *Maple Leaf* and *General Hunter* approached the wharves between Ocean and Market streets. As a shore party leaped to a wharf to secure the first vessel, a volley of musket fire wounded one of the sailors. A Confederate cavalry unit that had been in the town mounted their horses and rode rapidly to the west. "As soon as our boat was made fast," Appleton recalled, "the Rebels began to fire and we jumped ashore and started running up the wharf to the street."[42] Three of his companies deployed as skirmishers and began fanning through the streets, taking eleven prisoners. A company of the 1st Massachusetts Cavalry pursued the fleeing horsemen five miles beyond the town and returned with eleven prisoners. The 54th Massachusetts camped at the outskirts of town that first night. While marching through the streets, Appleton noticed that the women and children seemed "terribly afraid of our colored men. We assure[d] them that the men will not interfere with them," but he detected a general horror in the eyes of Southern whites when they saw former slaves wearing army uniforms and carrying guns.[43]

The landing operations continued for three more days, but already on the afternoon of the eighth a mounted brigade led by Colonel Guy V. Henry began a rapid advance toward the railroad town of Baldwin, where Gillmore hoped to gain "possession of a train if one has been brought in by the enemy." Henry carried orders to rendezvous with infantry units at a point on the railroad three miles west of town, but when the footsoldiers failed to arrive on time, Henry's men rode off to the west. What followed was a seventy-two-hour, fifty-mile dash described in great detail by Sawyer of the *Herald* and Whittemore of the *Times*, "saddle-embedded" war correspondents who accompanied the troops on horseback.[44]

Jacksonville Unionist William Alsop, a recent appointee to the Florida Direct Tax Commission, was the local guide as the riders spurred their horses over roads and through streams where bridges had been destroyed. When scouts reported that Confederates were drawn up in line of battle outside

Camp Finegan, Henry bypassed the camp and rode on to the west. Later that evening, Lieutenant Colonel Abner McCormick and the 350 healthy men under his command at Camp Finegan, using stealth and cover of darkness, traveled west to join Finegan at Camp Beauregard near Lake City.[45]

As Colonel Henry's cavalry resumed riding toward Baldwin, Whittemore of the *Times* "witnessed the most brilliant dash that a similar force of cavalry ever executed. It was upon an artillery camp situated like Camp Finegan on the line of the railroad at Ten Mile Run [today's Maccleny]. The rebel cavalry, having been cut off from Camp Finegan, no intelligence of our approach had reached the artillerists—the Milton Artillery—consequently they were taken by complete surprise." As the Union riders approached, they sighted the Confederate cavalry men "sitting near the fires in the act of preparing something to eat. Their horses and mules were standing ready harnessed, and their wagons were partly laden with officers' baggage. . . . In half a minute's time our cavalry had dashed into the center of the camp and surrounded it on all sides."[46]

Captain J. L. Dunham, in command of the Milton Light Artillery, was still in his tent when the Union cavalry approached. All but eighteen of his men were able to escape, but four guns, six wagons, forty-five horses and mules, and a large quantity of supplies were captured.[47] Henry's column rode off again at 4 a.m. on the ninth, passing through an area Whittemore described as "miserable country, all swamp." Three hours later they captured Baldwin without firing a shot, finding little more than unpainted shanties, a tavern, a warehouse, a hotel, and a railroad depot. One of the soldiers observed: "The whites who are living here . . . are wretchedly poor. It is a pitiful sight."[48]

Whittemore realized, however, that Baldwin had been an important railroad junction for freight and passengers on lines running west from Jacksonville to Tallahassee and running south from Fernandina to Waldo, Gainesville, and Cedar Key on the Gulf Coast. Its warehouse and railroad depot were filled with Confederate supplies awaiting shipment: cotton, rice, tobacco, turpentine, weapons, and other supplies and equipment valued at half a million dollars. A second telegraph operator was captured, along with "three railroad cars, two of which were filled with corn, and another carrying a 3-inch rifled gun and caisson."

By late on the ninth, advance Union infantry units occupied the town, accompanied by Gillmore and Seymour and their staffs. Gillmore informed Halleck: "We have taken, without the loss of a man, about one hundred prisoners, eight pieces of excellent field artillery well supplied with ammunition, and other valuable property to a large amount." He assured Dahlgren "the enemy will not make any resistance in East Florida for the present. They are panic-stricken."[49]

At the south fork of the St. Marys River, two companies of the 2nd Florida Cavalry under command of Major Robert Harrison opened fire as the Union cavalry approached the riverbank. One Union man was killed, and two were wounded. When Henry noticed that the Florida men were fighting dismounted, sheltered by trees, he sent skirmishers ahead on foot while a detachment of riders crossed the river at another ford in a flanking maneuver. The fight lasted only thirty minutes, but four Federals were killed and thirteen were wounded. Finegan praised the gallantry of the defenders for checking the enemy's "progress for several hours at the Saint Mary's Crossing."[50]

At dawn on February 10, Henry's men rode into Sanderson to the distant sound of a locomotive pulling a string of cars toward Lake City. Only minutes before, Confederate infantry had finished stripping Sanderson of all the supplies the train could carry. What they could not load in the train cars, they set on fire. "Three large buildings near the depot were in flames" when the cavalry reined in their horses, "one with 3,000 bushels of corn and another with 2,000 barrels of turpentine and resin. The remaining building contained commissary stores. The conflagration continued all that night and during the following day." Through the smoke and flames, Sawyer of the *Herald* identified the buildings still standing: a tavern, a few dwellings, a hotel, and a railroad depot.[51] At 2 a.m. on the eleventh, after the horses had been fed and rested, the men rode off again.

Three miles outside Lake City, the Federal column encountered a Confederate defensive formation consisting of 490 infantry and 110 cavalry, supported by two pieces of artillery.[52] A line of men in gray uniforms stretching for more than a mile was visible through the fog that prevailed that morning. After skirmishing briefly, Henry ordered his men to withdraw. Having succeeded in locating the main Confederate defense force, he wisely decided to call a halt.[53]

With infantry support more than thirty miles in the rear, lacking fresh mounts, and dependent on slow-moving horse-and-wagon conveyances for supplies, Henry decided to forgo a dash to the Suwannee River to torch the railroad bridge that spanned East and West Florida. Darkness was settling over the battlefield as his men rode back toward the east for several miles, posted pickets, and camped for the night during a torrential rainstorm. Orders from Seymour reached him in the morning to return to military headquarters at Sanderson.[54]

While Henry's cavalry unit was carrying out its mission, Appleton and the 54th Massachusetts occupied Camp Finegan. They arrived at what Appleton thought would be an abandoned camp, only to find figures clad in gray caps and cloaks huddled around a campfire. Sending men to the right and the left to surround the figures by the fires, Appleton "led the rush on the first fire" expecting to confront Rebel soldiers but instead found "ten or twelve women and lots of children with capes and coats. Everyone had a good laugh at my expense."[55] His soldiers slept around the fires that night while the women and children stayed in one of the few houses still standing. Throughout the night, deserters came into the camp to surrender.

The next morning Appleton sent soldiers to a nearby farm to investigate complaints by a white farmer that his turkeys had been stolen. Instead, the soldiers discovered enslaved men and women locked in a smokehouse to prevent them from escaping to the Union camp. Appleton informed the farmer of the Emancipation Proclamation, but the man ignored it and pleaded with his slaves to return to work. They refused, and walked to Jacksonville and to freedom.

Later that day, Appleton led eight companies of the 54th Massachusetts to Baldwin to guard the repaired telegraph line. He thought the tiny town was "a dismal place," its houses "all in ruins" and its residents "rabid secesh."[56] Deserters, prisoners under escort, and civilian refugees heading for Jacksonville passed through his camp, attracting little more than curious stares from the black troops. But when newly freed slaves entered the camp, Appleton's men became excited: "It makes our men's eyes shine as they go by. The men beg me to allow them to scout for slaves to free." Appleton gave them permission to raid nearby plantations and farms, where they emancipated with great enthusiasm the blacks they found still in bondage.

Appleton was shocked when a woman screamed at him that if he were captured he would surely be hanged. When asked why, she replied: "because you command Nigger troops."[57] He then realized that changing the attitudes of white Floridians would be a difficult task, but he was under orders to try to gain the respect and trust of loyal Florida citizens and convince them to return to their homes, take the oath of loyalty, and vote to return Florida to the Union. Union officers were ordered to "enforce in the strictest manner, and under the severest penalties, all existing orders and regulations forbidding the destruction or pillage of private property."[58]

On February 10, Gillmore and Seymour conferred for several hours at Baldwin concerning future operations in Florida. Gillmore returned to Jacksonville the following day, but they communicated through courier and telegraph frequently for the next three days.[59] On the eleventh Seymour wrote: "What has been said of the desire of Florida to come back now is a delusion, the backbone of the rebellion is not here, and Florida will not cast its lot with us until more important successes elsewhere are assured." Disappointed that so few deserters had crossed Union lines and that only one hundred prisoners had been taken, he urged Gillmore to call for "the immediate withdrawal of all Federal troops from the interior of Florida" and to occupy "only Jacksonville and Palatka."[60]

When Gillmore departed Jacksonville on February 14 to return to headquarters of the Department of the South, he and Seymour seemed to be in basic agreement on policy for the Florida campaign. The western headquarters was to be at Baldwin to maintain control of the vital railroad junction. Seymour had already endorsed Gillmore's explicit statement that it would be unwise to order a further advance toward the interior of the state until the risk of human casualties diminished. Seymour was ordered to oversee construction of fortifications at Jacksonville, Baldwin, and Palatka strong enough to withstand surprise attacks when garrisoned with only two hundred to three hundred men. Given the two regiments already on station at Fernandina and St. Augustine, it was Gillmore's opinion that an additional twenty-five hundred men would be sufficient to hold Florida and reinvigorate the local economy. He wanted loyal Union men living along the St. Johns to revive the lumber and turpentine trade and convince residents of the permanence of this fourth Union occupation; he had already asked Secretary Chase to reopen trade at the Jacksonville port.[61]

On February 15 Gillmore returned to Hilton Head, confident the Union campaign was proceeding successfully. The Federals controlled Fernandina and St. Augustine, along with key points along the St. Johns River (Mayport, Jacksonville, and Palatka) and the railroad junction at Baldwin. By controlling this enclave, Gillmore felt it would be possible to protect Union loyalists, revive agriculture and commerce, and conduct infantry and cavalry raids into rural areas to undermine the economy and the morale of Florida's secessionists.

Within hours of Gillmore's return to Hilton Head, communications from Seymour arrived that eroded his previous confidence in the Florida campaign. In messages sent February 16 and 17, Seymour announced that he had reversed his negative opinion concerning local support for the Union; he now believed that Florida residents were ready to renounce secession and rejoin the Union. More importantly, Seymour boldly declared that he was already in the process of moving his army to the interior of the state, a complete reversal of the policy the two generals had agreed to on February 11. On February 17, however, he announced he was "moving to Suwannee River . . . with the object of destroying the railroad near the Suwannee . . . probably by the time you read this I shall be in motion."[62] In addition, Seymour insisted on the impossible; he told Gillmore to immediately stage a feint movement at the Savannah River to occupy Confederate forces and prevent Beauregard from sending reinforcements to Florida.

Gillmore was aghast. He realized the entire Union force in Florida would be in grave danger if Seymour ordered the advance. The diversionary raid on the South Carolina coast had been terminated on February 16, and to revive such a venture would require days of planning and preparation, as well as the cooperation of Admiral Dahlgren and the Union navy. Realizing that Beauregard would be able to send reinforcements to Florida in sufficient numbers to endanger an invading army, Gillmore ordered his chief of staff, General John W. Turner, to travel with all speed to Jacksonville to demand that Seymour halt the advance.

Gillmore also told Turner to deliver a blunt message to Seymour: "You must have forgotten my last instructions." The two generals had agreed on future policy for the Florida campaign "at a personal interview," Gillmore wrote, but already Seymour had discarded the plans for a dangerous alternative that "not only involves your command in a distant movement, without provisions, far beyond a point from which you once withdrew on account of precisely the same necessity, but presupposes a simultaneous demonstration of 'great importance' to you elsewhere, over which you have no control, and which requires the co-operation of the navy. A raid to tear up the railroad west of Lake City will be of service, but I have no intention to occupy now that part of the State."[63]

Under normal conditions, Turner could have traveled from Hilton Head to Jacksonville in fourteen hours, but severe weather turned this emergency journey into a forty-eight-hour marathon. By the time Turner arrived at Jacksonville, Seymour had already ordered his entire force of 5,500 infantry and cavalry, supported by sixteen guns in the field artillery batteries, to advance toward Lake City. At 6 a.m. on February 20, Seymour initiated a colossal blunder that led to losses of tragic proportion at the Battle of Olustee.[64]

If it had been decided to move the Federal army into the interior of Florida on February 10, that action would have had a high probability of success. When Union forces steamed up the St. Johns on February 7, Finegan's entire East Florida command consisted of only 1,200 men, spread from the Suwannee River to Amelia Island and from Tampa Bay to Mosquito Inlet.

Finegan was able to concentrate those troops at Lake City, where they were joined by reinforcements from middle Florida as well as several hundred men from Savannah transferred by Beauregard. Even then the Federal troop advantage was approximately two to one, but by the morning of February 20 the Confederates had reduced the numerical edge to approximately 300 men, and it was Finegan who held the decided advantage of field position and preestablished defensive lines.

As soon as the Federal diversionary raid on the South Carolina coast ended on February 16, Beauregard released four regiments of Georgia troops, along with the Chatham Artillery, under command of Brigadier General Alfred H. Colquitt, and dispatched them by rail to Valdosta, Georgia. Because the region still lacked a north-south line connecting Florida and Georgia, the troops walked from Valdosta to Madison, Florida, a forty-five-mile march they accomplished in twenty-four hours. From Madison they rode on the Florida, Atlantic and Gulf Central Railroad to Lake City, arriving the evening of February 18. After a day's rest they took places in the defense line alongside Finegan's Florida men and waited for the Federals.[65]

In the days after the confrontation with Union cavalry outside Lake City, Finegan moved his defenders thirteen miles east of Lake City to a camp near Ocean Pond, outside the village of Olustee Station. Calling the site "the only strong position between Lake City and Barber's [Station]," Finegan ordered trenches dug from Ocean Pond on the north to a cypress pond on the south, intersected at half the distance by the tracks of the Florida, Atlantic and Gulf Central Railroad and the road from Jacksonville to Lake City.[66] On the morning of February 20, 5,200 determined Confederates defended the line.

Seymour was aware that Finegan's command had been reinforced. Seven days after he ordered the advance, in a personal letter to Adjutant General John T. Sprague, he said he had expected "to meet no more than 4500 of the enemy." One month later he informed Sprague: "The best information I could gain placed the enemy at 1800 cavalry & 2500 infantry. I knew I could thrash that number!"[67] Such brash overconfidence is troubling. Only seven months earlier, Seymour had ordered more than 5,000 men against 200 entrenched Confederates at Fort Wagner, an action that resulted in 1,800 Union casualties. It was a lesson learned again and again during this war, but too quickly forgotten by commanders whose men followed orders to charge and sacrificed their lives in assaults on entrenched defenders firing rifles with deadly accuracy.

Seymour had been warned by brigade commander Colonel Joseph R. Hawley of the 7th Connecticut that it was improbable a Federal army could hold a position in the interior of Florida after knocking out a Suwannee River bridge. With only a single locomotive operational on the Florida, Atlantic and Gulf Central Railroad, Hawley feared the Confederates would cut off the rail line, trapping the Federals with no access to supplies. Hawley's entreaties were disregarded; Seymour had already made up his mind to attack. On February 22, two days after the battle had ended, Seymour wrote: "The instant I could accumulate provisions enough to sally out, in pursuit of the original aim & end of the expedition, the destroying of communications by the Suwannee, that moment I advanced." It was only proper, he argued, that General Gillmore's orders be "modified as I have a right to modify them by a personal presence and command."[68]

On the morning of February 20, Union forces massed in the vicinity of Barber's Station, more than thirty miles west of Jacksonville. Seymour's order to march came at 6 a.m. He expected the enemy to be drawn up in strength at Lake City, and he ordered his officers to move the men rapidly to confront Finegan's defenders there. His plan was to order a frontal attack while Henry's cavalry bypassed the scene of battle and raced on to destroy the railroad bridges on the Suwannee River.[69]

Three columns of Federal troops marched westward throughout the morning, heading for Lake City without stopping for rest or food. Seymour was surprised when the enemy was sighted thirteen miles east of Lake City, drawn up in formation, waiting along a battlefront that extended for more than a mile. The defense line was positioned between a large swamp on the north and another on the south, which served to funnel the attackers in front of the defenders' rifles. The opposing forces were about equal in numbers and staffed with similar percentages of raw recruits and seasoned veterans. As the Federals approached in the early afternoon, Finegan ordered cavalry and infantry units forward to "skirmish with the enemy and draw them to our works."[70]

More than four hours of fierce fighting followed. Hundreds of brave men on both sides fell as rifle and artillery shells ripped through the ranks. As darkness settled over the now bloody field, the Federals withdrew, leaving behind large numbers of dead and wounded men. In panic, what remained of Seymour's army began a chaotic retreat toward Barber's Station, the point where they had begun their march at dawn that day.

General Colquitt reported "the enemy gave way in confusion. We continued the pursuit for several miles, when night put an end to the conflict. Instructions were sent to the cavalry to follow close upon the enemy and seize every opportunity to strike a favorable blow."[71] Finegan agreed: "The enemy retreated that night, hastily and in some confusion . . . leaving a large number of their killed and wounded in our possession on the field. . . . The victory was complete."[72]

Winston Stephens had been at the scene of the heaviest fighting and was confident that "men never fought better than our men did and God seemed to shield them in a great measure." The men from the North fought valiantly, "but our artillery and infantry opened and the boys yelled and went to work as men can only work who are in earnest. Then the scene was grand and exciting. I felt like I could wade through my weight in wild cats." Dead white and black Federal soldiers were left "strewn thick all over the field. We drove the yankees inch by inch for about two miles and then they left in a hurry." Blaming Finegan for a lackluster attempt to pursue the enemy, Stephens lamented: "we could have captured the whole army."[73]

The retreat became a demented nightmare for the Union soldiers. As one man remembered, they "wended or crawled along, the wounded filling the night air with lamentations, the crippled horses neighing in pain, and a full moon kissing the cold, clammy lips of the dying. The line of retreat was strewn with guns, knapsacks and blankets."[74] Defying normal limits of human endurance, the entire command reached Barber's Station during the night. Surgeon C. Macfarlane of the 115th New York remembered filling "every ambulance, wagon and gun carriage with the wounded" and seeing "great numbers" of walking wounded as well. "We all had the rebel prisons in our minds, and fear is a terrible spur to endurance." During the ensuing retreat "no one was allowed to speak above a whisper, to make the slightest noise, or even to scratch a match."[75]

Seymour sent a telegraph to Jacksonville: "Have met the enemy at Olustee and now falling back. Many wounded. . . . A devilish hard rub."[76] He ordered Appleton back toward Olustee with three companies of the 54th Massachusetts to form a perimeter defensive line. The order stated: "You will be attacked before morning, and you must hold your ground until I get the army in shape to relieve you."[77] Throughout an evening so bitterly cold it caused ice to form an inch thick, Appleton's men protected the wounded and disoriented Union soldiers that came down the lonely road, all the while dreading the approach of a pursuing army.[78] The next day, still expecting to be attacked by the Confederates, Appleton rejoined the rear guard and marched another twenty miles before nightfall. He ate one small potato before falling asleep, only to be rudely awakened when he rolled into the fire and burned a hole in his jacket.

The next day, just before reaching Camp Finegan, the entire 54th Massachusetts was ordered back to rescue a malfunctioning locomotive and train of railroad cars loaded with wounded soldiers. "Tired as our men were," Appleton remembered, "they pushed the train in to Jacksonville by hand. Some horses were sent out to help with the locomotive the last of the way. We had very little to eat, nothing but the army biscuit, and very little of that. I had a small drink of coffee this last day."[79] By the evening of February 22, Appleton and what remained of Seymour's army was back in Jacksonville, thankful they had not been captured and made prisoners of war, which would surely have happened had the Confederates pursued the retreating army immediately and vigorously. A wounded artillery officer wrote from a hospital ship anchored in the river off Jacksonville: "In ninety hours we have marched one hundred and ten miles, fought a battle of three hours' duration, got badly whipped, and what there is left of our little army is back again where we started from."[80]

On February 25, Seymour reported that of the 5,500 men he led into battle at Olustee, 203 were killed, 506 were missing, and 1,152 were wounded, a total of 1,861 casualties. Based on the "percentage of Union casualties," William H. Nulty has written, "the battle of Olustee was the third bloodiest of the entire war!" Seymour's report, however, almost certainly undercounted the number of Union dead. On February 22, two days after the fighting had ended, Finegan observed wounded Federal soldiers still being removed from the battlefield. Three days later he reported again, saying that approximately 400 Union men had been buried, another 200 captured, and "418 of their wounded were removed by us from the field."[81] Apparently, several hundred men whom Seymour listed as missing were instead dead, killed during or after the battle and buried in the six days that followed the Union retreat. It is probable that many of the uncounted dead men were black soldiers, wounded men left on the field of battle who were killed in the days that followed.

Historians William H. Nulty and David J. Coles have found convincing evidence that a small number of Confederate soldiers roamed the field after the battle and killed black soldiers they found among the wounded. After the Yankees had retreated, Captain William F. Penniman, 4th Georgia Cavalry, rode his horse over the scene of some of the worst fighting, picking his way through scores of dead and wounded Union soldiers and all the while hearing rifle fire that "seemed to be going on in every direction, until the reports sounded almost frequent enough to resemble the work of skirmishers." He was informed by one of his subordinate officers that the shots were coming from the men of his own regiment, who were "Shooting niggers Sir.

I have tried to make the boys desist but I can't control them." Penniman objected, but the officer said that "one young fellow over yonder told me the niggers killed his brother after being wounded, at Fort Pillow, and he was twenty three years old, that he had already killed nineteen and needed only four more to make the matter even, so I told him to go ahead and finish the job."[82]

The following morning Penniman retraced his route of the previous evening. He viewed "Negroes, and plenty of them, whom I had [previously] seen lying all over the field wounded, and as far as I could see, many of them moving around from place to place, now without motion, all were dead. If a negro had a shot in the shin another was sure to be in the head." About the few black soldiers who were taken for medical attention, Penniman wrote: "[they] were placed on the surgeons operating table—their legs fairly flew off, but whether they were at all seriously wounded I have always had my doubt."[83]

Winston Stephens also rode over the field in the daylight following the battle. He made no specific references to black soldiers, but he was in general tormented by what he viewed: "I went over the battle ground this morning on my way to camp and never in all my life have I seen such a distressing sight. Some men with their legs carried off, others with their brains out and mangled in every conceivable way, and then our men commenced stripping them of their clothing and leaving their bodies naked. I never want to see another battle or go on the field after it is over."[84]

Union general John P. Hatch, who investigated allegations of atrocities committed after the fighting ended at Olustee, reported: "It is well known that most of the wounded colored men were murdered on the field."[85] After a more recent and thorough investigation, David Coles concluded that the evidence "proves beyond any reasonable doubt that atrocities did occur at Olustee."[86]

Finegan tallied Confederate casualties on February 26. His official report listed "93 killed, and 841 wounded, a large proportion very slightly." He revised that estimate only slightly three weeks later, listing 93 killed, 847 wounded, 6 missing, for a total of 946 casualties. The Battle of Olustee had, indeed, been a bloody affair. The 10,700 men in blue and gray who engaged in combat on February 20 suffered a casualty rate of one in four.[87]

As soon as the retreating Federals reached Jacksonville, every available man was put to work strengthening the defense lines surrounding the town. Working day and night, veterans of the battle constructed earthworks, artillery mounts, and rifle pits under the protective cover of naval gunboats at battle stations on the St. Johns. Trees were cut down for a thousand yards in front of Union lines, and telegraph wire entanglements were staked in front of breastworks until the defense line incorporated McCoys Creek as a hindrance to enemy cavalry and stretched far enough for a thousand men to stand on guard duty.

After a tedious day of working on the fortifications, Appleton wrote: "this is my 24th night of sleeping or not sleeping in clothes and boots. Like all the rest of the men, my clothes abound in body lice. I often spend an hour or two picking over my garments and washing in some big puddle in some swamp." Seymour ordered the 54th Massachusetts to the extreme left of the defense line to occupy rifle pits dug a thousand yards in advance of the other Union forces. In the event of a cavalry attack, the men were instructed to let the enemy breach the line, then fall back slowly while continuing to fight.[88]

Gillmore returned to Jacksonville to communicate directly with Seymour and to ensure that his orders would not be countermanded again. He told Seymour to concentrate on the immediate goal of securing an impregnable defensive position at Jacksonville and to banish all thoughts of another advance to the interior of the state. He bluntly stated: "affairs in Florida will not warrant an advance of your command for the present; therefore you will only look to the security of your position at Jacksonville."[89]

It was a wise decision to communicate directly and bluntly with Seymour. In a private letter to his friend Adjutant General Sprague, Seymour blamed Gillmore and others for the defeat at Olustee and indicated that he might consider another advance: "It was a mistake to come here at all—but that's no fault of mine. And I doubtless made a mistake in trying to whip Mr. Reb. But it is an error I am likely to commit whenever the chance is offered & I have troops to do it with as I had on that day."[90] Morose and self-pitying during his final days in Florida, Seymour told Sprague he was "indifferent to all except the opinions of my friends." He was hoping for a transfer to another command in the Army of the Potomac, but he feared that his enemies in the military and the press "may *sacrifice* me as goats always have been from time immemorial."[91]

Gillmore urged vigilance in guarding against attacks on the naval vessels bringing men and supplies upriver to Jacksonville, warning Seymour that "guerrilla parties or ambuscades may annoy your transports." He recommended landing a regiment occasionally "at points below Jacksonville" in order to "scout the country a short distance into the interior."[92] With the river and Jacksonville secured, a steady movement of troop transports carrying reinforcements brought the Federal troop level to 12,000 men.

Two weeks after the Battle of Olustee, the New York Times reported: "the troops are entirely recovered from the slight shock imparted by the unfortunate result at Olustee, and are in excellent condition to again meet the enemy."[93] Working day and night, veterans of Olustee and the reinforcements who were rushed to Jacksonville in the days after the defeat constructed formidable defenses around the town under protective cover of naval gunboats on station in the St. Johns River. Some of the first fortifications were only three feet in height, but one soldier commented: "We could lie down behind them and be comparatively safe from the missiles of the enemy."[94] Small trees and limbs were cut down and dragged in front of the trenches, and "trip-wires were stretched along the front of the works to help prevent Confederate troops from entering."[95]

Men on picket stations at the outer line were spared the onerous labor that soldiers constructing the fortifications were subject to, but their duty was subject to other perils. Jacob Smith of Company D, 107th Ohio, complained that he was posted near the edge of a wooded area with instructions to "keep a sharp lookout for spies, guard-runners and rebel guerrillas. All the noise I heard while on post was the familiar hum of the southern mosquito; they were full of life and song and loved to keep up a close acquaintance. With them for company, we were not liable to become sleepy, and in resisting their attacks the hours would pass more rapidly by."[96]

At the end of their duty time, the men returned to crude campsites close to the outer lines. Trunks of palm trees were hollowed and lined with flattened tin cans to direct smoke from campfires up and away from the tents. William L. Hyde of the 112th New York Volunteer Infantry said, "it was surprising in how short a time old soldiers will make themselves comfortable, if there is any material lying around that can be begged, borrowed, or 'confiscated.'"[97]

When the defenses were completed in early March, they consisted of a vertical-log stockade, the timbers sharpened at the top, anchored on the St. Johns River at Hogan's Creek and McCoys Creek. The stockade stretched in a half circle around the town and incorporated several fortified redoubts. A twelve-foot-deep moat was dug outside the stockade's walls to further strengthen the defenses. Trees were felled for a thousand yards beyond the breastworks, and pits for riflemen were dug just behind. An entangling thicket of telegraph wire was placed at the outer limits to impede enemy cavalry. McCoys Creek on the west served as a further hindrance to attackers.

Forts Hatch, Foster, and Fribley, along with redoubt Sammons and battery Myrick, provided further protection for the western flank of the town.

These fortifications stood guard over the railroad line and three important roads: the Black Creek Road leading to Middleburg and other locations in Clay County, the Plank Road leading to Lake City, and the Kings Road heading northwest toward Georgia. North and east of the stockade, the redoubts McCrea and Reed and battery Hamilton protected the Panama Road leading to Trout River.[98] Thirty guns were mounted in the fortifications, including heavy coastal artillery, siege howitzers, and large-caliber rifled pieces. Eventually, three heavy forts were built outside the wall to protect the approaches to the five city gates. The main gate was to the west at the present intersection of Davis and Adams streets. Additional gates were located at Pearl and Ashley, Beaver and Main, Adams and Washington, and Bay and Water streets.[99]

The intimidating firepower of the Union navy's gunboats served as further warning that an attack on Jacksonville from the north and west would result in heavy casualties. Vessels assigned to cover Jacksonville from the St. Johns River in February and March were the *Mahaska*, a sloop of war that mounted a 100-pounder rifle and five other guns; the *Pawnee*, a steam sloop armed with eleven guns; and the gunboats *Norwich*, *Ottawa*, *Dai Ching*, and *Water Witch*, which mounted an additional twenty-one pieces of heavy artillery. Together the vessels carried 627 officers and sailors. Commander George R. Balch of the *Pawnee* told Admiral Dahlgren shortly after the Federal troops returned from Olustee that he had "abundant reason to believe that to the naval force must our troops be indebted for protection against a greatly superior force flushed with victory."[100]

As reinforcing troops settled into the camps around Jacksonville, defenses were strengthened along the east bank of the St. Johns. A blockhouse was erected atop St. Johns Bluff, and two small works for infantry were installed at Yellow Bluff. In Jacksonville, near the southwest corner of Forsyth and Pine (now Main) streets, a hundred-foot-tall signal tower was erected to communicate with a similar tower mounted at the new encampment at Yellow Bluff, and from there to a third tower installed at the naval gunboat base at the entrance to the St. Johns. This communications network kept Union headquarters at Jacksonville advised of enemy troop or guerrilla movements and maintained contact with gunboats patrolling the St. Johns.[101]

For several weeks in late February and early March, torrential rainfall immobilized the Union army at Jacksonville. On the night of March 10 a severe rainstorm with incessant lightning and thunder drenched the campsite of the 54th Massachusetts and washed away rifle pits and earthworks. Appleton heard the wind and rain strike the sides of his tent "like a watchman's rattle" and watched light from the electrical storm "fill the tent with twin-kling blue flames that seemed to play all over us for several seconds, and then came a crash like a heavy gun. The few camp fires that will burn, blow out horizontally, ten or twenty feet, and then long trains of sparks stream away into the darkness."[102]

Many of Appleton's men lacked blankets and overcoats, and some had to stand on duty in bare feet or with their feet wrapped in rags. They resembled "a set of rag-muffins: half shoes, no shoes, rags of pantaloons, shreds of blouses, old hats and caps. We have . . . new clothing, but not near enough to go around." Their only shelter came from a limited number of old wall tents set on platforms of scavenged bits of lumber. "These edifices are not very weather proof," Appleton lamented, "but they are the best we can do. I have crammed some old rubber cloths into the holes in the roof of our tent, where the water pours on my bed."[103] Following the storms, numerous men suffered from severe colds and coughed incessantly. Vaccination programs for smallpox were under way, but cases still occurred. When it proved impractical to send men to Jacksonville for confinement and care, a quarantine camp was established at McCoys Creek.

Appleton sought the counsel of his superior officer, Colonel Ned Hallowell, concerning the future of black men in America. Both officers were dedicated abolitionists who "felt the magnitude of our undertaking to raise the Colored man as far as we can in the Army," but they had become discouraged by the continuing "checks and rebuffs." The black soldiers had also become discouraged. A group of men from the 54th and 55th Massachusetts, which together composed the 3rd Brigade under Hallowell's command, had been sending letters to their field officers since early March, warning that they would refuse to fight if they were not soon paid. This was an old complaint for black soldiers, growing out of the discriminatory pay policy of the Union army. They were paid less than white soldiers, a policy that Governor John Andrews of Massachusetts had repeatedly asked the Lincoln administration to rectify. When the request was denied, the men of the 54th and 55th voted to refuse all payment until salaries were made equal for black and white soldiers. "Sometimes we almost despair of having justice done to our men in the matter of pay and proper recognition," Appleton wrote in his journal on March 12.[104]

The difficulty black soldiers faced was dramatized for Appleton when two of Beauregard's staff officers came to Jacksonville under a flag of truce. For the men of the 54th Massachusetts, no issue was more consequential than the fate of the black soldiers captured by Confederates at Olustee. When one of the Union officers asked the Confederates what they were going to do with captive black troops, one officer replied: "Hang them if President Lincoln is willing."[105] Appleton grimly concluded that the future of black freedmen in an America cleansed of slavery would be tied closely to the treatment of black soldiers during the course of the war. "If their wrongs are not righted," Appleton wrote prophetically, "this may be 'the Land of the Free,' but it is no land for the Freedmen. Well, we will neither despair nor grumble. Providence watches over us. Some must suffer for every great cause. Millions of free men are not born without a pang."[106]

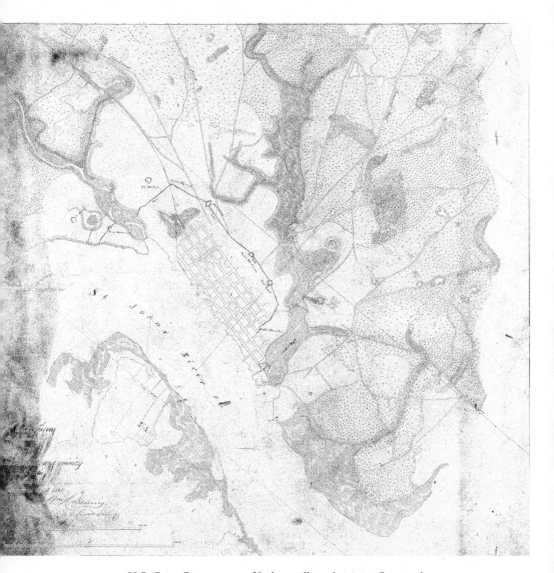

MAP 2. U.S. Coast Survey, map of Jacksonville and vicinity. Surveyed April 1864. The map shows the Federal defense works completed at Jacksonville in March 1864 to stop the advance of the pursuing Confederate army following their victory at the Battle of Olustee. A vertical-log stockade stretched in a half-circle around the town from Hogan's Creek on the east to McCoys Creek on the west. A twelve-foot-deep moat outside the stockade wall provided further protection. (Courtesy of National Archives and Records Administration.)

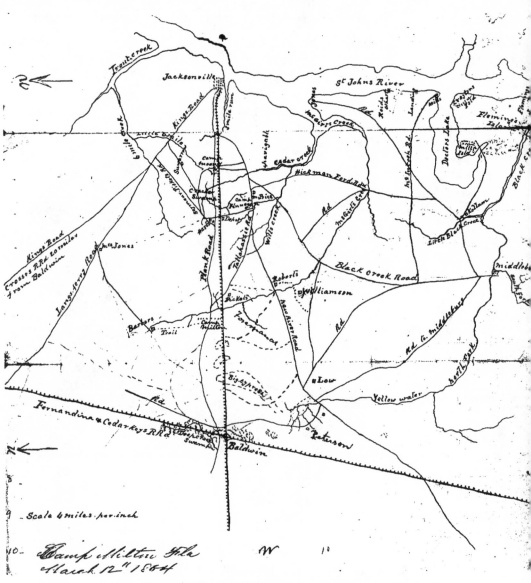

MAP 3. Drawn by George Washington Scott, lieutenant colonel, 5th Florida Cavalry, CSA. (Courtesy of Florida State Archives.)

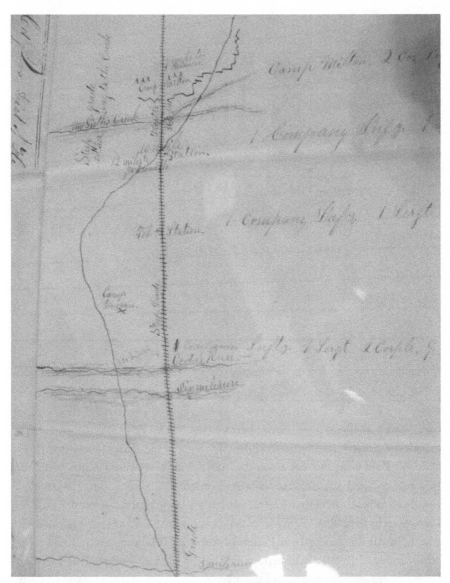

MAP 4. The route to Camp Milton. Hand-drawn map with the routes of the Florida Central Railroad and wagon roads, noting where various companies of the 75th Ohio Volunteers and the 104th Pennsylvania Volunteers were to be deployed: two companies at Camp Milton; one company at 10-mile station; one company at the telegraph station between Cedar Creek and 10-mile station; one company at Cedar Creek railroad bridge; one company at Cedar Creek on wagon road; one company at 3-mile station. Signed by Major Edward L. Rogers, AAG, Major 104th Pennsylvania Volunteers, August 1864. (Courtesy of Larry Skinner.)

10

Thunder on the River

Torpedo Warfare and the Struggle for Control of Northeast Florida

In the days after the Battle of Olustee, General Beauregard realized that the entire Union army should have been captured during its chaotic retreat. The victorious Confederates had missed a great opportunity to drive the Yankees out of Jacksonville and off the St. Johns River. With General Finegan in command, the pursuit had been so laggardly that the Confederate army did not arrive at Baldwin until February 24, more than forty-eight hours after the Federals reached the defense lines at Jacksonville. It took Finegan another two days to reach McGirts Creek, twelve miles west of Jacksonville. At Mc-Girts Creek, Brigadier General W. M. Gardner took command and ordered a "halt" until the strength of Federal forces could be determined. Gardner, commander of Confederate troops in Middle Florida, had returned to duty from sick leave in February and been given the additional command of Confederate forces in East Florida by General Beauregard. He was unable to assume command immediately, however, because he arrived in Ocean Pond only hours before the fighting began. He observed the action and accompanied the victorious troops as they pursued the fleeing Union army. Disappointed by the laggardly pursuit, Gardner realized that "the moment for reaping the fruits" of the great victory at Olustee "had been allowed to escape and the enemy had been allowed time not only to reorganize his defeated forces, but to receive reinforcements and to strengthen the strong position at

Jacksonville, where his gun-boats could be used against us." Gardner's most compelling reason for calling the halt, however, was his "utter want of confidence in the brigadier-general [Finegan] to handle an army on the field of battle, as manifested under my own eye at the battle of Olustee."[1]

Instead of ordering an attack, Gardner focused on building fortifications west of the town. He recognized the strategic importance of protecting the railroad junction at Baldwin and building defense works to impede a future Federal advance. Cavalry and some infantry were subsequently moved four miles to the east to temporarily reoccupy Camp Finegan as a base from which scouts and skirmishers could monitor Union activities. In early March, Beauregard arrived on the scene and initiated construction of a formidable Confederate defense line at the west bank of McGirts Creek. He named the new fortification Camp Milton in honor of Florida's Confederate governor, John Milton, and personally supervised construction of a two-mile breastwork to protect the rail line and the wagon road to Baldwin and Lake City.[2] The defensive network that emerged was described as "breast-works and stockades [that] were immediately constructed at [the west bank of McGirt's Creek] and similar fortifications of a more permanent character . . . at Baldwin, eight miles in the rear of McGirt's Creek, and at the intersection of the railroads running from Fernandina to Cedar Key and from Jacksonville to Lake City."[3]

By early March, approximately 8,000 troops from South Carolina, Florida, and Georgia were headquartered at Camp Milton. Beauregard was in the process of deploying an additional 2,000 Confederate cavalry and 15,000 infantry into Florida at the time, which delayed his plan to send 10,000 men to General Bragg's beleaguered command in Tennessee and weakened the defensive network at Savannah and other points along the Atlantic coast. Exceedingly frustrated by pressures from the War Department to storm the Federal position and liberate Jacksonville, Beauregard reported that the enemy "cannot be driven out of Jacksonville with our present means."[4]

Beauregard held the Confederate government responsible for failing to complete a rail line "between Lawton [Georgia] and Live Oak [Florida]" that would have connected the east-west railroads in the two states. Had a connector line been in place in February 1864, more troops could have been sent quickly and efficiently to Florida prior to the Battle of Olustee. Had that happened, and had a competent pursuit of General Seymour's defeated army occurred, the result might have been a fourth Federal evacuation of Jacksonville. Therefore, when pressured again to storm the Jacksonville defenses, Beauregard responded: "If . . . another officer can expel the enemy from Florida by prompt and decided measures, I will be most happy to sur-render the command to him."[5]

The other Confederate officers in the vicinity agreed with Beauregard. Major General James Patton Anderson, appointed by Beauregard to com-mand of the overall District of Florida in March, judged it possible to "carry the works around Jacksonville by storm. Of course it would be at great sac-rifice of life, and to no purpose, since his gun-boats would prevent us from holding it." General Colquitt estimated the Federal force at 12,000 effectives and said that "an assault . . . with our present forces would be attended with disastrous consequences. If it should prove successful the cost would be greater than the advantage gained." Finegan wrote: "Flanked as Jacksonville is by two creeks, and with their gun-boats in their rear, and being fortified in front, as they doubtless are, it seems to me entirely impracticable to take the place by assault without a very great loss to us, even if taken at all."[6]

On March 7, Beauregard ended the debate by writing: "The position of Jacksonville is naturally very strong, easily made much stronger, and with the five gun-boats now in the Saint John's is . . . impregnable except by regu-lar approaches."[7] Chief of Staff Thomas Jordan's response was prophetic for the future of the war on the St. Johns River: "I take for granted you want river torpedoes, and will send them quickly as possible."[8] Jordan realized that Beauregard was planning to drive the Federals out of Jacksonville and away from the St. Johns River valley through the use of torpedo warfare. The general intended to place torpedoes, better described as floating explosive devices, in the river to destroy the Federal gunboats and transports that had been navigating the river with few hindrances since 1862. Assisted by Con-federate artillery batteries planned for Fleming Island (upriver from Jackson-ville) and the entrance to Trout River (downriver), Beauregard believed the use of torpedoes could isolate the Federals and render them vulnerable.[9] In the months ahead, the war in Florida would be dramatized by the thunder-ous sounds of Confederate torpedoes detonating against the hulls of Federal vessels on the St. Johns River.

But first it was necessary to secure Confederate defenses and prevent a future Federal advance to the west of Jacksonville. Work on the fortifications at Camp Milton was disrupted in March 1864 by rainstorms that washed out barrier walls and several miles of railroad track, severing food supplies for thousands of men. In Baldwin, Anderson complained that work had been "retarded by the heavy rains preventing in great measure the work from progressing as it had to be done in water which stands in many places along the line of works."[10] Beauregard assigned a company of engineers under

Captain James W. McAlpine to supervise hundreds of enslaved black men working under emergency conditions. To assist in this vital project, Confederate agents impressed male slaves from as far away as Alachua and Marion counties. An agent with a small guard detachment visited plantations to gather the needed workers. If an owner failed to meet his assigned quota, guards marched away every one of the able-bodied male slaves residing at his property. If one of the slaves escaped, Confederate agents demanded a replacement from the same plantation. The impressed slaves were required to continue working until the fortifications were completed.[11] Progress on fortifications was also slowed by disaffection among Confederate troops, which led many to desert and seek sanctuary behind Union lines or hideouts in remote areas, while others quietly resumed their former civilian lives. That March, Confederate authorities asked Sheriff Elan Daniels of Clay County to arrest and turn over to the provost marshal at Baldwin fourteen deserters from that county.[12] Soldiers who stayed with their regiments were also causing trouble; members of the 32nd Georgia Volunteers sat idle for several days, refusing to work on the fortification at Baldwin.[13]

When Camp Milton was completed, it represented a formidable obstacle to potential Union attempts to advance toward the interior of Florida. A Federal officer who later inspected the fortification described the breastwork as "made of huge logs firmly fastened and covered with earth. . . . The log part was 6 feet wide at the bottom and 3 at the top. They were proof against field artillery. The stockades were composed of timber from 12 to 16 inches thick, with loopholes [for riflemen] two feet apart. Their base was protected by earth thrown up from a ditch which ran along the whole line of works." To provide protection for the rail line, two batteries were erected at the rear of the fortification that were described as "very strong" and "elaborately finished, having a sharpness of outline almost equal to masonry. This line extended about 1½ miles, when a new line began. Across the dirt road north of the railroad the works were of the same class as those described, except that the stockades had platforms and embrasures for field pieces. The works at that point were most solidly constructed and beautifully finished."[14]

As impressive as the defenses were at Camp Milton, they were never intended to be permanent. The massive earthwork was designed as a temporary obstacle to an army advancing toward the vital railroad junction at Baldwin. In a March 20 letter to Anderson, Beauregard wrote: "Your present defensive line in rear of McGirt's Creek is only for a temporary purpose—that is, until the works around Baldwin shall be sufficiently completed to enable you to give battle at that point, with all the chances of success in your favor, notwithstanding the disparity in numbers." In the event that Union forces moved out of their position at Jacksonville and commenced an advance on Baldwin, Beauregard advised Anderson to begin a slow retreat, "drawing [the enemy] after you. About one brigade will take position in the lines there, with some cavalry on the left; the other two brigades and main body of cavalry will take position on the right, ready to take the enemy in flank and rear by advancing between the Little and Big Cypress Swamps, should he attack the lines in front."[15]

In addition to the fortifications at Camp Milton and Baldwin, Beauregard devised a plan to defend against Federal raids on the farms and plantations along the St. Johns that were depleting valuable herds of beef and other commissary supplies needed by the men in gray in Florida and at battlefields to the north. Basic to the plan was a telegraphic network extending from stations at Camp Milton to Baker County, Lake City, Gainesville, Waldo, and Tallahassee. Anderson's April 7 requisition for supplies from the Gainesville area alone called for "4,000 lbs Bacon, 300 bushels shelled corn, 75 bushels peas" to be placed on railcars and delivered to Camp Milton. Orders were also given to the chief quartermaster, Major E. C. Simkins, to deliver twenty barrels of syrup and eighteen hogsheads of sugar from supplies on hand at Waldo.[16]

Confederate cavalry monitored the enemy's activities and harassed picket lines, with instructions to delay any concerted attacks emanating from Jacksonville or Palatka until infantry support could be dispatched by rail. Their orders were to skirmish with the enemy until infantry units could meet the challenge. At Palatka, Anderson stationed a cavalry unit under Captain J. J. Dickison just inland from the Federal defense works, with the primary task of restricting Federal access to the interior farms and plantations. Lieutenant Colonel John M. Martin was situated further south at Orange Springs to protect that flank if Union troops marched in that direction, and Colonel William B. Tabb and the 59th Virginia Infantry regiment were encamped at Waldo, near the rail line that ran to Gainesville. A telegraph message could result in one or all of the units converging at a threatened position. The Confederate command could call on a brigade of 2,500 infantry, six pieces of artillery, 400 men of the 6th Florida battalion, and another 400 men of the 4th Georgia battalion.[17]

For several weeks, scouts and skirmishers from both armies prowled the twelve-mile zone between the fortifications at Camp Milton and Jacksonville. A company of Confederate cavalry was subdued on February 27 by a battalion of the Independent Massachusetts Cavalry in the vicinity of Camp Finegan. The *New York Times* reported "the complete rout of the enemy with a loss of one killed and three wounded [Confederates]. No casualties on our side."[18] A few days later Colonel Henry led Federal cavalry and a company of horse artillery on a reconnaissance at Three Mile Run. They encountered mounted Rebels and forced them to retreat as far as Camp Finegan.[19]

Captain Winston Stephens and the men of the 2nd Florida Cavalry were among the Rebel troops skirmishing against their Union counterparts. That these were trying times for soldiers is clear from Stephens's February 27 letter to his wife: "Our Genl seems to think that our men and horses can live on wind. . . . My horses are mere skeletons . . . it is nothing strange for them to go 24 and 36 hours without feed and then get a few ears of corn and go again."[20]

On March 1 the 2nd Florida Cavalry engaged in a fierce five-hour fight in the vicinity of Cedar Creek, west of Jacksonville. Facing Stephens and his men were Colonel Henry's 4th Massachusetts Cavalry and the 40th Massachusetts Mounted Infantry. After skirmishing, Henry ordered the Federals to pull back toward Cedar Creek. One Union soldier was killed and four were wounded.

The Confederates suffered only one casualty that day. While still in the saddle, Stephens, who was well known to the Union cavalrymen for daring escapades on his "cream colored horse," was shot in the head by a Union sniper. A member of the 40th Massachusetts, Charles Currier, described Stephens as "the 'Sheridan' of the enemy's forces in Florida," well known to Union cavalrymen as "a gallant fellow, and much ammunition had been expended in attempts to unseat him." When the Union sniper's bullet hit Stephens, Currier said, "the shock of his death was so great, as to cause a temporary cessation of their fire, whereupon our men set up a wild cheer."[21]

Swepson Stephens had ridden "side by side" with his older brother that day, and heard the fatal shot. In a letter written months later to Winston's widow, Swepson described his brother's final moments: "He fell before I could reach him. I dismounted and took him up and [sat] him on my horse and got up behind him and took him out in that way leaning back against me. That look, the last look was full of love. His lips moved but no word escaped. I see that look now and ever will."[22]

Octavia Stephens was pregnant when she heard of her husband's death. From her temporary refuge near Thomasville, Georgia, she wrote one of the most poignant journal entries penned by a Floridian during the Civil War.

With a sad, sad heart I begin another journal. On Sunday Feb 28th, dear Mother was taken with a congestive chill. On Friday March 4th, Davis came with the news of the death of my dear dear husband, he was killed in battle near Jacksonville on the 1st of March. Mother grew worse and on Sunday, Mar 6th, she too was taken from us, between 12 and 1 o'clk she passed quietly away from Typhoid Pneumonia. At 7 o'clk p.m. I gave birth to a dear little baby boy, which although three or four weeks before the time, the Lord still spares to me. Mother was buried on the 7th, and Rosa was taken with fever, but recovered after two days. . . . I have named my baby Winston, the sweet name of that dear lost one my husband, almost my life. God grant that his son whom he longed for but was not spared to see may be like him. I now begin as it were a new life and I pray that the Lord will give me strength to bear up under this great affliction, and with His help and the examples of those two dear ones now with him I may be enabled to do my duty in this life and be prepared when the Lord calls to meet them in that "better world" where there will be no more parting and no more sorrow.[23]

While men in blue and gray lost their lives in skirmishes in the contested land between the rival fortifications, and others continued their lonely vigil on the picket lines, the Federals broke the impasse at Jacksonville by mounting an expedition up the St. Johns on the night of March 10 to capture and occupy Palatka. Beginning on the ninth, and lasting for two rain-drenched days, Colonel William B. Barton embarked men from the 47th, 48th, and 115th New York Infantry, along with the 55th Massachusetts and Company C of the 3rd Rhode Island Artillery aboard the *Maple Leaf, General Hunter,* and *Charles B. Houghton.* Traveling at night to avoid enemy sniper fire, two gunboats led the way. When the gunboats were secured and the troops debarked, the men fanned quickly through the streets of Palatka without a shot being fired. The town had been stripped of almost everything of value, and although the houses were still in good condition, the prewar population of five hundred residents had been reduced to only a half-dozen families.[24]

One soldier from the 55th Massachusetts described Palatka as having "suffered greatly from the ravages of a long and tedious warfare."[25] The men of the 48th New York built earthworks and gun emplacements with the intention of holding the town permanently. Barton installed two 18-pounders and one 32-pounder and assigned men from Battery C of the 3rd Rhode Island Heavy Artillery to command of the artillery. The defenses were strong enough that a Union infantryman thought the Confederates would not dare to risk an attack: "I don't believe that they are fool enough to come down here and get killed. We have got this place arranged so as to keep back a hundred thousand troops."[26]

On March 31, Barton heard rumors of an impending attack by as many as eight thousand Confederates and ordered his men to clear away woods and underbrush to deny cover to potential attackers. "Everything possible is being done to strengthen our line of works," Barton reported to Captain P. R. Chadwick. "I have taken the responsibility of directing that the houses in front of our left be so prepared that they can be destroyed in a moment if it becomes necessary."[27] Barton's vigilance was merited. If they conceded two impregnable positions on the St. Johns River—at Jacksonville and further upriver at Palatka—the Confederates would leave hundreds of farms and plantations east and west of the St. Johns vulnerable to raids by Union cavalry and infantry. Anderson was alarmed by "indications . . . of an advance by the enemy, and every preparation was made to meet him at McGirt's Creek . . . or in the event he should turn that position . . . [to make a stand] at Baldwin, where it was believed a successful defense might be made against three times our number."[28]

Anderson was also deeply worried about the possibility of losing hundreds of vital slave laborers, thereby forfeiting the support of their owners to Yankee raiders carried upriver by gunboats from Jacksonville and Palatka. A further concern was protecting the supply line of beef and other commissary supplies from Florida that had become vital to Confederate armies. Recent setbacks on the Mississippi and in Tennessee had resulted in drastic shortages for the major Confederate armies in the East; officials feared that the loss of Florida and its cattle herds would have catastrophic consequences. Regaining control of the St. Johns River was imperative if Florida was to remain in Confederate hands.

By March 1864, Confederate commanders had developed considerable expertise with the use of torpedoes in defense of many harbors and navigable rivers that reached into the interior farmlands along more than thirty-five hundred miles of coastline. At the outset of the war, the Confederacy was without a navy and without capacity to produce ships of war. The Federal navy was not much better equipped at first, but Secretary of the Navy Gideon Welles had quickly ordered the refitting of older vessels, the conversion of commercial craft for military use, and the building of several hundred new ships. When the Confederate secretary of the navy, Stephen Mallory, was unable to draw on such rich resources, inspired patriots produced hundreds of underwater explosives, known at the time as torpedo mines, powerful enough to destroy Federal ships.

General Lee had called on General Gabriel J. Rains, head of the Torpedo Division, to block a Federal advance on Richmond by placing more than one hundred torpedo mines in the James River.[29] Later in the war, Rains placed 123 torpedo mines.[30] Familiar with Rains's successes in South Carolina waters, Beauregard decided in March 1864 to utilize a similar policy of terror and torpedoes to defend the St. Johns. It was more than a coincidence, therefore, when Chief of Staff Jordan wrote to Beauregard that he would expedite shipments of river torpedoes.[31]

Beauregard intended to plant torpedo mines at strategic points in the St. Johns "so as to prevent its navigation."[32] In support, he called for shore batteries to be installed upriver from Jacksonville, at Fleming Island, and downriver at the entrance to Trout River. If all went according to plan, Federal forces would be trapped at Palatka and Jacksonville; without a source of commissary or military supplies, they would be forced to abandon these posts. Beauregard assigned Lieutenant Colonel M. B. Harris, the chief engineer for the Department of South Carolina, Georgia, and Florida, to Camp Milton. He also authorized Captain E. Pliny Bryan to be in charge of manufacturing and placing the torpedoes.[33]

Bryan had been a secessionist in the Maryland legislature prior to the start of the war. After enlisting in the 1st Virginia Regiment and participating in the First Battle at Manassas (Bull Run), he served in the Signal Corps and became skilled at manufacturing torpedoes.[34] Once in Florida, Bryan went to work immediately at the lower St. Johns, just upriver from Mayport. His initial efforts were foiled when men working on a Union naval transport found two large torpedoes. A *New York Times* correspondent described the weapons as consisting of "half an oil can, hermetically sealed," each containing "seventy-five pounds of rifle powder. The powder was to be fired by means of a gun-barrel, to which was attached a percussion cap, exploded by a hammer, the latter being operated by a powerful steel spring, controlled and weighted by a complete Yankee brass clock, manufactured at Connecticut."[35]

Materials for manufacture of the torpedoes were sent from Charleston to Lake City in care of Lieutenant Thomas E. Buckman, chief of ordnance for Florida, who forwarded the materials by train to Bryan at Camp Milton. Buckman often accompanied the shipments and assisted in planting the explosives in the river, but his presence also attracted the attention of Union informants.[36] Acting on reports that Buckman had been seen in the area, Captain Joseph H. Allen of the 169th New York Volunteers interrogated St. Johns resident Benjamin Falany and discovered two kegs containing one hundred pounds of gunpowder each, along with two assembled torpedoes carrying the same amount of explosives. Falany denied involvement, but Allen had already found "a beaten path" between Falany's dwelling and the location of the torpedoes.[37]

After conferring with Beauregard, Bryan decided to move his torpedo-assembly camp to a secluded location further upriver. Drawing on wagons, teams of horses, drivers, and rations from Camp Milton, along with five local men from the 2nd Florida Battalion, Bryan set up a new camp on Doctors Lake, twelve miles upriver from Jacksonville.[38] The local men were Joshua D. O'Hern, John Brantly, Musco C. Crenshaw, H. C. Crenshaw, and John Frisbee, all natives of either Clay or Duval County and familiar with the river and the secluded areas nearby.[39]

The explosives assembled at Doctors Lake became the main hope of Florida's Confederate command for driving Union forces away from the St. Johns River. Captain M. G. Gary's company of the 2nd Battalion of Florida Militia was detached to stand guard and to help remove equipment if the camp was endangered.[40] This measure of caution paid dividends when Union troops gained intelligence of Bryan's activities and sent a patrol to investigate. One report stated that one hundred men were in hiding at a camp near Doctors Lake actively building and placing torpedoes in the river.[41]

Bryan and his crew quickly abandoned the camp and moved to a more secure location. Henceforth, they exercised great caution and secrecy to avoid further Union patrols. Scouts were placed at strategic points along the river with orders to deliver twice-daily reports of Union activity.[42] Lieutenant A. J. Steadman, an officer in the Signal Corps, was to decipher messages sent back and forth between shore parties and the Union gunboats.[43]

By late March, Union naval commanders had become increasingly worried about security along the river. The army responded by detaching troops from the garrison at St. Augustine to help patrol the river. Picket camps were set up at Six Mile Creek in St. Johns County and at Black Creek in Clay County, and the *Norwich* was posted at the entrance to Black Creek. Twice each day, sailors in a small vessel inspected the shore and searched for signs of torpedoes in the river.[44]

Meanwhile, Bryan and his local men assembled torpedoes. Early in the morning of Wednesday, March 30, exercising great caution and using cover of darkness, they secured anchors to the bottom of the St. Johns off Mandarin Point and attached ropes that led upward to twelve torpedoes floating beneath the water but close enough to the surface that the hull of a boat passing over it would collide with enough impact to detonate the weapon.[45]

At 5 p.m. on the thirtieth, the transport *Maple Leaf*, a side-wheel steamer of 600 tons burden, arrived at Jacksonville from Hilton Head carrying the baggage of three regiments and several thousand dollars' worth of merchandise, horses, and military supplies. Also on board were sixty men from the 112th New York Infantry. After unloading some of the cargo, Captain Henry W. Dale took on board "87 cavalry horses and about that number of men" and departed for Palatka at 9 p.m., in convoy with the gunboat *Harriet A. Weed* and the transport *General Hunter*. The boats arrived at Palatka at 4 a.m. the following morning, having passed by the torpedoes without making contact. "After discharging the cavalry," Dale was ordered to leave for Jacksonville at 11:15 on the evening of the thirty-first.[46]

The *Maple Leaf* was considered one of the finest transports in the employ of the Department of the South. She was originally a commercial vessel based at Quebec, Canada, and her owners, Charles Spear and Joseph H. B. Lang, had leased the boat to the army quartermaster's department in September 1862. She "had great capacity" for transporting troops and horses and had a "large hold for freight." Dale thought the boat's "accommodation rather surpassed any of the boats around her" and that "she had a very good saloon and everything was in tip-top shape." The crew and captain of the *Maple Leaf* consisted of thirty-one men with a combined monthly salary of $1,252.[47]

Under the experienced guidance of government river pilot Romeo Murray, a forty-three-year-old free black man raised at Fort George Island on the St. Johns River, the *Maple Leaf* was steered into the channel of the St. Johns to begin its fateful journey north toward Jacksonville. For reasons of security, all the boat's running lights were turned off. Eight crew assisted Murray with navigation; six men stood watch on the deck searching throughout the night for anything suspicious.[48]

Murray remembered the night as "clear" and the river as so "still and smooth" he could have detected an object the size of a hat floating in it. At 4 a.m., as the *Maple Leaf* approached Mandarin Point, Murray steered the craft to the east of a sand shoal on the west bank of the river. This was the normal piloting procedure, but on this night it carried the *Maple Leaf* directly into the patch of the river where Bryan and his crew had planted torpedo mines on the thirtieth. As Murray guided the boat around the sand shoal, a thunderous explosion was heard that ushered in a new phase of the war on the river.[49]

Murray later testified that he heard "a loud noise right under the boat and the pilot house lifted right up. I was raised up and my head struck the top of the pilot house and I fell down.... When I got up the wire had stretched and set the whistle blowing."[50] When the keg torpedo struck thirty feet from the stern on the starboard side along the keel, seventy pounds of "small-grain" cannon powder exploded and ripped open a large hole in the underside of the boat. Samuel D. Jones was at the wheel when the explosion occurred and remembered hearing "a heavy report, something like a clap of thunder or a great volley of musketry and a cracking of timbers. It raised the upper deck and ... [threw] me against the top of the pilot house.... I shouldn't think it was over two minutes from the explosion till she settled to the bottom."[51]

Dale was waked by a "tremendous crash, and heavy report" and "a sickening stench" as water poured into the saloon.[52] Chief engineer Samuel L. Johnson jumped out of bed when he heard the crash and made his way to the deck to find the "whole forepart of the vessel ... smashed to pieces like an old building kicked over."[53] As the craft was sinking the crew swung the port-side boat over the water, but the *Maple Leaf* quickly settled on the river bottom and the crew had only to unhook the boat and let it float. Several crewmen followed Johnson to a boat on the hurricane deck for the rest of the crew to use. After a few moments, the pilothouse broke away and fell forward onto the partially submerged boat.

Sixty-three survivors rowed toward Jacksonville. The explosion had taken the life of four crewmen: firemen Benjamin Wiggins and Charles Sumner and deckhands Simeon Field and Eli Foster. Three Confederate prisoners were left behind on the portion of the boat that remained above the water line. The shipwreck victims reached Jacksonville early in the morning.[54] Dale reported the incident to the commanding officer, then immediately returned to the wreck aboard the *Norwich* to investigate. They arrived at noon to find the Confederate prisoners still stranded on the vessel. Dale judged the *Maple Leaf* a total loss but thought it might be possible to save some of her contents "if the saloon deck were torn off [and] the main deck ... opened to let the cargo up ... [or,] a tug might wrench off the bow, and so let the cargo float."[55] According to a soldier from the 112th New York Infantry, "the loss of personal property to officers was severe and embarrassing," leaving many with nothing but the "clothing that covered them."[56]

At Camp Milton, Anderson rejoiced that Bryan had inflicted a "heavy loss upon the enemy & taught him to be cautious in the navigation of our waters."[57] A detachment of 120 footsoldiers from the 1st Georgia Regulars and one section of field artillery was sent to destroy what remained of the *Maple Leaf*. Before the guns began firing, Bryan and two other men rowed out to inspect the sunken boat, finding a few "unimportant articles" before setting fire to the portion that was above the water line.[58] A *New York Times* correspondent later reported that the vessel was entirely below water except for "the top of her wheelhouse and a portion of the smoke stack. . . . During the day the rebels shelled away this visible portion of the wreck, so that nothing now is seen of it."[59]

On April 7 a correspondent for the *Jacksonville Peninsula* condemned the use of torpedoes: "Since this disaster a number of torpedoes, of devilish ingenuity, and of great destructive capacity, have been discovered and removed from the St. Johns from near where the *Maple Leaf* was lost. It has also been ascertained that these infernal machines came from Charleston very recently, being sent by Monsieur Beauregard . . . and reflect the diabolical instincts of rebeldom."[60] A week later, the *New York Times* called for Union forces to abandon Palatka and concentrate all Federal forces at Jacksonville until the river was made safe again.[61]

Immediately after the destruction of the *Maple Leaf*, the Union navy responded by installing crude devices on steamers and gunboats designed to push torpedoes away from the bottoms of vessels, and by dispatching men in rowboats to drag hooks to snag the submerged lines secured to the torpedoes. Within twenty-four hours a torpedo was discovered ten miles above Jacksonville, and twenty more were pulled from the river in the next six days. Major Appleton reported that one of the gunboats brought thirty prisoners and "five or six torpedoes, each containing a keg of powder" into Jacksonville on April 4.[62] Captain George R. Balch, commanding the naval forces on the St. Johns, assigned the gunboats *Mahaska* and *Norwich* to convoy all transports when they navigated the river, with strict orders to watch carefully for signs of torpedoes.[63]

Brigadier General John P. Hatch, who had succeeded General Seymour as commander of Union forces in Florida from March 28 to April 20, 1864, felt that the torpedo menace left the men at Palatka vulnerable to a severance of supply lines. On April 14 he ordered the evacuation of all troops and supplies, the destruction of gun platforms and powder magazines, and the loading of provisions, ordnance, and quartermaster stores on army transports for escort downriver by a gunboat. The soldiers still ashore crossed the river to East Palatka and proceeded to Picolata. At their new campsite they found only two houses and a wharf, but from its location on the east bank of the St. Johns it could be supplied overland from St. Augustine. Men from the 3rd New Hampshire constructed a small earthwork fortification.

On the morning of April 16 the gunboat *Norwich* led the *General Hunter* and the *Cosmopolitan* north from Palatka toward Jacksonville, unaware that

Bryan and his torpedo planters had returned to the waters near Mandarin Point the previous morning. The *General Hunter* was the third boat in the convoy, sailing under the command of Captain Augustus Crowell and a crew of twenty-seven. Built in 1862 and commissioned as the *Jacob H. Vanderbilt*, the 470-ton vessel had been purchased by the federal government for $80,000 at the request of General Hunter because of her "fancy" appearance and "handsome accommodations and considerable speed."[64]

At 8:30 a.m. the *General Hunter* turned into the same bend in the river where the *Maple Leaf* had been destroyed only two weeks before. Midway into the turn the *Hunter* struck a torpedo and was lifted into the air by a mass of water. The *New York Tribune* reported that the torpedo "blew the forward part of the hull to fragments" and shattered the ship so severely that she sank to the riverbed within three minutes of the explosion, killing one man and injuring another. Only a portion of the saloon deck stood above water. The destruction of the *General Hunter* led to the termination of the occupation of Palatka.[65]

Summing up the occupation of Palatka, a correspondent for the *New York Times* observed: "Now that our troops have evacuated Palatka, there will be no further occasion for transports to ply up and down the river, consequently we may presume that the torpedo disasters in the St. Johns River have come to an end."[66] The *Times* predicted the "infernal machines" had accomplished their nefarious purposes and the Union would concede the St. Johns and withdraw from Jacksonville. Confederate reports echoed this sentiment. The Union command did not; they instead decided to hold firmly to the superior defenses at the more strategically located Jacksonville and continue to patrol the river.

On April 21, four companies of the 157th New York Infantry boarded a transport to reinforce the new post at Picolata. The transport was equipped with a "torpedo-rake" on her bow to cut torpedoes loose from their moorings and float them to the surface where they could be exploded from a safe distance by rifle fire.[67] The Union command had ordered their ships equipped with new and improved devices to combat the torpedo menace. They had also stepped up surveillance activities along the river and begun raiding homes of known Confederate supporters.

In late April a Federal cavalry company galloped onto Fleming Island searching for Lieutenant Joshua O'Hern and Captain Bryan. Arriving late at night at the rural residence of the O'Hern family, the soldiers rigorously questioned the inhabitants regarding the whereabouts of the two Rebels, and of any other Confederate soldiers who may have helped seed the St.

Johns River with torpedo mines. Although O'Hern and Bryan were asleep in an upstairs room of the house when the soldiers arrived, one of the residents feigned ignorance of their whereabouts and persuaded the soldiers that O'Hern was at Camp Milton caring for his "seriously sick" wife. O'Hern and Bryan remained hidden and escaped detection while the soldiers ransacked the property. Vowing to continue searching throughout the area until they found the men responsible for destruction of the *Maple Leaf*, the Union soldiers departed.[68]

Raids continued at Fleming Island, causing much consternation for O'Hern's wife and five children. Lilly, the eldest daughter, remembered years later that at the approach of the soldiers during one raid the slaves all ran to the woods. After their departure, one of the slaves helped Mrs. O'Hern pack a wagon with "groceries, bedding, clothing and what it could hold." The family fled to Alachua County to live until the war's end.[69]

Increased Union security measures and the curtailment of transport traffic south of Jacksonville prompted Bryan to refocus his activities on strategic points downriver, between Jacksonville and Mayport. His efforts were hindered, however, by a shortage of supplies needed to manufacture the torpedoes. Anderson lauded Bryan's activities and joined in his request for additional materials from Charleston: "The torpedo operation in the District under the efficient management of Capt E. Pliny Bryan has been eminently successful & much more can be done if the materials are promptly forwarded."[70] At the time, demand for the weapons was intense from commanders across the Confederacy; consequently, Bryan was unable to manufacture the torpedoes as quickly as he desired.

The shortage was partly relieved by Lieutenant Buckman, who devised an ingenious torpedo that mixed mercury and gunpowder in such a way that the chemicals would explode on contact. A witness reported: "All the available thermometers were collected and broken, and the precious globule of mercury at the bottom was utilized as the base for the bombs, which were afterwards placed in the river." The witness stated that Buckman directed construction of the underwater explosives. "There were no chemicals available, so the mercury obtained from the thermometers was treated with certain acids and then mixed with powder and confined in large kegs. Probably in beer kegs. These were bound heavily with sheet iron, and iron bands were placed around the outer covering. The charge of fulminated mercury was so arranged that it would explode from shock—or a spark would be created from shock which would ignite the powder confined in the heavy kegs. . . . One half-pound of mercury would make a dozen torpedoes."[71] With Buckman's assistance, Bryan focused downriver from Jacksonville at the entrance to Trout Creek. On the evening of April 25, while Bryan met with men preparing twelve torpedoes, a scout from Corporal Jacob Mickler's detachment saw a shipload of Union soldiers land at the secret campsite. Mickler and his men remained silent as the Yankees marched by in the darkness, so close that Mickler could hear the soldiers talking. Warned of the danger, Bryan quickly loaded the torpedoes into horse-drawn wagons and made a hasty escape.

Mickler continued to scout river traffic, waiting for the propitious moment to plant torpedoes. On the night of May 3 an opportunity was created when the *Mahaska*, tasked with guarding that section of the river, left its post for a coal refill in Jacksonville. While in the town, an officer delayed the vessel's return so that he could be married. Given that unexpected opportunity, Mickler and his crew placed torpedoes near the mouth of Cedar Creek.[72] The next day, the commanding officer of the *Sumter* reported that he had captured a "boat used by the rebels laying down the torpedoes."[73]

On May 8 the Union transport *Boston* arrived off Mayport from Port Royal. On board were a number of ladies from Beaufort, South Carolina, many of them wives of Union officers stationed in the Department of the South, on a pleasure trip to see the land of sun and flowers. Dr. Esther Hill Hawks, the wife of a surgeon with the 33rd Regiment of U.S. Colored Troops, was one of the passengers, returning to the school she had established in Jacksonville earlier that year. Dr. Hawks was familiar with the passengers and remarked later that some of them made jokes about "the danger of the boat being blown up.[74]

Early in the morning of May 9, the convoy of vessels steamed upriver toward Jacksonville with the *Boston* in the lead and the *Harriet A. Weed* following approximately five hundred yards behind. The *Weed* was towing the *Caswell*, a schooner used to conduct the government's survey of coastal waters. Captain Charles Gaskill, familiar with these waters, was at the wheel of the *Weed*, traveling with the regular crew of twenty-one men, and on this day accompanied by a special detail of the 3rd U.S. Colored Troops assigned to the guns on the boat. Perhaps the wake of the forward vessels caused the gunboat and schooner to veer slightly from the main channel toward the north shore of the river.

Whatever the cause, the consequences were deadly. Passengers on the *Boston* looked back in horror when the *Weed* struck two torpedoes placed in the river by Corporal Mickler and his men. Dr. Hawks remembered thinking the ship was "blown into too many pieces to ever come together again."[75]

Another witness heard "a heavy, dull report, like a blast from a mine, with an immense cloud of smoke" rising amid "splinters, timbers, planks and fragments of machinery."[76] The ship was blown almost entirely out of the water and went down with the loss of five crewmen, victims of drowning, and injuries to several black soldiers. A picket boat from the *Mahaska* was immediately sent to the wreck, but the *Weed* sank in less that a minute.[77]

News of the destruction was invigorating to Orloff Dorman, a Confederate sympathizer residing in Jacksonville, who recorded in his journal the names of men whom he thought were responsible for planting the torpedoes: "Bryan, Brantley and Ohern for the upriver explosives, and Captain Latimore, and Bob Houston for downriver."[78] The *Times* correspondent was incensed by the tragic fate of the *Weed*. Only a few days prior to the sinking, another correspondent had reported: "One of the gunboats in passing up the St. Johns River discovered the dead body of a black floating in the stream, . . . attached to a torpedo. . . . The *Harriet A. Weed* makes the third vessel that has been destroyed on the St. Johns within a few weeks by means of torpedoes. . . . It would be a wise movement to abandon Jacksonville and place the troops where they would be of more service."[79]

On the morning of May 10, spotters on the deck of the *Vixen* detected a patch of water where small ripples broke the surface, near the spot where the *Weed* was sunk. Men in a small boat found six torpedoes lurking just beneath the surface of the water. One of the torpedoes was cut from its mooring and towed to shore, where an auger bit was used to drain the powder. The device was described as "very simple and effectual, consisting of a cask 2 feet long and 1.5 feet diameter at center. It has six strong iron hoops, and two solid wooden cones, each 1.25 high and 1.25 feet diameter at base, are strongly secured at each end. These act as buoys." Charles O. Boutelle, employed on the U.S. Coast Survey, sketched the keg-shaped weapon and sent a detailed report of the mechanism. Secretary Welles had the torpedo brought to Philadelphia for further examination.[80]

In a span of five weeks the Union army lost two transports and one gunboat to torpedoes on the St. Johns. Control of the river finally seemed within the reach of Confederate arms. Anderson summarized the impact of the torpedoes: "We were able to confine the enemy closely to his entrenchments around Jacksonville, and by blowing up two of his armed transports above Jacksonville and one below, put a complete stop to his navigation of the river above that city, and caused him to evacuate Palatka and to use the river below Jacksonville with the greatest caution."[81]

Northern newspapers clamored for a complete withdrawal from Jacksonville, but neither the Union army nor the Union navy would agree. Instead, they ramped up security and sought mechanical remedies for the plague of torpedoes. The crew of each new gunboat that arrived on the St. Johns River was briefed about the torpedo threat. When the *E. B. Hale* arrived, Admiral Dahlgren warned its captain to be careful when ascending the river. Should he suspect torpedoes to be in the water, the captain was to send men in two boats to opposite sides of the channel, trailing a weighted rope between them to "sweep 5 to 10 feet below the surface" to snag the lines that attached the torpedoes to moorings.[82]

Nevertheless, Mickler and his comrades continued to plant torpedoes, sheltered by residents of the Broward Neck area of the St. Johns who also wanted to drive Union forces from Florida. Mickler had grown up at Mayport Mills; he knew where to plant the weapons to have the best chances of striking Union vessels. Because of shifting tides, variable water levels, and the tendency for moorings to shift locations, keeping the weapons from being detected was a constant challenge. Mickler planted dozens of torpedoes, but vigilant Union sailors became adept at spotting them.

On July 5, sailors aboard the *Alice Price* sighted five torpedoes, and crewmen from the gunboat *Ottawa* found two more near Cedar Creek.[83] The weapons had all been manufactured locally and packed into "lager beer kegs" sent from Lake City by Captain Buckman. Within two weeks, men aboard the *Alice Price* would learn the painful lesson that no matter how many torpedoes they detected, determined Confederates could conceal other floating instruments of destruction and death.

In mid-July, Brigadier General William Birney initiated an offensive to end the torpedo threat by driving Confederate troops away from the St. Johns. The campaign had the secondary objective of disrupting Confederate communications between the St. Johns and St. Marys rivers. Relying on intelligence reports gathered from Confederate deserters, Birney landed infantry at Trout Creek on July 15, with orders to push inland, and dispatched cavalry to Callahan in Nassau County. In addition, a second party of soldiers on the *Alice Price* traveled up the Nassau River to capture and dismantle the Holmes Sawmill and bring the mill machinery to Jacksonville. Birney planned to reassemble the machinery, valued at $50,000 and capable of cutting up to 50,000 feet of lumber daily, at Empire Mills, two miles below Jacksonville at Little Pottsburg Creek.[84]

The *Alice Price* was a 151-foot-long side-wheeler that displaced only 383 tons, ideal for passing through the shallow rivers in northeast Florida. Once loaded with soldiers and mill machinery, the boat must have displaced more water than normal. Approximately eight miles short of Jacksonville, the steamer struck a mine near the entrance to Cedar Creek and sank rapidly. The blast severed the hull in three places.[85] This would be the last Union vessel lost to torpedoes on the St. Johns. Because of the navy's adaptation of torpedo catchers and the increased vigilance, the "infernal machines" claimed no further victims.

It is important to recognize, however, that the Confederate challenge to Union dominance of the St. Johns had been of major consequence. For a time, torpedo mines effectively limited the upriver mobility of Union naval vessels and minimized the threat of raids into the interior of Florida. The vital commissary supply lines leading to Confederate armies outside the state remained open. This Confederate challenge, following closely on the heels of the overwhelming victory at Olustee, served to unite the defenders in gray and boost the morale of soldiers in Florida whose overall strength was dwindling. If afforded additional men and materials, many on the Confederate side believed they could have succeeded in driving the Yankees out of Florida.

Confederate manpower needs were so great at the time, however, that the troops sent to Florida in February 1864 to stop the Union advance toward Lake City, along with all the infantry and artillery units from Florida, received orders to transfer to battlefields further north. All that was left for the defense of Florida was a pitifully small number of cavalry forces who were expected to combat the Federals on the St. Johns and throughout the rest of a very large state. When the Florida Brigade under Finegan was ordered to Virginia, Bryan accompanied them. General Lee was aware that Bryan "had been very successful in Florida" and wanted him to accomplish the same for Confederate forces in Virginia.[86]

For about six months Confederate forces had effectively challenged Union control of the St. Johns River. Ultimately, the resources for manufacture of the torpedoes and men to place them in the river were exhausted, but a few dozen determined and resourceful men, using beer kegs, black powder, ingenuity, and knowledge of the local terrain had held a superior foe at bay. When the St. Johns was cleared of Bryan's "infernal machines," the highway into Florida was reopened, with disastrous consequences for Confederate Florida.

FIGURE 25. The Union transport *Maple Leaf*, a side-wheel steamer sunk off Mandarin Point on April 1, 1864, by a Confederate keg torpedo. This painting is based on a photograph of the vessel. (Courtesy of Dr. Keith V. Holland.)

Wreck of Transport Steamers "Maple Leaf" and "Genl. Hunter" St Johns River. Florida Sunk by Torpedoes.

FIGURE 26. Wrecks of transport steamers *Maple Leaf* and *General Hunter*, St. Johns River, Florida. The two steamers were sunk by torpedoes. Sketch by Alfred R. Waud. (Courtesy of Library of Congress.)

FIGURE 27. Joshua O'Hern of Clay County, one of the men who secured the torpedoes that destroyed the transport steamers *Maple Leaf* and *General Hunter*. General Beauregard's attempt to use underwater explosives to spread terror among Union sailors and deny U.S. naval vessels access to the St. Johns River came close to succeeding. (Courtesy of Claude Bass, Kevin Hooper, and the Clay County Archives, Green Cove, Florida.)

FIGURE 28. "Confederate torpedoes, shot and shell in the Arsenal Yard," Charleston, South Carolina. (Courtesy of Library of Congress.)

FIGURE 29. Major General Quincy A. Gillmore, commander of the Department of the South during the fourth Federal occupation of Jacksonville in 1864. (Courtesy of Library of Congress.)

FIGURE 30. Brigadier General Truman Seymour commanded Federal troops during the Battle of Olustee. (Courtesy of Library of Congress.)

FIGURE 31. General Pierre Gustave Toutant Beauregard, commander of coastal defenses in South Carolina, Georgia, and Florida, 1863–64. Beauregard reviewed Confederate troops at Camp Finegan and Jacksonville, and personally supervised construction of Camp Milton. (Courtesy of Library of Congress.)

11

The Struggle for Allegiance of Florida Residents

As the torpedo threat diminished in the summer of 1864, Union commanders increased the tempo of cavalry and infantry raids on upriver troop encampments and on the farms and plantations of Confederate partisans. Confederate commanders repeatedly asked for reinforcements to counter the raids, but in April General Beauregard, faced with a daunting challenge at Charleston, demanded the return of the regiments sent to Florida in February 1864. General Anderson promptly complied. In May, Richmond called for an entire infantry brigade to be rushed to battlefields in Virginia. Anderson again complied, but warned: "this takes all the infantry force out of this district." Confederate military headquarters was moved inland from Camp Milton to Lake City, and all offensive operations in the state were suspended. With only a small number of cavalry units left under his command, Anderson decided "the best that can be done will be to defend points of greatest importance. . . . It will be readily perceived that this force is wholly inadequate to the protection of the country."[1]

Anderson and Brigadier General John K. Jackson, who followed him as commander of Confederate forces in East Florida, worried that the enemy would use gunboats to establish a stronghold on the upper St. Johns as a base for raids into Marion, Sumter, and Alachua counties. A "large negro population" was still at work in those counties; raids to capture those enslaved laborers would have drastic consequences, Anderson warned, by "break[ing] up the operations of our commissary agents in supplying beef-cattle from

South Florida."[2] In addition, such raids would undoubtedly strain the allegiance of Florida's planters to the Confederacy.

In August 1864, Jackson compiled data on Florida products being supplied to Confederate armies. He tallied "25,000 head of beeves, equal to 10,000,000 pounds, 1,000 hogsheads of sugar, 100,000 gallons of sirup, . . . 10,000 head of hogs, . . . 50,000 sides of leather . . . [and] 100,000 barrels of fish."[3] He quickly agreed with Anderson and Beauregard that it was essential for survival of the Confederacy to defend Baldwin against Union attacks and to construct a north-south rail line between Florida and Georgia. Jackson sent persuasive appeals to Richmond for reinforcements, but no additional troops or materials were authorized.[4]

The Union command was well aware of Confederate military deficiencies in Florida in mid-1864, and was determined to exploit them. Cavalry patrols clattered through Jacksonville's gates often in April 1864 to scout enemy positions and to skirmish with Confederate patrols between Jacksonville and Camp Milton.[5] Union gunboats captured and destroyed small watercraft on the river and, acting on tips from residents, captured the steamboats *General Sumter* and *Hattie Brock*. They searched in vain for the small paddle-wheeler *Silver Spring*, which carried freight, military materials, and passengers on the Oklawaha River and the St. Johns.[6] The policy of confiscating small boats along the river worked so well that the supplies of fish became scarce in 1864. Former mayor Halsted Hoeg and Calvin Robinson petitioned General Hatch for permission to license boats of loyal fishermen because "the stopping of the small boats in our river is cutting off a large source of supply of provisions to the inhabitants of Jacksonville and its vicinity. The poor people feel it very severely. Their privations and sufferings are already very great." The petitioners requested that the town's "principal fishermen, Josiah C. Grace, Hatch Cox, and David Vandegriff," described as men of "unquestionable loyalty," be permitted to continue fishing.[7]

On April 25 the 75th Ohio Mounted Infantry was sent on an expedition to the headwaters of the St. Johns and Kissimmee rivers. At Lake Harney the force divided, one squadron heading for New Smyrna to stop the flow of weapons smuggled in by blockade runners. While they marched, the men destroyed tar, resin, and turpentine as well as three salt furnaces; at New Smyrna they captured two schooners loaded with five hundred bales of cotton and forced the sailors and crew to carry them back to St. Augustine. A detail of fifteen men left at New Smyrna captured a third schooner and another hundred bales of cotton. While that excursion was under way, the second squad marched west from Lake Harney though scrub, pine forests, and swampland at the headwaters of the Kissimmee River and rustled nearly five thousand head of cattle. Reunited at St. Augustine, the entire 75th Ohio was ordered back to the headwaters of the St. Johns to protect Unionists from raids by the 2nd Florida Cavalry.[8]

On April 27, three companies of the 157th New York Infantry were transported from Picolata to Welaka to search for commissary supplies. They captured a blacksmith from the 2nd Florida Cavalry at one farm and roasted sweet potatoes at the home of Granville Priest before commencing a rustling expedition during an overland return to Picolata. Passing around the head of Dunns Lake on their hundred-mile journey, the Union troops drove fifteen hundred head of cattle through a pine woods and grassland wilderness to a grazing area near Pellicer Creek south of St. Augustine, arriving on May 4.[9]

Union commanders also encouraged civilians to rustle cattle and deliver them to Union posts for compensation of five dollars a head. A Union cavalry officer, Captain S. H. Swettland, was given authority to supervise and control these raiding operations and to find grazing lands near St. Augustine. William Turner and J. M. Underhill were praised by Colonel William W. Marple for driving fifteen hundred head of cattle into Union corrals from the herds of notorious Rebels. Brigadier General Birney praised "Old Peterson and his sons" for driving 250 cattle into Union corrals in June. Birney wanted to clear "all Secesh" out of Orange and Brevard counties by authorizing "enterprising raids of crackers" like "Old Peterson." Birney targeted one man in particular: the notorious "Old [Moses] Barber will be captured dead or alive if he can be found."[10] It was at Barber's former plantation west of Baldwin that General Seymour had assembled Union troops for the ill-fated invasion that resulted in the Battle of Olustee.

Union troops experienced numerous successes, but they came to realize that it was always risky to establish outposts or conduct raids south of Palatka, where the width of the river narrows from a waterway measured in miles to a winding, slow-moving, sometimes shallow river with the distance between the banks measured in yards. Above Palatka, enemy marksmen and field artillery units could inflict significant damage on passing gunboats from hiding places on the shore. Brigadier General George H. Gordon sent squads of infantry to establish posts at Volusia, Saunders, and Welaka as bases for raids on commissary supplies. Part of Gordon's motivation for the mission was a report he received concerning the "sufferings of Union men" who endured "untold horrors" living hidden in swamps, "their families had hungered for food, and their relatives had been hung; they were willing to fight for the Union."[11]

The men collected herds of cattle and liberated slaves with ease until the evening of May 19. Captain Dickison and fifty-four men of the 2nd Florida Cavalry crossed the river in small boats and captured fifty-six Union men at Welaka and Fort Gates. A spokesman for Anderson lauded the "gallant expedition" and the "patriotic endurance and daring displayed by Captain Dickison's command."[12]

In response, Gordon ordered the withdrawal of river sentinels posted opposite Volusia and Saunders and accompanied a relief expedition of nearly seven hundred men. The small steam tug *Columbine* was sent furthest upriver on a mission to protect the outpost at Volusia, stopping first at Picolata to pack sandbags on the gunwales for protection against snipers. The *Ottawa* was placed at the mouth of Dunns Creek to patrol and provide assistance if called upon. To avoid danger at the narrow river passes south of Palatka, Gordon debarked six hundred infantry and cavalry at Orange Mills, with orders to march east to the road from St. Augustine, then south to the crossing at Haw Creek and on to Volusia.

The general accompanied the marchers. "We moved out of the shade of the superb oaks that lined the banks of the river," he recalled. "It was a late start but we made nine miles, halting in the sight of a miserable hut on the south side of Haw Creek, where I slept on a floor surrounded by negroes, dogs, cats, and babies." The next day, Gordon assembled the local men and asked for a guide. One of the men refused in animated fashion, but whispered under his breath: "Take me—tie me by force." Realizing the man was surrounded by spies, Gordon seized him and made it appear the man would only accompany the troops against his will. He later said of this guide: "A better Union man, a tour guide, or a more interesting traveler I never met."

When the men at Volusia were found safe, Gordon ordered the cavalry units to march to St. Augustine and plunder "herds of beef-cattle" along the way, it being well known the cattle "were going north to feed rebel armies."[13] The 144th and 157th New York Infantry regiments marched back to Orange Mills, from where they commenced a rugged march through a landscape that Lieutenant James Harvey McKee described as "pine woods and monotonous flat country that kept the soldiers constantly puzzled with this query: 'what do we want with this forlorn, forsaken section of the country anyway?'"[14] Eventually, the soldiers returned safely to camps at St. Augustine, Picolata, and Jacksonville.

The men aboard the *Columbine* were not so fortunate. In one of the most celebrated Confederate actions of the war in Florida, Dickison and twenty marksmen from the 2nd Florida Cavalry, accompanied by thirty men of the Milton Artillery, captured the gunboat at Horse Landing on the St. Johns, a few miles from Palatka. The boat was a small side-wheel tug of 132 tons armed with two 25-pounder Dahlgren guns. It carried two officers, twenty-four sailors and crew, and twenty-five riflemen from Colonel James C. Beecher's 35th U.S. Colored Infantry.[15] At noon on May 23, as the *Columbine* rounded a bend in the river under command of Acting Ensign Frank Sanborn, it was hit by artillery fire that severed the chain from the rudder and prompted the pilot to jump overboard. Sanborn recalled that "the vessel almost immediately went ashore upon a mud bank."[16] The Confederates' continuing fire swept naval personnel from the deck and caused the infantrymen to jump ship and swim ashore, and the officers to surrender. Dickison reported that "the deck presented a horrible scene, the dead and wounded lay weltering in blood."[17] Without suffering a single Confederate casualty, Dickison captured sixty-five prisoners, including six wounded, and reported twenty enemy fatalities. He then burned the vessel.

The loss of the *Columbine* was a painful reminder that Confederate cavalry units knew every place along the St. Johns where effective attacks could be mounted. Undeterred, Gordon continued to call for gunboat patrols. The Union navy carried raiders far to the south, beyond Lake Monroe, to scout enemy activities, plunder commissary supplies, and liberate slaves.

Gordon was also determined to break the impasse to the west of Jacksonville by capturing Camp Milton and gaining control of the vital railroad intersect at Baldwin. Consequently, Union cavalry squads routinely pushed aggressively to the west of Jacksonville to skirmish with Confederate patrols. On May 25 four hundred infantrymen and two sections of artillery advanced toward Baldwin, meeting only scattered resistance until they neared Mc-Girts Creek. Gordon was content on this occasion to have the men return to Jacksonville with intelligence on the strength of Confederate defenses.[18]

On June 1, Gordon initiated a campaign aimed at the reduction of the elaborate Confederate fortification at Camp Milton. His intelligence reports indicated that the enemy's trenches were dug about three hundred yards west of McGirts Creek, extending for three miles from north to south and centered on the rail bed. Eliminating the fortifications would open the way for a later assault on Baldwin.

Gordon assembled two strike forces at Jacksonville, consisting of nearly 2,700 men. Colonel William H. Noble and the 17th Connecticut Volunteers led the first column, followed by units of the 157th New York, 3rd U.S.C.T., 35th U.S.C.T., and 107th Ohio. Noble had orders to board transports at Jacksonville in time to disembark at 3 a.m. on June 1 at the point where Cedar Creek and McGirts Creek merged. From there they were to march to the rear of Camp Milton, at the point where McGirts Creek intersected with the rail line and two wagon roads. By 6 a.m. his unit had reached the lower Jacksonville and Black Creek Road, where they stopped to rest and eat breakfast, and then commenced the "advance as rapidly as it was possible, under a burning sun, breathless air, and without water for six hours. The long-continued drought had dried up all the usual streams."[19] They arrived at their destination at 2 p.m. Noble ordered a company of the 107th Ohio to skirmish with enemy scouts to prevent them from informing defenders at Camp Milton of the Union advance.

The second column was led by Colonel James Shaw and included the 7th U.S.C.T., the 144th New York, the 75th Ohio (mounted), and the 3rd Rhode Island Artillery. Shaw's march started at the town gates and followed the dirt road that ran parallel to the railroad tracks. With a less rigorous terrain to traverse, six pieces of artillery and the cavalry squadron were assigned to the second column. Shaw was ordered to time his frontal attack to coincide with an attack at the rear by Noble's column. Gordon wrote in his report of the expedition, "The front and rear of the enemy's works were gained by the two columns about the same time, but too late to capture the enemy. Evidences of his hasty flight were apparent in a burning trestle-work upon the railroad and in abandoned stores and forage."[20] The enemy force withdrew quickly, driving cattle ahead of them but abandoning "several barrels of syrup, potatoes, hominy, bundles of clothing, cooking utensils, and about a thousand bushels of corn." The Federal land force had captured "extensive and formidable earth and timber defenses . . . without firing a gun." After close examination, Noble described the "three miles of most laborious and carefully constructed stockade, earth works, & breast works, erected only by great industry & skill . . . [but] rendered as useless to the enemy as structures of papers."[21]

After the enemy departed, Gordon personally inspected "the line of fortifications" and found them to be "of great strength, capable of offering a successful resistance to a very large force."[22] Gordon ordered the entire fortification "fired and completely demolished. The labor of thousands of men . . . was thus destroyed, and one of the most formidable barriers to the march of an army to Tallahassee removed." Noble said of the Union victory: "The blow this struck . . . is worth more than a battle and a victory. The result to him [the enemy] is a severe defeat. But what is of more consequence ... [is] the demoralizing conviction that here, piles of timbers & earth massed together upon lines of defenses, built with great strength, toil and engineering skill, are no longer of any avail."[23]

When the demolition work was complete, Gordon ordered the Federal columns to return to Jacksonville, which he had left under protection of the gunboats and emplaced field artillery but with only four hundred soldiers manning the trenches and barricades. Anderson, perhaps hoping to salvage a moral victory out of this debacle, reported that during the Union retreat his cavalry "met advanced guard of the enemy between Baldwin and McGirt's Creek [and] drove him back to Jacksonville."[24]

For the next six weeks the Union command focused on river-based raids and engaged in cursory skirmishing and reconnaissance activities to the west of Jacksonville. The Confederates strengthened their works at Baldwin and shored up interior communication and transportation lines, and in July they opened a new field of operations. Lieutenant Colonel A. H. McCormick moved the 2nd Florida Cavalry to the headwaters of Trout and Cedar creeks, from where mounted sentinels could monitor gunboat activity on the St. Johns. This was alarming to General Birney, who considered the lower St. Johns the weakest point of the Union's defense plan for Jacksonville. He determined to "move with what troops I have and drive the enemy from Trout Creek at all hazards."[25]

On July 15, Birney transported detachments from the 3rd U.S.C.T. and the 4th Massachusetts Cavalry to a landing at Trout Creek with orders to advance along the waterway to its source, plundering livestock and other Confederate property. They were contested by a party of Rebel horsemen in a skirmish that continued for hours and was fought over a distance of ten miles. After the black troops burned a bridge over the south branch of Trout Creek, Birney divided the column and sent the cavalry galloping west toward the St. Marys River and the black infantrymen marching toward Callahan. At Callahan, two railcars loaded with iron track and a telegraph office were destroyed, and horses, mules, rifles, cartridges, and gunpowder were seized. A dozen slaves abandoned their masters and joined the squad on its return to Jacksonville, along with several prisoners.[26]

While these diversionary efforts were under way, Birney unveiled the primary goal of the campaign: a third column aboard the *Alice Price* was transported up the Nassau River to the site of Holmes Saw Mill. Birney said the mill combined "gang, rotary, and circular saw machinery" and was worth "probably $50,000 when in operation." The machinery was successfully dismantled and loaded aboard the gunboat for reassembly at Little Pottsburg Creek, below Jacksonville, where Empire Mills had operated before the war (today Empire Point). Birney predicted a revitalized mill "will turn out 40,000 to 50,000 feet of lumber daily."[27]

The three Union squads were confronted by Confederate defenders at Broward's Neck, Callahan, and McGirts Creek. McCormick was in the saddle throughout the day, leading efforts to stop the invaders before they reached Baldwin. He reported that Federal troops destroyed bridges and railroad trestles, disrupting passage of Confederate troops and supply trains. His only encouraging news was that sentry posts had been reestablished along Cedar Creek and that Baldwin was still under Confederate control.[28]

In the Broward Neck and Trout River area, the Federals plundered the livestock, horses, and slaves of known Confederate partisans, and black soldiers captured Washington Broward and marched him to Jacksonville in chains. The Broward clan had come to be regarded as participants in the most damaging guerrilla actions in East Florida. Washington Broward was brought to Jacksonville in a fashion calculated to embarrass and infuriate: shackled and led by black troops in a column that included liberated slaves.[29]

On July 21 the last major action in the immediate vicinity of Jacksonville was launched. Following a plan devised by Birney, several columns of Federal forces headed away from the city in different directions, some by land and others by water. A diversionary attack in Nassau County initiated the campaign. Another column, under command of Colonel Beecher and involving the 35th U.S.C.T. and the 4th Massachusetts Cavalry, was transported four miles up Black Creek to a secret landing in the woods, a procedure that took three days to accomplish. Officers had compiled a list of local residents thought sympathetic to the rebellion and sent soldiers from house to house informing residents they were confined to premises for the next three days "under penalty of death."[30] A cavalry company gave the same warning to residents of nearby Middleburg, thereby ensuring a cloak of secrecy for an occupation that would last for several weeks.[31]

At the rain-swollen south fork of Black Creek, Union infantry and cavalry drove off a Confederate cavalry unit before proceeding on the Clay Hill Road toward Trail Ridge, skirmishing with the enemy most of the route. At the north branch of Black Creek a bridge was constructed to allow the infantry, field artillery, and supply wagons to pass over the flooded water.[32] Once across, Birney dispatched the horsemen of the 75th Ohio "to destroy the two small trestles near Trail Ridge," complementing the work of another company of the 75th that had—at 6 a.m.—burned the "great trestle-work on the Lake City railroad over the South Fork of the Saint Mary's." That company had endured a "night march of over 30 miles, making the circuit of one of the enemy's camps, fording several deep streams, and capturing the trestle guard with its officer."[33]

The main column followed "the Alachua trail" to Darby's Station on the Lake City rail line. With help from the mounted units, the raiders destroyed a long trestle located five miles west of Baldwin, thereby cutting rail transport to Lake City. Birney reported: "the infantry bivouacked some 4 miles in the rear. It was after midnight when the work at the railroad ceased. The day's work had been enormous."[34]

McCormick realized that the Union successes placed his men at Baldwin in great danger. He called a council of officers at 2 a.m. on July 26, at which time it was determined "to evacuate Baldwin and move by way of Brandy Branch and Lang's Ferry, on the Big Saint Mary's, to this position [Camp Jackson, Fla.], on the west side of the south prong of that river."[35] During the night and in the early morning hours of July 26, the Confederates evacuated Baldwin.

Birney reported that the goals of the complex expedition had been achieved beyond his expectations. "The trestle-works on the Cedar Key and Lake City railroads have been burned beyond Baldwin, and the enemy has been forced to evacuate . . . Baldwin and Camp Milton. Two locomotives and trains are cut off and must fall into our hands unless destroyed by the rebels." The results of the campaign were even more far-reaching. "The rail transportation of blockade-run goods from the southern ports of Florida is broken up for the present," Birney wrote, "and the abundant supply of corn and cattle from the southern and middle counties of Florida, for the rebel armies, is within our control."[36]

Birney exulted in the accomplishments of his troops in a brilliantly executed five-day campaign that suffered only six Federal casualties. "Their force was superior to mine, and mine were nearly all colored men, a fact which mortified our prisoners greatly. These colored troops were burning with desire to avenge Olustee." A veteran of the Olustee campaign and a commander of black troops, Birney ended his report with a haunting reminder: "We captured 19 prisoners, who will be held, I trust, for exchange for colored soldiers only."[37]

With the capture of Camp Milton and Baldwin, the Federals had secured their position at Jacksonville for the remainder of the war. The Union command increased the number of upriver raids, with some originating at

Middleburg on Black Creek, where a detachment of the 4th Massachusetts Cavalry remained after occupying the town on July 21. One of the soldiers described Middleburg as "a small place of perhaps fifty houses, more like a New England village than any other place we had seen in the south." When the soldiers rode into town, the residents—nearly all women and children—fled to "two large houses in the center of the town, where in terror they awaited the butchery they anticipated was at once to take place." When they realized the soldiers did not intend to harm them, a five-year-old boy emerged from one of the houses and asked: "if those were Yankees, where were their horns?"[38]

The Yankees captured a young man suspected of being a spy, George Washington Bardin, a former mail carrier between Middleburg, Trail Ridge, and Baldwin who joined the 2nd Florida Cavalry in 1862. Bardin's parents had resided near Black Creek since 1815 and were still in their home when the Union soldiers arrived. The older sons and the family-owned slaves had moved to a rented farm in Bradford County after the first Union occupation of Jacksonville in 1862. In July 1864, Bardin escaped Federal troops at Middleburg by swimming across Black Creek.[39] Two teenagers from Middleburg, George N. Bardin and Moses Joiner, participated in an attack on a Union encampment on Black Creek that claimed the lives of several black sentinels. The boys were declared murderers, and search teams scoured the woods for them. Bardin's father hurriedly enlisted his son in the Confederate army.[40]

Not all of the residents of Middleburg were hostile to the occupying forces. Martha Hendricks, for example, abandoned her rural Clay County residence when her family was attacked by Confederate partisans early in the war for pro-Union views. When the Union soldiers arrived in July, Martha warned them of Confederate spies and of plans to destroy the bridge spanning the north fork of Black Creek. Federal sentry posts established as a result of her warning saved the bridge from destruction.[41] Middleburg represented the furthest inland post occupied in 1864 by Union forces.

On August 8, General Hatch occupied Magnolia, upriver from Jacksonville, near the former Union outpost at Palatka. From this new post, Union troops launched raids on farms and plantations and threatened Waldo, Orange Springs, and Gainesville, towns that were important for the Confederates' defensive network and for commissary supplies. Since the 1820s the nearby Bellamy Road had provided a path to the interior towns; Hatch envisioned it would now help "refugees and negroes reach the river."[42] Hatch intended to fortify the town with installations near the river and to devise plans that would deter Confederate torpedo planters from sowing their deadly weapons in the area. Cavalry dispatched from Magnolia raided several miles inland, liberating slaves and confiscating horses, cattle, and other supplies. The rich stores the enemy had collected at Gainesville became a prime target for raiders.[43] Over the next several months troops from the 4th Massachusetts Cavalry, 17th Connecticut Infantry, and the 75th Ohio Volunteers stationed at Magnolia were under command of Colonel Noble. Later, men from the 34th and 102nd U.S. Colored Infantry would arrive.

When Union troops first arrived at Magnolia on August 9, the town was nearly abandoned. Only a few trusting souls remained, including Dr. Nathan D. Benedict, who had provided medical care to Magnolia citizens since the 1850s. Dr. Benedict agreed to provide his services to the Union soldiers and remained in Federal employment for a number of years.[44] After defensive works were completed at the site of the T. J. Hendricks plantation, former residents of the town returned to take oaths of allegiance and reestablish their domiciles. Many secured jobs with the military, under supervision of the quartermaster department. The presence of Union regiments created a demand for beef, hogs, poultry, corn, and other produce. Residents traded butter and eggs with the Union soldiers for coffee and flour. Several of these families asked Noble for assistance in moving their families inside Union lines.[45]

In mid-August two columns of Federal troops left Magnolia simultaneously, both heading southwest: one toward Cedar Key, on the Gulf Coast, the other toward Starke and Gainesville. The first column, led by Noble, marched beyond Lake George, burned a steam-powered cotton gin and twenty thousand pounds of cotton, and returned with seventy-five liberated slaves, captured horses, and mules.[46] Noble's praise for the work of the men under his command was apparently too effusive for Hatch. The general in charge of the District of Florida criticized Noble for taking the wrong route.

Colonel A. L. Harris and the second column, consisting of the 75th Ohio Mounted Volunteers, was surprised by Dickison's cavalry while looting private property at Gainesville. About 200 Federals scattered to the woods in panic, many of whom would find their way back to Union lines days later. Casualties were 5 Union men killed and 171 wounded or missing. Confederate casualties were 1 killed and 5 wounded. After interrogating the survivors, Hatch concluded that "Harris undoubtedly allowed his men to scatter through the town and, I fear, to pillage."

Hatch issued a severe reprimand to Harris: "The bad conduct of the troops under your command on the Gainesville raid has been reported to me from several different sources. Your men disgraced their country by their lawless pillaging.... You will be held strictly accountable for the acts of your men." Even more ominously, Hatch warned: "Colonel Noble has instructions to execute immediately any man found pillaging and to report to me the general conduct of your command." Noble was ordered to "exercise the greatest vigilance in protecting people from those bad soldiers who disgrace the arms of their country by pillaging. Immediate trial and execution of the offenders on the spot where the offense is committed will be resorted to if other means fail."[47]

Hatch had good reason to be upset by vandalism among his troops. Indiscriminate pillaging of private property violated a basic Federal policy. Although the Union force at Jacksonville no longer hoped for a decisive military victory in Florida, political objectives were still being vigorously pursued. Chief among these was the effort to undermine the already dwindling strength of the Confederate government in Florida by rewarding loyalty to the Union. Punishing the residents of the region for treason and rebellion was now deemed less important than persuading them to rejoin the Union. Private property—with the exception of human chattel and the belongings of firebrand secessionists—was to be respected. All who abandoned the Confederacy and swore to an oath of loyalty were promised amnesty, food, shelter, jobs, and security within Federal lines.

Hatch was so impressed by the Union loyalists he encountered in Florida that he began organizing a loyal regiment from among the male refugees. In September he informed Major General John G. Foster, commanding the Department of the South: "the really loyal men of Florida are the most earnest men I have seen, and can be trusted with the selection of their own officers.... Can you send me Spencer or Sharps carbines for them and furnish the quartermaster's department with money to buy the horses?"[48]

The response from Foster was less than encouraging. By October he was having second thoughts about the trustworthiness of Florida residents who took the oath of loyalty. He sent word to Hatch to "discourage as much as possible all males from entering your lines unless they agree at once to take the oath of allegiance and are willing to bear arms. The majority of the refugees in Florida have apparently done us more harm than good."[49] Foster's pessimistic attitude toward refugees, and especially prisoners of war, was shared widely by Union soldiers. A sergeant in the 54th Massachusetts commented: "There have been several hundred prisoners fall into our hands since the re-occupation of Jacksonville, and I am also certain the greater part . . .

returned within rebel lines." After a few days' captivity, they readily take "the oath of allegiance to a Government they certainly hate. Their families are living in the vicinity, and they naturally desire to be with them, and by taking the oath, they are immediately released and relieved from danger of enrollment in our army, and as long as they remain in our lines, from service in the rebel army." After observing that refugees who took the oath of loyalty were given jobs, and sometimes rations, the sergeant bitterly remarked: "I can not fail to contrast this treatment which rebels receive at the hands of authorities with that meted out to the negro soldiers by the rebel authorities."[50]

Other Union soldiers resented the refugees who enlisted for a bounty and who would "then desert to the Confederate Army at the first opportunity."[51] A sergeant major with the 8th U.S.C.T. expressed surprise at the freedom given to former Confederate soldiers in Jacksonville. He saw former Rebels given permission to open stores and restaurants and to engage in business, apparently in preference to Unionists from the North.[52]

The post at Magnolia drew a number of refugees and deserters behind Union lines. It also resulted in a number of successful raids on plantations owned by Confederate sympathizers, and contributed beef and commissary supplies to Union troops at Jacksonville and St. Augustine. But determined Confederate resistance minimized the post's overall importance and led to its demise. The disaster at Gainesville on August 17 had alerted Foster to the possibility that the post at Magnolia was harmful to the Union cause. He took decisive action in October, following another Union defeat at the hands of Dickison and the 2nd Florida Cavalry.

On October 24, Dickison encountered a raiding party of Union cavalry heading toward Middleburg, rustling cattle, liberating slaves, and burning Rebel properties as they advanced. Dickison engaged the Union force about six miles from Magnolia in a forty-minute skirmish that "resulted in a complete rout of the enemy, many of them so hotly pursued that they took for the swamp, bogging their horses."[53] Union casualties were ten killed, eight wounded, and twenty-three captured. The losses also included forty-two horses, fifteen rifles, twelve pistols, and other arms. Confederate losses were light: two troopers wounded and two horses killed.

On October 31, Foster issued unequivocal orders: Magnolia was to be evacuated and a new post established on the west side of the inland waterway between the St. Johns River and Fernandina. The intention was "to guard that passage from any attempt of the enemy to close it." Foster rebuked Hatch for establishing the post and said that a more desirable location would have been Baldwin. The consequence had been "furnishing the rebels with fine arms and horses, and encouraging the men to plunder and pillage and causing them to be demoralized and inefficient." Hatch was ordered to deemphasize use of cavalry units in the future and to send up to two hundred horses to Hilton Head.[54]

Hatch defended his actions and protested the diminution of his cavalry force: "our main trouble has been that we have not had sufficient cavalry here, not that we have too much." He shipped the horses to South Carolina but respectfully pointed out that doing so was a mistake. The cavalry force that remained in Florida would be "entirely inadequate for the protection of the country between the Saint John's and the sea-coast, [and] we may expect forays to be constantly made by the enemy into the counties of Volusia and Saint Johns."[55]

Foster refused to reconsider his orders. He continued to criticize Hatch and defend his decision to deemphasize reliance on cavalry. In the future the emphasis in Florida would be on infantry: "If our soldiers are taught to undertake long marches they will accomplish far more in the swamps east of the river than will a mounted force."[56] Foster also accepted Hatch's offer to resign his command in Florida and transferred him to a post in South Carolina.

By the end of 1864 it was clear that the major infantry and artillery engagements in northeast Florida had ended, yet alarms and raids were frequent enough in early 1865 to remind Jacksonville residents that the shooting had not ended. Federal cavalry parties continued to dash through the town's fortified gates into the countryside to conduct raids on unrepentant plantation owners and liberate their slaves, and also to capture guerrillas who terrorized Union supporters. Confederate resistance remained tenacious. In early February, Dickison's company struck a detachment of fifty-two men of the Jacksonville-based 17th Connecticut while on a raid to Welaka, killing one, wounding one, and capturing the rest. In early March a Federal raiding party was more successful on a foray to Newnansville, bringing back twenty-two slaves and as many captured horses and mules.[57]

On March 18 the *Florida Union* reported that companies detached from the 3rd and 34th U.S.C.T., supported by cavalry, had boarded gunboats on March 7 for transport upriver to Orange Mills. The infantry divided into two columns: one headed for Palatka, the other for Fort Gates near Ocala. Seventy-five slaves were emancipated during the expedition, and scores of horses and mules and several hundred barrels of cane syrup were confiscated. Outside a place called "Lake Church Hill," Rebel cavalry attacked the

Union raiders in a sustained battle fought with rifles and swords. According to the *Florida Union*, the campaign was an "expedition into Rebeldom" that resulted in twenty-six enemy killed and wounded, and one Union casualty.

On the same day that story was printed, Mrs. H. B. Greely, a teacher sent to Florida by the American Missionary Association, wrote to her supervisor with an eyewitness report on the condition of liberated black men, women, and children when they arrived in St. Augustine. Greely described them as "the most destitute objects I ever saw, many . . . almost entirely naked." The missionary teachers in the town quickly organized sales and otherwise raised money for clothing and other means of comfort. Greely reported that the soldiers "would have brought more people and more booty had they not been betrayed by a girl on a plantation where they had killed the Overseer, & burned the sugar mills with a quantity of syrup & whiskey and the body of the Overseer in the sugar house." The betrayal prompted an unsuccessful retaliatory attack by Dickison's cavalry. Greely praised the valor of the black soldiers, and said "they claim a little humanity, as they say they left several of the rebels so severly [*sic*] wounded and alone, as their companions had fled, they thought duty to go back, a few of them, and finish them. They say when the parties met they charged upon the rebels in the name of 'Fort Pillow.'"[58]

In March 18, William Clark, together with L. Wilson and his son, guided Union troops during a raid on the plantation of Philip Dell near New-nansville. The raiders confiscated twenty-four slaves and twenty horses and mules; Clark and Wilson returned to Jacksonville to receive a reward for the successful campaign.[59] On April 1 another raiding party was transported upriver to a landing at the headwaters of Clarks Creek. Two Confederate pickets were killed before the raiders returned to Jacksonville with five prisoners.[60]

Orloff Dorman condemned Union troops for humiliating the captured Confederates. In a private journal entry he complained that "some crackers, guides and spies, and negro soldiers" brought two prisoners into town. The prisoners were marched down the streets of the town "by negro soldiers, with bayonets fixed, before and behind, and one of them" held a cocked revolver in his hand.[61] Dorman expressed hostility toward Confederates who deserted and took an oath of loyalty, then joined Union raiding parties.

Months of warfare, economic dislocation, suffering and privation, and continuing Federal raids added to the increasing uncertainty of the Confederate cause, prompting many from the interior of the state to join the refugees streaming into the city. In March 1865 the *Florida Union* reported:

"a flag of truce came over from the other side Thursday last bringing some fifty persons, men, women and children." The correspondent remarked that the occasion was marked by elaborate "courtesies . . . and other civilities."[62]

The last significant military hostilities in the state occurred on March 18, 1865, at the Battle of Natural Bridge at the St. Marks River near Tallahassee. The *Florida Union* printed a report of the heroic actions and wounding of a native son, J. J. Daniel, who had risen to the rank of colonel, 1st Florida Reserve Regiment. The engagement was a minor affair, but the Federal defeat frightened many in Jacksonville. The correspondent for the newspaper urged the formation of "companies for local defense; to be properly officered by men of their own choice; to drill if they think proper . . . to assist . . . in repelling an attack of the rebels should occasion require."[63]

The Confederate cause was hopeless by this time, and no one resented it more bitterly than Florida's wartime governor, John Milton. On April 1, 1865, Milton committed suicide.[64] Lee's surrender at Appomattox Court House in Virginia was only eight days away. On April 25, Union general Israel Vogdes met at Jacksonville with Confederate general Sam Jones. The next day Vogdes wired headquarters of the Department of the South: "I have the honor to acknowledge the receipt of a telegram announcing suspension of hostilities."[65]

It was not until May 6 that the *Florida Union* verified the news of suspension of hostilities. "THE WAR ENDED. Yes, we are able at last to announce that to our readers. . . . From this [moment] . . . we may date the end of the war." Cautiously, the editor added: "the present is not a fitting time for comment. A sufficient time must first elapse for careful consideration and thought upon the new era upon which we are about to enter."

The war was over, but for Jacksonville one cruel reminder of past sufferings was yet to come. One of the most traumatic experiences of the war occurred just forty-eight hours after hostilities officially ended in Florida. Just before sunset on April 28, a ghostly army descended on the city. They came in twos and threes, in groups of a dozen, and sometimes in bands of a hundred or more. They were Yankee soldiers, but from their appearance they could have been a Legion of the Damned. The rags they wore, coated with Georgia clay and Florida dust, were no longer identifiable as uniforms. The columns were composed of men who had survived the Sumter Prison at Andersonville, Georgia. They had been marched by their guards to Florida and released outside Federal lines not far from Jacksonville. About fifteen hundred arrived that first day, and by May 6 more than twice that number had straggled into town. On their arrival "most of them took a course straight for the river, as if by instinct," the *Florida Union* reported. "Their appearance as they passed along was pitiable in the extreme. Their clothing was in tatters; their faces were begrimed with dirt and black smoke from pine wood; they nearly were all without shoes; many were without hats. Large numbers were affected with scurvy."[66]

The influx of Andersonville survivors compelled Union commanders to construct a special camp and hospital on the St. Johns, where the men were able to enjoy cool breezes and the sight of sunlight sparkling on the water. The military and civilian populations of the city scoured the countryside for clothing, bedding, and provisions. Within a week, uniforms, tents, and other supplies arrived aboard an army transport, and arrangements were made to ship convalescents to a camp in Maryland. About 250 of the sickest and weakest were treated at the St. Johns River post. The last of the Andersonville survivors had been transported north by June, prompting the editor of the *Florida Union* to comment: "Jacksonville has often been the scene of many of the terrible realities of the war, but never were the people so appalled with the horror as when the released Union prisoners arrived in our midst."[67]

12

"The Storm Has Ceased"

*Life for Jacksonville's White
Residents during the Federal
Occupation*

John Hay, Lincoln's personal secretary, accompanied Federal forces to Jacksonville in February 1864 with orders from the president to field-test the Proclamation of Amnesty and Reconstruction announced the previous December. Hay intended to administer the loyalty oath until the number of pledged men became equal to 10 percent of the number of Florida voters registered for the 1860 election. Federal officials could then call for the election of delegates to a convention to write a new state constitution. The next step would be an election to choose representatives for a government that would renounce secession and apply for readmission to the Union. The president had instructed Hay to offer amnesty to Unionists and Confederates alike; former Rebels could be pardoned and have rights of citizenship restored if they promised to abide by the government's emancipation policies. Hay decided to target audiences in four Florida cities that were occupied by the Federal military: Fernandina, Jacksonville, St. Augustine, and Key West.

In Jacksonville, Hay found soldiers dashing about the town, wagons and caissons clogging the streets, and ships lined up in the river waiting to pull up to the wharves. Civilian refugees crossed Union lines in Jacksonville every day in quest of protection; so many were arriving that George Bowerem of the *New York Tribune* concluded, "the task of supporting the refugees with food and shelter has already become very onerous."[1] Bowerem noticed Lincoln's Amnesty Proclamation "posted conspicuously in and around Jacksonville" and being "liberally distributed among the people in the line of march taken by the troops. All are anxious to return to the Union. . . . All deprecate the idea of the Union armies being withdrawn." Hay observed crowds of people gathered around the posted proclamations, "the lettered reading, the unlettered listening with something that looked like genuine interest."[2]

In the first days of the occupation—before the defeat at Olustee—Hay was confident he could find enough loyal citizens to bring Florida back into the Union. Many of the Confederate deserters arriving in Jacksonville said they no longer had the "heart to fight against the Union cause." Whit Whittemore of the *New York Times* wrote: "There can be no question that the rebel government has dealt severely with them, and pushed not only the young and vigorous, but the old and decrepit into the ranks of the army." Within two months, he predicted, there would be "but one popular sentiment in Florida, and that sentiment—the Union."[3]

On February 11, Hay addressed prisoners at the army guardhouse on Bay Street, explaining that anyone pledging allegiance to the United States would be allowed to return home, entitled to all the rights of U.S. citizenship, whereas those who refused would be shipped north as prisoners of war. After numerous questions, a man stepped forward and said, "Let's take the oath," after which "They all stood up in line and held up their hands while I read the oath."[4] Hay worried that some may not have been sincere, but overlooked it: "What I build my hopes on is the evident weariness of the war and anxiety for peace."[5]

Some former leaders of the town were reluctant to sign the loyalty oath. Samuel Burritt and Uriah Bowden told Hay that they feared the Federals would again abandon the town and leave them at the mercy of vengeful Confederates. Hay spread the word that the current occupation force was permanent: this time the Union had come to stay, and it would protect loyal citizens.

Hay traveled between Jacksonville, St. Augustine, Fernandina, and Hilton Head over the next few weeks, alternately elated and despondent over the uneven success of the amnesty project. The Union defeat at Olustee presented his major obstacle. In the aftermath of that battle, Union supporters became increasingly worried that Confederate soldiers would return to Jacksonville. Hay's hopes for a mass recruitment of oath takers vanished. "I am very sure that we cannot get the President's 10th," he wrote on March 1. He closed his registration books and returned to Washington.[6]

Hay's failure convinced Lyman Stickney that an alternate plan was needed. Stickney had opposed Lincoln's plan out of fear it would attract former Confederates who would be difficult to control politically after the war ended. He wanted voting rights restricted to true Union men, especially those who hailed from the North, to build a Florida Republican Party in harmony with Treasury Secretary Chase's views. After witnessing the reluctance of Florida residents to take the amnesty oath, Stickney advised Chase to push for a convention to change the suffrage and slavery provisions of the old Florida constitution. All residents of the state of lawful age at the time of the election would be eligible to vote, "and all the inhabitants thereof free." After that, the ports of Fernandina, St. Augustine, and Jacksonville should be opened to "remove hindrances to northern emigrants."[7]

In March 1864, Chase withdrew as a presidential candidate; three months later he resigned from Lincoln's cabinet, thus negating whatever influence Stickney had commanded.[8] Stickney's diminished status was evident on May 24, when several hundred Florida Unionists met at the Methodist church in Jacksonville to elect delegates to the Republican Convention. Calvin Robinson was chosen to preside over the meeting, and local men Paran Moody and John W. Price were given key committee assignments. Elected as delegates to the convention were Buckingham Smith of St. Augustine and John S. Sammis, Paran Moody, John W. Price, Philip Fraser, and Calvin Robinson of Jacksonville. A new Union Executive Committee for the State of Florida was also chosen and authorized to use "full power to take all necessary action and measures to organize a State Government."[9] At the June 7 Republican Party Convention in Baltimore, the Florida delegation was admitted and Robinson was appointed to the Republican National Committee.[10]

In Jacksonville it was clear that real power continued to reside with the occupation authorities of the Union army. The Federal occupation changed life in the city overnight. General Gillmore's armada of nearly forty troop transports, supply schooners, and gunboats reminded residents of the busy port scenes that had been commonplace before the war.[11] A locomotive with railcars came up the St. Johns by ship, repair commenced on the track west of Jacksonville, and Scott's sawmill was restored to operation. By February 18, the railroad was reopened to Baldwin and Barber's Station and commercial port activity was again under way. Whittemore of the *Times* predicted: "It will not be many weeks before we shall see Jacksonville alive with trade and commerce."[12]

After the defeat at Olustee, activity accelerated in the city as ships carrying troop reinforcements and mountains of equipment and supplies arrived at the port. Streets were jammed with artillery caissons, commissary wagons, and long rows of tethered replacement mounts for the cavalry. Quartermaster's troops, couriers, officers, and refugees jostled for passage in the town's dirt streets. Lieutenant C. W. Brown of the 3rd U.S. Colored Troops, before the war a resident of Genessee County, New York, was not bothered by the chaotic conditions. "This state is one of the most splendid to soldier in," he wrote in his diary. "Dry shady woods, grassy camping grounds, plenty of wood, good water and above all, mild, beautiful weather. . . . Fruit trees are now in bloom and flowers grow wild in the wilder forests. Our bivouacs in many places have been literally amongst the flowers." Brown was impressed by the signs of returning "life after the cruel storm of this war. . . . The dwellings are half covered with a profusion of vines and trellis work surrounding long broad piazzas [and] the streets are quite pretty, many of them being shaded with large overhanging trees." By late March, commerce had become "quite brisk and the fair sex flocking in until it makes one remember early life and habits ere war broke upon our quiet homes to change the whole dreams of early ambition."[13]

Brown read the signs of change accurately. The military was encouraging commerce, and civilian refugees and Confederate deserters were arriving in the town. As early as February 15, Gillmore had ordered amnesty proclamations posted on buildings in the city and on trees lining the roads beyond town limits. The proclamation invited all persons willing to take an oath of loyalty to return to Jacksonville and "resume their usual avocations." The U.S. government promised to "afford them all needful protection." Union officers were ordered to "enforce . . . all existing orders and regulations forbidding the destruction or pillage of private property."[14]

Some refugees arrived in Jacksonville after suffering extreme hardships outside Union lines. The New York Tribune reported on February 20 the case of a woman who arrived looking like "a gaunt specter of starvation"; for several months she had "subsisted on a quart of rice a day and had nothing but a tea-cup to cook it with." Civilians were still hiding in the woods from Confederate conscript officers, but General Birney witnessed incidents in which refugees came out of hiding and welcomed men in Union uniforms "as deliverers." The provost marshal in Jacksonville, T. A. Henderson, posted a proclamation promising refugees and deserters from Confederate armies "that they will not under any circumstances, be compelled to serve in the U.S. Army against the rebels" as long as they pledged to "forever desert the rebel cause." Birney also gave high priority to "protecting the loyal inhabitants of East Florida" living outside the defensive network at Jacksonville.[15]

He announced that Federal troops would be dispatched to places where refugees were in danger.

The Confederate victory at Olustee and the subsequent torpedo warfare campaign temporarily disrupted the flow of refugees and deserters, but Union naval personnel maintained protective contact with civilians along the St. Johns River. Detachments of infantry and cavalry were transported upriver to scout for enemy activity and discourage guerrilla operations. In April 1864 a Union cavalry brigade rode between the St. Johns River and the Atlantic Ocean south of Jacksonville as far as the southern part of Volusia County with orders to "assure the citizens of the protection and good will of the U.S. Government and arrest and send to Jacksonville all persons you may find endeavoring to intimidate loyal men or furnish information to the enemy."[16]

The result was an increase in the flow of refugees. Able-bodied males were to be enrolled as scouts or soldiers or employed "in the comissary department as herders and cattle drivers and in the quartermaster's department as teamsters and laborers." Those unable to labor for the government were to be given temporary rations and assigned land to cultivate. General Gordon instructed Colonel Noble to inform loyal citizens that "the Government of the United States is determined to give its aid and its power to their protection, [but] it also demands their most vigorous assistance."[17] These policies proved successful. On August 9, 1864, General Hatch informed General Foster: "A great many refugees are coming in or crossing the river above here [Jacksonville]. To this time over 700 men have taken the oath at this place."[18]

The refugees contributed to efforts to reconstruct Jacksonville by restoring buildings and constructing new housing. Sleeping space was at a premium for the duration of the war and for many months after it ended. Almost from the start of the final occupation the sound of hammer and saw was commonplace in the city as the Federals directed repair of wharves and buildings. "The laborers in the different departments here are crackers," one man wrote, "still attired in the dirty gray uniforms furnished to them by the Confederate Government."[19]

Once the refugees were inside town walls, the provost marshal imposed strict controls on their movements, and passes were required to exit or reenter the city. Even neighboring farmers needed permission to bring produce to the city market. Civilians were rarely given passes that would clear them in and out of enemy country, but mail and packages were passed through the lines, subject to inspection on both sides. Civilians discovered that passing objects or information that might aid the enemy was cause for imprisonment. Refugees, particularly deserters who took the oath of allegiance, were watched carefully; when their actions indicated they did not take the oath seriously, imprisonment followed.[20]

The tight procedures instituted by the provost marshal infuriated Orloff Dorman, particularly on April 22, 1864, when all civilians who had not taken the oath of loyalty were ordered out of Jacksonville. Dorman fulminated at the order as a typical example of Yankee tyranny intended to cause suffering. In a companion crackdown, Union authorities shipped William Clark, Forbes Doggett, and other prisoners who refused to take the loyalty oath to prisons in the North. Dorman refused to take the oath, but he was not bothered by the provost marshal because he "kept aloof." Or so he believed. He did acknowledge, however, that his brother, Rodney Dorman, a former mayor of the town and a Union army officer, spoke on his behalf to the provost marshal.

Judging from Dorman's journal entries, few limits were placed on his movements; the most serious was curtailment of his fishing excursions. Dorman wandered throughout the town, returned home to record his observations, and crossed the St. Johns without a pass on at least one occasion. In March he carried sacks of corn in a canoe across the river to John Sammis's Strawberry Mills (in present-day Arlington) to be ground into grits. A bad storm came up while the corn was being ground, stranding Dorman and two rowers on the south side of the river. An army barge, sent at the request of Mrs. A. A. Ochus, arrived to carry Dorman and two other men back to town. Mrs. Ochus was the wife of a Confederate officer, Captain Adams A. Ochus of Company D, 11th Florida Infantry, who had been a popular musician in Jacksonville before the war.[21]

Early in April, orders were issued to confiscate all small watercraft in the vicinity of Jacksonville. Thereafter, civilians entering the city by boat were required to use a designated wharf where their passes and any cargo or baggage could be inspected. Soldiers in the units camped outside Jacksonville were required to have passes to visit the downtown area, while traders and farmers authorized to visit the city on business were restricted to Bay Street. Anyone found beyond the restricted area was "subject to arrest as a spy."[22]

Soldiers were permitted to use government horses only on official business and were subject to disciplinary action if they galloped their mounts through the streets without orders bearing the authorized designation—"gallop"—on the envelope. Sailors caught ashore without passes were thrown in jail. A bugle played "Taps" at 9 p.m. to signal that everyone was to be off the

streets and lights darkened unless otherwise authorized. Civilians who violated curfew were jailed, and few were exempt. When former judge Samuel
Burritt violated the curfew, a soldier was promptly dispatched to his home
bearing a curt note from the provost marshal, T. M. Sweet: "Your home is
not on my books as having permission to burn lights after 9 P.M. I require
prompt explanation of such disrespect and that you at once furnish me with
evidence that said permission has been granted you."[23]

When residents known to have been secessionists or Rebel sympathizers ran afoul of military authorities, their records were used against them.
The provost marshal intervened in a dispute between former Confederate
Daniel Hart and his estranged wife, saying: "Mr. Hart is well known to be an
unprincipled man and deserving of no consideration. He was sentenced by
a Military Commission about one year ago to three years imprisonment for
shooting a Federal soldier."[24] Jackson Murray, a secessionist who returned to
Jacksonville in the summer of 1864, was executed for the murder of a Unionist two years earlier. A Federal officer reported: "the execution was a terrible
lesson to those who under guise of authority wantonly sacrifice the lives of
those who differ from them."[25]

On June 4, 1864, Margaret Broward was evicted from her home at Cedar
Creek on suspicion of assisting men who placed torpedoes in the river. Not
until four months after the war ended was she allowed to return, with a
warning that her property might be confiscated by the Freedmen's Bureau
and given to newly freed slaves. Occupation authorities also recommended
that "one of the Broward men" from the Cedar Creek area be arrested. "This
man Broward has returned to the vicinity of Yellow Bluff. He has been a
Guerrilla for the past four years. He erected temporary works on the St.
Johns and fired upon any Union Boat that passed. At one time he and his
brothers killed three men upon one Boat. I would recommend that he be
arrested and tried for larceny if no more heinous crime be found against
him."[26]

Union soldiers were also subject to strict military discipline. Officers as
well as enlisted men were arrested for "ungentlemanly conduct" and were
punished for "pillaging property," stealing, or getting drunk. When John Hay
witnessed the execution of a black soldier for "a rape on a woman in the
neighborhood," he recorded the grim details: "In the middle of the square a
gallows was erected. . . . A cart drove in & . . . was backed under the gallows;
the poor devil stood upright. . . . His sentence was read, the noose adjusted,
he said a few words to the crowd & the cart beginning to move he jumped up
& tried to break his neck but failed & gasped & jerked and struggled dread-

fully." Hay and the other witnesses stood in stunned silence until one of the bystanders "jumped up to his shoulders & hung on him swinging. No effect. Another man got on: he still gasped. At last they raised him up & jerked him down hard; & he ceased struggling & after a while the crowd dispersed." The next day Hay returned to the gallows and saw the "poor devil still fluttering his rags in the wind—his head horribly oblique, his eyes staring wide, his mouth open, and his blackened tongue protruding." A crowd of "negroes, boys & crackers" was gathered near the gallows listening "with intense relish" to tales of "the hideous show of the night before."[27]

Civilian offenses included violation of the oath of allegiance, disloyalty, murder, illegal selling of liquor, traveling without a pass, and conducting business without a license. Drunkenness was a chronic problem during the entire occupation period. Selling liquor was forbidden in 1864, unless by permission of the provost marshal. Licensing regulations were adopted and the fee varied from five to twenty-five dollars, increasing over time. The army generally approved of licensed sales of alcohol as an outlet for release of pent-up emotions and a means of reducing tension, although it often had the opposite effect. Before the war ended, saloons proliferated along Bay Street.[28]

After smallpox and yellow fever epidemics at Savannah and Charleston in the summer of 1864, the occupation authorities monitored public health and sanitation problems. In Jacksonville an intensive cleanup campaign was launched. After more than two years of being alternately occupied and abandoned, burned and pillaged, sanitation procedures were badly needed in the town. Hundreds of soldiers joined crews of civilians hired by the provost marshal to collect and burn rubbish, clean drainage ditches, and scout the wharves, creeks, and city streets for debris, while inspectors searched for the violators and brought them for adjudication.

On one occasion the provost marshal ordered the army's chief commissary officer to remove decaying vegetables that had accumulated on the wharf behind the commissary storehouse, as "the health of the town renders it necessary that the strictest sanitary measures should be observed." Merchants were also prodded into action. On June 21 the provost marshal ordered a trader to remove animal hides "exposed to the sun on the wharf nearly opposite Laura Street [which] are emitting a very offensive and contaminating effluvia."[29] In general, soldiers caused fewer sanitation problems than did civilians. From the moment the army established itself permanently in the city, a reporter for the *Peninsula* wrote, the camps of the soldiers were "models of neatness and kept faultlessly clean."[30]

Life under martial law included regulations to protect soldiers as well as to discipline them. When soldiers complained that prices were so high they could not afford to make purchases, the military established price controls. Unscrupulous military suppliers lost their licenses and were occasionally jailed. Hardly anything escaped the attention of the provost marshal. When one citizen refused to share his well with neighbors, an order was issued: "You will immediately on the receipt of this note replace the well bucket and rope in the well belonging to the house which you occupy and allow the neighbors to draw water whenever and as much as they please."[31]

Even former mayor Halsted Hoeg was subject to regulation. When Hoeg attempted to evict a newly freed slave from one of his properties, the provost marshal interceded: "Israel Hall will not be interfered with. He will occupy the house that he now lives in until further order." Morality was monitored and regulated as well. On June 21 an unmarried "colored woman calling herself Sarah Johnson" was arrested for living with a black soldier. The town's two jails, one for civilians, another for soldiers, became so crowded that some people in confinement were "lost" by the authorities. On August 7, two civilians were released from confinement when it was found they had been behind bars without charges being brought. No records could be found to indicate why the men had been arrested.[32]

Chronic housing problems required the military to arbitrate between whites and blacks contesting for the same housing accommodations. One record reads: "Application to have family removed from stable on Adams Street. . . . Permission granted negroes to live in stables." Similar petitions passed in a constant stream through the provost's office. The extent of suffering and deprivation is revealed in a poignant report written by the provost marshal: "A man living in a stable came to me last week and stated that his wife had recently come in from the interior and was on her way to St. Augustine. Reaching this place she was taken sick (has since given birth to a child) and could not proceed at once to [her] former home in St. Augustine." With all the available housing occupied, the provost was unable to arrange an accommodation. "The man is a shoemaker and is lame. His wife cannot be safely moved now. He promises to have . . . [the stable] neatly cleaned and whitewashed if he can be allowed to remain there until his wife is recovered."[33]

During the summer of 1864, military headquarters at Hilton Head ordered a census of the civilian population in the occupied towns of northeast Florida. The Jacksonville census, finished in September, tallied 557 civilians of both sexes and races over the age of fifteen, and 377 children age fourteen and younger living within the city's fortified walls. In addition to the 934 civilians, the town was populated by roughly two thousand soldiers of the garrison. The white male civilians were employed in several dozen occupations, from common laborer to journalist, printer, mason, confectioner, fisherman, shoemaker, lawyer, and doctor. Women worked as dressmakers, washerwomen, restaurant proprietors, and teachers.[34]

The census listed names of old Southern families who had abandoned property and prosperity when they fled the city in 1862 in solidarity with the cause of secession. They returned in 1864 and 1865 to find their businesses ruined and their properties confiscated or occupied by strangers. Listed on the census are the names of families who had resided in the region for generations: Hart, Doggett, Osteen, Bessent, Register, Baya, Genovar, DaCosta, Poinsett, Hudnall, and others.

Twenty adults refused to take the oath of allegiance. Seven were women, including Mrs. M. Doggett. Among the men were John Doggett and M. C. Doggett. Forbes Doggett was one of thirteen civilians jailed in the summer and fall of 1864 for "disloyalty." Others who languished in prison were local residents John M. Pons, James Turner, Alfred Moore, John Holmes, D. M. Saunders, Medicio Sanchez, George McCloud, Joseph Fitzpatrick, and John W. Scott.[35]

Of the white civilians in town in the fall of 1864, about half were born in the South; the others were either Northern- or foreign-born. Among those born outside the United States was the family of Adolph Ochus, a Confederate officer captured by Union soldiers in July. The German-born Ochus had lost his prewar music shop and was unemployed. His wife worked as a clerk at the Taylor House, a boarding establishment. George Peck of Connecticut operated a small watchmaker's shop, while Constantine Nicholas ran a restaurant. Dominic Damient was a candy maker, Bartolo Canova was providing the town with fish, and former merchant Calvin D. Oak was a storekeeper for Calvin Robinson, who was back in town and once again working as a merchant.

Following the 1862 Union evacuation, Robinson had found refuge in New York and Washington until late in November 1862, when he returned as assistant surveyor for the Direct Tax Commission in Fernandina. He worked only briefly for the tax commission, then began purchasing abandoned and confiscated merchandise from Federal authorities in anticipation of opening another retail establishment in Fernandina. When Colonel Higginson and the 1st South Carolina Loyal Volunteers occupied Jacksonville in March 1863, Robinson accompanied the regiment to investigate the possibility of reviving his retail store and sawmill. The Union evacuation of the town prompted Robinson to return to Fernandina.

In June 1863, when the tax commission began auctioning confiscated Rebel properties in Fernandina, Robinson was a major participant. The previous summer he had traveled to Boston to meet with creditors and discuss restitution of the $41,000 in debts he incurred in the burning of Jacksonville homes and businesses in March 1862. From assets of $125,000 at the beginning of the war, he had managed to salvage only $12,000 in Southern bank bills that he buried in his garden. An agreement was reached calling for Robinson to bid on Fernandina properties with the proceeds of his salvaged bank bills, and later transfer deeds to those properties to the creditors to pay down his debts. On an investment of $1,825 he gained $24,300 in credits on his old debts; the remainder of the debt was paid in full soon after the war ended.

While in Fernandina in the spring of 1863, Robinson arranged for medical treatment for the fifteen thousand freedmen who had found their way through Union lines. He was appointed superintendent of schools in Fernandina by General Saxton, and he bought lots for freedmen using money they had saved from wages earned for working for the army. He also purchased at auction the home of General Finegan, which the Direct Tax Commission had confiscated for nonpayment of taxes. Robinson transferred the title to Miss Chloe Merrick, who turned the Finegans' showplace home into an orphanage for African American children.

Robinson resided in St. Augustine briefly, serving as clerk of court under U.S. District Court judge Philip Fraser, another Jacksonville refugee. Robinson hurried to Jacksonville at the commencement of the fourth Union occupation of the town; he reopened his old business and became a leader of the Republican Party. It was Robinson who cast Florida's single vote for Abraham Lincoln at the Republican National Convention in 1864.[36]

John S. Sammis returned with Union forces in February 1864. Married to the youngest daughter of deceased planter and slave trader Zephaniah Kingsley and his African wife, Anta Majigeen Njaay Kingsley, Sammis had accumulated extensive plantation holdings and owned a major mercantile business prior to the war. He also owned a water-powered saw- and gristmill at Strawberry Creek in today's Arlington and a plantation with a large number of slaves.[37] Like Robinson, Sammis paid a heavy price for supporting the Union. In 1862, Confederates confiscated $75,000 worth of his properties.

Sammis and Robinson crossed paths often after fleeing from the town in March 1862, in New York and Washington, and in Florida as members of the Direct Tax Commission. Sammis resigned from the tax commission and returned to Jacksonville temporarily during the brief third Union occupation of the town. When Union forces came to Jacksonville again in February 1864, Sammis and business partner Thomas Ells purchased a shipload of merchandise in New York and resumed business at the Sammis Block on Bay Street. Two of Sammis's mixed-race sons, Edgar and Edward, and his son-in-law, John S. Driggs, joined the business as clerks. By the end of the war, Sammis had reestablished most of his old business connections and prestige. He later became an important figure in the postwar Republican Party and a leader in Jacksonville's economic recovery.[38]

During the first Union occupation in 1862, Eliza Hudnall sold baked goods and home-cooked meals to sailors aboard the gunboats and took an oath of loyalty aboard the *Ottawa*. Union officers suggested she establish a boardinghouse and put two confiscated houses on East Forsyth Street under her care. Two of her daughters married Federal officers. After the war, Mrs. Hudnall became the proprietor of the St. Johns House at Jacksonville during the city's golden era of tourism in the 1880s.

Mrs. Hudnall's popularity with Federal officers may also have been assisted by her willingness to inform on disloyal residents of the town. Six weeks after Jacksonville was occupied in 1864 she began informing on Southern sympathizers. When one of her civilian boarders used "disloyal and disrespectful language" at her dinner table, Mrs. Hudnall carried the tale to the provost marshal. At the man's trial she testified that he cursed the Stars and Stripes, expressed a longing to see the Confederate flag fly once again over Jacksonville, and threatened the life of a naval officer. She also said the man regretted taking the oath of allegiance.[39]

Beneath the surface of the entrepreneurial success stories occurring under Federal occupations, an explosive issue was dividing Jacksonville's Unionists and former Confederates. The ongoing auctions of tax-delinquent properties engendered bitter and lasting animosities. Prewar tax records for Duval County had been carried away early in the war, and assessing back tax bills could only proceed in areas already secured by the military. Consequently, most properties sold in 1864 were lots and houses within Jacksonville's corporate limits. On August 18, 1864, properties belonging to Redding W. Biggs, Abel S. Baldwin, Cyrus Bisbee, Antonio Canova, Charles Willey, George C. Powell, Theodore Hartridge, Lewis Flemming, George R. Foster, William Ledwith, Isadore V. Garnie, and Thomas O. Holmes sold in Jacksonville, at prices ranging from $32 to $1,075.[40]

Treasury Department records indicate that only a moderate volume of sales occurred in 1865. The steamer *St. Marys* sold at auction for $5,000. The Cowford Ferry, including its boats and properties, was confiscated from Confederate sympathizer W. A. Young and sold for an unrecorded sum.[41] Only days after the Yankees arrived in 1864, they reroofed Confederate captain Charles Willey's house and used it for a troop hospital. The house was later sold at auction to John S. Sammis for a residence, then sold to a third party. Orloff Dorman saw these sales as "stealing, it is nothing else." He paid the property taxes on his own town lots while calling the tax commissioners "the least civil sons of bitches," and complained that he and Charles Willey were victims of taxation without representation. Dorman vented his anger on the Willey case in annual journal entries from 1864 to 1878, when Willey's heirs finally recovered possession. In 1864 he warned in the pages of his private journal: "it may be the time will come when I may have a hand in punishing these usurpers for their misdeeds. Leniency in that case would be a sin to the world and God to surpass any other. An example is required of them all that will be lasting."[42]

While the passions of secession and war, the aggravations of confiscated property, and the exigencies of life under military rule continued to divide Jacksonville residents, there was one hopeful attempt to unify the population around a progressive measure. In February 1864, the first free public school in Jacksonville's history was established for white and black children. But bitter divisiveness surfaced as Jacksonville's white parents refused to permit their children to attend a racially integrated school.

The founder and first teacher at the school was Dr. Esther Hawks, a medical school graduate from New England and an abolitionist. She was married to another abolitionist, Dr. John Milton Hawks, a surgeon with the United States Colored Troops. Dr. Esther Hawks learned that racial prejudice would die a slow and painful death in Jacksonville. When the school opened on the second floor of the Odd Fellows Hall on Bay Street, she recorded first-day attendance at thirty students: twenty-nine whites and one "colored." On the second day, Mrs. Hawks reported an increase of sixteen colored children, but one of the white girls announced: "Miss, I can't come to school tomorrow. Ma says I shan't come if you teach the blacks." Disappointed, Mrs. Hawks told the child the school was free and open to whites and blacks. Later, she wrote in her diary, "said Mary is as ill-looking a cub as there is in the lot, but not to blame for her ma's prejudice."[43]

Among the initial white students were Mary Bacon, age twenty-two, and her three younger sisters, none of whom had attended school. They had never learned to read or write, but they were all eager to do so. The Tabeau brothers, Willis and Rajah, only attended for three days before their mother forced them to withdraw because black children were present. Rajah's reluctance to follow his mother's orders prompted an unpleasant incident, when "the mother came to the stairs and sent in the eldest boy to say that if Rajah didn't come away she'd break his bones."

Dr. Hawks's daily attendance records document the decline in white student participation. On April 8 she wrote: "Two families continued to send until this week, but the mother told me that, although she would be glad to have them come, the neighbors make so much fuss she should be obliged to keep them at home. The number of colored children increases faster than whites diminish."[44] At the end of six weeks, all but one white student had followed the Tabeau children's example. The lone white student was possibly Mary Bacon, who had vowed on the day after Rajah's forced departure: "They can't scare me—I mean to learn all I can. I don't care who stays away!"[45]

Late in March, Mrs. Apthorp, the wife of a Federal officer, joined Dr. Hawks at the school. L. A. Barrow, supervisor of the freedmen schools in the Department of the South, told the women to divide the teaching duties at the free school so that Dr. Hawks could also provide instruction at a separate school for soldiers of the black regiments stationed in Jacksonville. Barrow supported Hawks's decision on racial integration, telling her: "I think you took the right course respecting white and colored scholars. Show no preference for either; and let none be abused. Our mission is to all who wish to learn."[46] The two missionary teachers continued to experience difficulties in Jacksonville, both with the military authorities and with the residents of the town. One of Dr. Hawks's friends wrote on April 15: "I hope you will not get discouraged, hold on till help comes."[47]

Orloff Dorman scorned the missionary teachers with the same venom he used to denounce anything that reminded him of the Union. He believed the teachers were vile Yankees sent on a mission to create trouble for whites in Jacksonville. "They are simply mischief makers," Dorman wrote in his journal; "they make the negroes extremely insolent, wicked and depraved." Local residents who shared his biases refused to rent rooms to the women who taught in the free school, and shunned them socially.

For Esther Hawks there were compensating rewards, especially the responses of students she found "orderly and earnest" and eager to proceed with their daily lessons. She also taught daily lessons to soldiers who attended classes between their scheduled military duties. Former slaves learned to read and write and discussed the basics of citizenship as preparation for their future lives as freedmen and citizens of the United States once the shooting stopped. Dr. Hawks preserved dozens of letters from the grateful soldiers she taught. George Delevan, a soldier in the 54th Massachusetts, wrote to her from a hospital in Beaufort to request a personal memento to remember her by. "I will try to keep it for as long as I live, just for your sake," Delevan told his former teacher.[48]

Dr. Hawks finished the 1864 school year in spite of the difficulties and resumed teaching at the school in October. At five feet, seven and one-half inches in height, and with hazel eyes, a pale complexion, and dark hair, the twenty-eight-year-old teacher must have presented a handsome figure as she rode a horse through the town's streets. Captain George S. Pope issued standing orders to "let Mrs. Dr. Hawks have the big horse . . . if she would want to ride at any time."[49]

In addition to the missionary school that commenced instruction in February 1864, a "free school" that enrolled 115 students and employed four teachers was operating in March 1865. The founder of the school, General Hatch, instructed the provost marshal to levy a monthly tax on merchants to pay the salaries of the principal and teachers. Four other schools operated in Jacksonville during 1865, meeting at temporary locations that included the Odd Fellows Hall, Rev. John S. Swaim's Methodist Episcopal Church, Mrs. A. T. Howe's home at the corner of Forsyth and Washington streets, and the home of Jacksonville's prewar music master, A. A. Ochus.[50]

On June 3, 1865, the editor of the *Florida Union* advised Jacksonville's citizens to forget the past and look to the future by opening "regular communication with the North," boosting commerce at the port, and taking "steps to repair the wharves." Individual property owners could contribute by fixing sidewalks and fences and removing the debris accumulated during the war years. If accomplished, these projects would permit Jacksonville to again "present a city-like appearance."[51] Union soldiers and refugees working under supervision of the provost marshal had already cleared away the worst of the rubble; buildings had been repaired, ditches cleaned, streets patched, telegraph communication restored, and rail lines rebuilt. Commerce and port activity was stimulated by the repairs. Firm police control exercised by the army encouraged many skeptical former residents to return to their homes and businesses.

Ann P. Cooper came back to Jacksonville and petitioned the provost marshal for the return of her home and rental payment for the months it had been used as a military hospital by the Union army. Dr. J. W. Applegate, chief medical officer for the District of Florida, told the provost marshal the house had been seized as abandoned property in February 1864 for a hospital. He recommended payment of the rental fee and the continued use of the house as a hospital.[52]

A stage line was operating between Jacksonville and St. Augustine by June 1865. Less than a month later the first postwar train arrived from Lake City, connecting Jacksonville to Tallahassee by rail. The blockade of most Southern ports had ended in May, and port business showed signs of revival. By July, a steamship was operating between Jacksonville and Palatka, the City Gas Light Company had been reorganized, and reconstruction of sawmills destroyed during the war had begun.[53]

While restoration efforts were under way in Jacksonville, former U.S. senator David Yulee arrived in town to meet with Salmon P. Chase, now the chief justice of the U.S. Supreme Court, who was touring the South at the time. Yulee, a leading Florida secessionist and Confederate official, was promptly arrested by the provost marshal and confined in the home of attorney Samuel Burritt. Chase met with Yulee and afterward called him "ignorant" for insisting that no important changes had occurred between 1861 and 1865: "Slavery was dead—that much was hastily admitted—but what other changes the causeless Rebellion could have, or ought to have wrought, he didn't see." On May 29, Brigadier General Vogdes detained Yulee pending orders from Washington.[54]

Many of the town's prewar leaders had returned by July 1865, including John P. Sanderson, Dr. Asa Baldwin, John Holmes, Colonel John McCormick, Columbus Drew, and Dr. Theodore Hartridge.[55] Francis P. Fleming and some other Confederate veterans refused to return, and instead settled in other towns across the state. Fleming described Jacksonville as "a worse Yankee hole than ever. I would not live there again for anything." He and his brother Lewis, along with J. J. Daniel and Edward M. L'Engle, explored the possibility of establishing a colony in Brazil, where slavery was still legal, but abandoned the plan when they secured a contract to cut railroad ties for the Union military.[56]

On June 26, 1865, Orloff Dorman traveled outside Jacksonville for the first time since February 1862. He rode through the neighboring countryside and found it "torn up and broken up and destroyed and burned." The people, cattle, horses, and farm equipment were gone, "and all the negroes stolen." Alongside what he remembered as an idyllic country road he now found desolation, "only a part of three families remaining . . . and they had been robbed of pretty much everything they had."[57] Dorman was unable to rid himself of bitterness. By staying in Jacksonville rather than becoming a refugee, he had suffered the "torments of hell . . . [and] associated with fiends."[58]

He was resigned to defeat. The "good life" would always be an image of the past, contrasted to a deprived, depraved, and desolate future. The Yankees had seen to that! For the remaining years of his life, Dorman believed that the perfect society had been the one based on enslaved black laborers ruled by the superior race of white men of Jacksonville.

Others may have shared Dorman's despair, but they left their thoughts unrecorded while they attempted to rebuild their lives and fortunes. The economy expanded as fall approached. A drugstore opened, postal service was restored, and attorneys, physicians, dentists, and surgeons opened their doors. Calvin Oak returned to his previous business location in the Reed Building at Ocean and Bay after forming a partnership with George Peck in a jewelry and watchmaking business. Land and insurance agencies opened. John Oliveros returned from three years of Confederate service to restore his gun and locksmith shop on Bay Street. Miss Mary Lenihan opened a "Fashionable Millinery" at the corner of Washington and Forsyth streets.[59]

The Duval County Medical Society met in November 1865, reuniting such prominent professional men as A. S. Baldwin, Richard P. Daniel, Holmes Steele, E. T. Sabal, H. C. Vaughan, George H. McPherson, J. Todd, and Miles J. Murphy, all of whom had served the Confederacy.[60] Clubs like the Odd Fellows and Masons were reestablished, and church congregations reorganized and began rebuilding their burned-out sanctuaries. In August the *Jacksonville Herald* predicted the return of Northern tourists during the coming winter. A correspondent for the *New York Times* reported that the "Northern men, mostly discharged officers and soldiers, have gone into business [in Jacksonville], but the arrival of large quantities of cotton, much of it Sea Island cotton, has done more than anything else to set business in motion and direct attention from the calamities of the war."[61]

Twenty ships entered or left the port in the first two weeks of September 1865. Departing vessels carried machinery, leaf tobacco, lumber, and nearly two thousand bales of cotton. Regularly scheduled steamship service between Jacksonville, Savannah, and Charleston was restored that same month. In October, work on the first two-story building erected since 1861 was completed. "All our boarding houses are crowded and we have no building suitable for a hotel in this city," the *Florida Times* commented.[62]

The revival of business in Jacksonville focused people's attention on the future. "The music of fife and drum has given place to the more cheerful sound of the carpenter's hammer and saw," the *Florida Union* reported on September 9. "We think the prospect is very encouraging and that by another spring few traces will be left of the disastrous war that had driven the people from their homes and laid in ruins the fairest portion of what has been and what at no distant day will be again the fairest city in the South." A Jacksonville resident told a *New York Times* correspondent that the "conversation . . . has changed from war to business," the town "is assuming its former character," its wharves again "lined with schooners."[63]

On November 25, Colonel John T. Sprague, military commander at Jacksonville, issued a proclamation restoring municipal government. Halsted Hoeg, a Unionist who had been the town's mayor when the war began in 1861, was appointed to fill the term interrupted four years before. Before the year ended, a new Jacksonville City Council had repudiated the slave ordinances of earlier decades. In December the editor of the *Florida Union* heralded the coming year: "We notice on every hand a spirit of improvement. . . . New houses are being erected, old ones repaired, and dilapidated fences being overhauled. . . . A new steam saw mill is nearly completed, and three others are in process of erection."[64] The editor predicted that news of the progress and cooperative spirit would be heard in the North and prompt investors to "pour money" on the city rather than guns. On Christmas Day, a *New York Times* correspondent writing from Jacksonville looked back on the events of the past four years: "Florida has passed through the fiery ordeal, she has experienced a dark night and tempestuous weather; but the day has dawned, the storm has ceased."[65]

No one had a more vivid memory of a "dark night" or a "fiery ordeal" than Otis L. Keene. After the Judson House burned in March 1862, Keene returned briefly to Maine before moving to Washington to work for the Treasury Department. He met often with other exiled Florida Unionists when they visited Washington, often over dinners at the Willard House. In May and July 1865, Keene and his wife, Abbie, dined with Samuel Burritt, Columbus Drew, and Theodore Hartridge. They also entertained the man who would become the state's provisional governor, William Marvin, and its first elected postwar governor, Harrison Reed.[66]

On January 15, 1866, Keene stepped off a steamship at a Jacksonville wharf and registered at a boardinghouse. With conflicted memories, he walked about the town, stopping at an empty lot that had once been the site of Jacksonville's finest hotel, the Judson House. His thoughts returned to that "dark night" in March 1862 when he stood beside his wife in the rain watching flames and smoldering embers devour what remained of the Judson House. In the evening, he wrote in his diary that the weed-filled lot "certainly looks desolate and dreary."[67]

Keene pushed memories of that night in 1862 aside and refocused his thoughts on the future. The next day he repaid prewar debts and secured a position as purser on one of the steamships running from Palatka to Savannah. Like members of the Fraser, Mitchell, Robinson, and Sammis families, who had also opposed secession and war, Keene had decided to rebuild his life unburdened by the past. His goal was to reestablish friendships, social status, career, and prosperity. His acquaintances among the Daniel, Drew, Sanderson, Steele, and other families that had supported the Confederacy had come to similar conclusions. Decades of political conflict, secession, and war were all in the past, and now their thoughts were on the future. Whatever their patriotic alliances had been, Keene and the other white residents of Jacksonville had reason to be optimistic. The ongoing signs of economic revival provided reassurance that prosperous times were returning.

FIGURE 32. Battery Creighton, Jacksonville, Florida, 1864. Sketch by Alfred R. Waud. (Courtesy of Library of Congress.)

FIGURE 33. Chimney Point and an abandoned sawmill on the St. Johns River, 1864. Sketch by Alfred R. Waud. (Courtesy of Library of Congress.)

FIGURE 34. Federal campsite at Jacksonville, Florida, 1864, located at today's Hemming Plaza. Photograph by Sam Cooley, 1864. (Courtesy of Dr. Wayne W. Wood, from the Jacksonville Historical Society.)

FIGURE 35. Major John W. Appleton, 54th Massachusetts Regiment of United States Colored Infantry. Appleton's letters, preserved at the West Virginia University Library, chronicle the daily life of black soldiers during the fourth occupation of Jacksonville. (Courtesy of Florida State Archives.)

FIGURE 36. Federal signal tower, Jacksonville, Florida, 1864. Signals
went from this tower at today's Main and Forsyth streets to a similar
structure at Fort Yellow Bluff near today's Dames Point, and from
there were relayed to the gunboat base at Mayport Mills near the
entrance to the St. Johns River. The wood siding at the top of the
hundred-foot tower shielded the men from sniper fire. Photograph
by Sam Cooley, 1864. (Courtesy of Library of Congress.)

FIGURE 37. Federal sentry looking toward the wharf at Bay and Ocean streets. Photograph by Sam Cooley, 1864. (Courtesy of Dr. Wayne W. Wood, from the Jacksonville Historical Society.)

FIGURE 38. Commercial buildings located north of Bay Street, between Ocean and Newnan streets. Photograph by Sam Cooley, 1864. (Courtesy of Dr. Wayne W. Wood, from the Western Reserve Historical Society.)

FIGURE 39. City Market at Ocean Street and the St. Johns River, Jacksonville, Florida. Federal artillery and caissons crowd the market; the transport steamer USS *Cosmopolitan* and a second transport are at the wharf. John Clark's waterfront warehouse became the Federal boathouse. Photograph by Sam Cooley, 1864. (Courtesy of Dr. Wayne W. Wood, from the U.S. Army Military History Institute.)

FIGURE 40. Warehouse of Theodore Hartridge, facing north on Bay Street. Colonel Thomas W. Higginson billeted black Union soldiers on the second story of this building during the 1863 Union occupation of Jacksonville. In 1864 it became the warehouse of the provost marshal. Photograph by Sam Cooley, 1864. (Courtesy of Dr. Wayne W. Wood, from the U.S. Army Military History Institute.)

FIGURE 41. Federal troops drill outside the Jacksonville Reading Room, located south of Bay Street. The USS *Hellen Getty* and a second transport steamer are tied to wharves at the rear of the building. Photograph by Sam Cooley, 1864. (Courtesy of Dr. Wayne W. Wood, from the Western Reserve Historical Society.)

FIGURE 42. Dozens of emancipated slaves stand in front of the Provost Marshal's Office at Jacksonville, Florida, 1864. Federal officers are on the steps and porch. (Courtesy of Dr. Wayne W. Wood, from the National Archives and Records Administration.)

FIGURE 43. Farewell to a fellow soldier, circa 1900. Elderly veterans of United States Colored Infantry regiments pay last respects at the funeral of a Union veteran of the Civil War. (Courtesy of Eileen Brady, Special Collections, Thomas G. Carpenter Library, University of North Florida.)

A Troubled
Transition to Freedom

*Life for Jacksonville's Black
Residents during the Federal
Occupation*

The Federal occupation of Jacksonville in 1864 and 1865 resulted in stability and a revival of commerce, with an accompanying prospect of returning prosperity. However, beneath the surface calm lay troubling and persistent problems that defied reasonable solutions, the most vexing being racial conflict between former slaveholders and the black men and women recently freed by the Union army and by the Thirteenth Amendment. Judging by the antebellum Jacksonville newspapers, the deepest fears of the town's white residents prior to secession had been of Northern intentions to abolish slavery and the wave of anti-white violence that would inevitably follow. In 1848 the *Florida News* had warned that rich and poor whites were all "entirely dependent" on slavery and that only extreme measures could prevent abolition. If emancipation occurred, "insurrection" would surely follow, and whites would suffer murder and arson. These fears intensified in the 1850s and persisted throughout the war, becoming most apparent when former slaves, transformed into black Union soldiers carrying rifles, occupied the towns of northeast Florida. For a year after the armistice, armed black soldiers patrolled the streets of Jacksonville with the Federal occupation force. Whites had become a minority of the town's population, and their prewar fears persisted. With the racial controls inherent in the prewar slave codes no longer operative, the whites of Florida sought ways to reimpose white supremacy and to retain control of land and labor.[1]

The black residents of Jacksonville were also apprehensive. They had survived slavery and achieved freedom, but many questions remained concerning their future in the United States. As unpaid and forced laborers in their collective past, the recently freed black men and women of Florida hoped to become independent landowners, craftsmen, or laborers, working for the welfare of their families. They were aware, however, that if white Floridians had their way, the future for emancipated slaves would be limited to working for their former owners. Freedmen had become the majority of Jacksonville's population, and their first concerns were finding food and shelter for their families and securing jobs and income. The veterans of black Union regiments who settled in the town after discharge also expected to receive citizenship privileges, including the right to vote, in return for their military service. Blacks were attending meetings at local churches to discuss their future status in the Union; they were vitally interested in gaining the right to vote. Although they were rejoicing in their freedom, the black men and women of northeast Florida were worried about what the future would bring and aware that they faced a troubled transition to freedom.

A *Florida Union* correspondent speculated in May 1865 that "nearly all of the planters in this county and those adjoining immediately made satisfactory arrangements with their negroes to remain on their plantations and cultivate the crops, being compensated for their labor either in money or a share of the crop."[2] A very different conclusion was reached by a *New York Times* correspondent in mid-June when he found large numbers of black families arriving in Jacksonville from the farms and plantations of the area: "The planters are, many of them, turning off their negroes without pay for subsistence, and they come [into the town] in large numbers."[3] These conflicting reports reflect the divergent conditions and opinions that existed in the postwar months as some planters tried to adjust to the new era ushered in by the Union victory, while others resisted the full implications of emancipation and insisted on maintaining control of both land and labor.

A group of ninety freedmen arrived in Jacksonville on July 4, prompting a *New York Times* correspondent to write: "The negroes of Florida appear to have fallen into the too convenient mistake of a people suddenly released from bondage [believing] that the end of slavery meant the end of labor."[4] A *Jacksonville Herald* editorial deplored the "chronic abhorrence of idleness, vagrancy and dependence" and the large numbers of "people, white and black, living month after month on government rations." The *Herald* reported that every railroad depot between Jacksonville and Tallahassee was crowded with newly freed black men and women, "healthy, good looking negroes, the better portion of them females decked in their gayest attire."[5] A *New York Times* correspondent found a "swarm" of "the poor, infatuated creatures" in Tallahassee, carrying their "new liberty" too far in believing that their uncompensated work as slaves entitled them to own the land they had previously tended.[6]

The same complaint had been made earlier by T. M. Mickler, mayor of Lake City, who told the provost marshal in Jacksonville that former slaves in Columbia County were taking possession of plantation lands and threatening violence to their former owners. Mickler said the whites of Lake City feared for their personal safety and needed to be protected from blacks by the military.[7] In Alachua and Marion counties, a white Union officer, Captain George D. Blast of the 3rd U.S.C.T., heard rumors that the "freedmen were acting up," expecting to receive back wages for their unpaid labor as slaves. Tales being circulated that the government planned to feed, clothe, and pay former slaves prompted some local planters to talk of "using the lash on them" to keep them under control. Blast recommended strong laws to maintain "control [of] the colored," a remark that would undoubtedly have angered the black soldiers in the company he commanded.[8]

In the immediate aftermath of the war, complaints like these were heard frequently from disgruntled whites who had lost the war and their most valuable property—enslaved human beings. In the opinion of many planters, the major problem they faced after emancipation was finding a way to reestablish control over the black laboring population. Many whites in northeast Florida worried that, without the controls provided by the state and local slave codes, they would not have an available low-cost, dependable, and dependent labor force.

Had the newspaper correspondents also interviewed the black men and women they observed at the region's train stations, they might instead have written about black travelers attempting to reunite with loved ones after the massive family dislocations produced by slavery and the war. Unburdened by the restraints of slavery, freedmen could travel without permission of a white master and assert independent control of the conditions of their labor. It is reasonable to assume that a portion of the black travelers were lazy or irresponsible, as reported in the press, but others were seeking employment after being evicted by former owners or were departing voluntarily because they were still being treated like enslaved persons.

Some freedmen ridiculed the charge that they were unwilling to work by reminding their white detractors who it was that had done the work, provided the personal care and attention, and produced the income for owners while they were still enslaved. Now emancipated, they intended to do the same for themselves by moving to towns in quest of better jobs or educational opportunities for their children. Others were without food and seeking rations from charitable organizations and the Union army.[9]

The hundreds of white and black refugees crowding into Jacksonville in 1865 did create real and serious public health concerns. In a series of reports during 1865, army surgeon J. W. Applegate documented the problems they were encountering, including severe shortages of food and housing. In January the military provided rations to four hundred persons who, according to Applegate, "had no means of support." He recommended they be moved to a vacant plantation at the mouth of Pottsburg Creek and that jobs be created for black and white refugees alike. In some neighborhoods, houses were so overcrowded and unsanitary that Applegate suggested barracks or dwellings be constructed outside town boundaries, near vacant plantations, where homeless people could find shelter and garden space to plant the vegetables they needed for healthy diets. Excess produce could be sold at markets in Jacksonville to provide income for impoverished families.[10]

Mrs. H. B. Greely, a teacher with the American Missionary Association, commented on the degrading conditions experienced by some refugees. She knew of a white woman living in makeshift and slovenly quarters who kept "a fire in an iron basin, & the only place for the smoke to go out was the door." It was Greely's opinion that "poor whites seem to be as much—or more—degraded & in need than the colored people, for the latter are not afraid to work, the others have always thought work degrading; & even now it seems as if they would starve rather than work. There is a hope that when slavery is really dead, & the spirit of caste is banished, they may arise & be equal to the colored people." Greely had warm praise for a woman more than sixty years old who was "just beginning to spell, seems as if she could not think of anything but her book says she spells her lessons all the evening, then she dreams about it, & wakes up thinking about it. Her husband is a good old saint over 80 years. They were slaves & all their children are slaves; their master left them to take care of the house, & went off with their children when our people came."[11]

In June 1865, Applegate again observed that freed persons were living in "over crowded conditions" in Jacksonville. "Numbers of this class of persons are constantly coming in from the interior and stowing themselves away in

houses already filled to excess." As the recently appointed chief medical officer for the state of Florida, Applegate warned that, without fresh vegetables,
black refugees will "suffer from epidemic diseases, which will spread to the
other inhabitants." He inspected houses built to accommodate six persons
that had become the domiciles of fifteen to twenty, "without any accommodations whatever for cooking, eating, or sleeping."[12]

By July, Applegate was alarmed that troop barracks were being filled by
refugees as soon as soldiers transferred to other posts or mustered out of
the army. "As a sanitary precaution," he warned, the refugees "should all be
immediately sent from the town." In some barracks still occupied by white
soldiers, Applegate found large numbers of black women fictitiously claimed
"as their wives; and in such instances the soldier does not pretend to stay in
his camp or sleep in his quarters. In fact, you may visit these localities at any
time during the day or night, and you will find them full of soldiers, many
of them half intoxicated." He recommended the barracks be torn down and
reconstructed outside town limits.[13]

The commanding officer of the 34th U.S.C.T., Colonel William W. Marple, investigated conditions in northeast Florida in May 1865. His motivation
had been the unambiguous order issued by General Gillmore, commander
of the Department of the South, mandating that "Negroes are at all times,
whether a truce exists or not, and at all places, whether within or beyond
the lines, to be treated like white men."[14] Marple informed his superiors that
"large numbers of freedmen of both sexes, and of all ages, have reported to
these headquarters for counsel, protection, and support." He was confident
that the "freedom of the colored people is almost unanimously acquiesced
in" and that those "masters who are kind and humane to their servants and
disposed to hire them, paying reasonable wages, [will find] the freedmen disposed to remain in their old houses." Marple was, however, aware of former
slaveholders who had not become reconciled to emancipation and refused to
"have a free negro about them, and unless the colored people will consent to
remain in abject servitude, as before, they are driven off—sometimes with
violence—a few cases of strapping, whipping, and shooting are reported.
These statements are corroborated by both whites and blacks."[15]

A correspondent for the New York Tribune found corroborating evidence
that freedmen were still targets of violence and prejudice. "Severe flogging
with the whip and paddle has not entirely disappeared. A few instances of
shooting and other acts of violence have occurred . . . and plantation masters
generally have no ability to promote the social and moral elevation of the
colored people."[16]

Reports like these prompted General Vogdes to conduct an investigation in July. Congress had created the Bureau of Refugees, Freedmen, and Abandoned Lands in March, with a mandate to supervise relations between former slaves and their owners. It was May before Brigadier General Oliver O. Howard was appointed to command of the bureau, and freedmen's affairs remained under the jurisdiction of the army during the first half of 1865. Vogdes's July investigation and report was intended to facilitate the transition from regular army supervision to Freedmen's Bureau controls. Vogdes found that "peace and good order prevail within the limits of my command and that as a general rule contracts have been made on reasonable terms between planters and freedmen." Lacking a circulating currency medium, he urged participants to agree on compensation of one-third or one-half the crop to the freedmen, but advised Howard of an issue of more lasting consequence: "It will take some time to eradicate the previous idea that the labor of the negro belongs to the community, and not to himself, in a word that he is a chattel to be bought, sold or whipped at the will of an irresponsible master."[17]

While the war was being fought, the Union army maintained contrabands on abandoned plantations cultivating cotton and other cash crops, rather than place them on independent and self-sufficient small farms as they requested. After the war, the army issued food rations to destitute blacks and whites and established regulations governing compensated labor for the freedmen, but continued to press freedmen to return to their former workplaces until the Freedmen's Bureau announced its plans. Planters were told to enter into written agreements with workers concerning terms of labor and compensation. After receiving assurance that Union soldiers would supervise the contractual arrangements, many freed persons agreed to the terms of labor.[18]

To implement the policy, Vogdes also told officers at military posts in Florida to apprehend unemployed blacks in towns and return them to plantations, and to use force if it became necessary. This basic arrangement continued after the Freedmen's Bureau assumed control of labor contracts. Colonel Thomas W. Osborne, appointed in September 1865 to direct the bureau's operations in Florida, was convinced that freed slaves would become troublesome vagrants if they remained in the cities, and consequently he continued Vogdes's policy.[19]

On numerous occasions Howard announced that the goal of the bureau was to assist freed persons with a temporary helping hand, but also to convince them that their future depended on returning to work for their former owners for cash wages. That was also the plan of President Andrew Johnson, the man elevated to the presidency after the assassination of Abraham Lincoln. Johnson was a white supremacist who intended to ensure white ownership of land in the postwar South and thereby gain the political support of white conservatives.[20] Most whites in Florida agreed with Johnson that the freedmen's contribution to the economy and future of Florida would be as a permanent and landless class of low-salaried laborers.[21]

On December 1, 1865, the provost marshal abruptly terminated the food relief program in Jacksonville. "The Freedmen or colored persons within this command, are called upon to go to work, and earn an honest living by industry and good conduct, and commanders of posts are to forbid idlers and lazy persons being at their Posts and in the vicinity." Agents were instructed to "induce such persons to work, and if they have nothing to do, find something for them among the citizens requiring labor upon the farms in the surrounding country. The sooner colored persons can understand that they are to work for a living the better it will be." The freedmen and -women of Florida must realize, the provost marshal stated, that "the winter is approaching and the issue of rations by the Government being forbidden, they will find themselves and their families greatly benefited in accepting the employment offered them by their former masters."[22]

The white residents of Mose Dell, a small rural community near Jacksonville, protested to white army officials when a detachment of black troops was sent from Jacksonville to patrol their town. Philip J. Manucy wrote to the "Authorities of Jacksonville, Florida" to complain about the black soldiers patrolling his community. Manucy requested the return of the white soldiers who had been there on "River Picket for several months and who have gained all our confidence by their honerbel conduct. While on the contrary we feel very unprotected with these colored soldiers here. Hoaping that the general commanding will be so generos as to grant the request," Manucy signed the petition for the other residents.[23]

Lieutenant S. L. Kearney of the 3rd U.S.C.T. witnessed hostility directed against the black men under his command during a four-week expedition to administer amnesty oaths and supervise local elections. As he traveled across the state to a small town on the Gulf Coast south of Tampa, Kearney noticed that the whites he met were "unfriendly to Colored Soldiers and equally so, if not worse, against officers of colored troops, although the men had plenty of money and conducted themselves with great propriety." Kearney was vexed it had been "very difficult to buy anything on the road, the people apparently having no desire to sell or give and not even a drink of water if they dare refuse." The planters along the route complained vigorously about the freedmen being "lazy and indolent and often inclined to be insubordinate."[24]

It was not unusual for the black soldiers of the occupation force to become the focal point of white fears and anger. A rumor spread throughout the Southern states that freedmen were plotting a Christmas insurrection aimed at slaughtering whites and seizing their property. Visions of rampaging former slaves armed with guns and bent on vengeance frightened many former slaveholders, although no factual basis for the rumor was found. General Ulysses S. Grant toured the South in the fall of 1865, on one occasion instructing an officer in Louisiana to refuse requests from former black soldiers to buy their rifles when they left the army. Grant also urged Secretary of War Stanton to discharge all black regiments recruited in Northern states that were still at posts in the South. The general had concluded that posting black troops in regions with large black populations provoked violence. "The presence of black troops [who were recently] slaves demoralizes labor, both by their advice and furnishing in their camps a resort for the freedman for long distances around. . . . The freedman's mind does not seem to be [disabused] of the idea that the freedman has the right to live without care or provision for the future." Grant predicted that the presence of black troops would result in large numbers of jobless and lazy freedmen congregating in towns throughout the South, and that this would lead to "vice and disease . . . [and] extermination or great destruction of the colored race. It cannot be expected that the opinions held by men at the South for years can be changed in a day."[25]

On December 1, a violent incident occurred in Lake City that was blamed on a detachment of the Jacksonville-based 34th U.S.C.T. White community leaders accused black soldiers of provoking the violence, saying they "threatened to burn the city and have insulted our citizens without provocation, and our citizens have been beat by colored persons on more than one occasion, and some of the colored troops have publicly declared that they would not obey the commands of their officer." Spokesperson David Jones demanded that Provisional Governor William Marvin and the Union army remove "Colored troops . . . from this post as early as possible, that order may be restored and the civil laws executed."[26]

Captain James Montgomery, the son of Colonel James Montgomery, the first commanding officer of the 2nd South Carolina, 34th U.S.C.T., wrote a detailed report that blamed the violence on white men. On the day the fighting broke out, an election was in progress in Lake City. Anticipating trouble, Montgomery "closed the bar rooms," but he discovered that whiskey was available in sufficient quantity "to make everybody drunk." Some intoxicated white men taunted Montgomery. Later, a fight between white men broke out in a store, but when "the Sergeant of the Guard went in to quiet it, they drew weapons on him and struck him with a four pound weight." The public square of the town was "filled with an excited crowd of men who were fighting on all sides, and many prominent men . . . [doing] nothing at all to quiet the affair." Because Montgomery had forbidden his men to use rifles or sidearms, and the rioters were "armed with pistols and knives and shot guns," the guard was "powerless to do anything. When they would take a man in custody his friends would release him." Montgomery sent an emergency order to a company of black soldiers to immediately "turn out on the square with loaded muskets. This had the desired effect and the mob dispersed."[27]

The citizens of Lake City were "incensed" by the involvement of black troops and petitioned to have Montgomery removed from command. He insisted, however, that had he "not interfered, there would have been much bloodshed. The fight was begun by [Confederate] deserters, and ex-Rebel Soldiers between whom a very bitter feeling exists. They boast that when the troops are removed they are going to 'clean the deserters and niggers out.'"[28]

In Jacksonville as well as Lake City, black soldiers on duty with the occupation force encountered hostility from whites who had returned with prewar notions of racial superiority still intact. Supervised by the provost marshal, the black regiments functioned as a military police force, patrolling streets and enforcing martial law.[29] Bloody street fights, sometimes fought with knives and other weapons, occurred between black soldiers and Confederate veterans. The *Savannah Daily Herald* reported on July 27, 1865, that whites had become a minority in Jacksonville and were deeply resentful: "The negroes and the citizens . . . are on anything but friendly terms, and the colored troops that are now stationed in the city are difficult to control." A correspondent for the local *Florida Times* reported: "the younger white men were inclined to show the blacks 'what was what' and a race war was feared."[30]

Racial conflict was also a troublesome problem among the soldiers in the occupation force. Historian Joseph T. Glatthaar has written of the significant number of white officers of black regiments who held prejudiced racial views, and of the disputes, violent confrontations, protests, and even mutiny that resulted. Punishments ordered by such officers tended to be extreme and cruel, and reminded the black soldiers of the way slaves were treated by their white owners. Glatthaar discovered evidence of frequent protests that "escalated into small-and large-scale mutinies, with executions or long-term jail sentences as a result." Black soldiers represented "fewer than one of every thirteen Union soldiers" yet accounted for "nearly 80 percent of all soldiers executed for mutiny."[31] During postwar occupation duty, white officers of black regiments often interacted with whites of the town and sometimes found their own racial attitudes influenced by the views of the locals.

The 34th U.S.C.T. was based in Jacksonville for nearly six months in 1863 and 1864, and again from January 1865 to February 1866. The 3rd U.S.C.T. was stationed in the town from February 5 until October 31, 1865. A white officer in the 3rd U.S.C.T., Lieutenant C. W. Brown, kept a diary during the months he resided in Jacksonville, recording incidents of insubordination, fistfights, and violent confrontations. While in Jacksonville, Brown was involved in an incident that Glatthaar calls "the most shocking mutiny" of the entire war. The 3rd U.S.C.T. was ordered to muster out of Union service in Jacksonville and depart for Philadelphia by October 31, 1865. On October 29, after several days of confinement in their tents while a late-season hurricane lashed northeast Florida, the black soldiers emerged to discover one of their comrades tied by his thumbs to a scaffold on the parade ground for stealing a jar of molasses from the field kitchen. Angered by the sight, soldiers shouted for the man to be cut down. These were men who had risked their lives in combat since the regiment mustered in at Camp William Penn near Philadelphia in August 1863, yet they had been subjected to numerous types of cruel discipline in the "old-army way" during more than two years of military duty. In thumb-tying, the offender was generally stripped to the waist and tied by his thumbs to overhead scaffolding so that his toes barely touched the ground, causing immense pain to his thumb sockets and his arms and to the calves of his legs. Brown's diary documents several such punishments of soldiers in the 3rd U.S.C.T.[32]

Witnessing this punishment yet again, only two days before mustering out, sparked a furious protest. Thirty men started toward the platform shouting and gesticulating, some carrying weapons. The white officers stood their ground until the protesters were ten to fifteen feet away, when Lieutenant Colonel John L. Brower fired three shots into the crowd. Some enlisted men shot back, and wounds were inflicted on both sides. Fifteen soldiers were arrested and confined at the Bay Street stockade. Legal officer Alva A. Knight, a graduate of Amherst College, captain of Company B, 34th U.S.C.T., and a future lawyer, judge, and state senator in postwar Florida, filed charges of mutiny in a war zone against the men, which carried the possible sentence of death by firing squad.[33]

Only two days later, the court-martial trials commenced aboard a ship anchored in the St. Marys off the town of Fernandina. Thirteen convictions were returned, including six death sentences. The condemned mutineers were executed on December 1, 1865. What had begun as a petty theft of a jar of molasses ended only thirty-four days later in death by firing squad.[34]

The *New York Times* printed a vague and inaccurate report of the mutiny. "The colored soldiers have been acting very badly . . . of late and it seems to be the opinion of officers and citizens that the sooner the colored soldiers can be mustered out of the service and their places filled by white troops the better it will be for all concerned. . . . There have been several mutinies . . . of late in the Third and Thirty-fourth Colored Regiments."[35] In fact, there had been only one mutiny among the men of the 3rd, on October 29, 1865, in Jacksonville. None had occurred among the men of the 34th. The correspondent was reporting rumors that encapsulated the anti-black sentiment prevalent among whites at the time.

As part of the Federal occupation force in Jacksonville, the black soldiers were acutely aware of the continuing incidents of racial conflict, yet many decided to settle in the town after mustering out of the army. Hundreds of men from the 33rd, 34th, and 21st had been held in bondage in northeast Florida before escaping and joining Union regiments. Black veterans from other states who had served in the area also settled in the town, married local women, and secured jobs after discharge. White residents of the town, as well as Union commanders, were fearful that the presence of so many discharged black soldiers would provoke former Confederates to acts of violence.[36]

Many black veterans returned with rudimentary learning acquired during their time in the army. Some joined a communal farming venture at Hanson Town, named after Daniel Dustin Hanson, a surgeon with the 34th U.S.C.T. who purchased land north of the town boundary (today, the Florida Community College site on State Street) and sold parcels to soldiers from his regiment and to other blacks. He also encouraged the freedmen to join together to market their crops, to make bulk purchases of seed, fertilizer, and tools, and to pool their earnings to purchase additional land. Such assistance was sometimes necessary in the face of merchant boycotts of crops marketed by freedmen. Orloff Dorman, by no means an admirer, commented that Hanson had developed "quite a settlement" for his former army comrades.[37]

Hanson also planned a large communal settlement for freedmen on several thousand acres of land at Pottsburg Creek purchased from John and

Mary Kingsley Sammis, but a malarial condition acquired during army service led to Hanson's death in 1868. Hanson's investment partner, Colonel Marple, also of the 34th U.S.C.T. and the commander of Union forces at Jacksonville after the war, withdrew from the project and the land was returned to the former owners.[38]

Some communal ventures fared better. In August 1865 a *Jacksonville Herald* correspondent discovered a settlement of black refugees on an abandoned plantation in Duval County where "sweet potatoes and a few other vegetables were thriving. The women were engaged in gathering and preparing [Spanish] moss for the market—the men were making shingles and earning one dollar per day. An air of industry, thrift, and resolution to live, seemed to pervade the place," and the moss was priced at "four cents per pound in the Jacksonville market." In addition to communal ventures, individual veterans fared well in Jacksonville. Pension records of the black veterans document that after discharge they were employed as teamsters at town wharves, laborers at sawmills, waiters at hotels, carpenters, and a wide variety of other occupations.[39]

At the conclusion of their workdays, many blacks attended community meetings to discuss social welfare, education, and political issues. The *Jacksonville Herald* reported that "the colored citizens of Jacksonville hold monthly meetings at the Presbyterian Church for the purpose of considering the wants of their poor and making provisions for them." Black residents were preparing to participate as citizens in American society and holding meetings to discuss their "educational interests, their rights and duties as citizens, and the condition they will find themselves in when the military is removed. . . . The attendance of the last meeting was large, including some white soldiers and citizens."[40]

White residents of the town were also meeting and holding demonstrations to discuss the future. There was general consensus within the former ruling class that whites must continue to dominate relations between the races in the postwar years, and they sought to devise policies permitting them to reassert the racial controls implicit in the slave codes of the prewar years. William Marvin, appointed provisional governor in July 1865 by President Johnson, was in sympathy with their feelings. Marvin had been a Whig politician at Key West before the war, a Unionist after secession, and a racial conservative who believed in white supremacy. Jacksonville Unionists like Judge Philip Fraser and Otis L. Keene, along with men who served the Confederacy like Columbus Drew and Theodore Hartridge, were mutually comfortable with Marvin's racial and political views. These men backed

Marvin as he stumped Florida in the summer of 1865 seeking support for the president's reconstruction program.[41]

To end martial law in Florida, Marvin urged all of the state's white males to take an oath of allegiance and to register as voters. They could then elect delegates to a statewide convention to write a new state constitution and bring Florida back into the Union. The delegates would be required to repudiate secession and Confederate debts and accept the finality of emancipation. The only impediments to an early end to military occupation and martial law then remaining would be voter ratification of the new state constitution, election of state and national officials, and legislative ratification of the Thirteenth Amendment to the U.S. Constitution, the amendment that outlawed slavery.[42]

For the Florida freedmen, the crucial issue was whether or not they would be eligible to vote. Marvin's speeches stressed that suffrage eligibility was to be determined by each state. As the provisional governor of Florida, Marvin stated repeatedly that he wanted the vote limited to white males only. At every stop on a statewide speaking tour, he informed his white listeners that they need not, and should not, enfranchise freedmen. He reminded black Floridians that they were free but not equal to whites, and not entitled to voting rights.[43]

On October 10, 1865, adult white male voters who had pledged an oath of loyalty chose delegates to a statewide constitutional convention. With Federal occupation officers supervising the balloting, many whites formerly associated with secession and the Confederacy were elected as delegates. On October 25 the convention met at Tallahassee and voted to nullify the Ordinance of Secession. By a margin of only twenty-one to fourteen, the delegates approved the measure "that neither slavery nor involuntary servitude" would again exist in the state, and reluctantly repudiated Confederate war debts. The new constitution denied black residents of Florida the right to vote, hold public office, or serve on juries. Blacks would be allowed to testify against other blacks in the state's courts but were barred from testifying against whites. Vagrancy laws applying only to blacks were adopted as racial control measures. Whites in Florida applauded the delegates' work, but members of the U.S. Congress reacted angrily, charging that Florida was attempting to hold the freedmen in "semi-peonage," and denouncing the new constitution as "an instrument that begins by the denial of equality to nearly half of . . . [Florida's] citizens."[44]

The general election in November produced a legislature composed primarily of Confederates and former slaveholders. The new legislature dealt at length with race relations in order to make state laws compatible with the new constitution. The Thirteenth Amendment was ratified, but a severe "black code" was implemented that clarified the lawmakers' intention to discriminate against the freedmen and preserve white supremacy in law. Denied the franchise, segregated in schools and railway cars, subjected to a head tax, threatened by the whip, pillory, or prison if they violated stringent vagrancy laws, and denied the right to bear arms, Florida's freedmen faced a future without the benefits of freedom they had expected the Union victory to produce. By early 1866 the tempo of race relations had been established: white supremacy was enshrined in laws that resembled the prewar slave codes.[45]

An aroused U.S. Congress refused to admit the Florida delegation, invalidated the state constitution, and imposed a congressional and military reconstruction program that would last until 1876. Florida was again placed under martial law, new delegates to a constitutional convention were chosen, a new constitution was written, and a new government was formed. Adult black males gained the right to vote and to participate as citizens in a democratic state, at least temporarily. By the end of the century, however, the promise of citizenship for which many black men from northeast Florida had fought and died would be replaced by racial segregation, a legal substitute for the racial controls inherent in the prewar slave codes and an effective buttress for white supremacy that would persist for another century.

Acknowledgments

I am deeply grateful to many individuals and institutions for generous assistance with this manuscript, especially Joan E. Moore, my wife, for the constant love and support that makes my work possible.

A special thank-you is also extended to the University of North Florida Board of Trustees for grants that enabled history majors to travel to archives and train as historians while doing primary source research on Jacksonville during the Civil War. Generous contributions from the late Lewis Ansbacher and his wife, Sybil Ansbacher, assisted students with travel expenses that facilitated production of a related Web page on Florida History Online, a documentary history archive posted on the UNF server (www.unf .edu/floridahistoryonline).

The students who assisted with the research are Candace Clancy, Ruth Cook, Lawrence Dixon, Norman Feil, Wendy Flach, Dennis Galloway, Kathleen Kole, Lillian (Rosie) Kostandarithes, Daryll Kozee, Jeffery Krone, James Krumrine, John Kurth, John MacKenzie, Barbara Parrish, Stephanie Schropp, Shawn Shannon, William Stanton, Sandra Stratton, Christopher Thompson, Jason Venn, Jeanene Watters, John Weeks, and Corey Wesner. I am grateful for your contributions.

Students whose research helped shape a chapter are due special acknowledgment. They include Mary Bartholomew for research on the Forrester family of Clay County; Holly Bebernitz for insightful research on Octavia and Winston Stephens; Amanda Chanco for research on the black Union regiments and the third occupation of Jacksonville; Carol S. Clark for labor in the National Archives on logbooks of Union gunboats on the St. Johns and the letter books of their commanders; Bonita Deaton for a carefully researched essay on the Unionists of Magnolia, Florida; John F. (Buck) Fannin for a manuscript on the 1865 mutiny by soldiers of the 3rd regiment of the U.S. Colored Troops; Kevin Hooper for extensive work in the National Archives on Confederate and Union military records and on Clay County history; Elizabeth Lowman for work on the William L. Apthorp Papers;

Christina Luers for work at the U.S. Army Military History Institute and on the Dr. Seth Rogers manuscript; and James Vearil for finding countless primary documents and helping to expand coverage of events upriver far beyond the Duval County boundary. Kevin Hooper's contributions continued for many months and were invaluable.

I am also indebted to Dr. Wayne Wood for copies of photographs from his valuable collection of Jacksonville images; James R. Ward for contributions of maps and photographs; Gerard D. Casale for research in the National Archives; Dickie Ferrie for photographs, original letters, and books from his personal collection; Dr. Keith Holland for sharing his knowledge of the torpedo bombing of the *Maple Leaf*; Carmen Derrick for finding the 1859 Map of Jacksonville donated by G. D. Ackerly to the Jacksonville Main Library; and Professor Aaron Sheehan-Dean for insightful comments on the first draft. To the anonymous reviewer of drafts one and two of *Thunder on the River*, I appreciate your wise advice.

I benefited from the professional help of Charles Tingley of the St. Augustine Historical Society Research Library, James Cusick of the P. K. Yonge Library of Florida History, and Deborah Wynne of the Florida Historical Society Library and Archive. Dozens of archivists at the National Archives and Records Administration, the Library of Congress, U.S. Army Military History Institute, South Caroliniana Library, Florida State Archives, and other institutions assisted with the research. I am sorry I did not record their names.

Notes

CHAPTER 1. *"Raise the Banner of Secession":*
Sectional Debates in Jacksonville, 1845–1861

1. This chapter benefited from a scrapbook of news clippings compiled by Richard A. Martin and from an unpublished history of Jacksonville's newspapers that he wrote in the 1970s.

2. For Turner's rebellion see Oates, *Fires of Jubilee.*

3. *Jacksonville Courier*, August 20, 27, September 7, 1835.

4. For background on this sectional controversy and the compromise, Fehrenbacher's *Three Sectional Crises* and Moore's *The Missouri Controversy* were of great assistance. See also Remini, *Henry Clay*, 169–92.

5. Foner, "The Wilmot Proviso Revisited," 262–79; Quarles, *The Negro in the North*; Rawley, *Race and Politics.*

6. Holt, *Rise and Fall*, chs. 9–11.

7. *Florida News*, February 20, 1846, June 24, 1848; *New York Tribune*, May 15, 1848.

8. Drew quoted in *Florida News*, August 12, 1848.

9. Doherty, "Florida and the Crisis of 1850," 35, and "Union Nationalism in Florida," 84–85.

10. *Florida News*, August 12, 1848.

11. Ibid., August 12, November 11, 1848. The tally was Taylor 153 and Cass 93; elsewhere in Duval County: Cass 158 and Taylor 60.

12. *Florida Republican*, March 7, April 25, 1850; Jennings, *Nashville Convention.*

13. Remini, *Henry Clay*, 730–61.

14. *Florida News*, August 7, 1850.

15. Ibid.

16. Ibid.; for Budington, see Hooper, *Early History of Clay County*, 119.

17. *Florida News*, October 16, 1850.

18. Doherty, *Whigs of Florida*, 44–45, 51–52.

19. *Florida Republican*, February 7, 20, 1850.

20. Ibid., April 4, June 27, July 11, 1850.

21. Ibid., October 9, February 13, April 24, 1851, and January 10, July 3, October 9, 1852; *Florida News*, December 4, 1852.

22. *Florida News*, September 6, November 15, December 13, 1855, and January 24, 31, May 3, December 18, 1856. See also *Florida Republican*, August 6, November 15, 29, December 6, 13, 1855; *Jacksonville Semi-Weekly Republican*, May 12, 26, 29, August 6, December 10, 24, 1856.

23. *Florida News*, October 13, 1855.

24. *Florida Republican*, January 31, 1856.

25. F. F. L'Engle to Edward L'Engle, September 27, 1856, and Charlotte Porcher L'Engle to Edward L'Engle, January 29, 1857, Edward M. L'Engle Papers, SHC.

26. *Florida News*, January 23, 1846; *Florida Republican*, December 14, 1848, July 4, October 3, November 14, 1850, February 6, 1851, and December 3, 1856; *Florida News*, February 10, 1858; *Jacksonville Standard*, February 24, March 10, 1859.

27. *Florida Republican*, October 3, 1850.

28. *Florida News*, October 13, 1855; *Jacksonville Standard*, February 24, March 10, 1859.

29. *Florida Republican*, January 28, 1857.

30. Ibid.; *Jacksonville Standard*, March 10, 1859.

31. John Haddock probate file, Duval County Courthouse.

32. *Florida News*, January 23, 1846; *Florida Republican*, November 5, 1856.

33. *Florida Republican*, December 14, 1848.

34. Ibid., July 4, 1850.

35. Ibid.

36. Ibid.

37. Ibid., November 14, 1850.

38. *Florida News*, May 15, 1852.

39. Ibid., May 22, 1852.

40. Ibid.

41. Ibid.; Samuel Buffington, J. A. Barbee, Henry T. Titus, S. D. Fernandez, and Joseph Finegan comprised the Vigilance Committee.

42. Schafer, "'A Class of People'"; Landers, *Black Society in Spanish Florida*, is the best guide to slavery in Spanish Florida.

43. *Florida News*, June 5, 1852.

44. Mahon, *History of the Second Seminole War*, ch. 8. See also *Florida News*, August 14, 1852; *Florida Sentinel*, June 8, 1852; and Doherty, *Whigs of Florida*, 55.

45. *Florida News*, August 14, 1852; Doherty, *Whigs of Florida*, 55.

46. Holt, *Rise and Fall*, chs. 9–11.

47. Nichols, "The Kansas-Nebraska Act"; Doherty, *Whigs of Florida*, 58–60.

48. Eighth Census, 1860, Clay and Duval counties.

49. *Florida News*, September 30, 1854.

50. Ibid., October 7, 1854.

51. Ibid., October 7, 14, November 18, 1854.

52. Thompson, "Political Nativism in Florida," 49–53.

53. *Florida News*, May 19, 1855; *Florida Republican*, September 6, 1855. Phillip Fraser, Calvin Oak, George A. Turknett, Halsted H. Hoeg, S. W. Williams, and Dr. Abel S. Baldwin won town council seats.

54. *Florida Republican*, September 25, 1855.

55. Ibid., September 27 and October 5, 1855.

56. *Florida News*, October 6, 1855; *Florida Republican*, April 16, 1855. Francis I. Wheaton, Samuel Buffington, Halstead H. Hoeg, Walter Kipp, Calvin Oak, George A. Ward, and Samuel Williams were elected to the council. Wheaton was chosen intendant (mayor). Democrats were Rodney Dorman, A. M. Reed, Cyrus Bisbee, Felix Livingston, George C. Acosta, Henry E. Holmes, and David McCuen.

57. For comprehensive discussion of the political issues, see Foner, *Free Soil*.

58. *Florida Republican*, September 17 and 24, 1856.

59. Ibid., July 9 and 16, 1856.

60. Ibid., November 5, 12, December 3, 1856.

61. *Florida News*, November 15, 1856.

62. Ibid., January 14 and April 11, 1857. Democrats elected: A. A. Canova, R. W. Biggs, Henry Holmes, George Acosta, and Charles Somers; defeated: William P. De-Wees. Hart defeated William K. Cole. George Couper Gibbs and Halstead H. Hoeg

were the American Party winners. See also Thompson, "Political Nativism in Florida," 59–61.

63. Fehrenbacher's *Dred Scott Case* is an excellent source of background information.

64. W. W. Davis, *Civil War and Reconstruction*, 7; Oates, *To Purge This Land*.

65. *Jacksonville Standard*, April 5, 1860; W. W. Davis, *Civil War and Reconstruction*, 39.

66. For the convention see *East Floridian*, May 23, 1860.

67. Thompson, "Political Nativism in Florida," 61.

68. Ibid., 62.

69. *Jacksonville Standard*, April 5, 1860. Democrats elected: A. B. Canova, Florida, Cyrus Bisbee, Massachusetts. Constitutional Union elected: Columbus Drew, Virginia; Samuel N. Williams, Georgia; H. N. Gookin, Ireland; Halsted H. Hoeg and John Clark, New Hampshire; J. P. Bouse, New Jersey.

70. Ibid., May 31, 1860.

71. Ibid.

72. Ibid.

73. Ibid.

74. Ibid.

75. Merritt, *Century of Medicine*, 50; *Jacksonville Standard*, November 1, 1860; McPherson, *Battle Cry of Freedom*, ch. 7.

76. Proctor, "The Call to Arms," taken from Revels, "Grander in Her Daughters." Daughters were Florida, Helen, Maria, and Margaret Broward.

77. Donald, Baker, and Holt, *Civil War and Reconstruction*, ch. 5.

78. *Jacksonville Standard*, December 6, 1860.

79. Ibid.

80. Proctor, *Florida*, December 1860. Throughout this book, in all matters related to Abraham Lincoln, I have relied on Donald, *Lincoln*, and Potter, *Lincoln and His Party*.

81. Proctor, *Florida*, December 1860.

82. *Jacksonville Standard*, December 6, 1860.

83. Ibid.; Calvin L. Robinson, "An Account of Some of My Experiences in Florida during the Rise and Progress of the Rebellion," 35, JHS [hereafter cited as Robinson, "An Account"].

84. Washington M. Ives, Journal, 1860–1862, FSA.

85. Ibid.; Reiger, "Secession of Florida," 360.

86. W. W. Davis, *Civil War and Reconstruction*, 43; *East Floridian*, December 19, 1860; Eppes, *Through Some Eventful Years*, 135–36; Robinson, "An Account," 3.

87. W. W. Davis, *Civil War and Reconstruction*, 53; *Southern Confederacy*, April 12, 1861.

88. *Jacksonville Standard*, December 6, 1860.

89. Ibid. The resolution was adopted on November 29, 1860.

90. Martin, *The City Makers*, 1–15; *Florida News*, February 2, May 5, July 7, 1849; *Jacksonville Standard*, April 5, 1860.

91. Bessie S. Anderson, "Retrospective Experiences," May 3, 1901, JHS.

92. Robinson, "An Account," 3; Gold, *History of Duval County*, 127.

93. Schafer, "U.S. Territory and State," 228, quoting Brown, *Ossian Bingley Hart*. See also *Southern Confederacy*, February 1, 1861; Wooster, "The Florida Secession Convention," 383; and *Journal of the Proceedings of the Convention of the People of Florida, Begun and Held at the Capitol, in the City of Tallahassee* (Tallahassee, 1861), 3, 48–49.

94. Donald, Baker, and Holt, *Civil War and Reconstruction*, 134–36. Republicans voted 40 percent in favor.

95. South of Missouri, and all future territories.

96. Morrison, *Slavery and the American West*.

97. Holt, *The Fate of Their Country*, 3–4.

98. *Florida News*, August 7, 1850.

CHAPTER 2. *Jacksonville Prepares for War*

1. Otis Little Keene, "Jacksonville as It Was Fifty-three Years Ago," *Florida Times-Union*, September 26, 1908; Otis Little Keene, Diaries, 1863–1910, PKY; Otis Little Keene, Judson House Register, 1855–1862, FHSL; T. F. Davis, *History of Jacksonville*, 99–100, 114–15; *Jacksonville Metropolitan*, December 12, 1908, September 26, 1910; *Florida Times-Union*, September 29–30, 1910. Abbie Hurd Dunham Keene was from Vinland, New Jersey.

2. Keene, "Jacksonville as It Was Fifty-three Years Ago."

3. Martin, "Defeat in Victory," 6–8; Keene is the central character in Martin's article, which draws heavily on the Keene diaries.

4. Merritt, *Century of Medicine*, 56; Kirk, "History of the Southern Presbyterian Church," 162, 256.

5. *Florida Republican*, October 24, 1850; *Jacksonville Standard*, December 6, 1860; Doherty, "Union Nationalism in Florida," 91; Keene, Diaries, entries for 1863–65 in vol. 1, 1863–74. See also Martin, "Defeat in Victory," 33.

6. Anderson, "Retrospective Experiences."

7. *Southern Confederacy*, February 1, 1861.

8. Martin, *The City Makers*, 26–36.

9. Gold, *History of Duval County*, 264–65; Rerick, *Memoirs of Florida*, 1:428–29; Webb, *Webb's Historical*, 154.

10. Robinson, "An Account," 2, 17, 130; Rohrabacher, *Live Towns and Progressive Men*, 80–81; Esgate, *Jacksonville*, 137; *Jacksonville Standard*, February 24, 1859, April 5, 1860; *St. Johns Mirror*, May 7, 1861.

11. *Jacksonville Standard*, April 5, June 7, 1860; Robinson, "An Account," 2.

12. Robinson, "An Account," 2.

13. Garvin, "Free Negro in Florida," 9–17; Bates, "Legal Status of the Negro",159-81; Jackson, "The Negro and the Law"; Berlin, *Slaves without Masters*.

14. Eighth Census, 1860, Population Schedules.

15. Willie Bryant to Davis Bryant, October 30, November 2, 1861, S-BFP.

16. Willie Bryant to Davis Bryant, November 2, 1861, ibid.

17. *Florida Times-Union*, September 26, 1908; *New York Tribune*, March 24, 1862.

18. *St. Johns Mirror*, May 7, 1861. Forts Pickens, Taylor, and Jefferson remained in Union hands throughout the war.

19. Ibid.

20. Eighth Census, 1860, Population Schedules; *Florida Republican*, November 1, 1855; *Jacksonville Standard*, April 5, 1860.

21. Ives, Journal, May 11, 25, 27, and June 22, 1861.

22. *Southern Confederacy*, April 12, 1861.

23. Ibid.

24. *St. Augustine Examiner*, April 20, 1861.

25. *St. Johns Mirror*, May 7, 1861.

26. Ibid.

27. Robinson, "An Account," 8–9.

28. Ibid.

29. Deaton, "Magnolia, Florida," drawing from the claims of Bird Knowles, L. Jackson Knowles, and Martha L. Hendricks, nos. 11090, 8675, and 11089, respectively, in the Records of the Southern Claims Commission, RG 217, entry 732, NARA-CP.

30. Proctor, *Florida*, April 26, 1861.

31. Ives, Journal, April 26, 1861.

32. *Southern Confederacy*, February 1, 1861; Keene, Judson House Register, February 1861.

33. *Southern Confederacy*, February 1, 1861; *St. Johns Mirror*, May 7, 1861; Ives, Journal, April 26, 1861.

34. *St. Johns Mirror*, May 7, 1861.

35. Ibid.

36. Robinson, "An Account," 13–16.

37. Ibid., 16–19.

38. Keene, Judson House Register, March–June 1861.

39. Martin, "Defeat in Victory," 7–8; *Florida Times-Union*, September 26, 1908.

40. Martin, *The City Makers*, 32–33.

41. Ives, Journal, April 20, 24, 1861.

42. Ibid., May 18, 1861.

43. Ibid., May 28, July 1, 1861.

44. Ibid., May 25, 27, 31, June 12, 22, 1861.

45. Nulty, *Confederate Florida*, ch. 1.

46. Keene, Judson House Register, July 1861; Robertson, *Soldiers of Florida*, 77–99.

47. Martin, *The City Makers*, 33–44.

48. Ibid.; Rerick, *Memoirs of Florida*, 1:252–53.

49. Robertson, *Soldiers of Florida*, 41, 43, 77, 99, 118; *Florida Union*, October 14, 1865; Gold, *History of Duval County*, 374.

50. Octavia Stephens to Winston Stephens, August 7, September 7, 1861, and Mrs. J. W. Bryant, "Diary," April 29, 1862, S-BFP. Much of the correspondence in the Bryant-Stephens Collection has been published in Blakey, Lainhart, and Stephens, *Rose Cottage Chronicles*.

51. Winston Stephens to Octavia Stephens, September 10, 1863, S-BFP.

52. Winston Stephens to Octavia Stephens, n.d., ibid. Stephens's unit was mustered in as Company B, 2nd Florida Cavalry, November 1862.

53. Robinson, "An Account," 2–7.

54. Ibid., 8–13.

55. Ibid., 17.

56. Martin, "Defeat in Victory," 10–11; *Tri-Weekly Sun*, January 27, 1876.

57. Mueller, "East Coast Florida Steamboating."

58. Keene, Judson House Register, September 29, October 9, 1861; Gold, *History of Duval County*, 331. For the Union blockade of the Southern coastline see Browning, *Success Is All That Was Expected*, and for efforts to escape the blockade see Wise, *Lifeline of the Confederacy*. Buker, *Blockaders, Refugees, and Contrabands*, focuses on the Florida coastline.

59. Mueller, "The Way It Really Was," 16–17; Keene, Judson House Register, August 20–22, 1861.

60. Bavier, *The Schooner Yacht America*, 4.

61. Keene, Judson House Register, November 2, 1861; Boswell, *The America*.

62. Keene, Judson House Register, January 5, February 4, 1862; *New York Times*, January 29, 1862; Proctor, *Florida*, February 26, 1862.

63. See "Report of the Secretary of the Navy, C.S.A.," February 27, 1862, *ORN*, 18:830–31; Johns, *Florida during the Civil War*, 26–39; Keene, Judson House Register, December 3, 12, 31, January 6, February 4, March 6, 1862.

64. Robinson, "An Account," 16–17; Esgate, *Jacksonville*, 17–18.

65. Budd to Stevens, March 13, 1862, *ORN*, 12:699; *New York Tribune*, March 24, 1862; *New York Times*, March 24, 1862.

66. Rerick, *Memoirs of Florida*, 1:236.

67. *Journal of the Proceedings of the Convention of the People of the State of Florida, Called Session* (Tallahassee, 1861), 3, 6, 13–22. For an excellent discussion of this convention, see Johns, *Florida during the Civil War*, 15–22.

68. Lee to Trapier, March 1, 1862, *ORA*, 6:403–4. Lee had previously decided to withdraw troops from Amelia Island and other coastal islands in Florida vulnerable to attack by the Union navy. See Lee to Trapier, February 24, 1862, and Lee to Milton, February 24, 1862, ibid., 398–400. See also Trapier to Washington, March 28, 1862, ibid., 93–94, regarding the withdrawal of Confederate troops.

69. Winston Stephens to Octavia Stephens, December 1, 22, 1861, February 20, 28, March 6, 1862, S-BFP.

70. Du Pont to Gillis, February 27, 1862, *ORN*, 12:570–71, regarding plans for departure the following morning. See also Du Pont, "Memorandum of Instructions Regarding Plan of Operations," March 1, 1862, ibid., 772. See also *New York Times*, March 15, 1862.

71. *New York Times*, January 14, 1862; Wright to Du Pont, March 3, 1862, *ORN*, 12:581–82.

72. *New York Times*, March 11, 1862.

73. Ibid., March 11, 15, 1862.

74. Ibid., March 11, 1862.

75. Milton to Yulee, June 8, 1863, John Milton Letterbook, FSA.

76. Wright to Thomas W. Sherman, March 7, 1862, *ORA*, 6:239, 248–50.

CHAPTER 3. *A Pathway into the Heart of East Florida*

1. Robinson, "An Account," 19.

2. Ives, Journal, March 5–6, 10, 1862.

3. Robinson, "An Account," 20.

4. Boatner, *Civil War Dictionary*, 846; Proctor, *Florida*, October 22, November 1, 17, 22, 1861, January 30, February 19, 1862; Keene, Judson House Register, March 5–7, 1862.

5. Johns, *Florida during the Civil War*, 65; T. F. Davis, *History of Jacksonville*, 116–17; Martin, "The *New York Times* Views Civil War Jacksonville," 420–21.

6. *New York Times*, March 20, 1862; *New York Tribune*, March 24, 1862; ORN, 12:600–601.

7. Wright to Sherman, March 7, 1862, *ORA*, 6:239; Du Pont to Stevens, March 7, 1862, *ORN*, 12:586–87.

8. Wright to Sherman, March 7, 1862, and Wright to Whipple, March 7, 1862, *ORA*, 6:239–40; Sherman to McClellan, March 15, 1862, ibid., 247–48.

9. Wright to Sherman, March 8, 1862, and Sherman to Adjutant-General, March 9, 1862, ibid., 241–42, 242–43.

10. Wright to Sherman, March 7, 1862, ibid., 239; Du Pont to Stevens, March 7, 1862, *ORN*, 12:586–87.

11. Du Pont to Stevens, March 7, 1862, *ORN*, 12:586–87.

12. Ibid.

13. Robinson, "An Account," 19–20.

14. Martin, *The City Makers*, 38.

15. Ibid.

16. "The Story of Old Jacksonville," *Florida Times-Union and Citizen*, November 20, 1898.

17. Gold, *History of Duval County*, 131; Proctor, *Napoleon Bonaparte Broward*, 15–16.

18. Keene, Diaries, March 9, 1909.

19. Robinson, "An Account," 27–28; *New York Times*, April 2, 1862.

20. Keene, Diaries, March 10, 1862; Robinson, "An Account," 19; Trapier to Washington, March 20, 1862, *ORA*, 6:414–15.

21. *New York Tribune*, March 24, 1862; *New York Times*, March 20, 1862.

22. *New York Times*, March 20, 21, 1862.

23. Ibid., March 20, 1862.

24. *New York Tribune*, March 24, 1862.

25. Ibid.

26. Stevens to Du Pont, March 13, 1862, *ORN*, 12:599–600.

27. Ibid.

28. Stevens to Du Pont, March 11, 1862, ibid., 595.

29. Du Pont to Welles, March 13, 1862, ibid., 598–99.

30. *New York Tribune*, March 24, 1862.

31. T. F. Davis, *History of Jacksonville*, 117.

32. Robinson, "An Account," 21–22.

33. Keene, Judson House Register, March 7–11, 1862; *New York Times*, March 21, 1862.

34. *New York Tribune*, March 24, 1862; *New York Times*, March 21, 1862.

35. *New York Tribune*, March 24, 1862; *New York Times*, March 21, 1862; Robinson, "An Account," 22–23.

36. Robinson, "An Account," 22–23.

37. Ibid., 34–36.

38. Ibid., 29–30.

39. Cooley, "A Florida Story of War Times," 397. Florence Cooley was Maria's daughter. See also Gold, *History of Duval County*, 343.

40. Robinson, "An Account," 24–25, 32, 37.

41. Keene, Diaries, March 11, 1866.

42. Keene, Judson House Register, March 11, 1862.

43. Gold, *History of Duval County*, 131.

44. *New York Times*, April 6, 1862.

45. *New York Tribune*, March 24, 1862.

46. Stevens to Du Pont, March 13, 1862, ORN, 12:599–600.

47. Wright to Pelouze, March 15, 1862, ORA, 6:100.

48. Nulty, *Confederate Florida*, 37.

49. Ibid., 39.

CHAPTER 4. *The First Occupation of Jacksonville*

1. Stevens to Du Pont, March 13, 1862, ORN, 12:599–600.

2. Ibid.

3. Keene, Diaries, March 12, 1862; Robinson, "An Account," 26–28.

4. *New York Tribune*, March 24, 1862; T. F. Davis, *History of Jacksonville*, 118; Eighth Census, 1860, Population Schedules, Duval County; Stevens to Drayton, April 13, 1862, ORN, 12:739; Gold, *History of Duval County*, 115–19.

5. *New York Tribune*, March 24, 1862.

6. Stevens to Du Pont, March 13, 1862, ORN, 12:599–600.

7. *New York Tribune*, March 24, 1862.

8. Stevens to Du Pont, April 23, 1862, ORN, 12:640.

9. Boswell, *The America*, 162–71, 174–77; Mrs. Henry Clark interview, February 26, 1940, WPA; Eighth Census, 1860.

10. Stevens to Du Pont, March 17, 1862, ORN, 12:631–32.

11. Ibid.; see also Stevens to Du Pont, March 28, 1862, ibid., 638–39.

12. Stevens to Du Pont, April 23, 1862, ibid., 640.

13. Ibid.; see also pp. 638–39.

14. Mellen C. Greeley, "Musings of Mellen Clark Greeley, Written in His Anec-Dotage, 1880–1963," 14, JHS; Stevens to Du Pont, March 28, 1862, ORN, 638–39.

15. Ibid.

16. For insightful analysis of changing Union policy toward civilians in Union-occupied areas of the Confederate states, see Grimsley, *The Hard Hand of War*, and Ash, *When the Yankees Came*.

17. Stevens to Du Pont, April 1, 1862, ORN, 12:697–98.

18. Phena Hudnall Love interview, March 20, 24, 1936, WPA; *New York Times*, April 2, 1862.

19. Wright to Greenleaf, April 13, 1862, Provost Marshal's Office (Jacksonville), Records of Provost Marshal Field Organizations (Civil War), District of Florida, RG 393, NARA.

20. Wright to Davis, C.S.A., April 2, 1862, ORA, 4:127.

21. Winston Stephens to Octavia Stephens, March 10, 13, 17, 1862, S-BFP.

22. *New York Tribune*, March 24, 1862; *New York Times*, April 2, 1862; Robinson, "An Account," 33, 38, 42.

23. *New York Times*, March 20 and 26, 1862.

24. Sherman to Adjutant General, March 16, 25, 1862, ORA, 6:248–50.

25. *New York Times*, March 31, 1862.

26. Ibid.; Robinson, "An Account," 39.

27. Philip Fraser, chairman, enclosed with Sherman, "To the People of East Florida," March 20, 1862, ORA, 6:251–52. Sherman's message is also in ORN, 12:639–40;

28. Ibid.

29. Robinson, "An Account," 40.

30. *New York Times*, April 2, 1862.

31. Stevens to Du Pont, April 3, 1862, ORN, 12:698; Stevens, March 17, 1862, Letters sent by Commander Thomas H. Stevens, Letter Books of U.S. Naval Officers, RG 45, NARA.

32. Robinson, "An Account," 41; Esgate, *Jacksonville*, 19.

33. Wright to Pelouze, March 25, 31, 1862, ORA, 6:125, 253; Wright to Bisbee, April 10, 1862, and Wright to Ely, "Special Report," April 13, 1862, ORA, 130, 124; Stevens to Du Pont, April 3, 1862, ORN, 12:698.

34. Robinson, "An Account," 39–40.

35. Wright to Davis, April 2, 1862, Sherman to Adjutant General, March 25, 1862, and Wright to Pelouze, March 25, 1862, ORA, 6:127, 250, 253.

36. Pelouze to Wright, March 21, 1862, and Wright to Pelouze, March 25, 1862, ORA, 6:249–50.

37. Dilworth to Washington, April 15, 1862, ibid., 131–32; Wright to Pelouze, March 31, 1862, ibid., 125–26.

38. Wright to Pelouze, March 31, 1862, ibid., 125–26; see also *New York Times*, April 7, 1862.

39. Wright to Pelouze, March 31, 1862, ORA, 6:125–26.

40. Ammen to Du Pont, April 10, 1862, ORN, 12:712–13.

41. Stevens to Drayton, April 3, 1862, ibid., 705.

42. Wright to Pelouze, April 3, 1862, *ORA*, 6:128–29.

43. Hayes, *Du Pont*, 1:373.

44. Benham to Wright, April 2, 1862, *ORA*, 6:127–28; see also Hunter to Stanton, March 27, 1862, ibid., 254.

45. General Hunter, General Orders no. 26, March 15, 1862, *ORA*, 248–49; General Orders no. 1, March 31, 1862, ibid., 257–58; Hunter to Stanton, April 13, 1862, ibid., 263.

46. Wright to Ely, April 13, 1862, *ORA*, 124–25; Notice, April 7, 1862, ibid., 129.

47. Robinson, "An Account," 42.

48. Ibid., 42–43; see also W. W. Davis, *Civil War and Reconstruction*, 253.

49. Stevens to Du Pont, April 8, 1862, Stevens to Drayton, April 3, 13, 1862, and Ammen to Du Pont, May 3, 1862, *ORN*, 12:697–99, 705–6, 737–40, 748–50; Wright to Ely, April 13, 1862, *ORA*, 6:124–25.

50. Wright to Ely, April 13, 1862, *ORA*, 6:124–25.

51. Robinson, "An Account," 45; *New York Times*, April 22, 1862; *New York Herald*, April 22, 1862.

52. Stanton to Gerow, April 28, 1862, *ORA*, 6:131.

53. Robinson, "An Account," 46.

54. *St. Augustine Examiner*, May 1, 1862; *New York Times*, April 22, 1862.

55. Hayes, *Du Pont*, 2:69; see also 18.

CHAPTER 5. *Freedom Was as Close as the River*

1. Stevens to Du Pont, April 10, 1862, Stevens to Budd, April 10, 1862, Budd to Stevens, April 12, 1862, *ORN*, 12:728–29, 738–39.

2. Ammen to Du Pont, May 3, 1862, ibid., 748–50.

3. Sproston to Ammen, April 28, 1862, ibid., 751.

4. Ammen to Hopkins, April 28, 1862, ibid., 750.

5. See Ammen to Du Pont, May 3, 1862, ibid., 748–50; Hopkins to Headquarters, April 27, 1862, ibid., 750; Ives, Journal, April 17–19, 1862.

6. Ives, Journal, April 22–May 27, 1862.

7. Ammen to Du Pont, May 3, 1862, *ORN*, 12:749–50; Daniel Ammen, May 31, 1862, Letter Books of U.S. Naval Officers, RG 45, NARA.

8. *New York Times*, April 2, 1862; *New York Tribune*, March 24, 1862; *New York Herald*, September 12, 1862; Pearson to Floyd, April 8, 1862, *ORA*, 53:233.

9. Davis Bryant to Willie Bryant, July 27, 1862, and Winston Stephens to Octavia Stephens, July 17, 1862, S-BFP.

10. Ammen to Du Pont, May 9, 21, 1862, *ORN*, 12:804–6; Rebecca Bryant to Davis Bryant, May 11, 13, 1862, and J. W. Bryant to Octavia Stephens, May 11, 1862, S-BFP.

11. J. W. Bryant to Octavia Stephens, May 11, 1862, S-BFP; see also Winston Stephens to Octavia Stephens, n.d. (circa May 15, 1862), ibid.

12. Winston Stephens to Octavia Stephens, July 6, 24, 31, 1862; Octavia Stephens to Winston Stephens, August 8, 1862, S-BFP.

13. Nicholson to Du Pont, May 21, 1862, *ORN*, 12:806.

14. Ibid. Du Pont replied on May 22, 1862: "unless the vessels are fired upon from that vicinity, I do not wish that there should be any destruction of property." Ibid., 807.

15. Ammen to Du Pont, May 3, 21, 31, 1862, ibid., 12:749, 806, 13:64.

16. Ammen to Du Pont, June 8, 1862, ibid., 13:83–84. For Mosquito Inlet see Du Pont to Welles, March 24, 1862, and Rogers to Du Pont, March 23, 1862, ibid., 12:645–48; Dilworth to Washington, April 4, 1862, ibid., 651.

17. Ammen to Du Pont, June 8, 1862, ibid., 13:83–84.

18. Ibid.; Du Pont to Welles, June 11, 1862, ibid., 83; Nicholson to Du Pont, June 17, 27, 1862, ibid., 109, 147.

19. Nicholson to Rodgers, June 17, 1862, ibid., 109.

20. Ibid.

21. Nicholson to Du Pont, June 17, 1862, ibid., 110.

22. Nicholson to Du Pont, June 27, 1862, ibid., 147.

23. Du Pont to Nicholson, July 3, 1862, ibid., 167.

24. For Federal policy concerning civilians in occupied zones see the important analyses in Ash, *When the Yankees Came*, and Grimsley, *The Hard Hand of War*. Their findings closely match northeast Florida circumstances.

25. Du Pont to Lardner, March 1, 4, 1862, ORN, 12:572–74.

26. Stevens to Du Pont, March 7, 1862, ibid., 583–85.

27. Ibid.

28. Godon to Du Pont, March 30, 1862, ibid., 633–34.

29. Wright to Pelouze, March 10, 1862, *ORA*, 6:244; Nicholson, Report, March 21, 1862, *ORN*, 12:643; Andrew Fairbanks to George Fairbanks, August 30, 1860, May 24, November 21, 1861, February 4, 1862, FC; Proctor, *Florida*, April 26, 1861; Winston Stephens to Octavia Stephens, December 12, 1861, S-BFP.

30. Schafer, "Freedom Was as Close."

31. Samuel Fairbanks to George Fairbanks, April 21, 29, and May 4, 1862, FC.

32. Samuel Fairbanks to George Fairbanks, July 4, 1863, ibid.; Regimental Descriptive Books, Company G, 33rd USCT, RG 94, NARA.

33. Winston Stephens to Octavia Stephens, October 23, 1862, S-BFP; Samuel Fairbanks to George Fairbanks, April 21, 29, 1862, FC.

34. See the Regimental Descriptive Books, 21st, 33rd, 34th USCT, RG 94, NARA, and Civil War Pension Files, RG 15, NARA. Pension records used here are Cryer, 452,263; J. Adams, 254,507; H. Adams, 874,759; Murray, 689,587; Long, 125,870; McQueen, 343,261.

35. Men identified as free were in one or more censuses from 1830 to 1860; others were identified through relatives. For important prewar data regarding enslaved men and women, see Civil War Pension Files, RG 15, NARA. For pension files used here see Phillips, 839,924; Hannahan, 721,857; Forrester, 808,976 and 288,415.

36. See pension files for Pappy, 363,496; Long, 125,870; J. Lang, 166,518; Osborn, 998,333, 778,686, and 998,312, in Civil War Pension Files, RG 15, NARA. See also 1850 and 1860 Federal Censuses for St. Johns County.

37. Ammen to Stevens, April 2, 1862, Daniel Ammen, Letter Books of U.S. Naval

Officers, RG 45, NARA; Stevens to Du Pont, April 3, 1863, Thomas H. Stevens, Letter Books of the U.S. Naval Officers, ibid.

38. Stevens to Davis, April 15, 1862, Stevens, Letter Books of the U.S. Naval Officers, *NARA*.

39. Ibid.; Wright, Report, April 13, 1862, and Dilworth, Report, April 15, 1862, *ORA*, 6:124–25, 131–32.

40. Samuel Fairbanks to George Fairbanks, April 21, 1862, FC.

41. Ibid.; Stevens to Drayton, April 3, 1862, *ORN*, 12:705.

42. See McPherson, *Battle Cry of Freedom*, 352–58 and ch. 16, for policies on contrabands, Lincoln, and emancipation.

43. Stephen Fairbanks to George Fairbanks, July 10, 1862, FC.

44. Decklog, *Ellen*, April 8–10, 1862, Logs of Ships and Stations, RG 45, NARA. The research on Union gunboat deck logs and letter books was contributed by Carol S. Clark, Kingsley Plantation, Timucuan Ecological and Historic Preserve, Jacksonville, Florida.

45. Decklogs, *Patroon*, May–July 1862, Logs of Ships and Stations, RG 45, NARA.

46. Winston to Octavia Stephens, July 24, 1862, S-BFP.

47. Ammen to Du Pont, Letter Book, May 3, 1862, Letter Books of U.S. Naval Officers, RG 45, NARA.

48. See decklogs for the *Uncas, Paul Jones, Patroon*, and the *Water Witch*, Logs of Ships and Stations, RG 24, NARA. See also Maxwell Woodhull Letter Book, November 1862, Letter Books of U.S. Naval Officers, RG 45, NARA.

49. Samuel Fairbanks to George Fairbanks, August 27, 1862, FC; Winston Stephens to Olivia Stephens, September 11, 1862, S-BFP. A "single" escaping in July was David Flemming. See his pension file, no. 273,637, Civil War Pension Files, RG 15, NARA.

50. Long, *Florida Breezes*, 331.

51. Boye to son, September 23, 1862, Typescript, SAHSRL.

52. See Lee to Governor John Milton, April 8, 1862, *ORA*, 6:429; see also Jefferson Davis to Governor Milton, ibid.; J. Withers, Special Orders, April 9, 1862, ibid., 432.

53. Hateley to Nicholson, June 27, 1862, *ORN*, 13:147.

54. Nicholson to Hately, June 27, 1862, ibid., 148.

55. Proctor, *Florida*, April 29, 1862; Nicholson to Du Pont, July 14, 1863, *ORN*, 13:163.

56. Nicholson to Du Pont, July 14, 1863, *ORN*, 13:163.

57. Nicholson to Du Pont, August 4, 1862, ibid., 220. Balsam's house was saved, but he was later forced to flee to Fernandina with his family and his home was destroyed. Craig, "Steamboating Days," 147; and "New Berlin," from Thomas James Grey interview, April 30, 1937, and June 28 and July 12, 1855, WPA; *Florida News*, March 18, April 1, 1854, *Florida Republican*, January 20, 1855.

58. McKeige to Du Pont, August 9, 1862, *ORN*, 13:245–46.

59. Ibid.

60. Finegan to Cooper, May 7, September 12, 1862, and Finegan to Jordan, October 14, 1862, *ORA*, 14:122, 494, 638; Proctor, *Florida*, May 21, June 30, 1862.

CHAPTER 6. *Debacle at St. Johns Bluff, and the Second Occupation of Jacksonville*

1. Crane to Du Pont, September 9, 1862, *ORN*, 13:301–2. The Union navy solved a serious alcohol-abuse problem on the St. Johns in the summer of 1862. Regarding "floating grogships," see Drayton to Du Pont, April 14, May 14, 1862, ibid., 12:741; see also Nicholson to Du Pont, June 17, 1862, ibid., 13:108–9, McKiege to Du Pont, August 9, 1862, ibid., 245–46, and Snell to Du Pont, August 16, 1862, 261–62.

2. Winston Stephens to Octavia Stephens, September 11, 1862, S-BFP.

3. Adams, Pocket Diary, 1862, SLF. Thanks to Robert C. Tindall of Palatka for sending me a copy of this document.

4. Finegan to Cooper, September 15, 1862, *ORA*, 14:121; Crane to Du Pont, September 11, 1862, *ORN*, 13:324–25.

5. Crane to Du Pont, September 11, 1862, *ORN*, 13:324–25.

6. Finegan to Cooper, September 15, 1862, *ORA*, 14:121.

7. Du Pont to Steedman, September 15, 1862, *ORN*, 13:327. For tonnage, armament, etc., see Pratt, *The Navy*, 424–27.

8. Steedman to Du Pont, September 17, October 14, 1862, *ORN*, 13:329–30, 362–65.

9. Steedman to Du Pont, September 17, October 14, 1862, ibid.

10. Adams, Pocket Diary, September 17, 1862, SLF.

11. Finegan to Cooper, September 19, 1862, *ORA*, 14:122; Brannan to Prentice, October 13, 1862, ibid., 130–31.

12. Winston Stephens to Octavia Stephens, September 21, 1862, S-BFP.

13. Hopkins to Finegan, October 8, 1862, *ORA*, 14:138; Du Pont to Pendergrast, September 22, 1862, *ORN*, 13:341.

14. Du Pont to Steedman, September 20, 1862, *ORN*, 13:336–39, 346.

15. Du Pont to Mitchell, September 21, 1862, and Mitchell to Du Pont, September 24, 1862, *ORN*, 13:339, 446; Brannan to Prentice, October 13, 1862, *ORA*, 14:129.

16. Anonymous, from Schmidt, *47th Regiment of Pennsylvania Volunteers*, 203.

17. Ibid., 202–3.

18. Steedman to Du Pont, October 3, 1862, *ORN*, 13:355.

19. T. F. Davis, "Letter of Captain V. Chamberlain," 86–87.

20. Brannan to Mitchell, October 4, 1862, Brannan to Prentice, October 13, 1862, and Hopkins to Finegan, October 8, 1862, *ORA*, 14:127–32, 138–41.

21. Hopkins to Finegan, October 8, 1862, ibid., 139.

22. Finegan to Baker, October 2, 1862, ibid., 137–38.

23. Winston Stephens to Octavia Stephens, October 1, 1862, S-BFP.

24. Ibid.

25. Hopkins to Finegan, October 8, 1862, and Finegan to Jordan, October 14, 1862, *ORA*, 14:139–40, 638.

26. Woodruff, Company D, 47th Pennsylvania, Schmidt, *47th Regiment of Pennsylvania Volunteers*, 206.

27. Ibid.

28. Good to Lambert, October 2, 1862, *ORA*, 14:132–33; Woodhull to Steedman, October 3, 1862, *ORN*, 13:356.

29. Good to Lambert, October 3, 1862, *ORA*, 14:133–34; Schmidt, *47th Regiment of Pennsylvania Volunteers*, 207–9.

30. Private Brecht, 47th Pennylvania, Schmidt, *47th Regiment of Pennsylvania Volunteers*, 209–10.

31. Hopkins to Finegan, October 8, 1862, and Finegan to Jordan, December 24, 1862, *ORA*, 14:138–42; Winston Stephens to Davis Bryant, October 19, 1862, S-BFP.

32. Winston Stephens to Davis Bryant, October 19, 1862, S-BFP.

33. Octavia Stephens to Winston Stephens, October 10, 1862, ibid. Apparently, this letter was never mailed.

34. Adams, Pocket Diary, October 2–10, 1862, SLF.

35. T. F. Davis, "Letter of Captain V. Chamberlain," 89–90.

36. Brannan to Mitchell, October 4, 1862, and Brannan to Prentice, October 13, 1862, *ORA*, 14:127–30.

37. Finegan to Cooper, October 3, 1862, ibid., 138, 141.

38. Hopkins to Finegan, October 8, 1862, ibid., 13:138–41.

39. Nulty, *Confederate Florida*, 39; Winston Stephens to Davis Bryant, October 19, 1862, S-BFP.

40. William D. Mitchell, Report of the Court of Inquiry, October 11, 1862, *ORA*, 14:142–43.

41. Davis to Dancy, January 20, 1863, ibid., 53:277.

42. Steedman to Du Pont, October 4, 1862, *ORN*, 13:357.

43. Brannan to Prentice, October 13, 1862, *ORA*, 14:130–31.

44. T. F. Davis, "Letter of Captain V. Chamberlain," 90–91.

45. Ibid., 93–94.

46. Ibid.

47. Ibid., 92.

48. *Southern Rights*, October 4, 1862, microfilm, PKY.

49. Steedman to Du Pont, October 11, 1862, and Woodhull to Steedman, October 7, 1862, *ORN*, 13:380, 369.

50. Woodhull to Steedman, October 7, 11, 1862, Steedman to Du Pont, October 14, 1862, and Williams to Steedman, October 19, 1862, ibid., 361–67.

51. Woodhull to Steedman, October 7, 1862, ibid., 367–70. For a plan to destroy cornfields along the river see Brannan to Prentice, October 13, 1862, *ORA*, 14:130.

52. Preston to Du Pont, October 11, 1862, *ORN*, 13:378–79.

53. Samuel Fairbanks to George Fairbanks, October 6, 1862, FC.

54. Snell to Steedman, October 14, 1862, Steedman Letters, PKY.

55. Regimental Descriptive Books, 33rd and 34th regiments, USCT, RG 94, NARA; Thomas Holzendorf, pension file 752,605, Civil War Pension Files, RG 15, NARA.

56. Winston Stephens to Octavia Stephens, November 4, 1862, S-BFP; see also Samuel Fairbanks to George Fairbanks, October 7, 1862, FC.

57. "Diary of A. M. Reed," Duke University Library.

58. Winston Stephens to Octavia Stephens, November 4, October 15, 23, 1862, S-BFP; Finegan to Cooper, October 9, 1862, *ORA*, 14:633, 661.

59. Brannan to Prentice, October 13, 1862, *ORA*, 14:131; Boatner, *Civil War Dictionary*, 81; Preston to Du Pont, October 11, 1862, *ORN*, 13:379; Wilkerson Call, "Special Orders no. 1342, October 30, 1862," *ORA*, 14:661; Winston Stephens to Octavia Stephens, October 15, November 4, 1862, and Davis Bryant to Willie Bryant, December 21, 1862, both in S-BFP.

CHAPTER 7. *Unionists in Exile*

1. *New York Times*, April 20, 28, 1863, and February 4, 13, 1864.

2. Robinson, "An Account," 46.

3. U.S. House of Representatives, "An Act for the Collection of Direct Taxes," 126.

4. Keene, Diaries, passim.

5. G. W. Smith, "Carpetbag Imperialism," 107–8; *New York Times*, January 25, 1863.

6. *New York Times*, January 25, 1863; G. W. Smith, "Carpetbag Imperialism," 113–15.

7. See U.S. House of Representatives, "An Act for the Collection of Direct Taxes," 65, 72, 84, 90; G. W. Smith, "Carpetbag Imperialism," 110–11; Futch, "Salmon P. Chase," 164; Stickney, "Tropical Florida" and "Florida Soil, Climate and Productions."

8. See Schafer, "'A Class of People'" and *Anna Madgigine Jai Kingsley*.

9. U.S. House of Representatives, "An Act for the Collection of Direct Taxes," 88–89, 95; Esgate, *Jacksonville*, 135–36; Shofner, *Nor Is It Over Yet*, 5; G. W. Smith, "Carpetbag Imperialism," 118–21.

10. *New York Times*, October 25, 1862.

11. Ibid., October 16, 1862.

12. Ibid., October 18, 1862.

13. Ibid.

14. Ibid.; see also Cox, *Lincoln and Black Freedom*.

15. *New York Times*, January 13, 1863.

16. Ibid.

17. *New York Evening Post*, February 8, also January 25, 1863.

18. *New York Times*, October 3, 1863, February 4, 13, 1864; *New York Tribune*, February 9, 1863; G. W. Smith, "Carpetbag Imperialism," 128–29.

19. *Fernandina Peninsula*, April 18, July 2, 1863.

20. Du Pont to Steedman, March 9, 1863, *ORN*, 13:742.

21. Winston Stephens to Octavia Stephens, October 29, 1862, S-BFP.

22. Winston Stephens to Octavia Stephens, July 15, 1862, ibid.

23. Octavia Stephens to Winston Stephens, July 29, August 7, 1862, ibid.; T. F. Davis, *History of Jacksonville*, 93, locates a Crespo boardinghouse at the southeast corner of Adams and Ocean streets. The 1860 Census lists Jane Crespo, Florida born, age fifty-seven, boardinghouse keeper, with $7,000 in real and personal property, including four slaves. H. C. Wallace, a woman, age thirty-four, resided in the house.

24. Winston Stephens to Octavia Stephens, November 20, 1862, S-BFP.

25. Winston Stephens to Octavia Stephens, Camp Finegan, October 23, 1862, ibid.

26. Winston Stephens to Octavia Stephens, February 22, 1862, ibid. Each messmate paid two dollars monthly to Felix's owner. See also Winston Stephens to Octavia Stephens, December 1, 4, 1861, and August 4, 1862, ibid.

27. Winston Stephens to Octavia Stephens, January 15, 27, February 8, March 4, 1863, ibid.

28. Winston Stephens to Octavia Stephens, January 27, 1863, ibid.

29. Ibid.

30. Winston Stephens to Octavia Stephens, October 29, 1862, ibid.

31. Davis Bryant to Willie Bryant, January 12, 1863, in Blakey, Lainhart, and Stephens, *Rose Cottage Chronicles*, 187 n. 1.

32. Ibid.

33. Winston Stephens to Octavia Stephens, December 1, 1862, S-BFP.

34. Octavia Stephens to Winston Stephens, January 31, 1863, ibid.

35. Octavia Stephens to Winston Stephens, February 14, 1863, ibid.

36. For the diary entry see Blakey, Lainhart, and Stephens, *Rose Cottage Chronicle*, 212. For the visit to Jacksonville see George Bryant to Willie Bryant, March 14, 1863, ibid., 212.

37. Davis Bryant to Willie Bryant, March 15, 1863, ibid., 213–14.

38. Glatthaar, *Forged in Battle*, ch. 1.

39. Ibid.

40. Berlin, Reidy, and Rowland, *Freedom's Soldiers*, 4; see Hargrove, *Black Union Soldiers*, 36–37.

41. Cornish, *Sable Arm*, 35.

42. Hunter, General Orders, no. 11, May 9, 1862, *ORA*, 14:342. See also Hunter, General Orders, no. 7, April 13, 1862, ibid., 333, and Cornish, *Sable Arm*, 35.

43. Quoted in Cornish, *Sable Arm*, 39.

44. President Abraham Lincoln, General Order no. 11, May 19, 1862, *ORA*, ser. 3, 2:42–43; see also Cornish, *Sable Arm*, 35; Hargrove, *Black Union Soldiers*, 40; Berlin, Reidy, and Rowland, *Freedom's Soldiers*, 85; Rose, *Rehearsal for Reconstruction*, 145.

45. *New York Times*, July 14, 1862.

46. Ibid., June 9, 1861, August 6, 10, 1862; see Wesley, "Negroes as Soldiers in the Confederate Army."

47. Berlin, Reidy, and Rowland, *Freedom's Soldiers*, 7; Westwood, *Black Troops*, 65; Ash, *Firebrand of Liberty*, 32–34.

48. Westwood, *Black Troops*, 67; Saxton to Stanton, August 16, 1862, and Stanton to Saxton, August 25, 1862, *ORA*, 14:374–76, 377–78; Cornish, *Sable Arm*, 80; Berry, *Military Necessity*, 47; Berlin, Reid, and Rowland, *Freedom's Soldiers*, 39.

49. Westwood, *Black Troops*, 67; Rose, *Rehearsal for Reconstruction*, 152–53.

50. Circular, August 5, 1862, United States Army, Headquarters, Beaufort, S.C., Rufus Saxton Papers, SCL.

51. Trowbridge, Reminicences, SCHS.

52. *Minneapolis Journal*, December 24, 1907.

53. Beard to Saxton, November 10, 1862, *ORA*, 14:189–92.

54. Saxton to Stanton, November 12, 1862, ibid., 189–93; Schafer, "Freedom Was as Close."

55. Saxton to Stanton, November 12, 1862, *ORA*, 14:189–90.

56. Ibid., 189–92.

57. Ibid.

58. Wilson, "Shadow of John Brown," 308; Glatthaar, *Forged in Battle*, 14.

59. Howard N. Meyer, introduction to Higginson, *Army Life*, 7–23, 29.

60. Cornish, *Sable Arm*, xvi.

61. Higginson, *Complete Civil War Journal*, 435; see also Cornish, "The Union Army as a School for Negroes."

62. Higginson, *Complete Civil War Journal*, 441.

63. Higginson to Company G, November 25, 1862, General Order no. 1, Order Books, 33rd USCT, Regimental Records, RG 94, NARA.

64. Higginson, "The First Black Regiment," 528. Dr. Esther Hill Hawks also praised the Florida men while saying about South Carolina men: "it is an undeniable fact that the negroes of these Sea Islands are of the lowest type." See Hawks, *A Woman Doctor's Civil War*, 38.

65. Higginson, *Army Life*, 42.

66. Muster and Descriptive Books, 33rd, 34th, and 21st regiments, USCT, RG 94, NARA. See also the Eighth Census, 1860, Florida, Slave Schedules.

67. Higginson, "The First Black Regiment," 528. See Berlin et al., *Free at Last*, 517. Glatthaar concluded: "If the black troops had misbehaved . . . the results would have been catastrophic for the black race and the USCT" (*Forged in Battle*, 141).

68. Higginson, *Army Life*, 73–74, 78–79.

69. Seth Rogers, Letters, February 5, 1863, MHI.

70. *New York Times*, February 10, 1863.

71. Ibid.

72. Higginson, *Complete Civil War Journal*, 94–95; Higginson, "Up the St. Mary's," 432.

73. Rogers, Letters, January 30, 1863, MHI.

74. *New York Times*, February 10, 1863.

75. Hawks, *A Woman Doctor's Civil War*, 42–43.

76. Rogers, Letters, February 1, 1863, MHI.

77. Winston Stephens to Octavia Stephens, February 8, 1863, and Davis Bryant to Willie Bryant, April 2, 1863, S-BFP.

78. Higginson to Saxton, February 1, 1863, *ORA*, 14:195–98; Higginson, *Army Life*, 80–105.

79. Saxton to Stanton, February 2, 1863, *ORA*, 14:194.

80. Woodhull to Du Pont, December 11, 1862, *ORN*, 13:477; U.S. House of Representatives, "An Act for the Collection of Direct Taxes," 75, 100.

81. Hayes, *Du Pont*, 2:326–27.

82. Saxton to Stanton, March 6, 1863, *ORA*, 14:42–43.

83. Higginson, *Army Life*, 107.

84. Ibid., 108.

85. *New York Daily Tribune*, February 27, 1863.

CHAPTER 8. *"These Are United States Troops and They Will Not Dishonor the Flag": The Third Occupation of Jacksonville*

1. Ash, *Firebrand of Liberty*, 86.
2. Higginson, *Army Life*, 109.
3. Ibid., 110.
4. Rogers, Letters, March 7, 1863, MHI.
5. Higginson, *Army Life*, 112.
6. Ibid.; see also Higginson, "Up the St. John's River," 314.
7. *New York Times*, March 25, 1863.
8. Winston Stephens to Octavia Stephens, March 15, 1863, S-BFP.
9. William Lee Apthorp, "Montgomery's Raids," typescript, HMSF.
10. Ibid.
11. Ibid.
12. Higginson, *Army Life*, 113.
13. Higginson, *Complete Civil War Journal*, 109.
14. Ibid., 110.
15. Rogers, Letters, March 12, 1863, MHI.
16. Higginson, *Army Life*, 114–15; Ash, *Firebrand of Liberty*, 117.
17. Higginson, *Army Life*, 115; *New York Tribune*, April 8, 1863.
18. Higginson, *Complete Civil War Journal*, 109.
19. Higginson, "Up the St. John's River," 315; Ash, *Firebrand of Liberty*, 115.
20. Muster and descriptive rolls, 33rd and 34th regiments, USCT, RG 94, NARA; Dyer, *Compendium*, 3:1636.
21. Higginson, *Army Life*, 19–20.
22. Higginson, *Complete Civil War Journal*, 110.
23. Higginson, *Army Life*, 12–14; *New York Times*, March 25, 1863.
24. Higginson, *Complete Civil War Journal*, 109.
25. Rogers, Letters, March 12, 1863, MHI.
26. Finegan to General Jordan, *ORA*, 14:837–38; Higginson to McCormick, March 18, 1863, ibid., 839. See also Higginson, *Army Life*, 122, and Ash, *Firebrand of Liberty*, 131–32.
27. Hattie Reed to Davis Bryant, March 22, 1863, and Octavia Stephens to Davis Bryant, April 2, 1863, S-BFP.
28. Anonymous to Dear Loulie, April 4, 1863, ibid.
29. Higginson, *Army Life*, 116.
30. Albert C. Sammis, Case no. 136,412, Civil War Pension Files, RG 15, NARA. See Schafer, *Anna Madgigine Jai Kingsley*.
31. Sammis pension record (n30 above), specifically the depositions by Mary Kingsley Sammis and Henry Adams; see also *Jacksonville City Directory*, 1870, 1882, 1889.
32. Higginson, *Complete Civil War Journal*, 66–67.
33. Ibid., 114.
34. Identified from testimony in the Sammis pension record.
35. See Higginson, "Reoccupation of Jacksonville in 1863," 467–68, 472.

36. Higginson, "Up the St. John's River," 320; Higginson, *Complete Civil War Journal*, 113.

37. Higginson, *Army Life*, 114, 122–23; Rust to Halpine, April 2, 1863, ORA, 14:227–28; U.S. House of Representatives, "An Act for the Collection of Direct Taxes," 14–15, 75, 100–101, 177; *Fernandina Peninsula*, April 30, 1863.

38. Rogers, Letters, March 22, 1863, MHI.

39. Cadwell, *The Old Sixth Regiment*, ch. 5.

40. Finegan to Jordan, March 14, 1863, *ORA*, 14:227–28.

41. "Enclosure no. 2," ibid., 229.

42. Winston Stephens to Octavia Stephens, March 16, 1863, S-BFP.

43. Seddon to Cobb, March 24, 1863, ORA, 14:840.

44. Beauregard to Finegan, March 21, 1863, ibid., 839–40.

45. Higginson, *Army Life*, 118; Finegan to Jordan, March 14, 1863, ORA, 14:226–29.

46. Apthorp, "Montgomery's Raids," HMSF.

47. Ibid.

48. Higginson, *Complete Civil War Journal*, 116.

49. Apthorp, "Montgomery's Raids," HMSF.

50. Higginson, *Army Life*, 120.

51. Finegan to Jordan, March 20, 1863, ORA, 14:226–29.

52. See M. E. Dickison, *Dickison and His Men*, xv.

53. Rerick, *Memoirs of Florida*, 1:461; Rohrabacher, *Live Towns and Progressive Men*, 92.

54. Finegan to Jordan, March 31, 1863, ORA, 14:234; Higginson, *Army Life*, 129–30.

55. Diary of Alfred Walton, published in the *Jacksonville Evening Telegram*, October 30, 1893. Taken from T. F. Davis, *History of Jacksonville*, 129–30.

56. Ibid.; Finegan to Jordan, March 31, 1863, ORA, 14:234; Cadwell, *The Old Sixth Regiment*, ch. 5.

57. William M. McArthur, "Journal of Expedition to Jacksonville," April 2, 1863, Beaufort, South Carolina. A special thank-you to Mr. "Dickie" Ferry for use of this original document from his personal collection.

58. T. F. Davis, *History of Jacksonville*, 72; see also Higginson, *Army Life*, 126–29; Rust to Halpine, April 2, 1863, ORA, 14:233.

59. McArthur, "Journal of Expedition to Jacksonville."

60. Dickison to Call, March 27, 1863, and Russell to Finegan, April 2, 1863, ORA, 14:237–39, 860–61; *New York Tribune*, April 8, 1863.

61. Lincoln to Hunter, April 1, 1863, in Nicolay and Hay, *Abraham Lincoln*, 2:321; Saxton to Stanton, March 14, 1863, ORA, 14:226; Higginson, *Army Life*, 130.

62. Saxton to Stanton, March 14, 1863, ORA, 14:226.

63. Rogers, Letters, March 24, 1863, MHI.

64. Higginson, *Army Life*, 130.

65. Apthorp, "Montgomery's Raids," HMSF.

66. Rogers, Letters, March 28, 1863, MHI.

67. Saxton to Stanton, April 4, 1863, ORA, ser. 3, 3:116–17.

68. Ibid.

69. Ibid.; Ash, *Firebrand of Liberty*, 200–202.

70. *New York Tribune*, April 8, 1863.

71. Cadwell, *The Old Sixth Regiment*, ch. 5.

72. T. F. Davis, *History of Jacksonville*, 132. Walton returned the prayer book and manuscript after the war.

73. Robinson, "An Account," 53–54. Ledwith was at the southwest corner of Ocean and Adams; Pierson was at the northeast corner of Monroe and Market; Bisbee and Canova was at Main and Laura, south of Bay.

74. *New York Tribune*, April 8, 1863.

75. *New York Times*, April 17, 1863.

76. Higginson, "Some War Scenes Revisited," 1.

77. Cornish, *Sable Arm*, 141; Rogers, Letters, March 29, 1863, MHI.

78. Higginson, *Complete Civil War Journal*, 135.

79. Winston Stephens to Davis Bryant, April 8, 1863, S-BFP.

80. Letter describing the impact of the fire, April 14, 1863, ibid.

81. *New York Tribune*, April 8, 1863.

82. *Cotton States*, April 14, 1863.

83. Rust to Halpine, April 2, 1863, *ORA*, 14:234–36.

84. Finegan to Jordan, March 31, 1863, ibid., 234–36.

85. Beauregard to Gillmore, July 4, 1863, ibid., 28, pt. 2:11–12.

86. Higginson, "Up the St. John's River," 325.

87. Rogers, Letters, April 2, 1863, MHI.

CHAPTER 9. *"To Redeem Florida from the Rebels":*
The Fourth Occupation of Jacksonville

1. Martin, *The City Makers*, 53.

2. Reiger, "Deprivation, Disaffection, and Desertion"; see also Reiger, "Anti-War and Pro-Union Sentiment."

3. Winston Stephens to Octavia Stephens, June 1, 1863, S-BFP.

4. Winston Stephens to Octavia Stephens, June 7, 1863, ibid.

5. Ibid.

6. Davis Bryant to Willie Bryant, June 8, 1863, ibid.

7. Octavia Stephens to Winston Stephens, June 10, 1863, ibid.

8. Ibid.

9. Octavia Stephens to Winston Stephens, June 18, 19, 1863, ibid.

10. Octavia Stephens to Winston Stephens, July 25, 1863, ibid.

11. Octavia Stephens to Winston Stephens, August 5, 1863, ibid.

12. Willie Bryant to Davis Bryant, July 26, 1863, in Blakey, Lainhart, and Stephens, *Rose Cottage Chronicles*, 252.

13. Winston Stephens to Octavia Stephens, August 12, 1863, S-BFP.

14. Winston Stephens to Octavia Stephens, August 4, 1863, ibid.

15. Ibid.

16. Davis Bryant to Winston Stephens, September 8, 1863, ibid. In his letter to Stephens, Davis Bryant secretly enclosed the letter from his father, along with a warning of the danger his father would be in if Union authorities learned of the letter.

17. Octavia Stephens to Winston Stephens, October 30, November 6, December 12, 1863, ibid.

18. Winston Stephens to Octavia Stephens, January 4, 1863, ibid.

19. Winston Stephens to Octavia Stephens, January 26, 1864, ibid.

20. Meriam to Dahlgren, October 18, 1863, *ORN*, 15:51.

21. Dahlgren to Breese, November 19, 1863, and Breese to Dahlgren, November 27, 1863, ibid., 128–29, 147–48.

22. Stickney to Chase, December 11, 1863, Chase Papers, LC.

23. Stickney to Chase, April 16, 17, 1863, Chase Papers, LC; and Stickney to Chase, April 27, 1863, Journal of the Direct Tax Commission of Florida, Records of the U.S. Direct Tax Commission, RG 58, NARA.

24. Stickney to Chase, December 11, 1863, Chase Papers, LC; *New York Herald*, September 8, 1863. For Gillmore see Boatner, *Civil War Dictionary*, 301.

25. Coles, "Far from the Fields of Glory," 33–34. See also Futch, "Salmon P. Chase," 163–88; G. W. Smith, "Carpetbag Imperialism," 260–99; and Martin and Schafer, *Jacksonville's Ordeal by Fire*, 122–29, 168–78.

26. *Fernandina Peninsula*, December 24, 1863; G. W. Smith, "Carpetbag Imperialism," 278–79.

27. Stickney to Chase, January 7, 1864, Chase Papers, LC; see also U.S. House of Representatives, "An Act for the Collection of Direct Taxes," 17, 61.

28. Sandburg, *Lincoln: The War Years*, 3:5–6.

29. Lincoln to Gillmore, January 13, 1864, *ORA*, 35, pt. 1:278.

30. Gillmore to Halleck, January 14, 1864, and Gillmore to Stanton, January 15, 1864, ibid.

31. Halleck to Gillmore, January 22, 1864, ibid., 279.

32. Gillmore to Halleck, January 31, 1864, ibid.

33. Dennett, *Lincoln and the Civil War*, 155–56.

34. Stickney to Chase, January 21, February 5, 1864, Chase Papers, LC.

35. Dennett, *Lincoln and the Civil War*, 156; G. W. Smith, "Carpetbag Imperialism," 283–84.

36. Gillmore to Dahlgren, February 3, 1864, Gillmore File, Generals' Papers, RG 94, NARA.

37. First quotation: Cyrus W. Brown, Diary, February 4, 1864, Florida Room, JPL. See also Gillmore to Seymour, February 4, 1864, *ORA*, 35, pt. 1:280; and Dahlgren to Welles, February 15, 1864, *ORN*, 15:276. Second quote: Bornet, "A Connecticut Yankee Fights at Olustee," 242.

38. Gillmore to Seymour, February 4, 1864, *ORA*, 35, pt. 1:280.

39. Meriam to Dahlgren, February 11, 1864, and Dahlgren to Welles, February 15, 1864, *ORN*, 15:176–77, 280–81; *New York Tribune*, February 20, 1864; Finegan to Jordan, February 26, 1864, *ORA*, 35, pt. 1:330.

40. Balch to Dahlgren, February 21, 1864, *ORN*, 15:282; Meriam to Dahlgren, February 11, 1864, *ORA*, 35, pt. 1:476–77; and Dahlgren to Welles, February 15, 1864, *ORN*, 15:176–77, 280–81.

41. Appleton Papers, February 7, 1864, WVUL.

42. Ibid.

43. Ibid.

44. Seymour to Turner, February 17, 1864, *ORA*, 35, pt. 1:295; *New York Times*, February 20, 1864. For the train, see Gillmore to Seymour, February 5, 1864, *ORA*, 35, pt. 1:280–81.

45. Finegan to Jordan, February 26, 1864, *ORA*, 35, pt. 1:330–33.

46. *New York Times*, February 20, 1864.

47. Ibid.; Seymour to Turner, February 17, 1864, and Dunham to Thomas, March 18, 1864, *ORA*, 35, pt. 1:296, 346–47.

48. Yonge, "The Occupation of Jacksonville," 265–66.

49. *New York Times*, February 20, 1864; Gillmore to Halleck, February 9, 1864, and Gillmore to Dahlgren, February 10, 1864, *ORA*, 35, pt. 1:282; Dahlgren to Welles, February 15, 1864, and Gillmore to Dahlgren, February 10, 1864, *ORN*, 15:277–78.

50. Finegan to Jordan, February 26, 1864, *ORA*, 35, pt. 1:330–33. Confederate losses were two killed and three wounded. For the Union account see Seymour to Gillmore, February 11, 1864, ibid., 281–82; and *New York Times*, February 20, 1864.

51. *New York Herald* and *New York Times*, both February 20, 1864.

52. Finegan to Jordan, February 26, 1864, *ORA*, 35, pt. 1:330–33.

53. *New York Times*, February 20, 1864; Nulty, *Confederate Florida*, ch. 4.

54. General Orders no. 5, February 17, 1864, *ORA*, 35, pt. 1:297.

55. Appleton Papers, February 11, 1864, WVUL.

56. Appleton Papers, February 12, 1864, ibid. The order came from Gillmore.

57. Ibid.

58. See General Orders no. 15 in *ORA*, 35, pt. 1:481.

59. The Gillmore/Seymour correspondence for February 11–18, 1864, can be seen in ibid., 281–86.

60. Seymour to Gillmore, February 11, 1864, ibid., 281–82.

61. Gillmore to Halleck, February 13, 1864, ibid., 293.

62. For the exchange of letters see Seymour to Gillmore, February 17, 1864, and Gillmore to Seymour, February 18, 1864, ibid., 284–85, 285–86.

63. Gillmore to Seymour, February 18, 1864, ibid., 285–86.

64. Seymour to Gillmore, February 22, 1864, ibid., 286–88; Nulty, *Confederate Florida*, 203.

65. Jordan to Finegan, *ORA*, 35, pt. 1:580. See Nulty, *Confederate Florida*, ch. 5, and Coles, "Far from the Fields of Glory," ch. 2. See also Shofner and Rogers, "Confederate Railroad Construction."

66. Finegan to Jordan, February 26, 1864, *ORA*, 35, pt. 1:331.

67. Seymour to Sprague, February 27, March 26, 1864, Seymour to Sprague, date, Seymour file, Generals Papers, RG94, NARA.

68. Seymour to Turner, February 22, 1864, *ORA*, 35, pt. 1:287.

69. *New York Times*, March 1, 1864; Seymour to Gillmore, March 25, 1864, *ORA*, 35, pt. 1:286–87; see also Grant to Harris, April 27, 1864, ibid., 340.

70. Finegan to Jordan, February 26, 1864, and Smith to Call, February 24, 1864, *ORA*, 35, pt. 1:331, 351–52.

71. Report of General Colquitt, February 26, 1864, ibid., 343–45.

72. Finegan to Jordan, February 26, 1864, ibid., 331.

73. Winston Stephens to Octavia Stephens, February 21, 1864, S-BFP.

74. *New York Times*, February 28, 1864.

75. Macfarlane, *Reminiscences of an Army Surgeon*, 46, quoted in Coles, "Far from the Fields of Glory," 144.

76. Seymour to Turner, February 20, 1864, *ORA*, 53, pt. 3:101–2.

77. Appleton Papers, February 20, 1864, WVUL.

78. A. J. Sanger to Dear Parents, February 21, 1864, original in the private collection of Mr. "Dickie" Ferrie.

79. Ibid.

80. *New York Times*, February 28, 1864.

81. Seymour, "Return of Casualties," *ORA*, 35, pt. 1:298; Nulty, *Confederate Florida*, 203; Finegan to Jordan, February 26, 1864, *ORA*, 35, pt. 1:330–33.

82. Penniman Reminiscences, pp. 60–61, no. 2747-z, SHC.

83. Ibid.

84. Winston Stephens to Octavia Stephens, February 22, 1864, S-BFP.

85. Hatch to Hitchcock, September 25, 1864, *ORA*, ser. 2, 7:876.

86. Coles, "Far from the Fields of Glory," 181, 176–77.

87. Finegan to Jordan, February 26, 1864, *ORA*, 35, pt. 1:330–33; Hatch to Hitchcock, September 25, 1864, ibid., ser. 2, 7:876; Gardner to Beauregard, March 7, 1864, ibid., ser. 1, 35, pt. 1:334–37.

88. Appleton Papers, February 28 and March 31, 1864, WVUL.

89. Gillmore to Seymour [through Ed. Smith], Hilton Head, S.C., March 7, 16, 1864, *ORA*, 35, pt. 2:9–10, 18. Seymour continued to call for an attack on the Confederate forces. See Seymour to Turner, March 14, 17, 1864, ibid., 18, 23.

90. Seymour to Sprague, March 26, 1864, Seymour file, Generals' Papers, RG 94, NARA.

91. All the quoted material is from ibid.; see also Seymour to Sprague, February 27, March 21, 1864, ibid.

92. Turner (sending Gillmore's orders) to Seymour, March 7, 1864, *ORA*, 35, pt. 2:9–10.

93. *New York Times*, March 8, 1864.

94. J. Smith, *Camps and Campaigns*, 164.

95. Barlow, *Company G*, 161.

96. J. Smith, *Camps and Campaigns*, 164.

97. See Hyde, *History of [112th] N.Y. Volunteers*, 69–70.

98. The forts on the west were named after General John P. Hatch, General John Foster, and Colonel Charles Fribley of the 8th U.S. Colored Troops. Fribley was killed at Olustee. Military maps show an unnamed fortification near the present Old City Cemetery north of State Street that connected to the stockade area via a ribbed log road laid down like corduroy. Military reports at the time indicate the area was cleared of tree cover to deny potential cover for enemies, and also for construction of a fortification that was later deemed unnecessary.

99. "Jacksonville and Vicinity, Florida," Fortifications Map File, Dr. 129, Sheet 29, Civil Works Map File, Records of the Topographical Bureau, RG 77, NARA-CP.

100. Balch to Dahlgren, February 23, 1864, *ORN*, 15:285–86.

101. Seymour to Turner, March 15, 1864, *ORA*, 35, pt. 2:19; *New York Times*, April 1, 1864.

102. Appleton Papers, March 10, 1864, WVUL.

103. Ibid.

104. Ibid., March 12, 1864; for analysis of discriminatory salary policy of the Union army, see Glatthaar, *Forged in Battle*, ch. 9.

105. Appleton Papers, March 17, 1864, WVUL. The incident occurred on March 4.

106. Ibid.

CHAPTER 10. *Thunder on the River: Torpedo Warfare and the Struggle for Control of Northeast Florida*

1. Gardner to Beauregard, March 7, 1864, *ORA*, 35, pt. 1:334.

2. Barth, Special Orders, March 7, 1864, ibid., 35, pt. 2:340.

3. General James Patton Anderson to Feilden, May 14, 1864, ibid., 35, pt. 1:368.

4. Beauregard to Cooper, March 6, 1864, ibid., 35, pt. 2:333–34; Barth to Cooper, March 7, 1864, ibid., 340.

5. Beauregard to Cooper, March 6, 1864, ibid., 333–34.

6. Anderson to Bryan, Colquitt to Beauregard, Finegan to Bryan, Colonel George P. Harrison to Bryan, and Gardner to Bryan, all March 5, 1864, ibid., 334–37.

7. Beauregard, Report, March 7, 1864, ibid., 339.

8. Jordan to Beauregard, March 7, 1864, ibid., 339.

9. Beauregard to Cooper, March 25, 1864, ibid., 35, pt. 1:323–24; Beauregard to Anderson, March 20, 1864, ibid., 35, pt. 2:366–67.

10. Anderson to Jordan, March 30, 1864, Records of Confederate Military Organizations, Records of Armies and Geographical Commands (Confederate), Department of South Carolina, Georgia, and Florida, 1861–65, RG 109, NARA.

11. Circular Letter, Barth, April 13, 1864, ibid.

12. Barth to Tabb, March 31, 1864, ibid.

13. Barth to Harrison, April 1, 1864, ibid.

14. Gordon to Burger, June 4, 1864, *ORA*, 35, pt. 1:402. For the site of Camp Finegan see William M. Jones, "A Report on the Site of Camp Finegan," Jones Papers, UNF.

15. Beauregard to Anderson, March 20, 1864, *ORA*, 35, pt. 2:366–67.

16. Barth to Simkins, April 7, 1864, Records of Confederate Military Organizations, Records of Armies and Geographical Commands (Confederate), Department of South Carolina, Georgia, and Florida, 1861–65, RG 109, NARA.

17. Lay to Harris, March 15, 1864, ibid.

18. *New York Times*, March 8, 1864.

19. Ibid., March 14, 1864.

20. Winston Stephens to Octavia Stephens, February 27, 1864, in Blakey, Lainhart, and Stephens, *Rose Cottage Chronicles*, 323–24.

21. Charles A. Currier, "Recollections of Service with the Fortieth Massachusetts Infantry Volunteers," 89–90, Charles A. Currier Papers, MHI, quoted in Coles, "Far from the Fields of Glory," 189–90.

22. Swepson Stephens to Octavia Stephens, October 20, 1866 (written seventeen

months after the war ended), in Blakey, Lainhart, and Stephens, *Rose Cottage Chronicles*, 329.

23. Octavia Stephens, journal entry, March 15, 1864, ibid., 328–29.

24. *New York Times*, March 17, 30, 1864.

25. Trudeau, *Voices of the 55th*, 83.

26. Trimble, *Brothers 'Til Death*, 68.

27. Barton to Chadwick, March 31, 1864, *ORA*, 35, pt. 1:378–79.

28. Anderson to Feilden, May 14, 1864, ibid., 368.

29. Rains, "Torpedoes," vol. 3, nos. 5 and 6, reprinted at www.civilwarhome.com/torpedoes.htm.

30. Ibid., vol. 3, no. 5.

31. Jordan to Beauregard, March 7, 1864, *ORA*, 35, pt. 2:339; Beauregard to Headquarters, March 7, 1864, ibid.

32. Beauregard to Anderson, March 20, 1864, ibid., 366; Beauregard to Jordan, March 10, 1864, ibid., 346.

33. Beauregard to Anderson, March 20, 1864, ibid., 366–67.

34. Gallagher, *Fighting for the Confederacy*, 68.

35. *New York Times*, March 14, 1864; see also Marcus, *New Canaan Private*, 57.

36. Statement of Benjamin Falany, Records of Districts, District of Florida, RG 393, NARA.

37. Allen to Pierce, Jacksonville, Florida, March 14, 1864, ibid.

38. Barth to Colquitt, Camp Milton, March 21, 1864, Records of Confederate Military Organizations, Records of Armies and Geographical Commands (Confederate), Department of South Carolina, Georgia, and Florida, 1861–65, RG 109, NARA.

39. Anderson, Special Order no. 14, March 21, 1864, ibid.

40. Barth to Finegan, March 25, 1864, ibid.

41. Gordon, *War Diary*, 296.

42. Anderson to Jordan, March 30, 1864, Records of Confederate Military Organizations, Records of Armies and Geographical Commands (Confederate), Department of South Carolina, Georgia, and Florida, 1861–65, RG 109, NARA.

43. Anderson, Special Order no. 14, March 21, 1864, ibid.

44. Warren to Chatfield, Picolata, May 22, 1864, Records of Districts, District of Florida, RG 393, NARA; M. L. S. Jackson, Diary, 144th New York Volunteers, Lewis Schmidt Collection, M91-100, FSA.

45. Case Files for General Jurisdiction Cases, Claim 3705, RG 123, NARA.

46. Testimony of Captain Henry W. Dale and testimony of Charles H. Farnham, Proceedings of a Board of Survey, April 2, 1864, Records of the Quartermaster General, Entry 1403, RG 393, NARA. See also Hatch to Turner, April 1, 1864, *ORA*, 35, pt. 1:380, and mapleleafshipwreck.com/Book/Chapter5/chapter5.htm.

47. Case Files for General Jurisdiction Cases, Claim 3705, RG 123, NARA.

48. Testimony of Romeo Murray, April 2, 1864, Proceedings of a Board of Survey, April 2, 1864, Records of the Quartermaster General, Entry 1403, RG 393, NARA.

49. Ibid.

50. Ibid.

51. Testimony of Samuel D. Jones, ibid.

52. *Boston Herald*, April 14, 1864.

53. Testimony of Samuel L. Johnson, Proceedings of a Board of Survey, April 2, 1864, Records of the Quartermaster General, Entry 1403, RG 393, NARA.

54. *New York Herald*, April 13, 1864.

55. Testimony of Henry W. Dale, Proceedings of a Board of Survey, April 2, 1864, Records of the Quartermaster General, Entry 1403, RG 393, NARA.

56. Hyde, *History of [112th] N.Y. Volunteers*, 71.

57. Anderson, Camp Milton, April 3, 1864, Records of Confederate Military Organizations, Records of Armies and Geographical Commands (Confederate), Department of South Carolina, Georgia, and Florida, 1861–65, RG 109, NARA.

58. Barth to Grieve, April 1, 1864, ibid.

59. *New York Times*, April 13, 1864.

60. *Jacksonville Peninsula*, April 7, 1864.

61. *New York Times*, April 13, 1864.

62. Appleton Papers, April 5, 1864, WVUL. See also *Danbury Times*, April 28, 1864.

63. Balch to Rowan, ORN, 15:312.

64. *New York Tribune*, April 26, 1864; see also Thomas to Stanton, Proceedings of a Board of Survey, April 2, 1864, Records of the Quartermaster General, Entry 1403, RG 393, NARA. Hatch was also in command of Union forces in the District of Florida from August 4 to November 10, 1864.

65. *New York Tribune*, April 26, 1864.

66. *New York Times*, April 23, 1864; see also *Jacksonville Peninsula*, April 21, 1864; Hatch to Turner, April 16, 1864, *ORA*, 35, pt. 1:387–88; and Balch to Rowen, April 17, 1864, *ORN*, 15:314.

67. Barlow, *Company G*, 166.

68. "Yesterday, Family Legends," L. O. Dunham Papers, Clay County Archives.

69. Ibid.

70. Anderson to Bryan, Camp Milton, May 11, 1864, Records of Confederate Military Organizations, Records of Armies and Geographical Commands (Confederate), Department of South Carolina, Georgia, and Florida, 1861–65, RG 109, NARA.

71. Anonymous, undated typescript, JHS. See also Mayer to Shaw, June 7, 1864, *ORA*, 35, pt. 2:116.

72. Mickler to wife, May 2, 1864, Mickler Letters, PKY.

73. Balch to Tilghman, May 4, 1864, *ORN*, 15:423. See also the *New York Daily Tribune*, May 18, 1864.

74. Hawks, *A Woman Doctor's Civil War*, 72.

75. Ibid.

76. *Philadelphia Inquirer*, May 4, 1864.

77. Hatch to Townsend, May 12, 1864, *ORA*, 35, pt. 1:392; Balch to Dahlgren, May 10, 1864, *ORN*, 15:426; *Philadelphia Inquirer*, May 18, 1864.

78. Orloff M. Dorman, "Memoranda of Events," May 22, 1864, LC.

79. *New York Times*, June 3, 1864.

80. Wells to West, May 24, 1864, M 1091, Subject File of the CSA Navy, 1861–1865, Roll no. 11, Records of the Confederate Navy Department, RG 109, Navy Department, NARA. Three more torpedoes were found at the St. Johns River and Cedar Creek.

For a sketch of one of the torpedoes and a description of the firing apparatus, see *ORN*, 15:426–28, 436–38.

81. Raab, *James Patton Anderson*, 70.

82. Dahlgren to Mitchell, May 29, 1864, *ORN*, 15:463–64.

83. Logbook, *Ottawa*, November 3, 1863–October 12, 1864, Entry July 5, 1864, Logs of Ships and Stations, RG 45, NARA.

84. Birney to Burger, Jacksonville, July 20, 1864, *ORA*, 35, pt. 1:410.

85. Foster to Meigs, August 8, 1864, ibid., 35, pt. 2:225; Birney to Burger, July 7 and 12, ibid., 171–72. See also Burger to Birney, July 16, 1864, ibid., 176–77, and Testimony Regarding the Torpedoed Ship *Alice Price*, Records of the Quartermaster General, Entry 1406, RG 393, NARA.

86. Lee to Ewell, July 11, 1864, *ORA*, 40, pt. 2:764. Bryan died in Charleston of yellow fever in the summer of 1864.

CHAPTER 11. *The Struggle for Allegiance of Florida Residents*

1. Anderson to Feilden, May 19, 1864, Beauregard to Anderson, April 14, 1864, Barth to Finegan, April 18, 1864, and Anderson to Cooper, May 17, 1864, *ORA*, 35, pt. 2:491–93, 427, 441–42, 488.

2. Anderson to Feilden, May 19, 1864, ibid., 491–93.

3. Jackson to Cooper, August 12, 1864, ibid., 606–8.

4. Jackson to Stringfellow, August 22, 1864, ibid., 35, pt. 1:436.

5. *Jacksonville Peninsula*, April 7, 1864; *New York Times*, April 13, 1864.

6. Breese to Balch, February 23, 1864, *ORN*, 15:286.

7. Hoeg and Robinson to Hatch, September 16, 1864, and Hatch to Hoeg and Robinson, September 17, 1864, Records of Provost Marshal Field Organizations (Civil War), Part 2, Entry 1314, RG 393, NARA. The men resided at today's Empire Point.

8. Reid, *Ohio in the War*, 2:436–38; see also Ladley, *Hearth and Knapsack*, 169–74.

9. Barlow, *Company G*, 167–73.

10. Swettland to Captain Scott, May 11, 1864, Marple to Scammen, August 28, 1864, and Birney to Sweatland [*sic*], June 9, 1864, all in Records of Districts, District of Florida, Part 2, Entry 1312, RG 393, NARA.

11. Gordon, *War Diary*, 293–303.

12. Barth, General Orders, May 24, 1864, Jones to Cooper, May 27, 1864, and Gordon to Burger, May 27, 1864, *ORA*, 35, pt. 1:393–98. For raids at Welaka, see Silliman, *New Canaan Private*, 68–74.

13. Gordon to Burger, May 27, 1864, *ORA*, 35, pt. 1:393–98.

14. McKee, *Back "in War Times,"* 158–62.

15. Gordon to Burger, May 27, 1864, *ORN*, 15:441–44.

16. Ibid.

17. Dickison to Barth, May 24, 1864, *ORA*, 35, pt. 1:397.

18. Gordon to Hatch, May 26, 1864, ibid., 399.

19. Noble to Scott, June 2, 1864, Records of Districts, District of Florida, Part 2, CN 63, Letters Received, 1864–1866, RG 393, NARA.

20. Gordon to Burger, June 4, 1864, *ORA*, 35, pt. 1:401–3.

21. Noble to Scott, June 2, 1864, Records of Districts, District of Florida, Part 2, CN 63, Letters Received, 1864–1866, RG 393, NARA.

22. Gordon to Burger, June 4, 1864, *ORA*, 35, pt. 1:401–3.

23. Noble to Scott, June 2, 1864, Records of Districts, District of Florida, Part 2, CN 63, Letters Received, 1864–1866, RG 393, NARA.

24. Anderson to Jones, June 3, 1864, *ORA*, 35, pt. 1:403.

25. Bailey to Burger, July 7, 12, 1864, ibid., 35, pt. 2:193–94.

26. Birney to Burger, July 20, 1864, ibid., 35, pt. 1:410.

27. Ibid.

28. McCormick to Barth, August 3, 1864, ibid., 411–13.

29. Ibid.

30. Bailey to Shaw, July 22, 1864, Bailey to Commanding Officer, Picolata, Florida, July 22, 1864, and Shaw to Bailey, ibid., 35, pt. 2:182–84.

31. Charles A. Currier, "Recollections of Service," MHI.

32. Birney to Burger, Report of Brig. Gen. William Birney, July 27, 1864, *ORA*, 35, pt. 1:419–21.

33. Ibid.

34. Ibid.

35. McCormick to Barth, August 15, 1864, ibid., 421–23.

36. Birney to Burger, Report of Brig. Gen. William Birney, July 27, 1864, ibid., 419–21.

37. Ibid.

38. Currier, "Recollections of Service," MHI.

39. Confederate Pension Record: George Washington Bardin, FSA.

40. Confederate Pension Record: Henry S. Bardin, FSA.

41. Claim of Martha Hendricks, Settled Case Files for Claims Approved by the Southern Claims Commission, RG 217, NARA-CP.

42. Hatch to Foster, August 9, 1864, *ORA*, 35, pt. 2:229.

43. Hatch, "Report," August 15, 1864, ibid., 35, pt. 1:426.

44. For Dr. Benedict, see Records Relating to Medical Personnel, RG 94, NARA.

45. Testimony of James U. Smith, Claim of Joseph Brooker, Settled Case Files for Claims Approved by the Southern Claims Commission, RG 217, NARA-CP. For example, see record of John Revels, farmer, employed as a guide for Company B, 4th Massachusetts Cavalry: Case MM1750, Records of the Immediate Office of the Judge Advocate General (Army), Correspondence and Related Records, RG 153, NARA.

46. For details of the two Union raiding columns that departed Magnolia in mid-August 1864 and the results and consequences of those raids, see the following official correspondence in *ORA*, 35, pt. 1:427–35: Hatch to Foster, August 19, 22, September 6, 1864, Hatch to Burger, August 23, 1864, Noble to Hatch, September 4, 1864, Noble to Burger, September 23, 1864, and Harris to Burger, September 23, 1864. For Confederate accounts of the raids and of Captain Dickison's victory at Gainesville see ibid., 436–40: Jackson to Stringfellow, August 22, 1864, McCormick to Headquarters, August 25, 1864, Dickison to Barth, August 17, 1864, and Moreno, General Orders no. 41, August 26, 1864.

47. General Hatch's severe rebuke of Colonel Harris is in Hatch to Harris, September 27, 1864, ibid., 35, pt. 2:303, and his order calling for the "immediate trial and execution" of "bad soldiers" found guilty of pillaging is in Hatch to Noble, September 27, 1864, ibid., 304.

48. Hatch to Foster, September 22, 1864, and Anderson to Birney, June 6, 1864, ibid., 301, 113–14.

49. Burger to Hatch, October 31, 1864, ibid., 319.

50. Redkey, *A Grand Army of Black Men*, 43–46.

51. Westervelt, *Diary of a Yankee Engineer*, 115–16.

52. Redkey, *A Grand Army of Black Men*, 48–52.

53. Dickison to Barnes, October 31, 1864, *ORA*, 35, pt. 1:446–47.

54. Foster to Hatch, October 31, 1864, ibid., 35, pt. 2:319–20.

55. Hatch to Foster, November 1, 1864, ibid., 322.

56. Foster to Hatch, November 5, 1864, ibid., 324–25; for the order relieving Hatch of his Florida command see Burger, General Orders, no. 152, November 5, 1864, ibid., 323–24. Foster appointed Brigadier General E. P. Scammon to replace Hatch as commander of the District of Florida.

57. Burger to Scammon, January 29, 1865, and Robinson to Foster, February 11, 1865, ibid., 47, pt. 2:165, 392; *Florida Union*, March 11, 1865.

58. Greely to Whipple, March 18, 1864, in Richardson, "'We Are Truly Doing Missionary Work,'" 181–82.

59. Dorman, "Memoranda of Events," March 7, 1865, LC. See also Dorman's entries for April 3 and 6, 1865.

60. *Florida Union*, March 18 and April 1, 1865.

61. Dorman, "Memoranda of Events," January 16, 1865, LC.

62. *Florida Union*, March 18 and April 1, 1865.

63. Ibid., April 18, 1865.

64. Ibid., April 8, 1865.

65. Vogdes to Burger, April 26, 1865, *ORA*, 47, pt. 3:318.

66. *Florida Union*, May 6, 1865; see also the *New York Times*, May 13, 1865.

67. *Florida Union*, June 3, 1865; *New York Times*, May 13, 1865.

CHAPTER 12. *"The Storm Has Ceased": Life for Jacksonville's White Residents during the Federal Occupation*

1. *New York Tribune*, February 20, 1864.

2. Dennett, *Lincoln and the Civil War*, 159–60.

3. *New York Times*, February 20, 1864.

4. Dennett, *Lincoln and the Civil War*, 160–61.

5. Ibid., 161–62.

6. Ibid., 164–66; Dennett, *Lincoln and the Civil War*, 43–44.

7. Stickney to Chase, February 16, 24, 1864, Chase Papers, LC.

8. Ibid.

9. *New York Tribune*, June 3, 1864; *New York Times*, June 4, 1864.

10. *New York Times,* June 1, 9, 1864; G. W. Smith, "Carpetbag Imperialism," 292–94; Mann, "Fernandina," 42–57.

11. Dennett, *Lincoln and the Civil War,* 159.

12. *New York Times,* February 23, 1864; *New York Tribune,* February 20, 1864.

13. Brown, Diary, March 5, 6, 8, 28, 1864, JPL.

14. *New York Tribune,* February 20, 1864; Records of Districts Provost Marshal Field Organizations, District of Florida, General Gillmore, February 15, 1864, Part 4, Entry 1614, vol. 53, RG 393, NARA.

15. *New York Tribune,* February 20, 1864; see also Birney to Burger, May 6, 1864, *ORA,* 35, pt. 1:388–89; *Jacksonville Peninsula,* April 7, 1864.

16. *Jacksonville Peninsula,* April 7, 1864; Hatch to Foster, August 9, 1864, *ORA,* 35, pt. 2:54, 114, 194, 229.

17. Gordon to Colonel Wiliam H. Noble, May 17, 1864, *ORA,* 35, pt. 2:94–95.

18. Hatch to Foster, August 9, 1864, ibid., 229–30.

19. *New York Herald,* March 30, 1865.

20. Orders of the Provost Marshal, April 28, May 1, 3, 12, 15, 21, 27, July 9, November 22, 1864, Records of the Provost Marshal Field Organizations, District of Florida, Jacksonville, RG 393, NARA.

21. Dorman, "Memoranda of Events," February 8, 18, April 21, May 20, 22, June 27, September 18, 1864, LC.

22. Orders of the Provost Marshal, March 22, 1864, Records of the Provost Marshal Field Organizations, District of Florida, Jacksonville, RG 393, NARA.

23. Orders of the Provost Marshal, May 20, 1864, ibid.

24. Hart correspondence, June 8, 1865, ibid.

25. Brown, Diary, JPL.

26. See the correspondence related to the Broward family, June–August 1865, in Records of the Provost Marshal Field Organizations, District of Florida, Jacksonville, RG 393, NARA.

27. Dennett, *Lincoln and the Civil War,* 163–64.

28. See March–November 1864, Records of the Provost Marshal Field Organizations, District of Florida, Jacksonville, RG 393, NARA.

29. Ibid.

30. *Jacksonville Peninsula,* April 21, 1864.

31. See March–November 1864, Records of the Provost Marshal Field Organizations, District of Florida, Jacksonville, RG 393, NARA.

32. Orders, May 20, June 21, August, December 15, 1864, ibid.

33. Orders, July 27–28, 1865, ibid.

34. Special Census of Jacksonville, conducted by the Provost Marshal, 1864, 1865, ibid.

35. Guard House records, ibid.

36. Robinson, "An Account."

37. For Zephaniah Kingsley and his African wife, see Schafer, *Anna Madgigine Jai Kingsley.*

38. Claim nos. 16,153 and 21,901, M67, Roll 13, Settled Case Files for Claims Ap-

proved by the Southern Claims Commission, RG 217, NARA-CP. See also the claim by Thomas Ells, no. 15,718.

39. Phena Hudnall Files, April 25, 1864, June 24, 1865, Records of the Provost Marshal Field Organizations, Jacksonville, Florida, RG 393, NARA; Phena Hudnall Love interview, March 20, 24, 1936, WPA.

40. Journal of the Direct Tax Commission of Florida, September 15, 1862–April 13, 1867, Records of the Florida Direct Tax Commission (Boxes 1276, 1278, 1303), RG 58, NARA. See also the *Florida Union*, November 5, 1864, issue no. 12, in Box 1303. Merchandise was also auctioned, including bales of yellow Jessamine Root, animal hides, 1,200 empty bottles, and two rafts of cedar logs.

41. A Register of Confiscation Suits brought in the Northern District of Florida, April 12 and August 6, 1866, RG 206, NARA.

42. Dorman, "Memoranda of Events," February 13, 1864, March 25, 1865, LC.

43. Papers of J. M. and Esther Hawks, II, folio 320, LC [hereafter cited as Hawks Papers].

44. Ibid.

45. Ibid.; see also Hawks, *A Woman Doctor's Civil War*.

46. Barrow to Hawks, March 14, 1864, folios 327–28, Hawks Papers, LC.

47. Anonymous to Hawks, April 15, 1864, and Barrow to Hawks, April 16, 1864, folio 339, ibid.

48. Undated letter, folio 261, ibid.; see also folios 348, 351, and 352, ibid.

49. Provost Marshal certificate, November 27, 1864, folio 441, ibid.; Pope to Leonard, folio 337, ibid.; Shofner, *Nor Is It Over Yet*, 72–73. After the war ended, Dr. Hawks and her husband, Dr. John Milton Hawks, founded a colony for freedmen at Port Orange, Florida.

50. *Florida Union*, March 11, September 4, October 7, 1865; *Jacksonville Herald*, October 13, 1865; *New York Times*, December 27, 1865. Censuses of Jacksonville conducted in 1864 and 1865 and information on teachers' salaries are in Records of Provost Marshal Field Organizations (Civil War), District of Florida, Letters Received 1864–1866, RG 393, NARA. See also Richardson, "'We Are Truly Doing Missionary Work,'" 184–86.

51. *Florida Union*, June 3, 1865.

52. Applegate to McHenry, July 21 and 23, 1865, Provost Marshal's Office, Records of Provost Marshal Field Organizations (Civil War), Letters Received, RG 393, NARA.

53. *Florida Union*, May 27, June 17, July 5, 22, August 19, September 4, 9, 1865; *New York Times*, June 16, 24, 1865. See also Dorman, "Memoranda of Events," May–July 1865, LC.

54. The arrest was mentioned in Dorman, "Memoranda of Events," May 12–18, 1865, LC. The quoted material is from Proctor, *Florida*, May 20, 1865, as is the mention of Vogdes.

55. *Florida Union*, July 22, August 5, 19, 26, November 4, 1865; see also *Jacksonville Herald*, August 31, 1865.

56. Martin, *The City Makers*, 74–75; Shofner, *Nor Is It Over Yet*, 21–22; *New York Times*, October 1, 1865.

57. Dorman, "Memoranda of Events," June 27, 1865, LC.

58. Ibid., July 19, 1865.

59. *Jacksonville Herald*, August 31, September 22, October 13, 31, 1865.

60. *Florida Union*, November 4, 11, 18, 1865.

61. *Jacksonville Herald*, August 31, 1865; *New York Times*, August 17, 1865.

62. *Jacksonville Herald*, September 22, 1865; *Florida Times*, October 5, 1865.

63. *Florida Union*, September 9, 1865; *New York Times*, August 17, 1865.

64. *Florida Union*, December 16, 1865.

65. *New York Times*, December 25, 1865.

66. Keene, Diaries, 1864 and 1865.

67. Ibid., January 15, 1865.

CHAPTER 13. *A Troubled Transition to Freedom: Life for Jacksonville's Black Residents during the Federal Occupation*

1. *Florida News*, August 12, 1848. On the antebellum racial fears of whites, see chapter 1, Blakey, *Parade of Memories*. Historian Arch F. Blakey states that although prewar race hostility existed, there was "little, if any, hatred. This changed throughout Florida during 1865 and 1866 since many Union soldiers stationed in the State were black," 97.

2. *Florida Union*, May 27, 1865.

3. *New York Times*, June 16, 1865.

4. Ibid., July 22, 1865; for similar reports see August 1, 1865.

5. *Jacksonville Herald*, August 31, 1865.

6. *New York Times*, August 1, 1865.

7. Mickler to McCaughan, May 24, 1865, Records of Districts, Letters Received 1864–1866, Volume 17, Part 2, District of Florida, RG 393, NARA.

8. Blast, Inspection Report, July 7, 1865, ibid.

9. Foner, *Reconstruction*, 77–123.

10. Applegate to McHenry, January 31, 1865, Provost Marshal's Office (Jacksonville), Letters Received, Records of Provost Marshal Field Organizations (Civil War), District of Florida, RG 393, NARA.

11. Greely to Jocelyn, February 4, 1865, in Richardson, "'We Are Truly Doing Missionary Work,'" 185.

12. Applegate to McHenry, June 10, 1865, Provost Marshal Records, Letters Received, RG 393, NARA.

13. Applegate to McHenry, July 18, 1865, ibid. He named the engineers of the 75th Ohio and the 4th Massachusetts Cavalry as leading malefactors.

14. Gillmore to Vogdes, April 30, 1865, Records of Districts, Letters Received 1864–1866, Volume 16, Part 2, District of Florida, RG 393, NARA.

15. Marple to McHenry, May 26, 1865, ibid.

16. *Tribune* quoted in Proctor, *Florida*, June 12, 1865.

17. Vogdes to Howard, July 31, 1865, Records of Districts, Letters Received 1864–1866, Volume 16, Part 2, District of Florida, RG 393, NARA.

18. See McFeely, *Yankee Stepfather*, 150–65.

19. Richardson, *The Negro in the Reconstruction of Florida*, 53–70; see also Shofner, *Nor Is It Over Yet*.

20. Trefousse, *Andrew Johnson*, chs. 12 and 13.

21. Shofner, *Nor Is It Over Yet*, 27–29, 65. Shofner argues that the imposition of a temporary labor system imposed in Florida evolved into "the free labor system which, with its tenancy, sharecropping, crop liens, ruinous credit arrangements, and one-crop concentration, plagued the agricultural areas of Florida for decades." For reactions of white southerners to emancipation, see Carter, *When the War Was Over*, and Litwack, *Been in the Storm So Long*.

22. *Florida Union*, December 6, 1865.

23. Manucy to "Authorities of Jacksonville," Mose Dell, Florida, February 18, 1865, Provost Marshal's Office (Jacksonville), Letters Received, Records of Provost Marshal Field Organizations (Civil War), RG 393, NARA.

24. Kearney to Marple, October 24, 1865, Records of Districts, Letters Received 1864–1866, Volume 16, Part 2, District of Florida, RG 393, NARA.

25. "Report of General Grant," *New York Times*, December 20, 1865; see also *Florida Union*, December 6, 1865.

26. Jones and others, Resolutions for the Removal of the Company of Colored Troops, Records of Districts, Volume 16, Part 2, District of Florida, Letters Received, RG 393, NARA.

27. Montgomery to Samms, Florida, December 1, 1865, ibid.

28. Ibid.

29. Glatthaar, *Forged in Battle*; see also Bentley, *History of the Freedmen's Bureau*, and McFeely, *Yankee Stepfather*.

30. *Florida Times*, October 5, 1865; see also "Important Document: Report of the Special Committee on Reconstruction," *Macon Journal and Messenger*, January 10, 1866. For South-wide resentment of armed black soldiers in Union occupation forces, particularly General Grant's views that such troops inflamed passion and instigated violence, see "Report of General Grant," *New York Times*, December 20, 1865.

31. Glatthaar, *Forged in Battle*, 114.

32. Brown, Diary, JPL, documents several instances of thumb-tying soldiers in the 3rd U.S.C.T. For a list of officers and enlisted men of the U.S.C.T. regiments, see the Web site "Civil War Soldiers and Sailors System" (www.itd.nps.gov). This discussion of the mutiny is based on the careful research of Jacksonville attorney and historian John F. Fannin. Fannin's master's thesis, "The Jacksonville Mutiny of 1865," drew on extensive research in Records of the Office of the Judge Advocate General (Army) in the National Archives, Washington, D.C. See, for example: Testimony of Capt. William H. Walrath, Private Samuel Harley, Transcript of general court-martial 001477, Court-Martial Case Files and Related Records, RG 153. For analysis by another legal scholar, see Bennett, "The Jacksonville Mutiny."

33. Bennett, "The Jacksonville Mutiny," 157–72. Although the war had ended five months earlier, Florida was still officially in a state of rebellion, thus the charge carried the possible death sentence.

34. *Florida Union*, December 3, 1863. The *Florida Union* correspondent viewed the executions during an excursion on the *St. Marys* hosted by the army, featuring

horseback riding, sightseeing, lodging, and a party atmosphere. The executed men were James Allen, 25; David Craig, 23; Joseph Green, 19; Thomas Howard, 21; Joseph Nathaniel, age unknown; and Jacob Plowden, 46. Ages are found in Descriptive Book, 3rd USCT Infantry, Regimental Records, RG 94, NARA.

35. *New York Times*, December 25, 1865.

36. Schafer, "Freedom Was as Close," and Kenney, "LaVilla, Florida, 1866–1877."

37. Hanson, file no. 362,152, Civil War Pension Files, USCT, RG 15, NARA; Dorman, "Memoranda of Events," May 3, 1866, LC.

38. Hanson pension file. See also Archibald Records, May 3, 1901, Duval County Courthouse; and Dorman, "Memoranda of Events," August 16, 1866, LC.

39. *Jacksonville Herald*, August 31, 1865. For the job diversity documented in Union pension records, see "Black Floridians and the Civil War: The 21st, 33rd, and 34th United States Colored Infantry Regiments" (http://www.unf.edu/floridahistory online/CIR/index.htm).

40. *Jacksonville Herald*, August 31, 1865.

41. Shofner, *Nor Is It Over Yet*, 32, 37–39; Keene, Diaries, 1864 and 1865.

42. For clear and succinct background, see Benedict, *A Compromise of Principle*.

43. Ibid.

44. Martin, *The City Makers*, 83.

45. Shofner, *Nor Is It Over Yet*, 46–58. See also Blakey, *Parade of Memories*, 91–94, and Tebeau, *A History of Florida*, ch. 16.

Bibliography

Manuscript Collections

Clay County Archives, Green Cove Springs, Florida
  Dunham, L. O. Papers.
Duke University Library, Durham, North Carolina
  Reed, A. M. Diary, 1848–99. Typescript copy.
Duval County Courthouse, Jacksonville, Florida
  Archibald Transcription of Duval County Deed Records.
  Records of the Court of Probate.
Florida Historical Society Library, Cocoa
  Keene, Otis Little. Judson House Register, 1855–62.
  Palmer, David L., Darius Ferris, and Thomas O. Holmes. Papers.
Florida State Archives, Tallahassee
  Confederate Pension Records.
  Ives, Washington M. Journal, 1860–62.
  Record Group 101: Territorial and State Governor's Letterbooks.
    Milton, John. 1861–65.
  Schmidt, Lewis G. Collection.
Florida State University Libraries, Special Collections, Tallahassee
  Fairbanks Collection.
Historical Museum of Southern Florida, Miami
  Apthorp Family Papers.
Jacksonville Historical Society, Jacksonville, Florida
  Anderson, Bessie S. "Retrospective Experiences."
  Greeley, Mellen C. "Musings of Mellen Clark Greeley, Written in His Anec-Dotage,
    1880–1963." Transcribed and edited by Cynthia Lacy Parks, 1963.
  Robinson, Calvin L. "An Account of Some of My Experiences in Florida during the
    Rise and Progress of the Rebellion." Typescript.
Jacksonville Public Library, Jacksonville, Florida, Florida Room
  Brown, Cyrus W. Diary.
Library of Congress, Manuscripts Division, Washington, D.C.
  Chase, Salmon P. Papers, 1755–1874.
  Dorman, Orloff M. "Memoranda of Events That Transpired at Jacksonville, Flor-
    ida, and in Its Vicinity, with Remarks and Comments Thereon." 5 vols. (vol. 1
    missing).

Foster, Major General John G. Letter Books.

Hawks, John Milton, and Esther Hill Hawks. Papers.

Works Progress Administration Federal Writers' Project Collection.

National Archives, College Park, Maryland

Record Group 77: Records of the Office of the Chief of Engineers.

Record Group 217: Records of the Accounting Officers of the Department of the Treasury.

National Archives, Washington, D.C.

Record Group 15: Records of the Department of Veterans Affairs.

Record Group 24: Records of the Bureau of Naval Personnel.

Record Group 45: Naval Records Collection of the Office of Naval Records and Library.

Record Group 58: Records of the Internal Revenue Service.

Record Group 94: Records of the Adjutant General's Office.

Record Group 109: War Department Collection of Confederate Records.

Record Group 123: Records of the United States Court of Claims.

Record Group 153: Records of the Office of the Judge Advocate General (Army).

Record Group 206: Records of the Solicitor of the Treasury.

Record Group 233: Records of the United States House of Representatives.

Record Group 393: Records of the U.S. Army Continental Commands, 1821–1920.

P. K. Yonge Library of Florida History, University of Florida, Gainesville

Keene, Otis Little. Diaries of Otis Keene, 1863–1910.

L'Engle, William Johnson. Papers.

Mickler, Jacob E. Papers, 1860–66.

Robinson, Calvin L. "Manuscript of His Residence in Jacksonville during the Civil War." Typescript.

Sanchez, Edward C. Papers, 1829–79.

Steedman, Charles. Letters, 1862–64.

Stephens-Bryant Family Papers.

Richard Ferrie Private Collection, MacClenny, Florida

McArthur, William M. Journal. Typescript copy.

Robert W. Woodruff Library, Emory University, Atlanta

Tuttle, Edwin. Papers.

South Carolina Historical Society, Charleston

Trowbridge, Charles T. Reminiscences.

South Caroliniana Library, University of South Carolina, Columbia

Hunter, David. General Order 17, March 6, 1863. Printed copy.

Saxton, Rufus. Papers, 1824–1908

Southern Historical Collection, University of North Carolina, Chapel Hill

L'Engle, Edward M. Papers, 1834–97.

Penniman, William Frederick. Reminiscences, 1901.

State Library of Florida, Tallahassee

Adams, Richard Joseph. Pocket Diary, 1862.

St. Augustine Historical Society Library, St. Augustine, Florida
Boye, Christian. Letters. Biographical File.
United States Army Military History Institute, Carlisle, Pennsylvania
Currier, Charles A. Papers.
Rogers, Seth. "War-Time Letters from Seth Rogers, M.D., Surgeon of the First
South Carolina Afterwards the Thirty-Third USCT, 1862–1863." Typescript.
University of North Florida, Thomas G. Carpenter Library, Special Collections, Manuscripts and Personal Papers, Jacksonville
Jones, William M. Papers.
White, Eartha M. M. Collection.
West Virginia University Library, Morgantown, West Virginia
Appleton, John W. M. Papers, 1861–1913.

Government Documents

Acts and Resolutions of the General Assembly of the State of Florida, 1850–1865. Tallahassee, Florida, 1850–65.

Cadwell, Charles K. *The Old Sixth Regiment: Its War Records, 1861–1865.* New Haven, Connecticut, 1875.

Journal of the Proceedings of the Convention of the People of Florida, Begun and Held at the Capitol, in the City of Tallahassee. Tallahassee, 1861.

Journal of the Proceedings of the Convention of the People of the State of Florida, Called Session. Tallahassee, 1861.

Journal of the Proceedings of the General Assembly of the State of Florida at the Twelfth Session. Tallahassee, 1862.

Journal of the Proceedings of the House and Senate, 10th Session. Tallahassee, 1860.

Official Records of the Union and Confederate Navies in the War of Rebellion. 30 vols. Washington, D.C.: Government Printing Office, 1894–1922.

Original Returns of the Seventh Census. Washington, D.C.: Government Printing Office, 1854.

Original Returns of the Eighth Census. Washington, D.C.: Government Printing Office, 1864.

Stickney, L. D. "Florida Soil, Climate and Productions." *Report of the Commissioner of Agriculture for the Year 1862.* Washington, D.C.: Government Printing Office, 1862.

———. "Tropical Florida." *Report of the Commissioner of Patents for the Year 1861.* Washington, D.C.: Government Printing Office, 1862.

U.S. House of Representatives. "An Act for the Collection of Direct Taxes in Insurrectionary Districts in the United States, and for Other Purposes." Executive Document No. 18, 38th Congress, 2nd Session, 126.

War of the Rebellion: A Compilation of the Official Records of the Union and Confederate Armies. 70 vols. in 128 parts. Washington, D.C.: Government Printing Office, 1880–1901.

Newspapers

Boston Herald, 1864

Cotton States, Gainesville, 1863

Danbury Times, Danbury, Connecticut, April 28, 1864

East Floridian, Fernandina, 1860

Fernandina Peninsula, 1863–64

Florida News, Jacksonville, 1846, 1848–50, 1852, 1854–58

Florida Republican, Jacksonville, 1846–57

Florida Sentinel, Tallahassee, 1852

Florida Times, Jacksonville, 1865

Florida Times-Union, Jacksonville, 1908, 1910

Florida Times-Union and Citizen, Jacksonville, 1898

Florida Union, Jacksonville, 1864–65

The Floridian and Journal, Tallahassee, 1864

Georgia Journal and Messenger, Savannah, 1864

Jacksonville Courier, 1835

Jacksonville Herald, 1865

Jacksonville Metropolitan, 1908, 1910

Jacksonville News, 1846, 1848, 1852

Jacksonville Peninsula, 1864

Jacksonville Semi-Weekly Republican, 1856

Jacksonville Standard, 1859–60

Macon Journal and Messenger, 1866

Metropolis, Jacksonville, 1908, 1910

Minneapolis Journal, 1907

New York Daily Tribune, 1862–64

New York Evening Post, 1863

New York Herald, 1862–64

New York Times, 1861–65

New York Tribune, 1848, 1862–64

New York World, 1864

Philadelphia Inquirer, 1864

Sentinel, Tallahassee, 1866

Southern Confederacy, Jacksonville, 1861

Southern Rights, Jacksonville, 1862

St. Augustine Examiner, 1861–62

St. John's Mirror, St. Augustine, 1861

Tri-Weekly Sun, Jacksonville, 1876

Primary and Secondary Sources

Ash, Stephen V. *Firebrand of Liberty: The Story of Two Black Regiments That Changed the Course of the Civil War*. New York and London: Norton, 2008.

———. *When the Yankees Came: Conflict and Chaos in the Occupied South, 1861–1865*. Chapel Hill: University of North Carolina Press, 1995.

Barlow, R. A. *Company. G: A Record of the Services of One Company of the 157th New York Volunteers in the War of Rebellion, from September 19, 1862 to July 10, 1865.* Syracuse, N.Y.: A. W. Hall, 1899.

Bates, Thelma. "The Legal Status of the Negro in Florida." *Florida Historical Quarterly* 6, no. 3 (1928): 159–81.

Bavier, Robert N., Jr. *The Schooner Yacht America.* New York: Schaefer Brewing, 1967.

Bearss, Edwin C. "Military Operations on the St. Johns, September–October 1862 (Part 1): The Union Navy Fails to Drive the Confederates from St. Johns Bluff." *Florida Historical Quarterly* 42, no. 3 (1964): 233–48.

———. "Military Operations on the St. Johns, September–October 1862 (Part 2): The Federals Capture St. Johns Bluff." *Florida Historical Quarterly* 42, no. 4 (1964): 332–51.

Benedict, Michael Les. *A Compromise of Principle: Congressional Republicans and Reconstruction, 1863–1869.* New York: Norton, 1974.

Bennett, Captain B. Kevin. "The Jacksonville Mutiny." *Military Law Review* 134 (1990): 157–72.

———. "The Jacksonville Mutiny." *Civil War History* 35, no. 1 (1992): 39–50.

Bentley, George R. *A History of the Freedmen's Bureau.* Philadelphia: University of Pennsylvania Press, 1955.

Berlin, Ira. *Slaves without Masters: The Free Negro in the Antebellum South.* New York: Viking Press, 1976.

Berlin, Ira, Barbara J. Fields, Steven F. Miller, Joseph P. Reidy, and Leslie S. Rowland, eds. *Free at Last: A Documentary History of Slavery, Freedom, and the Civil War.* New York: New Press, 1992.

Berlin, Ira, Joseph P. Reidy, and Leslie S. Rowland, eds. *Freedom's Soldiers: the Black Military Experience in the Civil War.* Cambridge, U.K.: Cambridge University Press, 1998.

Berry, Mary Frances. *Military Necessity and Civil Rights Policy: Black Citizenship and the Constitution, 1861–1868.* Port Washington, N.Y.: Kennikat Press, 1977.

Bittle, George C. "Florida Prepares for War, 1860–1861." *Florida Historical Quarterly* 51, no. 2 (1972): 144–53.

Blakey, Arch Fredric. *Parade of Memories: A History of Clay County.* With an update by Bonita T. Deaton. Jacksonville: Drummond Press, 1995.

Blakey, Arch Fredric, Ann Smith Lainhart, and Winston Bryant Stephens Jr., eds. *Rose Cottage Chronicles: Civil War Letters of the Bryant-Stephens Families of North Florida.* Gainesville: University Press of Florida, 1998.

Boatner, Mark Mayo, III. *The Civil War Dictionary.* New York: David McKay, 1959.

Bornet, Vaughn D. "A Connecticut Yankee Fights at Olustee: Letters from the East." *Florida Historical Quarterly* 27, no. 3 (1949): 237–59.

Boswell, Charles. *The America: The Story of the World's Most Famous Yacht.* New York: David McKay, 1967.

Boyd, Mark E. "The Federal Campaign of 1864 in East Florida." *Florida Historical Quarterly* 29, no. 1 (1950): 4–38.

———. "The Joint Operations of the Federal Army and Navy near St. Marks." *Florida Historical Quarterly* 39, no. 2 (1950): 96–124.

Brown, Canter, Jr. "The Florida, Atlantic and Gulf Central Railroad, 1851–1868." *Florida Historical Quarterly* 69, no. 4 (1991): 412–30.

———. *Ossian Bingley Hart: Florida's Loyalist Reconstruction Governor*. Baton Rouge: Louisiana State University Press, 1997.

Browning, Robert M., Jr. *Success Is All That Was Expected: The South Atlantic Blockading Squadron during the Civil War*. Washington, D.C.: Potomac Books, 2002.

Buker, George E. *Blockaders, Refugees, and Contrabands: Civil War on Florida's Gulf Coast, 1861–1865*. Tuscaloosa: University of Alabama Press, 1993.

———. *Jacksonville: Riverport-Seaport*. Columbia: University of South Carolina Press, 1992.

Carter, Dan T. *When the War Was Over: The Failure of Self-Reconstruction in the South, 1865–1867*. Baton Rouge: Louisiana State University Press, 1985.

Clancy, Anne Robinson, ed. *A Yankee in a Confederate Town: The Journal of Calvin L. Robinson*. Sarasota: Pineapple Press, 2002.

Colburn, David R., and Jane L. Landers, eds. *The African American Heritage of Florida*. Gainesville: University Press of Florida, 1995.

Coles, David James. "Far from the Fields of Glory: Military Operations in Florida during the Civil War, 1864–1865." Unpublished doctoral diss., Florida State University, 1996.

Cooley, Florence Murphy. "A Florida Story of War Times." *Confederate Veteran*, September 1916, 397–98.

Cornish, Dudley Taylor. *Sable Arm: Negro Troops in the Union Army*. New York: Norton, 1966.

———. "The Union Army as a School for Negroes." *Journal of Negro History* 37, no. 4 (1952): 368–82.

Cox, LaWanda. *Lincoln and Black Freedom: A Study in Presidential Leadership*. Columbia: University of South Carolina Press, 1981.

Craig, James C. "Steamboating Days." *Papers, Jacksonville Historical Society*, 3:138–45. Jacksonville: Jacksonville Historical Society, 1954.

Cushman, John D. *A Goodly Heritage: The Episcopal Church in Florida*. Gainesville: University of Florida Press, 1965.

Dancy, James M. "Reminiscences of the Civil War." *Florida Historical Quarterly* 37, no. 1 (1958): 81–90.

Davis, T. Frederick. "Engagements at St. Johns Bluff, St. Johns River, September-October, 1862." *Florida Historical Quarterly* 15, no. 2 (1936): 78–85.

———. *History of Jacksonville, Florida, and Vicinity, 1513 to 1924*. St. Augustine: Florida Historical Society, 1925.

———. "Letter of Captain V. Chamberlain, 7th Connecticut Volunteers." *Florida Historical Quarterly* 15, no. 2 (1936): 86–96.

Davis, William Watson. *The Civil War and Reconstruction in Florida*. 1913. Gainesville: University of Florida Press, 1964.

Deaton, Bonita. "Magnolia, Florida: Unionism in a Southern Community." Unpublished paper, Department of History, University of North Florida, 1995.

Dennett, Tyler, ed. *Lincoln and the Civil War in the Diaries and Letters of John Hay*. New York: Dodd, Mead, 1939.

Dickison, John J. "Military History of Florida." In *Confederate Military History*, ed. Clement Anselm Evans, vol. II, pt. 2:1–198. Atlanta: Confederate Publishing Company, 1898.

Dickison, Mary Elizabeth. *Dickison and His Men: Reminiscences of the War in Florida.* Gainesville: University of Florida Press, 1962.

Dodd, Dorothy. "The Secession Movement in Florida, Part I." *Florida Historical Quarterly* 12, no. 1 (1933): 4–25.

———. "The Secession Movement in Florida, Part II." *Florida Historical Quarterly* 12, no. 2 (1933): 46–67.

Doherty, Herbert J., Jr. "Florida and the Crisis of 1850." *Journal of Southern History* 19, no. 1 (1953): 32–47.

———. "Union Nationalism in Florida." *Florida Historical Quarterly* 24, no. 2 (1950–51): 84–96.

———. *The Whigs of Florida, 1845–1854.* Gainesville: University of Florida Press, 1959.

Donald, David Herbert. *Lincoln.* New York: Simon and Schuster, 1995.

Donald, David Herbert, Jean Harvey Baker, and Michael F. Holt. *The Civil War and Reconstruction.* New York: Norton, 2001.

Duncan, Russell, ed. *Blue-Eyed Child of Fortune: The Civil War Letters of Colonel Robert Gould Shaw.* Athens: University of Georgia Press, 1992.

Durden, Robert F. *The Gray and the Black; The Confederate Debate on Emancipation.* Baton Rouge: Louisiana State University Press, 1972.

Dyer, Frederick H. *A Compendium of the War of the Rebellion.* 3 vols. New York: Thomas Yoseloff, 1959.

Emilio, Luis F. *History of the Fifty-fourth Regiment of Massachusetts Volunteer Infantry, 1863–1865.* Boston: Boston Book, 1891.

Eppes, Susan Bradford. *Through Some Eventful Years.* Macon, Ga.: Burke, 1926.

Esgate, James. *Jacksonville: The Metropolis of Florida.* Boston: W. G. M. Perry, 1885.

Fannin, John F. "The Jacksonville Mutiny of 1865." Unpublished master's thesis, University of North Florida, 2006.

Fehrenbacher, Don E. *The Dred Scott Case: Its Significance in American Law and Politics.* New York: Oxford University Press, 1978.

———. *The South and Three Sectional Crises.* Baton Rouge: Louisiana State University Press, 1980.

Fenlon, Paul. "The Florida, Atlantic and Gulf Central Railroad." *Florida Historical Quarterly* 32, no. 2 (1953): 72–90.

Foner, Eric. *Free Soil, Free Labor, Free Men: The Ideology of the Republican Party before the Civil War.* New York: Oxford University Press, 1970.

———. *Reconstruction: America's Unfinished Revolution, 1863–1877.* New York: Harper and Row, 1988.

———. "The Wilmot Proviso Revisited." *Journal of American History* 56, no. 2 (1969): 262–79.

Freehling, William W. *The Road to Disunion: Secessionists at Bay, 1776–1854.* New York: Oxford University Press, 1990.

Futch, Ovid L. "Salmon P. Chase and Civil War Politics in Florida." *Florida Historical Quarterly* 32, no. 3 (1954): 164–89.

Gallagher, Gary W. *Fighting for the Confederacy: The Personal Recollections of General Edward Porter Alexander.* Chapel Hill: University of North Carolina Press, 1989.

Garvin, Russel. "The Free Negro in Florida before the Civil War." *Florida Historical Quarterly* 46, no. 1 (1967): 9–17.

Glatthaar, Joseph T. *Forged in Battle: the Civil War Alliance of Black Soldiers and White Officers.* New York: Free Press, 1990.

Gold, Pleasant D. *A History of Duval County, Including History of East Florida.* St. Augustine, Fla.: Record Co., 1920.

Gordon, George H. *War Diary of Events of the War of the Great Rebellion, 1863–1865.* Boston: Houghton Mifflin, 1885.

Graham, Thomas S. "Florida Politics and the Tallahassee Press, 1845–1861." *Florida Historical Quarterly* 46, no. 3 (1968): 235–43.

———. "Letters from a Journey through the Federal Blockade, 1861–1862." *Florida Historical Quarterly* 55, no. 4 (1977): 440–57.

Grimsley, Mark. *The Hard Hand of War: Union Military Policy toward Southern Civilians, 1861–1865.* New York: Cambridge University Press, 1995.

Hadd, Donald R. "The Irony of Secession in Florida." *Florida Historical Quarterly* 41, no. 1 (1962): 230–29.

Hargrove, Hondon B. *Black Union Soldiers in the Civil War.* Jefferson, N.C.: McFarland, 1988.

Harris, William C. *With Charity for All: Lincoln and the Restoration of the Union.* Lexington: University Press of Kentucky, 1997.

Hawks, Ester Hill. *A Woman Doctor's Civil War: Esther Hill Hawks' Diary.* Ed. Gerald Schwartz. Columbia: University of South Carolina Press, 1984.

Hayes, John D., ed. *Samuel Francis Du Pont: A Selection from His Civil War Letters.* 3 vols. Ithaca: Cornell University Press, 1969.

Heitman, Francis B. *Historical Register and Dictionary of the United States Army, 1789 to 1903.* Washington, D.C.: Government Printing Office, 1903.

Higginson, Thomas Wentworth. *Army Life in a Black Regiment.* Intro. Howard N. Meyer. New York: Collier, 1962.

———. *The Complete Civil War Journal and Selected Letters of Thomas Wentworth Higginson.* Ed. Christopher Looby. Chicago: University of Chicago Press, 2000.

———. "The First Black Regiment." *Outlook* 59 (1898): 521–31.

———. "The Reoccupation of Jacksonville in 1863." *Civil War Papers Read before the Commandery of the State of Massachusetts, Military Order of the Loyal Legion of the United States,* 2:467–76. Boston: Published by the Commandery, 1900.

———. "Some War Scenes Revisited." *Atlantic Monthly,* July 1878, 1–10.

———. "Up the St. John's River." *Atlantic Monthly,* September 1865, 311–25.

———. "Up the St. Mary's." *Atlantic Monthly,* April 1865, 422–36.

Hodges, Ellen E., and Stephen Kerber, eds. "'Rogues and Black Hearted Scamps': the Civil War Letters of Winston and Octavia Stephens, 1862–1863." *Florida Historical Quarterly* 57, no. 1 (1978): 54–82.

Holland, Dr. Keith, Lee B. Manley, and James W. Towart, eds. *The Maple Leaf: An Extraordinary American Civil War Shipwreck.* Jacksonville: St. Johns Archaeological Expeditions, 1993.

Holt, Michael F. *The Fate of Their Country: Politicians, Slavery Extension, and the Coming of the Civil War*. New York: Hill and Wang, 2004.

———. *The Political Crisis of the 1850s*. New York: Norton, 1983.

———. *The Rise and Fall of the American Whig Party: Jacksonian Politics and the Onset of the Civil War*. New York: Oxford University Press, 1999.

Hooper, Kevin S. *The Early History of Clay County: A Wilderness That Could Be Tamed*. Charleston, S.C.: The History Press, 2006.

Hyde, William L. *History of the One Hundred and Twelfth Regiment N.Y. Volunteers*. Fredonia, N.Y.: McKinistry, 1866.

Jackson, Jesse J. "The Negro and the Law in Florida, 1821–1921." Unpublished M.A. thesis, Florida State University, 1960.

Jennings, Thelma. *The Nashville Convention: The Southern Movement for Unity, 1848–1851*. Memphis: Memphis State University Press, 1980.

Johns, John E. *Florida during the Civil War*. Gainesville: University of Florida Press, 1963.

Jones, Samuel. "The Battle of Olustee, or Ocean Pond, Florida." In *Battles and Leaders of the Civil War*, ed. Robert U. Johnson and Clarence C. Buell, 4:76–80. New York: Yoseloff, 1888.

Jones, William M. "A Report on the Site of Camp Finegan." *Florida Historical Quarterly* 39, no. 4 (1961): 367–74.

Jordan, Ervin L., Jr. *Black Confederates and Afro-Yankees in Civil War Virginia*. Charlottesville: University Press of Virginia, 1995.

Keene, Otis L. "Jacksonville, Fifty-three Years Ago: Reflections of a Veteran." *Florida Historical Quarterly* 1, no. 4 (1909): 9–15.

Kenney, Patricia. "LaVilla, Florida, 1866–1877: Reconstruction Dreams and the Formation of a Black Community." In *The African American Heritage of Florida*, ed. David R. Colburn and Jane L. Landers, 185–206. Gainesville: University Press of Florida, 1995.

Kirk, Clifford C. "A History of the Southern Presbyterian Church in Florida, 1821–1891." Unpublished M.A. thesis, Florida State University, 1966.

Ladley, Oscar Derostus. *Hearth and Knapsack: The Ladley Letters, 1857–1880*. Ed. Carl M. Becker and Ritchie Thomas. Athens: Ohio University Press, 1988.

Landers, Jane. *Black Society in Spanish Florida*. Urbana: University of Illinois Press, 1999.

Litwack, Leon. *Been in the Storm So Long: The Aftermath of Slavery*. New York: Knopf, 1979.

Long, Ellen Call. *Florida Breezes; or, Florida New and Old*. Gainesville: University of Florida Press, 1962.

Macfarlane, C. *Reminiscences of an Army Surgeon, 1861–1865*. Oswego, N.Y.: Lake City Print Shop, 1912.

Mahon, John K. *History of the Second Seminole War, 1835–1842*. Rev. ed. Gainesville: University Presses of Florida, 1991.

Mann, Jesse T. "Fernandina: A City in Turmoil, 1863–1888." Unpublished M.A. thesis, Florida State University, 1971.

Marcus, Edward, ed. *A New Canaan Private in the Civil War: Letters of Justus M. Sil-*

liman, *17th Connecticut Volunteers.* New Canaan, Conn.: New Canaan Historical Society, 1984.

Martin, Richard A. *A Century of Service: St. Luke's Hospital, 1873–1973.* Jacksonville: Privately published, 1973.

———. *The City Makers.* Jacksonville: Convention Press, 1972.

———. "Defeat in Victory: Yankee Experience in Early Civil War Jacksonville." *Florida Historical Quarterly* 53, no. 1 (1974): 2–33.

———. "A History of Jacksonville, to 1865." 2 vols. Unpublished manuscript, circa 1980.

———. "The *New York Times* Views Civil War Jacksonville." *Florida Historical Quarterly* 53, no. 4 (1975): 410–28.

Martin, Richard A., with Daniel L. Schafer. *Jacksonville's Ordeal by Fire: A Civil War History.* Jacksonville: Florida Publishing Company, 1984.

McFeely, William S. *Yankee Stepfather: General O. O. Howard and the Freedmen.* New Haven: Yale University Press, 1968.

McKee, James. *Back "in War Times": History of the 144th New York Volunteer Infantry.* New York: Times Office, 1903.

McPherson, James M. *Battle Cry of Freedom: The Civil War Era.* New York: Ballantine, 1989.

Merritt, Webster. *A Century of Medicine in Jacksonville and Duval County.* Gainesville: University of Florida Press, 1949.

Moore, Glover B. *The Missouri Controversy, 1819–1821.* Lexington: University of Kentucky Press, 1953.

Morrison, Michael A. *Slavery and the American West: The Eclipse of Manifest Destiny and the Coming of the Civil War.* Chapel Hill: University of North Carolina Press, 1997.

Mueller, Edward A. "East Coast Florida Steamboating, 1831–1861." *Florida Historical Quarterly* 40, no. 3 (1962): 241–61.

———. "Now This Is the Way It Really Was." *Jacksonville Seafarer*, May 1973, 16–17.

Nichols, Roy Franklin. "The Kansas-Nebraska Act: A Century of Historiography." *Mississippi Valley Historical Review* 43 (1956): 187–212.

Nicolay, John G., and John Hay. *Abraham Lincoln: A History.* 10 vols. New York: Century, 1890.

Norton, Oliver Wilcox. *Army Letters, 1861–1865.* Chicago: O. L. Deming, privately printed, 1903.

Nulty, William H. *Confederate Florida: The Road to Olustee.* Tuscaloosa: University of Alabama Press, 1990.

Oates, Stephen B. *The Fires of Jubilee: Nat Turner's Fierce Rebellion.* New York: Harper and Row, 1975.

———. *To Purge This Land with Blood: A Biography of John Brown.* New York: Harper and Row, 1970.

Peek, Ralph. "Lawlessness in Florida, 1848–1871." *Florida Historical Quarterly* 40, no. 2 (1961): 165–86.

Potter, David M. *Lincoln and His Party in the Secession Crisis.* New Haven: Yale University Press, 1942.

Pratt, Fletcher. *The Navy, a History: The Story of Service in Action.* Garden City, N.Y.: Garden City Publishing, 1941.

Proctor, Samuel. "The Call to Arms: Secession from a Feminine Point of View." *Florida Historical Quarterly* 35, no. 3 (1957): 266–77.

———, ed. *Florida: A Hundred Years Ago.* Tallahassee: Florida State Library, 1963.

———. "Jacksonville during the Civil War." *Florida Historical Quarterly* 41, no. 4 (1963): 344–56.

———. *Napoleon Bonaparte Broward: Florida's Fighting Democrat.* Gainesville: University of Florida Press, 1950.

Quarles, Benjamin. *The Negro in the North.* Chapel Hill: University of North Carolina Press, 1996.

Raab, James W. *James Patton Anderson, Confederate General: A Biography.* Jefferson, N.C.: McFarland, 2004.

Rains, Gabriel G. J. "Torpedoes." *Southern Historical Society Papers*, vol. 3, nos. 5 and 6 (May and June 1877).

Rawley, James A. *Race and Politics: "Bleeding Kansas" and the Coming of the Civil War.* Philadelphia: Lippinicott, 1969.

Redkey, Edwin S., ed. *A Grand Army of Black Men: Letters from African-American Soldiers in the Union Army, 1861–1865.* Cambridge: Cambridge University Press, 1992.

Reid, Whitelaw. *Ohio in the War: Her Statement, Generals, and Soldiers.* Columbus, Ohio: Eclectic Publishing Company, 1893.

Reiger, John F. "Anti-War and Pro-Union Sentiment in Confederate Florida." Unpublished M.A. thesis, University of Florida, 1966.

———. "Deprivation, Disaffection, and Desertion in Confederate Florida." *Florida Historical Quarterly* 48, no. 3 (1970): 280–99.

———. "Florida after Secesssion: Abandonment by the Confederacy and Its Consequences." *Florida Historical Quarterly* 50, no. 2 (1971): 129–43.

———. "Secession of Florida from the Union-A Minority Decision?" *Florida Historical Quarterly* 46, no. 4 (1968): 359–69.

Remini, Robert V. *Henry Clay: Statesman for the Union.* New York: Norton, 1991.

Rerick, Rowland H. *Memoirs of Florida: Embracing a General History of the Province, Territory and State.* Ed. Francis P. Fleming. 2 vols. Atlanta: Southern Historical Association, 1902.

Revels, Tracy J. "Grander in Her Daughters: Florida's Women during the Civil War." *Florida Historical Quarterly* 77, no. 3 (1993): 261–82.

———. *Grander in Her Daughters: Florida's Women during the Civil War.* Columbia: University of South Carolina Press, 2004.

Richardson, Joe M. *The Negro in the Reconstruction of Florida, 1865–1877.* Tallahassee: Florida State University, 1965.

———. "'We Are Truly Doing Missionary Work': Letters from American Missionary Association Teachers in Florida, 1864–1874." *Florida Historical Quarterly* 54, no. 2 (1975): 179–96.

Rivers, Larry E. *Slavery in Florida: Territorial Days to Emancipation.* Gainesville: University Press of Florida, 2000.

Robertson, Fred L., comp. *Soldiers of Florida in the Seminole Indian, Civil, and Spanish-American Wars*. Live Oak, Fla.: Democrat Book and Job Print Company, 1903.

Rohrabacher, C. A. *Live Towns and Progressive Men*. Jacksonville: Times-Union and Publishing House, 1887.

Rose, Willie Lee. *Rehearsal for Reconstruction: The Port Royal Experiment*. New York: Vintage Books, 1967.

Sandburg, Carl. *Abraham Lincoln: The War Years*. 4 vols. New York: Harcourt, Brace, 1939.

Schafer, Daniel L. *Anna Madgigine Jai Kingsley: African Princess, Florida Slave, Plantation Slaveowner*. Gainesville: University Press of Florida, 2003.

———. "'A Class of People Neither Freemen nor Slaves': From Spanish to American Race Relations in Florida, 1821–1861." *Journal of Social History* 26, no. 3 (1993): 587–609.

———. "Freedom Was as Close as the River: African Americans and the Civil War in Northeast Florida." In *The African American Heritage of Florida*, ed. David R. Colburn and Jane L. Landers, 157–84. Gainesville: University Press of Florida, 1995.

———. "U.S. Territory and State." In *The New History of Florida*, ed. Michael Gannon, 207–30. Gainesville: University Press of Florida, 1996.

Schmidt, Lewis G. *A Civil War History of the 47th Regiment of Pennsylvania Veteran Volunteers: The Wrong Place at the Wrong Time*. Allentown, Penn.: Published by the author, 1986.

———. *The Civil War in Florida: A Military History*. 4 vols. Allentown, Penn.: Published by the author, 1989–92.

Shofner, Jerrell H. *Nor Is It Over Yet: Florida in the Era of Reconstruction 1863–1877*. Gainesville: University of Florida Press, 1974.

Shofner, Jerrell H., and William Warren Rogers. "Confederate Railroad Construction: The Live Oak to Lawton Connection." *Florida Historical Quarterly* 43, no. 3 (1965): 218–29.

Silliman, Justus. *A New Canaan Private in the Civil War: Letters of Justus Silliman, 17th Connecticut Volunteers*. New Canaan, Conn.: New Canaan Historical Society, 1984.

Smith, George Winston. "Carpetbag Imperialism in Florida, 1862–1868." *Florida Historical Quarterly* 27, no. 2 (1948): 99–130; 29, no. 3 (1949): 259–99.

Smith, Jacob. *Camps and Campaigns of the 107th Regiment Ohio Volunteer Infantry, from August, 1862, to July, 1865*. n.p., 1910. Reprinted by Mark L. Gaynor, Indian River Graphics. Navarre, Ohio, 2000.

Smith, John David, ed. *Black Soldiers in Blue: African American Troops in the Civil War Era*. Chapel Hill: University of North Carolina Press, 2002.

Strickland, Alice. "Blockade Runners." *Florida Historical Quarterly* 36, no. 2 (1957): 86–94.

Tebeau, Charlton W. *A History of Florida*. Miami: University of Miami Press, 1971.

Thompson, Arthur W. "Political Nativism in Florida, 1848–1860: A Phase of Anti-Secessionism." *Journal of Southern History* 15, no. 1 (1949): 39–65.

Trefousse, Hans L. *Andrew Johnson: A Biography*. New York: Norton, 1989.

Trimble, Richard M., ed. *Brothers 'Til Death: The Civil War Letters of William,*

Thomas, and Maggie Jones, 1861–1865: Irish Soldiers in the 48th New York Volunteer Regiment. Macon, Ga.: Mercer University Press, 2000.

Trudeau, Noah Andre. *Like Men of War: Black Troops in the Civil War.* Boston, Little, Brown, 1998.

———, ed. *Voices of the 55th: Letters from the 55th Massachusetts Volunteers, 1861–1865.* Dayton, Ohio: Morningside Press, 1996.

Waters, Zach C. "Florida's Confederate Guerrillas: John W. Pearson and the Oklawaha Rangers." *Florida Historical Quarterly* 70, no. 3 (1991): 134–50.

Webb, Wanton S., ed. and comp. *Webb's Historical, Industrial and Biographical Florida.* New York: W. S. Webb, 1885.

Wesley, Charles H. "The Employment of Negroes as Soldiers in the Confederate Army." *Journal of Negro History* 4, no. 3 (1919): 239–53.

Westervelt, John H. *Diary of a Yankee Engineer: The Civil War Story of John H. Westervelt, Engineer, 1st New Work Engineer Corps.* Ed. Anita Palladino. New York: Fordham University Press, 1997.

Westwood, Howard C. *Black Troops, White Commanders, and Freedmen during the Civil War.* Carbondale: Southern Illinois University Press, 1992.

Williamson, Edward C. "Francis P. Fleming in the War for Southern Independence." *Florida Historical Quarterly* 28, no. 3 (1950): 206–11.

Wilson, Keith. "In the Shadow of John Brown: The Military Service of Colonel Thomas Higginson, James Montgomery, and Robert Shaw in the Department of the South." In *Black Soldiers in Blue: African American Troops in the Civil War Era,* ed. John David Smith, 306–35. Chapel Hill, N.C.: University of North Carolina Press, 2002.

Wise, Stephen R. *Lifeline of the Confederacy: Blockade Running during the Civil War.* Columbia: University of South Carolina Press, 1991.

Wooster, Ralph A. "The Florida Secession Convention." *Florida Historical Quarterly* 36, no. 4 (1958): 374–86.

Yonge, J. C., ed. "The Occupation of Jacksonville, February 1864, and the Battle of Olustee: Letters of Lieutenant C.M. Duren, 54th Massachusetts Regiment, U.S.A." *Florida Historical Quarterly* 32, no. 4 (1954): 263–88.

Index

Page references in italics refer to illustrations.

Batten Island (Florida): contrabands at, 90; Federal protection of, 93

Battery Creighton (Jacksonville), 257

Battle of Natural Bridge, 236

Battle of Olustee, x, 28, 184, 186–89; aftermath of, 188–89, 198–200, 239, 242; atrocities at, 188–89, 193; black soldiers following, 188–89, 229; casualties at, 188, 189; effect on refugees, 242; Finegan and, 186–87, 189, 198, 199; Seymour and, 187, 188, 190, 223; Stephens at, 187, 189

Bay Street (Jacksonville), commercial buildings of, 260

Beard, Oliver, 135–36

Beauregard, Pierre G. T., 93, 220; on burning of Jacksonville, 162; at Camp Finegan, 172, 199; defense of Florida, 198–202; following Battle of Olustee, 198–200; reinforcement of Florida, 184, 185; and third Jacksonville occupation, 152; troop deployment under, 199, 221; use of slave labor, 200–201; use of torpedo warfare, 200, 210, 218

Beecher, James C., 225, 228

Belvidere (side-wheeler), 98

Benedict, Nathan D., 35, 231, 309n44

Biggs, R. W., 149

Billings, Liberty, 157

Birney, William, 214–15, 223; Jacksonville actions of, 228–29; refugee policy of, 241–42; St. Johns River campaign of, 227–29

Bisbee, Cyrus, 44

Black Creek, Union Army at, 228, 230

Blakey, Arch F., 313n1

Blast, George D., 267

Blockade, Union, 80, 287n58; effect on contrabands, 83; effect on Jacksonville, 44; effect on northeast Florida, 42; end of, 253

Blockade runners, 44–45; Union vigilance against, 77

Boston (gunboat), 142, 157; pleasure trips aboard, 213

Boutelle, Charles O., 214

Bowden, Uriah, 39; and loyalty oath, 239

Bowerem, George, 179, 238–39

Boye, Christian, 91

Brady, John W., 41

Bragg, Braxton, 173

Brannan, John M., 110, 114, 116; at Greenfield plantation, 117; occupation of Jacksonville, 119

Brazil, Confederates in, 253

Breckinridge, John C., 19

Brevard, T. W., 112–13

Brock, Jacob, 44, 95

Broward, Charles, 15

Broward, John, 5; defense of Savannah, 54; secessionism of, 21; sons of, 29

Broward, John, Jr., 39

Broward, Margaret, 244

Broward, Napoleon Sr., 54

Broward, Washington, 228

Broward family, partisan activity by, 92, 228, 244

Brower, John L., 274

Brown, Cyrus W., 178, 241, 274

Brown, John, 16, 19

Bryan, Pliny: death of, 308n86; torpedo mines of, 206, 207, 209–10, 211, 213, 214; Union search for, 211–12

Bryan, Stephen, 87–88

Bryant, Davis, 79, 130, 172; on former slaves, 148; and Stephens's death, 204; warning to father, 302n16

Bryant, James W., 5, 31–32, 41; concern for family, 173–74; refuge in Mayport, 80; son's warning to, 302n16

Bryant, Rebecca, 41, 80, 131

Bryant, William Cullen, 127

Bryant, Willie, 140, 173

Buchanan, James, 17, 18

Buckman, Thomas E., 7, 29, 107; militia service of, 28; sale of property, 37; torpedo mines of, 206, 212–13, 215

Budd, William, 77–78

Buddington, Belle, 60

Budington, Ozias, 5

Bureau of Refugees, Freedmen, and Abandoned Lands, 270–71

Burritt, Samuel L., 64, 88, 253; curfew violations by, 244; and loyalty oath, 239

Butler, Benjamin, 132

Butler, John, 7

Cadwell, Charles K., 151, 159

Calhoun, John C.: Nashville convention of, 4–5

California, admission to Union, 5

Call, Keith, 23
Callahan (Florida), Union Army at, 227
Cameron, Simon, 88
Camp Beauregard, 180
Camp Finegan, 128–30; Confederate defenses at, 151; Confederate reoccupation of, 199; deserters from, 171–72; during third Jacksonville occupation, 146; troop strength at, 128; Union occupation of, 182
Camp Milton, 199; Confederate fortification of, 200–201, 225, 226, 227; map of, 196, 197; skirmishes around, 202–3; Union occupation of, 226–27
Camp Virginia, 40
Camp William Penn, 274
Canova, Bartolo, 247
Canova, Paul B., 23–24; militia service of, 33
Cass, Lewis, 3
Caswell (schooner), 213
Cavalry, Confederate: attacks on Infantry, 234–35; defense of Jacksonville, 118–19; defense of St. Johns River, 216, 225; under Dickison, 118–19, 155, 231, 233, 235; at Palatka, 202. See also Florida Cavalry, 2nd
Cavalry, Union: Dickison's rout of, 233; under Hatch, 234; at Jacksonville, 222, 234; provisioning raids by, 224, 231; on St. Johns River, 221
Cavalry horses, Confederate, 106
Cecile (steamboat), 34; blockade running by, 44
Cedar Creek: skirmish at, 203; torpedo mines on, 213
Chadwick, P. R., 205
Chamberlain, Valentine, 111, 116, 117, 118; on destruction at Jacksonville, 119; spoof newspaper of, 119–20
Chambers, W. E., 112, 113
Charles B. Houghton (transport), 204
Charleston (South Carolina): Democratic convention at, 19; epidemics at, 245; Federal action against, 152, 158, 162, 178, 221
Chase, Salmon P.: and Direct Tax Law, 124, 126; meeting with Yulee, 253; presidential ambitions of, 175; resignation from cabinet, 240
Chatham Artillery, 185
Chimney Point (St. Johns River), 257

Cimarron (gunboat), at St. Johns Bluff, 108
Civilians, Federal policy towards, 66, 290n16, 292n24
Clark, Henry, 29
Clark, William, 235; refusal of oath, 243
Clay, Cassius M., 127
Cobb, Howell, 152, 155
Cole, William K., 14
Coles, David J., 188, 189
Colonization plans: Lincoln and, 128; for northeast Florida, 125, 126, 127–28, 240
Colquitt, Alfred H., 185, 186
Columbine (steam tug), 224; capture of, 225
Commerce (Jacksonville), 29–30, 247–48, 260, 261; under martial law, 246; revival of, 249, 252–56, 265
Committee of Vigilance (Jacksonville), 11, 54, 283n41. See also Regulators
Compromise of 1850, 5, 12, 13
Confederate Army: burning of Jacksonville, 58–61, 143; conscript officers of, 241; defense of Jacksonville, 18, 144–45; defense of St. Johns River, 80, 91, 129, 205, 206; disavowal of regulators, 78; fortifications on St. Johns River, 31, 33, 34, 35–46, 47; freedmen in, 86–87; Jacksonville volunteers in, 41; living conditions of, 173, 174; militia units in, 46; morale in, 171–72, 173; occupation of Jacksonville, 74, 77–94; outside Jacksonville, 71–72; provisioning of, 129, 174, 205, 216, 221–22, 229; retreats from Jacksonville, 61; sharpshooters, 66, 72, 223; at St. Johns Bluff, 33, 45–47, 51, 92, 106–7, 116–17; truce at Jacksonville, 77–79, 291n14; use of slave labor, 133, 200–201, 205. See also Cavalry, Confederate; Deserters, Confederate; Soldiers, Confederate
Confederates. See Secessionists; Soldiers, Confederate; Whites
Confederate States of America: currency of, 37, 38; Florida's importance to, 121, 205; provisional government of, 25
Confiscation Acts: First (1861), 83, 132; Second (1862), 88
Congress, U.S.: on Florida Constitution, 277; Florida delegation to, 277–78
Connecticut (gunboat), 84
Connecticut Battery, 1st, 114
Connecticut Infantry, 17th, 225, 231, 234

Drayton, Percival, 76
Dred Scott v. Sanford (1857), 18
Drew, Columbus, 3–4, 276; on election of 1850, 5–6; in elections of 1854, 14; Unionism of, 28
Driggs, John S., 249
Dunham, Joseph L., 106, 108–9, 180
Du Pont, Samuel F., *100*; capture of Port Royal, 45; on contraband question, 82; on first Jacksonville occupation, 72–73, 76; flagship of, *99*; Florida expedition of, 47–48, 49, 56, 63; on Higginson expedition, 140–41; on Jacksonville truce, 291n16; and second Jacksonville evacuation, 128; and St. Johns Bluff engagement, 107–8, 110
Duval County (Florida): antebellum demographics of, 13–14; black refugees in, 276; black soldiers from, 147; in elections of 1855, 15; freedmen of, 86; Unionists of, 51; volunteers from, 23–24, 33, 34, 41; Wright expedition in, 50–51
Duval County Medical Society, 254
Duval County Minutemen, 23–24, 33
Duval Cowboys, 33, 34; casualties of, 39; occupation of Jacksonville, 77; at St. Johns Bluff, 54

E. B. Hale (gunboat), 118, 215; at St. Johns Bluff, 108
Elections: of 1848, 2, 3–4; of 1850, 5–6, 12; of 1854, 14; of 1855, 15; of 1856, 15, 16–17; of 1857, 18, 283n62; of 1860, 19, 21–22, 23, 284n69; of 1865, 277
Ellen (side-wheeler), 55, 56; refitting of, 66
Ells, Thomas, 249
Emancipation Proclamation, 89; promulgation of, 138, 153, 182

Fairbanks, Samuel, 90; on contrabands, 122; escaped slaves of, 84–85, 87–88; on second Federal occupation, 121
Falany, Benjamin, 206–7
Fannin, John F., 314n32
Farrand, Ebenezer, 32, 45; defense of Jacksonville, 51
Felix (cook), 129, 131, 297n26
Fernandina (Florida): black refugees at, 89; Confederate abandonment of, 46–48;

Confederate defenses at, 46; Confederate refugees from, 50; confiscated property in, 248; contrabands at, 122; Federal amnesty program at, 238; Hay at, 177–78; Unionist refugees at, 79, 92; Union occupation of, 48–49, 50, 183
Fillmore, Millard, 12, 16–17
Finegan, Joseph, *102*; and Battle of Olustee, 186–87, 189, 198, 199; and black Union troops, 154–55; on burning of Jacksonville, 162; call for weapons, 93–94; confiscation of home, 248; Jacksonville assault of, 155; at Lake City, 186; morale efforts of, 172; at Nashville convention, 5; at Ocean Pond, 185; replacement of Trapier, 62; runaway slaves of, 91; St. Johns offensive of, 93–94, 105–18; Stephens on, 118, 130; during third Jacksonville occupation, 151–53; troop strength of, 184–85
Fishing, Union interference with, 222
Flagg, George, 27
Fleming, Charles Seton, 24
Fleming, Francis P., 253
Fleming, Lewis, 9, 27
Fleming Island, Union raids at, 212
Florida: Beauregard's defense of, 198–202; black soldiers in, 137, 138–39, 175, 271; Confederate government of, 232; confiscated land in, 125, 176, 248, 249–50, 252–53; Constitutional Convention, 238, 277; defense of interior, 62; Federal government for, 68, 69–70, 124, 176, 177–78, 183–84; Federal installations in, 32; free black settlers in, 127, 128; importance to Confederacy, 121, 205; Lee's policy on, 91; provisions from, 205, 216, 221–22, 229; race relations in, 31; rail destruction in, 229; readmission to Union, 238; during Reconstruction, 278; secession of, 27, 32, 277; slave code of, 30; under Spanish rule, 2, 11, 15; supply lines from, 216; telegraphic network of, 202; white supremacy in, 277–78
Florida (newspaper), 234, 235; on refugees, 235–36
Florida, Atlantic, and Gulf Central Railroad, 27, 40, 186; evacuations by, 50; troop transport on, 185

Florida, northeast: antebellum prosperity in, 6–8, 9; anti-Union violence in, 35; black soldiers from, 137; cotton industry in, 6, 7, 254; demographics of, 28; economic distress of, 46; effect of Union blockade on, 42; Federal troop level at, 190; freedmen of, 85, 86; industries of, 6–7; labor shortage in, 7–8, 9, 14; militias of, 23–24, 33–34, 40, 47; northern colonization plans for, 126, 127–28, 240; occupied towns of, 246; profitability of slavery in, 7–8; railroads of, 7, 27, 40, 180, 183, 186, 201; secessionists of, 21, 22–24; slave self-emancipation in, x, 121–23; timber industry of, 6, 37; unionists of, 4; wartime destruction in, 253–54

Florida battalion, 6th, 202

Florida Brigade, in Virginia, 216

Florida Cavalry, 2nd, 42, 129, 152; capture of *Columbine*, 225; Cedar Creek engagement of, 203; Company B, 287n52; skirmish at St. Marys River, 181, 303n50; victories by, 233, 309n46

Florida Direct Tax Commission, 126–28; auctioning of merchandise, 312n40; sale of property, 176, 248, 249–50

Florida Infantry: 2nd Regiment, 40; 3rd Regiment, 41; 4th Regiment, 41, 78; 5th Regiment, 91–92

Florida legislature: "black code" of, 278; Democrats in, 6; former slaveholders in, 277

Florida News, 6; on anti-white violence, 265; on slave abduction, 10

Florida Railroad, evacuations by, 50

The Florida Republican (newspaper), 15, 17; on timber industry, 6

Florida Times, on racial violence, 273

Florida Union (newspaper): on Andersonville survivors, 237; on black soldiers, 314n34; on commerce, 252; on plantation labor, 266; on reconstruction, 255; on war's end, 236

Flotard, Thomas, 44

Foote, Andrew, 46

Forrester, Cyrus, 86

Forrester, Lewis, 86

Fort Barrancas, 32

Fort Clinch, 47

Fort Foster, 191, 304n98

Fort Fribley, 191, 304n98

Fort Gates, 115, 234

Fort Hatch, 191, 304n98

Fort Higginson, 146

Fort Jefferson, 286n18

Fort Marion (St. Augustine), 32

Fort Montgomery, 146

Fort Pickens (Santa Rosa Island), 32, 286n18

Fort Steele, 31, 32; armaments at, 47; completion of, 45; Confederate abandonment of, 49; Union occupation of, 55

Fort Sumpter, Confederate attack on, 25, 33, 34

Fort Taylor, 286n18

Fort Wagner, 185

Foster, John G., 232, 304n98; rebuke to Hatch, 233–34

Fraser, Philip: activism in exile, 126; evacuation from Jacksonville, 74, 75; during first Jacksonville occupation, 63–64, 69; intimidation by regulators, 67–68; murder plot against, 57, 58; in New York, 75; at Republican Convention, 240; at St. Augustine Unionist meeting, 176; in St. Augustine, 248

Freedmen: abduction of, 8, 9; in antebellum censuses, 292n35; aspirations of, 266; black soldiers and, 272; citizenship for, 278; in Confederate Army, 86–87; destitution of, 235, 268; education of, 250–52; during fourth Jacksonville occupation, 265–78; Hanson Town commune of, 275–76; head tax on, 31; Inquiry Commission on, 136; in labor force, 266, 267–68, 270–71, 314n21; land ownership by, 267; medical treatment for, 248; of northeast Florida, 85, 86; ordinances regulating, 11; on plantations, 266, 270; Port Orange settlement of, 312n49; Pottsburg Creek settlement of, 268, 275–76; refugees, 81, 82; in South Carolina Loyal Volunteers, 85; of St. Augustine, 86, 235; of Tallahassee, 267; travelers, 267–68; in Union Army, x, 131–41; violence against, 269; voting rights for, 266, 277; white opinion on, 31;

under white supremacy, 277–78. *See also* Contrabands; Slaves, runaway

Freedmen (Jacksonville): evacuation of, 30–31; living conditions of, 268–69

Freedmen's Bureau, 270–71

Free-Soil Party, 3, 12, 13; in Kansas, 16

Frémont, John C., 13, 17, 18, 88

Fribley, Charles, 304n98

Fugitive Slave Act, 5, 12, 25

Gainesville (Florida): Dickison's victory at, 231, 309n46; Union raid on, 231–32, 233

Gardner, W. M.: command of northeast Florida, 198–99; fortifications of, 199

Gaskill, Charles, 213

General Burnside (transport), 142, 154

General Hunter (transport), 204, 208; torpedoing of, 210–11; wreck of, 217

General Sumter (gunboat), Union capture of, 222

George Mooney Shipyard (Jacksonville), 45, 57

Georgia battalion, 4th, 202

Georgia Regulars, 1st, 209

Gillmore, Quincy Adams, 175, 219; amnesty proclamation under, 241; at Baldwin, 182; on burning of Jacksonville, 162; Florida campaign of, 176–79, 183–85; goals for Florida, 177; meeting with Hay, 177; occupation of Jacksonville, 180–81, 190, 240; on treatment of blacks, 269

Glatthaar, Joseph T., 273–74, 298n67

Godon, S. W., 84

Good, Tilghman H., 110; at St. Johns Bluff, 113–14

Goodwin, Joseph, 156

Gordon, George H., 223; Camp Milton expedition of, 225–27; refugee policy of, 242; relief expedition of, 224

Governor Milton (steamer), 106–7; Federal capture of, 120

Grace, Josiah C., 222

Grant, Ulysses S., 46, 272, 314n30

Greeley, J. C., 66

Greely, Mrs. H. B., 235, 268

Green, Joseph, 315n34

Greenfield plantation, 117

Grothe, William, 27

Guerrillas. *See* Regulators

Gulf Coast, Union expedition to, 231

Gunboats, Confederate: burning of, 54–55, 57; Union capture of, 222

Gunboats, Union: deck logs of, 293n44; defense of Jacksonville, 191, 192; effect on slaveholders, 84–85; in first Jacksonville occupation, 53, 57, 61; guerrilla attacks on, 190; in Higginson's expedition, 138; at Mayport Mills, 45, 77; at Mosquito Inlet, 81; at St. Johns Bluff, 108; on St. Johns River, x, 53, 55, 56, 57, 189–90, 207; in third Jacksonville occupation, 142–43; torpedoing of, 200, 208–11, 213–14

Guss, Henry R., 70

Haddock, Esther, 37

Haddock, John, 8, 29

Haddock, William H., 96

Hall, Israel, 246

Halleck, H. W., 176–77

Hallowell, Ned, 193

Hamlin, Hannibal, 124, 125

Hanahan, Henry, 86

Hanson, Daniel Dustin, 275, 276

Hanson Town, black commune at, 275–76

Hardee, Lucius, 29; evacuation of St. Johns Bluff, 54; militia service of, 34, 39; in Seminole Wars, 33

Harmon, Stephen, 8

Harriet A. Weed (steamer), 178, 208; torpedoing of, 213–14

Harris, A. L., 231–32, 310n47

Harris, M. B., 206

Harrison, Robert, 181

Hart, Daniel: estranged wife of, 244

Hart, Hubbard L., 106

Hart, Oscar, 26, 37; defense of Jacksonville, 51; during first Federal occupation, 66

Hartridge, Theodore, 276; warehouse of, 261

Hatch, John P., 304n98; anti-pillaging order of, 232; on Battle of Olustee, 189; command of District of Florida, 307n64; Foster's rebuke of, 233–34; free school of, 252; occupation of Magnolia, 230–31; petition from Jacksonville to, 222; reliance on cavalry, 234; replacement of, 310n56; reprimand to Harris, 231–32, 310n47; and torpedo mines, 210; on Unionists, 232

cavalry at, 222, 234; Federal defense of, 155–56, 190–91, 227; Federal evacuation (first), 73–76; Federal evacuation (second), 124, 128; Federal evacuation (third), 157–63; Federal fortifications at, 70, 72, 189–91, 146, 151, 152, 189–91; Federal looting of, 120; Federal martial law in, 243–50, 255, 271, 277; Federal occupation of, x, xi; Federal occupation of (first), 52–62, 63–77; Federal occupation of (second), 118–23; Federal occupation of (third), 141, 142–58; Federal occupation of (fourth), 163, 180–81, 190–94, 238–56, 265–78; Federal signal tower at, 259; food shortages in, 81, 222; foreign-born residents of, 247; home guard of, 41, 43; isolation of, 43–44; loyal government for, 126; lumber industry of, 37; maps of, *xii–xiii*, 195; metal collection drives in, 45; militias of, 21, 23–24, 38–39, 40, 41; Northerners in, 14, 28–30, 34–35; petition to Hatch, 222; Provost Marshal's Office, 242, 252, 263, 271, 273; racial conflict in, 265, 273–74; racial integration in, 250–51; railway depot, 58; Reading Room, 262; reconstruction of, 242, 254; refugees from interior in, 235–36; saloons of, 245; schools of, 250–52; sea traffic at, 253, 254; sectional debates in, 1–26; shipbuilding at, 45; slavery ordinances of, 11–12; stage line to, 253; surrender to Wright, 64; telegraph communications with, 34; and torpedo mine campaign, 214–15; tourism in, 249, 254; truce at, 77–79, 291n14; two-party system in, 1; U.S. Coast Survey map of, *195*; Unionist Convention (1861), 69–70; vagrancy laws of, 277; vigilantes of, 58–60; at war's end, 236; white supremacy in, 266, 276, 277

Jacksonville Courier, support for slavery, 2

Jacksonville Herald: on black refugees, 276; on freedmen, 266, 267

Jacksonville Light Infantry, 21, 36; charter members of, 27–28; fortifications by, 39; occupation of Jacksonville, 77; at outbreak of war, 34; resolution of, 24, 284n89; retreat from Jacksonville, 58; in 3rd Florida Infantry, 38; uniform of, 28

Jacksonville Standard, 22, 23; secessionist stand of, 27

Jake, long legged, 122, 148

James River, torpedo mines in, 206

Jaudon, Elias, 41

Jaudon, Maxey, 29, 39

Jeff Davis (privateer), 44

John Adams (steamer), 138, 141; in third Jacksonville occupation, 143

Johnson, Andrew, 271

Johnson, Samuel L., 209

Joiner, Moses, 230

Jones, Andrew M., 39

Jones, David, 272

Jones, Samuel D., 209, 236

Jordan, Thomas, 200

Judson House (Jacksonville), 27; burning of, 59, 60–61, 255; Confederate militia at, 38, 57–58; effect of war on, 36–37

Kansas: admission to Union, 18, 19; violence in, 16

Kansas-Nebraska Act, 13

Kearney, S. L., 271–72

Keene, Abbie, 27; during first Jacksonville expedition, 57

Keene, Otis Little, 27; activism in exile, 125, 255; on the *America*, 45; on burning of Jacksonville, 60–61; evacuation of, 75; during first Jacksonville expedition, 57, 63; intimidation by regulators, 38; militia service of, 34, 38; return to Jacksonville, 255–56; Unionism of, 32, 43; at Unionist Convention, 70

Kentucky: Lincoln's conciliation of, 88; Union victories in, 46

Key West (Florida), Federal amnesty program at, 238

Kingsley, Anta, 248, 311n37

Kingsley, Zephaniah, 248, 311n37

Kissimmee River, Union expedition at, 222, 223

Knight, Alva L., 274

Knowles, Jack, 35

Labbaker, James S., 7

Labor force (Florida): freedmen in, 266, 267–68, 270–71, 314n21; Irish in, 7; shortages in, 7–8, 9, 14

Lady of the Lake (schooner), 10

Lake City (Florida): Confederate occupation of, 181, 186, 221; Finegan at, 186; racial violence in, 272–73; rail transport to, 229, 253; secessionist violence in, 36; Union advance on, 216; white fear in, 267

Lake Harney (Florida), Union Army at, 222, 223

Lancaster, Abraham, 86

Lane, James, 132

Lang, Joseph H. B., 208

Laurel Grove plantation, Union capture of, 154

Ledwith, Thomas L., 5, 38, 160

Lee, Robert E., 206; coastal defense orders of, 46–47, 51, 287n68; defeats in Pennsylvania, 173; Florida policy of, 91; and torpedo mines, 216

Lelar, Robert, 89

L'Engle, Charlotte Porcher, 7

L'Engle, Edward M., 39, 253

L'Engle, Francis F., 7; departure from Jacksonville, 53; militia service of, 33

L'Engle, John C., 39; fortification work by, 31

Lenihan, Mary, 254

Leon Rifles, 39

Leuders, Frederick, 64

Lincoln, Abraham: Amnesty Proclamation of, 175–76, 177, 238–40, 241; assassination of, 271; and black troops, 131, 157; call for militia, 34; and colonization plan, 128; on contrabands, 88, 134; election of, 22; emancipation of slaves, 89, 138, 153, 182; on expansion of slavery, 18; on first Jacksonville evacuation, 75; on Florida loyalist government, 176; and Hunter's emancipations, 133; meeting with Jacksonville exiles, 124; policy on noncombatants, 66; policy on slaveholders, 83; Stickney's visit to, 175; support for Florida campaign, 175

Livingston, Felix, 4

Long, Ellen Call, 90–91

Long, Thomas, 86, 147

Loyalty oaths, Confederate, 34–35, 71

Loyalty oaths, Union, 146, 176, 232–33; by Confederate soldiers, 243; in Federal amnesty program, 238–41; refusal of, 243, 247

Macfarlane, C., 187

Magnolia (Florida): refugees at, 233; Union evacuation of, 233; Unionists of, 35; Union occupation of, 230–31, 309n46

Mahaska (sloop), 192; in St. Johns River expedition, 178, 179; at Weed torpedoing, 214

Maine, 8th Regiment, 160, 161

Mallory, Stephen R., 32, 205

Manucy, Philip J., 271

Maple Leaf (transport), 204, 217; casualties aboard, 209; in St. Johns River expedition, 179; torpedoing of, x, 208–9, 210, 211; wreck of, 217

Marple, William H., 269, 276

Martial law (Jacksonville): curfew during, 243–44; end of, 255, 277; food relief program of, 271; during fourth occupation, 243–50; housing problems under, 246; price controls in, 246; public health during, 245; travel under, 243, 245; violations of, 245

Martin, Richard A.: Jacksonville's Ordeal by Fire, ix

Marvin, William, 70, 272, 276–77

Massachusetts Cavalry: 1st, 110, 179; 4th, 228, 230, 231; Independent, 203

Massachusetts Emigrant Aid Society, 125

Massachusetts Regiment, 54th, 182, 187–88, 190; at Jacksonville, 192; morale in, 193

Massachusetts Regiment, 55th, 193, 204

Maxwell, John, 77

Mayport Mills, 97; Confederate fortification of, 31; contrabands at, 122; Federal gunboats at, 77; Higginson at, 143; refugees at, 89–90; regulator raid on, 105, 106; Union gunboats at, 45; Unionists of, 23; Union troops at, 110–11, 112

McAlpine, James W., 201

McArthur, William M., 155, 156

McCormick, Abner H., 180, 227, 229

McCoys Creek, 195; Federal defenses at, 190, 191; quarantine at, 193

McGirts Creek, Confederate Army at, 71, 198, 201, 225

McKee, James Harvey, 224

McKeige, Edward, 93

McQueen, Charles, 86

Reed, Harrison, 126
Reed, Hattie, 148
Refugees: from Fernandina, 50; during
Jacksonville truce, 79; loyal regiment of,
232; Union transport of, 72
Refugees (from Jacksonville), 50;
Confederate, 76; during first Federal
evacuation, 73–76; during first Federal
occupation, 53–54, 57, 61, 66; meeting
with Lincoln, 124; and reopening of
St. Johns River, 124; return of, 247, 253;
during third Federal occupation, 148
Refugees (to Jacksonville): Confederate
soldiers, 242; employment for, 242;
during fourth occupation, 238–39,
241–43; housing of, 269; from interior,
235–36
Refugees, black: in Duval County, 276; at
Fernandina, 89; harassment by regulators, 81–82; as river pilots, 121. *See also*
Contrabands
Regulators: Army's disavowal of, 78; and
first Jacksonville occupation, 54, 58–60,
67–68, 69; following Union evacuations, 128; harassment of blacks, 81–82;
intimidation of Unionists, 38, 42–44,
57, 67–68, 69; during Jacksonville truce,
79, 81; pre-secession violence by, 23;
raid on Mayport, 105, 106
Republican Party: American Party support for, 16; founding of, 12
Rhode Island Artillery, 3rd, 204, 226
Richard, Francis, 86
Richard, John C., 109
Robinson, Calvin: aid to freedmen, 248;
commercial interests of, 29–30, 247–
48; on Direct Tax Commission, 248–
49; and Federal burning of Jacksonville,
160; on Fernandina occupation, 50;
on first Jacksonville evacuation, 73, 75;
during first Jacksonville occupation,
64; on food shortages, 222; during
fourth Jacksonville occupation, 248;
intimidation by regulators, 38, 42–43,
67–68; on loyalty oath, 35; murder plot
against, 57, 58, 60; in New York, 75; at
Republican National Convention, 240,
248; on shipbuilding, 45; St. Augustine
residence, 248; at Unionist meetings,

70, 176; on wartime conditions, 43–44;
wartime losses of, 37–38
Robinson, Elizabeth, 59
Rodgers, C. R. P., 70
Rogers, James, 145
Rogers, Seth, 138, 139–40, 157, *167*; on
black soldiers, 148, 151; on burning of
Jacksonville, 161; on third Federal evacu-
ation, 158, 162–63; in third Jacksonville
occupation, 145
Rushing, Richard P., 27
Russell, Albert J., 33
Russell, Thomas T., 156–57
Rust, John D., 150, 161

Sabal, Emile, 24
Sadler, Hal M., 7, 24
Sadler, Nathan B., 33–34; sale of planta-
tion, 37
Sailors, Union: insubordination among,
120; at Jacksonville, 66
Sammis, Albert C., 86, 149–50, *168*
Sammis, Edgar, 249
Sammis, Edward, 249
Sammis, John S., 275; commercial inter-
ests of, 248, 249; confiscated property
of, 248; on Direct Tax Commission,
126, 248–49; former slaves of, 149–50;
mill of, 243; at Republican Convention,
240; residence of, 250; sale of property,
37
Sammis, Mary Kingsley, 126, 149, 276
Sams, F. W.: slave family of, 9
Sanderson (Florida), Union occupation
of, 181
Sanderson, John P., 145; departure from
Jacksonville, 53; at Nashville convention, 5; residence of, 53, 161, *169*; secessionism of, 28; at Tallahassee convention, 24–25
Santa Rosa Island, fortification of, 32–33
Savannah (Georgia): Confederate defenses of, 199; epidemics at, 245
Savannah Daily Herald, on Jacksonville
race relations, 273
Sawmills, 32, 130, 215; reconstruction of,
253; on St. Johns River, 6, 9–10; Union
capture of, 227–28
Sawyer, Oscar, 179, 181

influence on freedmen, 272; in Jacksonville, 131, 142, 144–51, 160–61, 265, 273; Lincoln and, 131, 157; under Montgomery, 142; at Moses Dell, 271; mutiny by, 274–75; from northeast Florida, 137, 157, 158; officers' treatment of, 273–74; postwar occupation duty by, 273–74; salary policy for, 193, 305n104; service with whites, 150–51, 159; in St. Johns River expeditions, 153; thumb-tying of, 274, 314n32; white anger at, 147, 148, 154, 179, 182, 271, 272, 275, 313n1, 314n30; white soldiers' support for, 159. *See also* South Carolina Loyal Volunteers; United States Colored Troops

Soldiers, Confederate: amnesty for, 175–76, 238–40; concern for families, 173; following Battle of Olustee, 188–89, 193; living conditions of, 173, 174; refuge in Jacksonville, 242; sale of property, 37. *See also* Deserters, Confederate

Soldiers, Union: from Andersonville prison, 236–37; foraging by, 143; during fourth Jacksonville occupation, 244–45; view of refugees, 232–33

Soule, Francis, 155

South Atlantic Blockading Squadron, 45

South Carolina coast, Union raid on, 184, 185

South Carolina Loyal Volunteers, 1st, 164, 247; former slaves in, 85; Hawks on, 298n64; recruitment into, 142, 162; Saxton on, 136; in St. Johns River expeditions, 141. *See also* United States Colored Troops

Southern Confederacy (newspaper), 30, 33

Southern Rights (newspaper), Union confiscation of, 119–20

Southern states, northern migration to, 125–26. *See also* Colonization plans; Northerners (Jacksonville)

Spear, Charles, 208

Sprague, John T., 185, 190, 255

Sprotson, John G., 81

St. Augustine (Florida): confiscated property at, 176; Federal amnesty program at, 238; free blacks from, 86, 235; stage line to, 253; Unionist meeting at, 176;

Unionist refugees at, 79; Union occupation of, 183

St. Johns (blockade runner), 44

St. Johns Bluff: Confederate abandonment of, 54, 115–18, 121; Confederate fortification of, 33, 45–46, 47, 51, 92, 106–7, 116–17; engagement at, 105–18; Federal bombardment of, 108–9

St. Johns Grays, 38–39

St. Johns House (Jacksonville), 249

St. Johns Light Infantry, 39

St. Johns Rangers, 42, 47; at St. Johns Bluff, 109, 112

St. Johns River: blockade of entrance, 74; civilian morale along, 174–75; Confederate defense of, 80, 91, 129, 205, 206, 207; Confederate fortifications on, 31, 33, 34, 45–46, 47; corn crop of, 82; Federal defenses on, 192; Finegan's offensive at, 93–94; Gillmore's campaign at, 176–79; headwaters of, 222; Higginson's expedition at, 141; reopening to Confederacy, 124; sawmills on, 6, 9–10; torpedo mines in, 206, 207–16; Union gunboats on, x, 53, 55, 56, 57, 207; Unionists of, 70; Union land force at, 110–16, 221; Union supremacy on, 118; Wright's expedition at, 49, 50–51, 52–53, 55–57

St. Marks River, battle at, 236

St. Marys (steamer), 47, 65, 314n34; blockade running by, 44; sale of, 250

St. Marys River: cavalry skirmish at, 181, 303n50; Emancipation Proclamation at, 138

St. Simons Island, contrabands at, 84

Stanton, Edwin M., 132, 175, 177; and black soldiers, 134–35, 136; on first Jacksonville evacuation, 75

Starratt, Harrison, 29

Steadman, A. J., 207

Steedman, Charles, 108, 128; at St. Johns Bluff, 110, 118

Steele, Holmes, 19, 29; fortification work under, 31, 34; militia organization by, 21, 27, 39

Stephens, Belle, 130

Stephens, Clark, 85

Stephens, Octavia Bryant, 115, *170*; on
Beauregard, 172; and Crespo Boarding
House, 128–29; death of daughter, 130,
173; and husband's death, 203–4; move
to Georgia, 174; slave management by,
173; during third Jacksonville occupation, 152; view of war, 41–42, 130–31; at
Welaka, 41, 42
Stephens, Swepson, 203
Stephens, Winston, 41, 42, *170*; at Battle
of Olustee, 186, 189; and burning of
Jacksonville, 161; capture of runaways,
89; on Confederate morale, 172; on
contrabands, 90, 122; and Crespo
Boarding House, 128–29; death of, 170,
203–4; death of daughter, 130, 173; on
Finegan, 118, 130; on Higginson expedition, 140; morale of, 173; on occupation
of Jacksonville, 66; relocation of family,
174; runaway slaves of, 85; snipers under,
66; St. Johns River service of, 80; at St.
Johns Bluff, 109, 112, 114–15; in St. Johns
Rangers, 47; during third Jacksonville
occupation, 152
Stephens, Winston, Jr., 204
Stevens, Thomas Holdup: command of
Ottawa, 56; on Jacksonville evacuation,
76; meeting with Confederates, 77–78;
occupation of Jacksonville, 61–62, 63,
64; relations with slaveholders, 87; St.
Marys mission of, 83–84; and St. Johns
River inhabitants, 66; in St. Johns River
expedition, 52–53, 55–57, 63; on Union-
ists, 70; and yacht *America*, 65
Stickney, Lyman D., 125–26; on black
troops, 140, 150; on loyalty oath, 240;
northern colonization plans, 126, 240;
reorganization plans for Florida, 176,
177; visit to Lincoln, 175
Stockton, William T., 40
Sutton, Robert, 138–39
Sweet, T. M., 244
Swettland, S. H., 223

Tabeau, Rajah, 250–51
Tabeau, Willis, 250–51
Talbot Island, Confederate fortification
of, 33

Tallahassee: engagement at, 109; freedmen
of, 267; "People's Convention" at, 22,
24–25, 39, 68
Taney, Roger B., 18
Tatnall, Isaac, 47
Taylor, James, 35
Taylor, Zachary, 3; death of, 12, 16
Teachers, missionary, 251, 312n50
Tennessee, Union victories in, 46, 173
Texas, annexation of, 2–3
Thayer, Eli: colonization plan of, 125, 126,
127
Thomas, Lorenzo, 51
Thompson, Arthur W., 14, 19–20
Timber industry: effect of war on, 37; of
northeast Florida, 6
Tombs, Aggie, 31
Torpedo mines, Confederate, x, 205–16,
218, 231; Beauregard's use of, 200;
casualties from, 209; consequences of,
216; effect on refugees, 242; impact on
Jacksonville, 214–15; improvised, 212–13;
Lee on, 206; manufacture of, 206, 207,
212–13, 216; materials for, 206–7, 212–13,
216; mechanisms of, 206, 214, 308n80;
placement of, 207; Union capture of, 214
Toussaint-Louverture, 138
Township (Florida), black soldiers at,
138–39
Trapier, James Heyward, 40, 58, 61; con-
flict with Milton, 51; replacement of, 62
Trout Creek, Union Army at, 227
Trowbridge, Charles, 134, 135, *166*
Turner, John W., 184
Turner, Nat, 2
Turner, William, 223

Uncas (gunboat): refugees on, 92; at St.
Johns Bluff, 105, 107; in third Jacksonville expedition, 143, 152, 155
Underhill, J. M., 223
Underwater explosives. *See* Torpedo mines,
Confederate
Union Army: civilian policy of, 66, 290n16,
292n24; contrabands in, 122, 131–41,
147, 162, 275; Department of the South,
76, 175, 236; evacuation of Jacksonville
(first), 73–76; evacuation of Jacksonville

(second), 124, 128; evacuation of Jacksonville (third), 157–63; Expeditionary Corps, 47; fortification of Jacksonville, 70, 72, 189–91, 146, 151, 152, 189–91; at Mayport Mills, 110–11, 112; occupation of Jacksonville, x, xi; occupation of Jacksonville (first), 52–62, 63–77; occupation of Jacksonville (second), 118–23; occupation of Jacksonville (third), 141, 142–58, 163; occupation of Jacksonville (fourth), 163, 180–81, 190–94, 238–56; pillaging by, 120, 231, 232, 310n47; pro-abolition officers in, 83; provisioning of, 223–24; at St. Johns River, 110–16; Tennessee victories of, 46, 173; treatment of prisoners, 235; truce at Jacksonville, 77–79, 291n14

Unionists (Florida), 4; confiscation of property from, 92; of Duval County, 51; Federal encouragement of, 232; of Mayport Mills, 23; of Middleburg, 230; privation of, 223–24; at Republican Convention, 240; St. Augustine meeting of, 176; of St. Johns River, 70

Unionists (Jacksonville), 28; activism in exile, 124–25; declaration of rights, 69–70; desire for compromise, 19–20; and Direct Tax Commission, 126; in first Federal evacuation, 73–76; during first Federal occupation, 58–59, 61, 63; during fourth occupation, 239; in home guard, 43; intimidation of, 38, 42–44, 57, 67–68; Northern exile of, 75, 124–41; at outbreak of war, 35; racial views of, 276–77; surveillance of, 42; at Tallahassee convention, 25; Whigs, 4

United States Colored Troops, 137; 23rd, 213; 33rd, 85, 165; 7th, 226; 35th, 226, 228; white officers of, 314n32. See also South Carolina Loyal Volunteers, 1st

United States Colored Troops, 3rd, 226, 227, 234; mutiny by, 274–75; postwar duty, 274; thumb-tying in, 274, 314n32

United States Colored Troops, 34th, 234; postwar duty, 274; white accusations against, 272–73

Utah, admission to Union, 5

Vandegriff, David, 222

Veterans, black: aspirations of, 266; funeral of, 264; occupations of, 276, 315n39

Vigilantes. *See* Regulators

Villard, Claudia, 37

Villepigue, F. L., 106

Virginia, Florida troops in, 216, 221

Vogdes, Israel, 236; and freedmen's affairs, 270

Volusia (Florida), Union Army at, 223, 224

Wabash (gunboat), 56, 99

Wallace, H. C., 296n23

Walton, Alfred, 155, 159–60; rescue of prayer book, 160, 301n72

Ward, George T., 40

Warrock, Loudwick, 27

Watercraft, Federal confiscation of, 243

Water Witch (gunboat), 192

Welaka (Florida): Octavia Stephens at, 41, 42; Union Army at, 223, 234

Welles, Gideon, 205, 214

Western territories, extension of slavery into, 2–3, 4–5, 13, 15–16, 21, 25–26

West India, freedmen of, 21

Whig Party: anti-immigrant bias of, 14; demise of, 12–13; in election of 1848, 4; in election of 1850, 12; following elections of 1850, 13; position on slavery, 2–3

Whig Party (Jacksonville), 1–2, 14; in elections of 1850s, 6, 18; Unionism of, 4

Whipple, J. T., 51, 64–65

Whites: anger at black soldiers, 147, 148, 154, 179, 182, 271, 272, 275, 313n1, 314n30; antebellum racial fears of, 22, 23, 265, 313n1; under Jacksonville fourth occupation, 238–56; opinions on freedmen, 31, 266, 267–68; poor, 268; racial control measures by, 276, 277; reaction to emancipation, 271, 314n21

White supremacy, 278; in Jacksonville, 266, 276, 277

Whittemore, Whit, 179, 180, 239, 240

Willard, Albert, 39

Willard Hotel (Washington), Jacksonville activists at, 125

Wilmot, David, 3

Wilson, L., 235

Wilson, Miller and Company, 37

DANIEL L. SCHAFER is professor emeritus of history, University of North Florida. Elected a Distinguished Professor in 1996, he taught at the University of North Florida for thirty-five years. He is the author of numerous articles and book chapters about African American and Florida history. His books include *William Bartram and the Ghost Plantations of British East Florida*; *Zephaniah Kingsley Jr. and the Atlantic World: Slave Trader, Plantation Owner, Emancipator*; *Governor James Grant's Villa: A British East Florida Indigo Plantation*; *St. Augustine's British Years, 1763–1784*; and *Anna Madgigine Jai Kingsley: African Princess, Florida Slave, Plantation Slaveowner*. He is also the creator and editor of Florida History Online (www.unf.edu/floridahistoryonline).

9 780813 060545